Knut Hamsun, Novelist

PETER LANG
New York • Washington, D.C./Baltimore • Bern
Frankfurt am Main • Berlin • Brussels • Vienna • Oxford

Sverre Lyngstad

Knut Hamsun, Novelist

A Critical Assessment

PETER LANG
New York • Washington, D.C./Baltimore • Bern
Frankfurt am Main • Berlin • Brussels • Vienna • Oxford

Library of Congress Cataloging-in-Publication Data
Lyngstad, Sverre.
Knut Hamsun, novelist: a critical assessment / Sverre Lyngstad.
p. cm.
Includes bibliographical references and index.
1. Hamsun, Knut, 1859–1952—Criticism and interpretation. I. Title.
PT8950.H3Z727   839.8'236—dc22   2004027919
ISBN 0-8204-7433-9

Bibliographic information published by **Die Deutsche Bibliothek**.
Die Deutsche Bibliothek lists this publication in the "Deutsche
Nationalbibliografie"; detailed bibliographic data are available
on the Internet at http://dnb.ddb.de/.

Cover design by Sophie Boorsch Appel
Cover art courtesy of Gyldendal Norsk Forlag, Oslo, Norway

The paper in this book meets the guidelines for permanence and durability
of the Committee on Production Guidelines for Book Longevity
of the Council of Library Resources.

∞

© 2005 Peter Lang Publishing, Inc., New York
275 Seventh Avenue, 28th Floor, New York, NY 10001
www.peterlangusa.com

All rights reserved.
Reprint or reproduction, even partially, in all forms such as microfilm,
xerography, microfiche, microcard, and offset strictly prohibited.

Printed in Germany

For Eléonore

Table of Contents

Acknowledgments ix

Foreword xi

1. Modernist Breakthrough and Absurdist Experiment 1

2. Satiric Interlude: *Roman à Clef* and Polemical Melodrama 37

3. Two Lyrical Novels 53

4. Love's Comedy and Sentimental Education 81

5. A Counter-Development Triptych: Ironic Pastoral, Rustic Bohemia, Bucolic Fantasy 121

6. Nostalgic Myth and Critique of Modernity: Novels of Social Change 159

7. *Growth of the Soil*: Primitivist Epic or Utopian Fantasy? 193

8. A Universe of Chance: From the Bizarre to the Macabre 217

9. Toward a Contrapuntal Novel: Romantic Nostalgia versus Pseudo-Faustian Adventure 251

10. The Human Comedy: Satiric Fantasy and Mock Apocalypse 275

11. Absurdism Revisited 307

Summary Evaluation 327

Notes 339

Selected Bibliography 373

Index 385

Acknowledgments

Parts of chapters one and three have appeared in the introductions to four translations of Hamsun novels published by the Penguin Group and are reprinted here by permission.

Foreword

Fortune has not smiled on Knut Hamsun in the English-speaking world. Whereas collected editions of his works were published in Germany and Russia in the early twentieth century, it was not until after 1920, the year in which Hamsun was awarded the Nobel Prize in Literature, that most of his novels began to be translated into English. But no collected edition has appeared. Moreover, the quality of most of the translations was mediocre at best. The first versions of *Hunger* and *Mysteries* were expurgated, and the new English translations of these novels that were made a few decades ago did little credit to Hamsun: one was egregiously faulty, the other abbreviated and simplified. Whether the difficulty of creating a literary space for Hamsun in England and America has been partly due to poor translations, as has been suggested,[1] and partly to Hamsun's similarity to Dickens, on the one hand, and D. H. Lawrence, on the other,[2] may be unanswerable questions. As for the latter possibility, the discovered resemblances would in any case affect only specific features of Hamsun's work rather than his overall achievement as a writer of fiction.

Another obstacle to a more general recognition is much clearer. There can be no doubt that Hamsun's involvement with Nazism during the German occupation of Norway (1940–1945) has greatly hampered and retarded his acceptance as a classic modern writer, along with contemporary European authors such as Thomas Mann, Franz Kafka, Marcel Proust, and James Joyce, whose works occupy a permanent place in the literary canon. At the end of the war in 1945, no one knew better than Hamsun himself to what extent his literary stock had depreciated.[3] It took a long time before the public was ready to place his pro-German activities in abeyance, and for the critics to deal with him as they would with any other creative writer. Consequently, at a time when the New Criticism was focusing on the intensive analysis of individual literary works, Hamsun tended to be bypassed in favor of less controversial authors. Worse than critical neglect was the dominant position acquired, in the 1970s, by ideological criticism in the assessment of Hamsun's work. The practitioners of this criticism, already started by Leo Lowenthal, a member of the Frankfurt School, in the 1930s,[4] tended to find crypto-fascist tendencies in just about everything written by Hamsun. Aasmund Brynildsen's critique of his oeuvre from an anthroposophical perspective is almost equally biased.[5] Applying a biographical method in reverse, the ideological critics derived the qualities and meaning of Hamsun's literary texts from his activities and opinions as a citizen, thereby stamping his entire production with the stigma of fascism.

There is no denying, of course, that Hamsun's fiction evidences conservative, even reactionary, ideas and attitudes, but to conclude from this that his total production is an expression of a fascistic ideology is absurd. However awkward it may be to split an individual into different personae, it is necessary to do so in Hamsun's case if we want to insure a fair judgment of his literary achievement. This necessity, however, arises only after his literary career is well on its way, since the political views of the early Hamsun seem to have been close to anarchism, tempered by nationalism where Norway's relations with Sweden were concerned. Moreover, at this time, during the 1890s, Hamsun's journalism—the principal vehicle through which he expressed his views—was mainly literary. But about 1910, with the death of the much admired Bjørnstjerne Bjørnson (1832–1910), Hamsun felt called upon to enter the breach left open by his idol, who was a great political leader as well as author. This was a role for which Hamsun was temperamentally ill-suited, and the political and social journalism that he subsequently produced does scant credit to his judgment and impugns his humanity. It is replete with political naiveté, social prejudice, and moral bigotry. His extreme anglophobia, together with a profound gratitude toward Germany for opening up a European market for his works, eventually led to his espousing the cause of Vidkun Quisling and, after the outbreak of war, to engaging in those polemics against the Norwegian Resistance for which he was prosecuted after the war.

Hamsun was basically a non-political person, in the sense that he neither had a gift for, nor any understanding of, the world of politics.

Several critics have called him a political imbecile or idiot.[6] Woefully mistaken about the Nazis, whom he equated with the German people, and obsessed by his nationalist dream of having Norway occupy a worthy place in the great Germanic union envisaged by Hitler, he imagined that his preeminent position as the country's most beloved author would sway his beleaguered countrymen to listen to him rather than to their legitimate leaders. This was a most tragic delusion. To an outsider, his decision to endorse Quisling and the Nazi occupation looks like an egregiously self-destructive act. Not only did it cause him to lose his honor, it also ruined him financially. At his death in 1952, Hamsun was a poor man, having forfeited his considerable fortune to the state after being found guilty of collaboration with the enemy.

In my analysis of Hamsun's achievement as a writer of fiction, I shall limit myself to the novels, making references to the poetry, plays, and short stories only where they cast a light on the particular work being discussed. Similarly, his biography, expertly treated by Robert Ferguson,[7] will be invoked only insofar as it will help elucidate the novels. It follows, as a corollary, that his political views fall outside my study, except where they are felt to intrude upon, or damage, a work's artistic quality. Given the wide range of Hamsun's fiction, my analysis will focus on the themes, structure and, to a lesser extent, style of each novel, and each cluster of novels, while attempting to demonstrate the links between one work and another, and between one cluster of works and another, where such links are apparent.

At this stage of Hamsun studies, one cannot avoid drawing upon the analyses and interpretations of previous critics; hundreds of articles and books are available on the subject. The books available in English, however, are few,[8] and none of them examines the totality of his novelistic output in depth. In attempting to remedy this situation, I shall obviously have to rely on the findings of previous scholars and critics, whose contributions will be acknowledged wherever it seems appropriate. Moreover, envisaging literary criticism as a collaborative enterprise, I have endeavored to include, in the notes, brief summaries of viewpoints and interpretations that differ from the readings which I have presented. Though not necessarily original, those readings are my own, even where they coincide with those of other Hamsun critics. I have throughout sought to capture the uniqueness of each text, while attempting to define its place within the changing phases of Hamsun's evolution as a writer.

It is an old-fashioned manner of criticism, and distinctly subjective, as it includes an evaluative component. I shall not flinch from making value judgments about the novels. Because Hamsun's oeuvre is rather uneven in quality, value judgments are quite in order, if for no other reason than to highlight the sterling quality of his finest works. A sampling of reviews and other critical appraisals, from at home and abroad, will serve to broaden the evaluative spectrum, while at the same time giving some idea of the ways in which the novels have been received.

CHAPTER ONE

Modernist Breakthrough and Absurdist Experiment

When the anonymous fragment of *Hunger*—substantially Part Two of the four-part novel—appeared in the Copenhagen journal *Ny Jord* (New Earth) in November 1888, it set off a flurry of conjectures as to who could have produced such an extraordinary piece of writing. The favorite candidate was Arne Garborg (1851-1924), well known for having depicted poverty among rural students in Kristiania (now Oslo) five years earlier. But Garborg's novel *Bondestudentar* (1883; Peasant Students), written in the spirit of naturalism, had an explicit social tendency that set it apart from the newly published piece.

A Norwegian newspaper, *Verdens Gang* or *VG* (The Way of the World), soon revealed the identity of the author, while stating, mistakenly, that he was living in America. Hamsun, who had wanted to retain his anonymity until the book was completed, now found himself famous overnight and a welcome guest in the drawing rooms of Copenhagen's intellectual luminaries. He was invited to lecture on America under the auspices of the Copenhagen Student Association and earned praise from Georg Brandes (1842-1927), the eminent critic. It was the latter's brother, Edvard Brandes (1847-1931), editor of the daily *Politiken*, who had "discovered" Hamsun and persuaded Carl Behrens (1867-1946) to publish the fragment in his journal, *Ny Jord*. Hamsun decided to expand his lectures about America into a book, *Fra det moderne Amerikas Aandsliv* (1889; *The Cultural Life of Modern America*, 1969), which forced him to postpone work on *Hunger*. The complete text appeared only in 1890.

The success of Hamsun's first novel recalls the instant fame that came to Dostoyevsky in 1846 with the appearance of *Poor Folk*, which ushered in the Natural School in Russian literature. The Danish author and critic Erik Skram called the publication of *Hunger* "a literary event of the first rank,"[1] and a distinguished Norwegian critic, Carl Nærup, wrote in 1895 that it had laid "the cornerstone of a new literature in Scandinavia."[2] It was translated into German the same year, into Russian in 1892. An English translation, severely mutilated by the exclusion of the erotic passages, had to wait until 1899. Many critics consider the novel to be Knut Hamsun's best, though he went on to write twenty more in a literary career that had begun much earlier and exceeded seventy years.

By the time the fragment came out in 1888, Hamsun had served a literary apprenticeship of more than ten years and experienced life on two continents. That life, never an easy one, was often marked by severe hardship. Born to an impoverished peasant family at Skultbakken, Vågå, in central Norway in 1859,[3] Knut Pedersen, to use his baptismal name, had a difficult childhood. In the summer of 1862, when Knut was less than three years old, his father, a tailor, moved with his family to Hamarøy, north of the Arctic Circle, where he worked the farm Hamsund belonging to his brother-in-law, Hans Olsen. From the age of nine to fourteen Hamsun was a sort of indentured servant to his uncle, since the family was financially dependent on him. The boy's beautiful penmanship made him particularly valuable to Hans Olsen, who suffered from palsy and needed a scribe for his multifarious business, from shopkeeper to librarian and postmaster. The uncle treated him rather cruelly; he would rap his knuckles with a long ruler at the slightest slip of the pen. And on Sundays the boy had to sit indoors and read edifying literature to Hans and his pietist brethren, painfully aware that his friends were outside, waiting for him to join them. No wonder Knut loved to tend cattle at the parsonage, where his uncle lived, an occupation which allowed him to lie on his back in the woods dreaming his time away and writing on the sky with his index finger.[4] Very likely, these hours of solitary musings away from the tyranny of his uncle acted as a stimulus to young Hamsun's imagination. His schooling, starting at the age of nine, was sporadic, and his family had no literary culture. However, the local library at his uncle's place may have provided a modicum of sustenance for his childish dreams.

Modernist Breakthrough and Absurdist Experiment

During his adolescence and youth Hamsun led a virtually nomadic existence, at first in various parts of Norway, later in the United States. After being confirmed at Lom, a neighboring township of Vågå, in 1873, in the same church where he had been baptized, he was a store clerk in his godfather's business in Lom for a year, then returned north to work in the same capacity for a merchant, Mr. Walsøe, not far from his parents' place. Here, at Tranøy, Hamsun seems to have fallen in love with the boss's daughter, Laura. It is uncertain whether the young man was asked to leave because of his infatuation with Laura, or because Mr. Walsøe was hurt financially by the failure of the herring fisheries in 1875.[5] In the next few years Hamsun supported himself as a peddler, shoemaker's apprentice, schoolmaster, and sheriff's assistant in different parts of Nordland. After the failure of his literary ventures in the late 1870s, the school of life took the form of road construction work for a year and a half (1880-81).

Hamsun's dream of becoming a writer had been conceived at an early age, amid circumstances that gave him no choice but to fend for himself. If ever a writer can be said to have been self-made or self-taught, Hamsun was one. Not surprisingly, the two narratives published in his teens, *Den Gådefulde* (1877; The Enigmatic One) and *Bjørger* (1878), were crude and insignificant, products of literary imitation. The former is an idyllic tale in the manner of magazine fiction, in a language more Danish than Norwegian. The latter, a short novel, was modeled on Bjørnstjerne Bjørnson's peasant tales of the 1850s. In 1879, with the support of a prosperous Nordland businessman, E.B.K. Zahl, Hamsun wrote another novel, "Frida," which he presented to Frederik Hegel at Gyldendal Publishers in Copenhagen. It was turned down without comment. The manuscript of this story—which was dismissed by Bjørnson as well—has been lost. Bjørnson suggested he become an actor. Thus, in early 1880, shortly after his twentieth birthday, the first period of Hamsun's literary apprenticeship came to an end.

The 1880s were marked by hard physical labor and renewed literary efforts. During the period he was employed in highway construction, he made his debut as a public lecturer. His next decision was not unusual for a poor, ambitious Norwegian in the 1880s: emigrating to America. However, Hamsun's ambition was not chiefly to improve his fortune; instead, he foresaw a future for himself as the poetic voice of the Norwegian community in the New World. Needless to say, the dream quickly foundered, though the lecturing activity was continued. To support himself he worked as a farm hand and store clerk, except for the last six months or so of his two-and-a-half years' stay, when he was offered the job of "secretary and assistant minister with a salary of $500 a year" by the head of the Norwegian Unitarian community in Minneapolis, Kristofer Janson (1841-1917).[6] This was Hamsun's first significant encounter with an intellectual milieu. While he did not share Janson's religious beliefs, he clearly enjoyed browsing in his well-stocked library. But his stay was cut short: in the summer of 1884 his doctor diagnosed "galloping consumption," and in the fall of that year Hamsun returned to Norway, apparently resigned to die. He was twenty-five years old. His illness turned out to be a severe case of bronchitis.[7]

Back in Norway, Hamsun's endeavors to support himself by writing stories, articles and reviews for the newspapers, while working on a "big book,"[8] brought only a meager harvest financially, despite a considerable amount of publishing activity. Worthy of mention is his article on Mark Twain in the weekly paper *Ny illustreret Tidende* (New Illustrated Gazette) in March 1885, important because by a compositor's error the "d" in his name, Hamsund, was left out.[9] The young aspiring writer adopted this spelling of his name for the rest of his life.

After a couple of years in Norway, at times in severe want, Hamsun returned to America, but now for purely economic reasons: to finance his literary ambition. From New York he wrote to a friend in Norway that it had become "impossible" for him at home.[10] However, the challenges posed by America were still formidable. Only toward the end of his two-year stay, after supporting himself as a streetcar conductor in Chicago and a farm laborer in the Dakotas, was he able to turn his attention to literature. Having returned to Minneapolis in the fall of 1887, he delivered a series of lectures there during the winter of 1887-88. These lectures, which dealt with such literary figures as Balzac, Flaubert, Zola, Bjørnson, Ibsen and Strindberg, demonstrate Hamsun's painfully acquired familiarity with the literary culture of his time. By July 1888 we find him in Copenhagen. In a brief sketch of his early life recorded in 1894 he says he "hid on board a day and a half"[11] when the ship reached Kristiania, bypassing the city that had so bitterly frustrated his literary dreams.

The young Norwegian who appeared in the editorial office of *Politiken* one morning in the fall of 1888 has been described, in the words of Edvard Brandes, by the Swedish writer Axel Lundegård. When he visited Brandes that same evening, the latter told him: "I have seldom seen anybody so down-and-out. Not just that his clothes were tattered. But that face! As you know, I'm not sentimental. But the face of that man moved me." Reading through the manuscript Hamsun had brought, he quickly realized that here was something out of the ordinary, worthy of Dostoyevsky. In the middle of his reading, he told Lundegård, "it struck me that the author was walking about town hungry. I was overcome by a sense of shame and ran like crazy to the post office and mailed him ten kroner."[12]

Brandes' suspicions were fully justified. The condition indicated in the title of Hamsun's book was one which the author had experienced several times in his life, in Kristiania as well as in Copenhagen: in early 1880, when he was staying at 11 Tomte Street, where the hero of *Hunger* lives in Part Three and Four of the book; in the winter of 1885–86; in 1888, and at other times. In a letter of December 2, 1888, Hamsun says he is living in an "attic where the wind blows through the walls; there is no stove, almost no light, only a single small pane in the roof,"[13] a description substantially replicated in the novel. About a week later he writes to the same person: "During the last six weeks I have had to wrap a kerchief around my left hand while I was writing, because I couldn't stand my own breath on it." That summer had been particularly bad, he writes: "A couple of times I was quite done for; I had pawned all I owned, I didn't eat for four days on end, I sat here chewing dead matchsticks."[14] Another letter reveals that the night spent by the hero of *Hunger* in the city jail is based on an actual episode from the summer of 1886.[15]

While periods of want and near starvation contributed the main substance of the novel, its imagery and motif structure also draw on other experiences of the young Hamsun, most notably the feelings of revolt and defiance that possessed him in the summer of 1884, when he was "sentenced to death" by his Minneapolis doctor. In an extraordinary letter to Erik Skram at Christmas in 1888, he expresses the sense of outrage he felt at this news; he confesses that it inspired a "desperate desire to go down to a brothel in town and sin[,] ... sin in grand style and kill myself doing so. I wanted to die in sin, whisper hurrah and expire in the act."[16] Here may be the germ of the novel's "fanatical whore" in the hero's last literary project, a character who sins from a "voluptuous contempt of heaven," as well as a source of his general cosmic revolt (I: 120). The follow-up in the letter is equally relevant to *Hunger*. For when his desire to die sinning was foiled, Hamsun tells Skram, his "passion broke out in other ways: I took to *loving light*." He calls it a "downright sensual love, carnal lust," which made him understand Nero's "exultation at the burning of Rome." Indeed, one night he set fire to the curtains in his room: photomania turned into pyromania. "And as I lay there watching the flames," he writes, "I literally had the feeling, in all my senses, that I was 'sinning.'"[17] While light and fire in general are important elements in the image structure of *Hunger*, one is particularly struck by their erotic connotations. In Part Three, being reminded of Ylajali, the young woman he has just become acquainted with, the hero experiences the same phenomenon described in Hamsun's letter: the voluptuous light that "penetrates" his mind becomes in the end an all-consuming, apocalyptic fire (96).

The presence of these "crazy states of mind," as Hamsun calls them, should make the reader beware of giving a too narrow, physiological explanation of the hero's bizarre mental states in *Hunger*. Referring to the "oddities" in Dostoyevsky's books, Hamsun tells Skram that, to him, they are nothing out of the ordinary; he says he experiences "far, far stranger things just going for a walk. ... Alas!"[18]

Hamsun's apparent boast can neither be proven nor disproven by the story of *Hunger*, in which the nameless central character, a young would-be writer, is permanently on the verge of starvation. From the novel's first moment, which shows the hero waking up in his "broken-down coffin" of a rented room in the Norwegian capital, his consciousness is focused on images of food and reminders of mortality. They both come to him by way of some old issues of a conservative daily, *Morgenbladet*, with which his drafty room is papered: a "fat, swelling ad for freshly baked bread" and another for shrouds at "Madam Andersen's, main entrance to the right" (I: 7). However, while the threat of death is intermittent, the hero's hunger pangs are continuous, except for brief intervals during which nothing worth reporting seems to happen. Strangely, the effect of his enforced fasting is suggestive of a drug taker's high, a similarity picked up by an American reviewer who speaks of the hero's "hallucinated consciousness." And, in a more recent review, George Steiner writes, "It is the nuanced enactment of every stage of hallucination via hunger that gives the novel its authority."[19] Hamsun himself saw his book as "an attempt to describe the strange, peculiar life of the mind, the mysteries of the nerves in a starving body."[20] One could say that it is this consciousness, with its sudden changes from euphoria to desperation, that plays the pivotal role in Hamsun's novel, and the city—its streets, its shops, its lodging houses—appears as a stage for a modern tragedy of mind.

Hamsun's chagrin at the opinion of Georg Brandes, who had found the book "monotonous,"[21] is quite understandable in view of the wide range of moods and states of mind it evokes. While he admits that it "plays on a single string," it "attempts to draw hundreds of notes from it."[22] True, each of the four fairly equal parts tells the same story, that of hope and expectation giving way to failure and frustration, but the basically downward curve of action and feeling varies from one part to another. The denouements also differ, ranging from the ecstasy of having a story accepted, in Part One, to the humiliation of sexual defeat in Part Three; from a friend's generosity, which opens the door to a week of "joy and gladness" (I: 71) in Part Two, to flight from the city as a deck hand on a ship bound for Cádiz at the end. And within each mini-story, the urban wanderer is trying to support himself by his writings, which go increasingly against the taste of the bourgeois society that constitutes his public, either because of his refusal to compromise with his aesthetic ideals, or because there is "too much fever" in what he writes (60). In any event, the interplay between the vicissitudes of fortune, including hunger and other deprivations, and the hero's mercurial temper, quirky intensity, and quixotic integrity produces, rather than monotony, a kaleidoscopic literary texture in which revolt against heaven alternates with mock humility, erotic fantasies with compulsive pranksterism, and instances of petty dishonesty with shame and remorse.

Hamsun's intention in writing *Hunger* is directly related to this strange internal landscape. In numerous letters he expresses contempt for the stereotypic novel—in fact, he says *Hunger* is not a novel, meaning it has nothing that could be called plot: there are "no weddings, no balls, no picnics."[23] He finds "character" equally suspect, following in this the example of August Strindberg (1849-1912), who in the preface to *Miss Julie* (1888) notes that his "people" are "somewhat characterless."[24] In a letter to an American friend in late 1888, Hamsun speaks about what the subject of literature should be in terms similar to those he would use in his programmatic article "Fra det ubevidste Sjæleliv" (From the Unconscious Life of the Mind), published in *Samtiden* (The Contemporary) in 1890: "The mimosas of thought—delicate fractions of feeling; one wants to delve into the most subtle tissues of psychic life. Delicate observations of the fractional life of the psyche."[25] He expresses similar ideas in an article about Kristofer Janson that appeared in the same issue of *Ny Jord* as the fragment of *Hunger*. Moreover, that essay champions a new literary language, one that commands "all the scales of music," a language whose "vibrant" words have "over- and undertones," even "lateral" tones, and can turn into "color, into sound, into smell." The writer must know the "secret power" of words, so as to be capable of combining a "hectic, passionate intensity" with a "latent . . . tenderness." The development of such a richly diverse language, the article implies, is necessary to express the above-cited fractional feelings, along with the whole "unconscious mental life that even today remains virtually uninterpreted."[26] Strangely, in his letter of complaint to Georg Brandes, Hamsun emphasizes the mere number rather than the depth of the mental states explored in his book, claiming that, if counted, they would be found to equal in number those of, for example, *Crime and Punishment* or the Goncourt brothers' *Germinie Lacerteux*.[27]

Consistent or not, Hamsun's various aesthetic pronouncements show that he had his finger on the intellectual pulse of his times. In the wake of Dostoyevsky and Nietzsche, pioneers in revolutionizing the human image, and influenced by Darwin's epochal discoveries, writers of fiction were articulating a more complex concept of man. Joseph Conrad was to show the unexplored depths of the psyche in *Heart of Darkness* (1902), as was André Gide in *The Immoralist*, published the same year.[28] The early Hamsun finds his place among these proto-modernists, both thematically and formally. Thematically, the recently translated novels of Dostoyevsky cast doubt upon the very foundations of the western humanistic tradition. Dostoyevsky's depth-psychological concept of the "broad" Karamazov nature[29] opened up the entire realm of the irrational, with divided consciousness, gratuitous acts, and the cult of intuition.

The formal corollary of this new focus is the outsider hero, internal monologue, and a novelistic strategy that draws as much on the principles of music as on those of traditional narrative. Thus *Hunger*, with its four roughly equal parts, employs the musical form of variations on a theme some dozen years before Thomas Mann used the sonata form in *Tonio Kröger* (1903). Gide's *The Immoralist*, with its three-part structure, offers a nice parallel: both Hamsun and Gide were dealing with marginal experiences, such as could not be contained within the old plot schemata. Gide chose a strict, tripartite geometrical form to convey his explosive emotional content; similarly, Hamsun's external form is very strict, whereas the substance often borders on frenzy, plunging the reader into a vortex of the most intimate personal experiences.[30]

To suggest the nature of the sensibility that manifests itself in Hamsun's *Hunger*, I shall let the book speak for itself before pursuing my analysis. The passages I have selected express central themes and illustrate characteristic narrative strategies. In the first, from Part One, what I shall call the Yahweh motif is introduced and developed. Thinking back on his "adversities," the hero first explains his "increasing weakness" by the idea of a grotesque animal incursion: "a swarm of tiny vermin had forced its way inside me and hollowed me out." Then he asks himself, "What if God simply intended to annihilate me?" As "cadences of the Bible" ring in his ears, he speaks "softly" to himself: "Wherefore did I take thought what I should eat, what I should drink, and wherewithal I should clothe this wretched bag of worms called my earthly body?" After an allusion to being provided for like the "sparrows of the air" and shown the "grace" of being pointed at by the "heavenly Father," the text, while continuing in the same Biblical tone, turns eerily sinister:

> God had stuck his finger down into the network of my nerves and gently, quite casually, brought a little confusion among the threads. And God had

withdrawn his finger and behold!—there were fibers and delicate filaments on his finger from the threads of my nerves. And there was a gaping hole after his finger, which was God's finger, and wounds in my brain from the track of his finger. But where God had touched me with the finger of his hand he let me be and touched me no more, and allowed no evil to befall me. He let me go in peace, and he let me go with that gaping hole. And no evil shall befall me from God, who is the Lord through all eternity.... (I: 17-18)

Begun on a mockingly ironic note, the passage develops an allusion to scriptural instances of God's finger, mostly metaphorical,[31] into an uncanny and physical reality. The incongruity between the solemn Biblical style and the macabre content deepens the initial irony. The imagery of being hollowed out not only ties in with the theme of hunger, but also connotes all the other lacks—economic, social, sexual, professional—which define the existence of the urban wanderer throughout his sojourn in the capital. Similarly, the religious parody introduces a stylistic element that pervades the entire novel. In this particular instance, the reification of the Biblical finger appears to be facilitated by Michelangelo's "The Creation of Adam," which Hamsun annuls by a virtual "Un-Creation of Man."

The scene in the city jail in Part Two can be seen as a hyperbolic expression of the constant threat of mortality the hero faces.[32] Just as the initial Kristiania-inflicted mark noted in the book's first paragraph turns into a wound made by God's finger, the shroud at Madam Andersen's has its grim successors. Acting on the suggestion of a police officer, the hero opts to stay overnight in the city jail, under the highly respectable name of Tangen. The fear caused by the total darkness in the cell makes him think, "What if I myself were to be dissolved into darkness, made one with it?" His anguish is temporarily diverted by his invention of a word, *kuboå*, which he thinks is "suited to mean something *spiritual*, a feeling, a state of mind." But the darkness—that "same unfathomable black eternity which my thought recoiled from and couldn't grasp"—remains. That does not prevent him from trying to understand it, and to express the inexpressible: "I made the most desperate efforts to find a word black enough to signify this darkness for me, a word so horribly black that it would dirty my mouth when I uttered it." Once again, as in the instance of God's finger, a metamorphosis takes place, the word becoming a thing, showing the hero teetering on the verge of madness, as he is himself aware: "All at once the thought flashed through my brain that I had gone mad." At the same time he confirms his conception of the word as a way of escaping death: "Who said I was going to die? Having found the word myself, I have the right to decide what it shall mean," he tells himself (I: 49–52).

In a broader perspective, the hero's confrontation with darkness and death is reminiscent of the mythical night journey, a symbolic descent into the realm of the unconscious followed by a return to daylight and rationality. Put in mind of the ships in the harbor, seen as "those black monsters" lying in wait for him, he conjures up a fearsome prospect:

> They wanted to suck me up and sail with me by sea and land, through dark kingdoms that no humans had ever seen. I can feel myself on board, pulled out to sea, soaring in the clouds, descending, descending. . . . I give a hoarse scream of terror and clutch the bed; I had been on such a perilous journey, had whizzed down through space like a faggot! How wonderful it was to feel safe again as I clapped my hand against that hard bunk bed! (I: 51)

Although the journey as described largely consists of flying, the experience is one of a terrifying descent, making the hero reflect, "This is what it's like to die" (51). The ordeal seems to go on for most of the night. Only after a glimmer of light penetrates the cell does he finally close his eyes in sleep, having anticipated the war-damaged Hemingway hero's ontological insomnia.

In Part Three the sexual theme, broached at the very outset by having the hero stalk and annoy the above-mentioned Ylajali, reaches a climax of sorts. Not sufficiently developed to constitute a plot, it is significant nonetheless. Beforehand, the hero's sexual deprivation has been forcefully evoked: he reacts to sex much the way he does to food after being forced to do without: with nausea. The "mating hour" on Karl Johan Street is described with vehement disgust: "The entire street was a swamp, with hot vapors rising from it." But though repelled, he is also attracted and searches his pocket for the necessary two kroner. "The passion quivering in every movement of the passersby, the dim light of the street lamps, the tranquil, pregnant night—it was all beginning to affect me: this air filled with whispers, embraces, trembling confessions, half-spoken words, little squeals. Some cats are making love amid loud shrieks in Blomquist's entranceway. And I didn't have two kroner." The next moment, however, the sex-starved young man looks "disdainfully" at the couples pairing off: "These easily satisfied, candy-chewing students who thought they were cutting loose in Continental style if they could feel a seamstress' bosom! These . . . boulevard dandies who didn't even turn up their noses at sailors' wives, fat duckies from the cattle market who would flop down in the nearest doorway for a crock of beer! What sirens!" Nothing less than a "long spit" can express his feelings about what is going on. Afterwards he acts like a paragon of virtue: "I lifted my head and felt deep down how blessed I was to be able to follow the strait and narrow." Meeting a streetwalker, he feigns shock at her invitation to "come along" and ends by playing the role of savior: "My name, by the way, was such and such, Pastor this or that. 'Good night! Go, and sin no more!'" (I: 75–77).

In his subsequent rendezvous with Ylajali, whose euphonious palindrome of a name, the hero's invention, evokes the dreamlike image he cherishes of her, the young man comes a cropper, despite a promising beginning: her mother, with whom she lives, being away, she feels free to invite him in. As long as they engage in sexual banter, everything goes swimmingly, but his courage collapses at the first sign of resistance, causing her to make gentle fun of him: "'There, see!' she said. . . . 'All it takes to knock you over is a tiny frown, you look sheepish as soon as one moves a little away from you'" (I: 107). The ensuing kisses, embraces, undoing of buttons and so forth come to an abrupt end when she notices that his hair is falling out, a discovery that makes her insist he tell her what sort of life he has been leading. But when, tired of "putting on an act and taking a lot of trouble over all these moves," he drops all pretenses and speaks to her as one human being to another, the romantic image *she* has obviously cherished of *him* is destroyed. The young man's honesty as he "seized the opportunity and told her everything," including that he "had walked off with five kroner one evening," caused her to turn "pale, frightened, her shining eyes quite troubled." When she buttons her dress again, he reflects, "Would she have thought better of me if I had turned myself into a roué?" (108).[33]

Before making his exit, after giving Ylajali a glimpse of his despair by telling her, "You have plucked me thoroughly clean, made me more wretched than I've ever been," he attempts to regain his dignity through bits of playacting. Among other things, he implies that he possesses extraordinary powers of perception, something like ESP, together with exceptional sensitivity, gifts that he owes in no small part to his poverty, which he declares to be an advantage rather than the opposite: "The intelligent poor individual was a much finer observer than the intelligent rich one. The poor individual looks around him at every step, listens suspiciously to every word he hears from the people he meets; thus, every step he takes presents a problem, a task, for his thoughts and feelings. He is alert and sensitive, he is experienced, his soul has been burned" (I: 111). But whatever mental superiority his "burns" have allegedly endowed him with, the dismal monologue with which the rendezvous ends comes across as a pathetic fantasy, especially when compared with his acting the Redeemer in his fleeting contact with the streetwalker.

The scene I have selected for comment in Part Four shows Hamsun's capacity for heightening, if that is the appropriate word for a curve that takes the hero into increasingly lower depths. When, unable to think of an alternative, he returns to his lodgings though no longer welcome, he finds the landlord in the hall playing Peeping Tom: looking through the keyhole, he watches his pregnant wife coupling with a newly arrived customer, a ship's mate. This is the hero's ultimate ordeal, one that shows up the phoniness of the literary project he is working on, a one-act drama with a mediaeval subject entitled "The Sign of the Cross." Apart from the bizarre external situation, one in which the landlord, "laughing with a quiet, excited laughter," invites the evicted client to share his fun—"Take a peep! Hee-hee! There they lie" (I: 130)—the peepshow looks like a mock on his own drama, one about a "gorgeous fanatical whore who had . . . sinned at the very foot of the altar . . . simply from a voluptuous contempt of heaven" (120). For the scene watched through the keyhole also has a sacrilegious aspect, as the following description suggests: "In the bed, right below Christ's oleograph and directly opposite me, I could see two figures, the landlady and the strange mate; her legs gleamed white against the dark quilt. And on the bed by the other wall sat her father, the paralyzed graybeard, looking on" (130).

Here, in a sordid, low-life corner of Kristiania, the aspiring writer has the opportunity to watch a burlesque mockery of his high-sounding defiance of heaven and, collaterally, of his literary ambition in general. No wonder the spectacle threw all his thoughts "into merciless confusion and upset . . . [his] rich mood" (I: 130). With life turning into a sex show for perverted minds, creativity is stymied. The hero is as helpless as the paralyzed old man, the fornicator's father, or as the Crucified Christ, to whom reference is made repeatedly in the lodging house section of Part Four. His identification with Christ, while anomalous, is not unexpected, in view of his above-cited words to the prostitute, "Go, and sin no more!"[34]

While the first-person novel was not very common at the time, it had been used by a Kristiania bohemian, Hans Jæger (1854–1910). His book *Fra Kristiania-Bohèmen* (1885; From the Kristiania Bohème) is a shameless self-revelation by a counter-cultural intellectual whose slogan was to "write one's life." But while Hamsun uses this narrative strategy with staggering virtuosity in *Hunger*, his version of "writing one's life" accomplishes something incomparably broader than his predecessor in the genre. While we follow the personal vicissitudes of Hamsun's hero with intense interest, we are simultaneously made to contemplate the human condition in general. The struggling fin-de-siècle artist in Kristiania becomes in the reader's mind a representative of humankind, facing the possibility of failure and, yes, even death in an alien world, a world that has no use for him. A comment Hamsun made in a letter to Edvard Brandes in 1888 may be relevant here; he says he "hadn't wanted to write for Norwegians. . . . I wanted to write for *human beings* wherever they found themselves." He felt more of a European than a Norwegian, he says.[35] Hamsun's breakthrough novel may owe its wide appeal, in part, to this broad perspective.

The ancestor of Hamsun's wanderer in the streets of Kristiania can be traced to the Romantic hero, now become a kind of flâneur by virtue of finding himself down-and-out. In the spirit of that hero, he is in revolt against heaven and at odds with men. Like Cain—a favorite of the Romantics—he is a marked man whose adversities echo the curse on the Biblical outcast. But whether the outcast status and cruel suffering of the urban wanderer recall Cain, Job, or some other figure of legend or myth, all playthings of God or fate, an occasional use of romantic irony imbues his rebellion with a tinge of self-mockery. This is clearly evidenced by his elaborate curse of God in Part Three—

which he afterward sees as "nothing but rhetoric and literature" (I: 99)—and by the way he dismisses his final appeal to Ylajali as "being claptrap and rhetoric again" (110).[36] This device turns the light of parody on the hero's pretensions; cutting him down to size, it makes him distinctly modern.

The accompanying disenchantment suggests comparison with a theme central to such nineteenth-century realistic novels as Balzac's *Père Goriot* (1834–35) and *Lost Illusions* (1837–43) as well as Dickens' *Great Expectations* (1861): that of a young man from the provinces trying to make his career in the capital. In Hamsun's case, the hero's only worthy antagonist is the city of Kristiania, which will eventually "set its mark upon" everybody who goes there (I: 7); significantly, the book begins and ends with a reference to that city. However, whereas the "campaigns" waged by the heroes of Balzac to conquer the city bring a modicum of practical success, in recompense for lost illusions, the battle of the Hamsun hero assumes the form of petty, often imaginary skirmishes with individuals, typified by his run-in with a little old man in Palace Park whom he hopes to drive from the field "in grand style" (22). By contrast with such pusillanimous battles, Rastignac, an embodiment of the Napoleonic motif so widespread in nineteenth-century fiction, issues his challenge to the city of Paris at the end of the book in a spirit of the utmost self-assurance: "A nous deux maintenant!" Though the hero, or anti-hero, of *Hunger* displays an inkling of that motif—he envisages himself as a "white beacon in the midst of a turbid human sea with floating wreckage everywhere" (36) and shows a superb contempt for "the brutes" or "the scum" (133)—his sense of superiority is sustained largely by a proclivity for self-aggrandizement, whether aristocratic pretensions, a lofty moral tone, or a would-be writer's braggadocio. Underneath the virtual mythomania, which produces an impressive succession of masks, metonymies for alternative selves, the slow process of deterioration continues unabated.

While naturalism, with its affinity for decline and attrition, may provide part of the answer to the hero's failure, his artistic ambition is clearly the root cause. With editors being able to use only what is "popular" (I: 73), his Romantic notion of creativity—shown when he exclaims after his "burst of inspiration" in Part One, "It's God! It's God!" (28)—never leads to anything that will satisfy the expectations of bourgeois society. Consequently, he loses out in the struggle for existence. His situation is not unlike that described by Marmeladov in *Crime and Punishment* when he implies that he has "nowhere . . . to go"[37]: the city has become a labyrinth, a place without exit, and society a dead end street. However, unlike Dostoyevsky, Hamsun accentuates the absurd aspects of this quandary.

This may be the feature which we find most congenial today, namely, the hero's awareness of the absurdity of all things human. Twenty-five years before Kafka created Gregor Samsa, man as an insect, and more than fifty years before Camus popularized the absurd hero as a modern Sisyphus, Hamsun in *Hunger* did both. The book swarms with insects and insect images, applied in describing the hero as well as other figures: "I felt I was myself a crawling insect doomed to perish, seized by destruction in the midst of a whole world ready to go to sleep" (I: 25). Like Sisyphus, the hero keeps rolling his rock without letup: "When a piece was finished I began a fresh one, and I wasn't very often discouraged by the editor's no," he writes (8). The book's very form, with each of four parts representing a new beginning, expresses the Sisyphean struggle and defeat, followed by renewed efforts.

Specific similarities with Camus' notion of the absurd include, from the very outset, the hero's ceaseless confrontation with death, which is the more poignant because of his vulnerable physical condition. Much of his strange behavior, as well as his *joie de vivre* — so paradoxical under the circumstances — can only be understood in the light of a perceived threat against his very existence. When he eventually pulls through, it is largely due to his unrelenting pride: metaphorically as well as physically, he wants to "die on . . . [his] feet" (I: 133).[38] While the thought of suicide does occur to him, it never becomes a real possibility; nor does he seek solace in a transcendent hope, metaphysical consolation. As in Camus' work, the accent is on a peculiar kind of modern heroism, one totally devoid of metaphysical guarantees.[39] It is not, however, devoid of metaphysical humor, as when the hero parodies Biblical language in a reversal of the man-God relationship: he will turn his back on the hypothetical God he addresses, he says, because "you did not know the time of your visitation." Like Stephen Dedalus, he proclaims *Non serviam*: "I shall renounce all your works and all your ways," he says, parodying the Christian vow to forgo the Devil (99).

Modernist Breakthrough and Absurdist Experiment 17

It is a staple of Hamsun criticism that the social perspective is non-existent in *Hunger*, by contrast to the overt socio-critical tendencies in the naturalistic literature of the period. This view overlooks the fundamentally ironic mode of the book's narrative discourse. The hero is as much out of tune with bourgeois society as he is with the order of creation, supposedly guaranteed by an all-powerful, all-knowing God. Indeed, Hamsun seems to conflate official Christianity with the middle-class social order. Here it stands him in good stead that the name of the city is Kristiania (or Christiania, which highlights the Christ connection); but beyond that, there are references to "Christ's Cemetery," "the clock of Our Savior's," and a businessman named Christie who refuses to give him a job because he cannot handle numbers. The clock, symbol of regulated, conventional bourgeois life, is associated with major social institutions: the university, the church, and the jail. The hero, having pawned his own watch, is dependent on these official indicators of public time, but he clearly has difficulty attuning his own private life to its mechanical rhythms. Thus, he is constantly either too early or too late for his appointments. Ironically, even the promise of salvation is dependent on observing regular office hours: when he arrives at the pastor's, "the hour of grace was past" (I: 63).[40] Policemen seem to be the favorite targets of the hero's nonconformist rage; they become the lightning rod for his metaphysical as well as his social defiance. Implicitly, if not explicitly, *Hunger* abounds in criticism of the established order, from a seemingly anarchistic perspective.

But this is only one side of the coin. Due to his inability to follow the clock, the hero is relegated to the role of a clown. Yes, Hamsun anticipates Picasso, Thomas Mann, and many other modernists in portraying the artist as clown—a superfluous man who knows the depths of human suffering but makes light of it, turning it into entertainment both for himself and others. The hero of *Hunger* approximates such a figure. Most often he plays a clown to himself, but at times he also plays to the public, accepting his hopelessly irrelevant position in a society that judges everything by monetary values.

Some critics contend that the hero's excessive generosity is evidence of a compulsive desire to starve, to be a hunger artist much like Kafka's famous character, arguing that his state of hunger is a necessary condition of his creative afflatus.[41] This, it seems to me, casts the hero of *Hunger* in a more abnormal role than the text justifies. True, he does say he was once "good at starving" (I: 74), as though going hungry were a kind of art, and he is incapable of holding on to his cash. But his openhandedness seems little more than a temperamental tic, indicative of his visceral contempt for material values. The narrative absence of the carefree periods in his life conforms to one of the most banal facts of human experience: happiness is aesthetically uninteresting, as Tolstoy was well aware judging by the first sentence of *Anna Karenina* (1875-77): "Happy families are all alike, every unhappy family is unhappy in its own way." It is also worth noting that, while the hero experiences an abundance of extravagant moods and fantasies during his periods of want, the story is written in retrospect: his creative efforts while going hungry amount to very little. But he can play the clown, which he does to the hilt.

The psychology of *Hunger* has given rise to many studies, including a book-length psychoanalytic critique in German.[42] Too much may have been made of Hamsun as a depth psychologist on a par with Freud and other delvers into the subconscious. What Hamsun describes in *Hunger* is the phenomenology of consciousness—if not "the shower of innumerable atoms . . . as they fall," in Virginia Woolf's parlance,[43] then something very close to it: the novel offers a minute, moment-by-moment evocation of the hero's stream of thought, at times with near-hallucinatory effect. But the narrator does not analyze unconscious motives, at least not to any depth; he simply records the vagaries of conscious and semi-conscious life—the flux of thought, feeling, and fantasy in a person whose sensibilities have been brought to a supernormal pitch by virtual physical collapse. It is perfectly legitimate, of course, to go behind and beyond the explicit narrative, to apply explanatory models that reach beneath the text to get at the dynamics of its genesis, as has been done by Atle Kittang in his pioneering study of Hamsun's so-called "novels of disillusionment."[44] And it can be tempting to link the book's sexual symbols, such as the wounded finger and damaged foot, with the hero's seeming sexual ineptness, the presence of a primal scene and so forth, and in consequence diagnose Hamsun as the victim of a castration or inferiority complex.[45] My final comments, however, will touch on some surface phenomena.

Modernist Breakthrough and Absurdist Experiment

Any reader of *Hunger* will be struck by a number of truly astounding psychological facts: first, the contingency of mental states, their sheer arbitrariness, whereby what happens in one moment is separated by vast lacunae from what precedes and follows. The life of the mind is depicted in Hamsun's first novel as discontinuous. Secondly, the book orchestrates several levels of perception, thought and feeling, some only half conscious, producing representations of a divided psyche: several selves may inhabit one and the same body simultaneously. In *Hunger*, this is shown through the many self-identifications of the hero, with the crippled old man, a little boy spit in the head by a red-bearded man, even with the oleograph Christ, who seems to observe the scandalous scene of the landlady's adulterous coupling along with the hero. While the device recalls Dostoyevsky's treatment of the double, Hamsun uses it in a novel manner. Often, the self-division becomes the occasion for humorous playacting as the hero launches into interior dialogues between one part of his psyche and another. Nevertheless, in the midst of the breaches in his mental landscape, he stubbornly insists he is of sound mind, at one with himself. And indeed, through an unrelenting stoic battle, he manages to maintain a modicum of psychic unity amid the chaos of impressions and impulses that make up his stream of thought.

In the last analysis, however, what holds the hero together is nothing but his emaciated body, which to a large extent determines the behavior of his mind. The very imagery of the book, with its wealth of physiological metaphors for mental happenings, supports this view. From this perspective, *Hunger* is a vivid example of "the writing of the body."[46]

Eventually, any theory of how to read Hamsun's *Hunger* comes up against the work's subjective mode of presentation. The epigraph of Hamsun's book on America reads, "Truth is disinterested subjectivity."[47] The force of this quasi-Kierkegaardian slogan permeates Hamsun's early novels. Though *Hunger*, for example, is written retrospectively, the point of view shows little resemblance to the Wordsworthian "emotion recollected in tranquillity," since the narrator tends to merge with the character he describes. Hamsun's choice of such a technique, which presents experience as refracted by an "eccentric" center of consciousness, with displacements, distortions and emotional projections, produces a veritable phantasmagoria of the inner life. Hence the intensity of Hamsun's style in *Hunger*: a psychological impressionism with a notable expressionist ingredient,[48] it verges on the surreal and the grotesque where states of reverie and psychic dissociation are depicted and exerts a virtually hypnotic effect.

Only occasionally does the narrator step back to cast an ironic glance at the character whose experiences he is relating. But he rarely judges him. The book contains no self-evident standard of truth or value that might help the reader take the measure of the hero's behavior. The same action is viewed in different lights at different times, and narrative distance fluctuates with the constant tense shifts from past to present and back again. The reader must find his own way among the welter of impressions, passions, and fantasies that make up this strange work.

Though the character who is the bearer of this wildly subjective world may not be immediately attractive—in fact, he is sometimes quite the contrary—he does elicit our interest and occasionally tugs at our heartstrings. If, in addition, the reader should recognize, with a shudder of delight or horror, some of the hero's strange proclivities in his or her own soul, "disinterested subjectivity" has been vindicated, proven capable of combining the portrayal of psychological uniqueness with a broad humanity.

Hamsun's first two novels, *Hunger* and *Mysteries*, form a natural duo, each sprung from the same protean sensibility and evoking the emotional experiences of a species of romantic anti-hero. Apart from being written in the third person, *Mysteries* differs from *Hunger* largely by a sustained element of intellectual debate and by the more radical form assumed by Hamsun's use of interior monologue. This development, along with the novel's markedly programmatic aspect, is closely related to a simultaneous critical campaign waged by the ambitious young author. During the time when he was working on the book that became *Mysteries*, Hamsun was engaged in a crusade against the direction of contemporary Norwegian literature. Already in 1890, the year in which *Hunger* appeared, he had published the previously cited essay "From the Unconscious Life of the Mind," in which he championed a new literary psychology, one that focused on the intangible, elusive aspects of consciousness, the very stream of thought. Concurrently, he emphasized the unpredictable nature of the process of thought and its roots in the subconscious mind. In 1891 he extended his crusade by going on a lecture tour of Norwegian cities, ending up in Kristiania in October of that year. In these lectures, the contents of which were only known through newspaper reports until 1960, Hamsun repeated his call for a new literature, while attacking the reigning deities on the Norwegian Parnassus, Ibsen, Bjørnson, Kielland, and Lie, the so-called "Four Greats." Ibsen had received a special invitation to the Kristiania lecture and sat in the front row, beside Nina and Edvard Grieg. The lectures caused a sensation, but the reviews were mixed. Many critics found the attacks to be outrageously unfair as well as churlish and cast Hamsun as a Yankee self-booster, a reference to his recent sojourns in the United States. Others found them to be intellectually shallow, such as Olav Thommessen, editor of the daily *Verdens Gang* and the model for the "Commander" in *Hunger*, who wrote that "a course in ignorance, superficiality, and impudence of a full three hours" was just too much.[49]

This largely hostile public reaction to the young author/critic is an essential part of the background to *Mysteries*, which appeared in 1892. The book has a distinct polemical component, as Hamsun continues the debate on a wider scale through his central character, Johan Nilsen Nagel, whose life mirrors in some ways that of his creator. During the period of the novel's genesis, Hamsun was very much on the move, between Kristiania and Copenhagen, between Copenhagen and the Danish island of Samsø, and from one Norwegian town to another. Moreover, despite excellent reviews, *Hunger* was selling poorly, and his finances were precarious. These circumstances were bound to have an impact on the book he was writing. Indeed, in creating the central figure of *Mysteries* Hamsun produced an aggravated or heightened version of his own provisional life: Nagel, whose rootlessness is global, represents the extreme limit of an existential condition with which his creator was intimately familiar.[50] In effect, he can be seen as a virtual self of the author, whose artistic vocation helped prevent its real-life actualization.

Although the genesis of *Mysteries*, like *Hunger*, can be traced to a decidedly personal predicament, more than any other of Hamsun's novels it was written with a particular aesthetic in mind. The book was intended to vindicate his new theory of literature, spelled out, however vaguely, in his lectures and in the above-mentioned article. In that theory, which in reality was not that new,[51] an author was envisaged as a "subjectivity" whose depiction of life and people flows from his own feelings, leaving nothing but derision for what Hamsun calls literary depiction by dint of "science and numbers."[52] In particular, the lectures included a broadside against the traditional novel, found wanting for applying a superficial psychology and showing a utilitarian concern with social problems. In contrast to his elders, who were criticized for their allegedly stereotypic character portrayal, Hamsun expressed a preference for the changeable and divided mind, for individuals "in whom inconsistency is literally their fundamental trait."[53] He wants to see the "soul illuminated and scrutinized every way, from all viewpoints, in every secret recess"; "I will," he says, "transfix its vaguest stirring with my pin and hold it up to my magnifying glass," prepared to examine "the most delicate vibrations." Significantly, the emphasis on emotional nuances also includes a preference for depicting mental phenomena in a state of becoming: he wants to direct attention to the "first germ" of thought and feeling rather than the "final bud" or flower. This accounts for his relative neglect of external action, since elements of plot—balls, outings, and so forth—show nothing but *the result* of a psychic process rather than that process "in its first germ and in its unfolding." "Thoughts," he says, "rise and change at the slightest impressions, and decisions and actions ripen by means of thoughts."[54]

Of particular importance for *Mysteries* is a statement in his 1890 article about the function of the unconscious in literature. If we want literature to give a more faithful representation of the mental life of contemporary people, he writes, it is necessary to know something about the "mimosa-like" sensitivities of the psyche,[55] the "secret stirrings" that take place "in the remote parts of the mind, the incalculable welter of emotions, . . . the random wanderings of thought and feeling, the uncharted, trackless journeys of heart and brain, the mysterious activities of the nerves, the whisper of the blood, the entreaty of the bones, all the unconscious life of the mind."[56] In the same article, Hamsun stresses the unconscious element in literary creation, following in this the German philosopher Eduard von Hartmann (1842–1906), whom he greatly admired.[57]

Modernist Breakthrough and Absurdist Experiment 23

While these premises seem intellectually exciting, they may have presented Hamsun with a dilemma of selection. A writer bent on representing the process of thought, along with the subconscious stirrings behind it, finds himself between the devil and the deep blue sea. On the one hand, the necessity of an aesthetic design calls for formal discipline; on the other, the ambition to reproduce the "unconscious life of the mind" militates against that discipline. The logic of the undertaking would call for an uninhibited outpouring of psychic contents, however trifling or absurd, and readers may have felt in 1892 – as some do today – that Hamsun sacrificed decorum and a satisfying form in favor of a misapplied notion of psychological mimesis. The extraordinary number and length of the cuts he made in subsequent editions of the book are a tacit admission of his dissatisfaction with the final product.[58] Apart from the setting, which remains the same throughout, the novel's sole unifying element seems to be the consistent presence – in every chapter except the last – of the central character, whose life and death struggle, interspersed with farce, allows the reader to forget about any perceived aesthetic lapses.

A one-sentence summary of *Mysteries* might read somewhat like this: a stranger appears in a small South-Norwegian coastal town, conceives a passion for the town beauty and, failing to win her love, commits suicide by jumping off the town jetty. While quite correctly outlining the novel's plot, this description is a caricature of Nagel's story, reducing it to the dimensions of a backwater melodrama. A more nuancé formulation, one taking account of the novel's texture as well as the bare bones of its plot structure, would rather leave the impression of a peculiarly modern type of tragedy. However, neither one nor the other is suggested by the opening sentence, which strikes a light, airy tone by the announcement of "some highly unusual events"[59] and the description of the stranger as "a remarkable, eccentric charlatan who did a lot of curious things and then disappeared as suddenly as he had come" (I: 143). But the breezy beginning is deceptive. First, in an early conversation between Nagel and the owner of the hotel where he is staying, it is revealed that, a few days earlier, a dead body was found in the adjacent woods, that of a young theologian named Karlsen, and in the next chapter we witness a scene of physical and mental torture in the hotel café. The torturer, a deputy judge by the name of Reinert – that is, a pillar of small-town society –

tries to force a disabled middle-aged coal carrier who goes by the name Miniman to drink beer sprinkled with cigar ash and to perform other degrading acts for money. While the scene casts a sinister light on middle-class society,[60] it enables Nagel to step forth as a hero, defending the defenseless and humiliating the victimizer. From this moment on, Nagel wages a kind of campaign against the town and everything it stands for,[61] while at the same time becoming more and more deeply involved with it.

During his stay, some two months, Nagel undergoes a series of emotional upheavals, though the external events are relatively few. His relationship with Miniman, whom he helps out with money and clothes, becomes closer and more complex; eventually it develops into a cat and mouse game, in which Nagel attempts to expose his friend as a pious hypocrite. After he despairs of winning the affections of Dagny Kielland, a parson's daughter engaged to a navy lieutenant, Nagel develops an interest in a poor, white-haired fortyish woman, Martha Gude, whom he invites to a charity bazaar in town, an event that represents a first climax to the novel's external action and includes a succession of scenes of scandal. Most important of these is Nagel's sudden appearance as a skilled violinist, though he has protested all along that he does not know how to play. But his virtuoso performance—of "a ballad, a barcarole, a dance, a Hungarian dance by Brahms, a passionate potpouri"—is brusquely interrupted by "some ghastly strokes, a desperate howl, a sound of woe so intolerable, so shocking, that nobody knew any longer where he was going; he made three or four strokes and then abruptly broke off" (I: 313). After the bazaar Nagel proposes to Martha and is accepted, however reluctantly.

When that relationship also comes to nothing, chiefly through the jealous intervention of Dagny, Nagel decides to make use of the vial of Prussian acid he carries in his vest pocket. However, by this time the poison has been replaced with water by Miniman, to whom Nagel, in a quaint gesture of generosity, gave his vest at a drunken party in his hotel room. Hamsun exploits the incongruity between the actual harmlessness of the vial and Nagel's conviction that its contents are deadly to produce one of the novel's most powerful sequences.[62] As Nagel staggers about the woods calling for water after drinking the "poison," he is swept up into a turmoil of fear and hope, regretting his act and reaffirming life. And in the aftermath his chagrin at having been cheated of the death he yearned for recedes in favor of relief, even joy, at still being alive.

But Nagel's euphoria is short-lived. He becomes increasingly anxiety-ridden, haunted by the apparition of a woman who had drowned herself the morning after they met in a San Francisco opium den. Nagel's own suicide by drowning occurs in a confused, semiconscious state, triggered by a feverish condition contracted from exposure in the woods and turning into virtual delirium, climaxed by a paranoid dream. In this dream, he sees himself being pursued by a "scaly beast with a slack belly . . ., a horrible hieroglyph with arms jutting out from its head and a yellow claw on its nose" (I: 372).[63] More important, it is during this three-page dream sequence that Nagel discovers the absence of, and desperately searches for, his iron ring,[64] symbol of his secular faith, which he had tossed into the sea before his attempted suicide. The failure of his dream search determines his fate. As his watch "falls to the floor" at twelve midnight, the deadline he has set himself for retrieving the ring, the now awake Nagel is propelled into headlong action, "racing toward the harbor" as though driven toward his death by some demonic force.[65] His plunge into the sea does more than end the life of the hero of *Mysteries*; it effectively dramatizes the importance which Hamsun attributed to the unconscious in human behavior.

In the rest of my discussion I shall suggest a way of reading *Mysteries*, a novel which has elicited a great deal of commentary, including a book-length study.[66] Critical evaluations varied widely from the start, Bjørnson calling it one of the "great books of literature," whereas the distinguished critic Carl Nærup found it to be "crude" and suggested, in a later evaluation, that "mystification" would have been a more appropriate title.[67] One reviewer wrote, "Here there is no longer a question of nature, only of hysterical ravings, moods drenched in delirium, and feverish hallucinations."[68] In the nineteen hundreds, the Danish critic Jørgen Bukdahl claimed that *Mysteries* was Hamsun's "best and most honest novel," in contrast to the judgment of his countryman Peter Kirkegaard that it is a "rather unsuccessful book," and that of the Norwegian novelist Knut Faldbakken, in whose opinion it is an "abortive masterpiece."[69] Hamsun's English biographer, Robert Ferguson, on the other hand, calls it an "extraordinary novel," giving one a "sensation of being actually and physically close to another consciousness."[70] American opinions of the novel range from the rhapsodic praise of Henry Miller to the largely negative reaction of John Updike.[71] Whatever one thinks of the work, it is hard to disagree with the statement by another critic that *Mysteries* is "one of the most provocative works of late nineteenth-century fiction."[72] If nothing else, these disparate appraisals attest to the complexity of Hamsun's novel, as well as of the book's central character. They both transcend the Norwegian or Scandinavian context; as a Dutch critic has said, Nagel "belongs to *European* literature."[73] One feels tempted to quote a statement by Charles Marlow in Joseph Conrad's *Heart of Darkness*: "All Europe contributed to the making of Kurtz,"[74] with the addition that, in Nagel's case, one would have to add America as well.

Nagel's story, that of a "mysterious stranger" who suddenly turns up in the small Norwegian town and as suddenly disappears, conforms to the outsider plot. However, Nagel is an outsider not only socially, like Turgenev's "superfluous men" to whom Hamsun's early heroes, or anti-heroes, have been compared,[75] but also metaphysically—"an alien, a stranger on earth," as he calls himself (I: 335). At its deepest level, his story is archetypal: the subtext traces the destiny of a modern Christ, presented in a spirit of near parody. Thus, Nagel voices a blanket condemnation of contemporary life and thought, befriends the poor and the despised, whom he helps "in secret" according to Holy Scripture,[76] and gains the love of two women suggestive of Mary and Martha, sisters of Lazarus. He is also in the habit of using stories to convey his thoughts. Though Nagel is a failed Christ, returning to the sea by which he came, he is resurrected on the novel's last page as the two women commemorate his quasi-miraculous powers.

The near-parodic aspect of the Christ analogy is shown throughout, most explicitly perhaps in chapter eighteen, where Nagel reflects on his "beautiful dream of a mission" while at the same time envisaging his suicide "in the fullness of time" (I: 330). Like Myshkin in Dostoyevsky's *The Idiot*, another Christlike figure, Nagel feels a need to play providence to people.[77] But he also, like Ivan in *The Brothers Karamazov*, comes close to being a moral nihilist, articulating a kind of negative theodicy. Ivan tells his brother Alyosha that, while he

Modernist Breakthrough and Absurdist Experiment 27

accepts God, he cannot accept "God's world," or any "eternal harmony" that history might bring about. He will "respectfully return him [God] the ticket" of admission and, on reaching thirty, "smash the cup [of life] to the ground" — clearly hinting at suicide as one way out.[78] Nagel combines these contrary positions: on the spur of the moment, the providential role he wishes to play is brusquely negated, as he reflects, in a moment of nervous exhaustion: "What concern was it of his that the good Lord arranged a collision with loss of life on the Erie Railroad far inside America. None, to be sure. Well, he had just as little to do with Martha Gude, a respectable lady of this town" (235). In his moral elusiveness, Nagel seems most akin to another Dostoyevskian character, Nikolai Stavrogin, the mysterious figure in *Demons* whose ambiguous nature, divided between noble and vicious impulses, leads him to death by his own hand.[79]

Within this overall pattern of *Mysteries*, a parodic version of the Christ story with its associated motif of righting the wrongs of this world, Hamsun accommodates a novelistic structure consisting of two basic elements: romance and intellectual debate. The model may derive from Ivan Turgenev (1818–83), whose novel *Rudin* (1855) is referred to in the text. Like most Turgenev novels, *Rudin* combines a failed romance with veritable orgies of discussion, and as in *Mysteries* the discussion often takes the form of quasi-monologues. Since the debates, dealing with issues of the day, will seem less and less relevant as time goes on, the double structure tends to privilege the romance element. In the working out of that element, Hamsun is closer to Dostoyevsky than to Turgenev: like Myshkin, Nagel shuttles between two women, both of whom play a fateful role in his life.

The novel's narrative progression is largely determined by the vicissitudes of the love stories. Since Nagel is consistently at the focus of the action, its dynamic depends chiefly on him; that dynamic is determined by two contrary forces, contingency and fatality. Nagel's mental reservation of suicide as a last resort places him in a world of utter contingency, one in which anything can happen. The problems caused by the total freedom this condition entails become evident at the very outset, by his difficulty in deciding whether to disembark from the steamer or not: for him, this is a Hamletic moment of to be or not to be. The acceptance of suicide removes all rational motives of action in favor of sheer caprice, turning the novel into a succession of gratuitous acts. On the other hand, once his passion for Dagny develops, the reader may begin to wonder: Will he follow in the wake of Karlsen, who apparently killed himself for love of her, or will he succeed where Karlsen failed? Eventually, one perceives a growing sense of fatality, as Nagel's attempts to control his life fail, turning his clairvoyance into a fearful prefiguration of destruction.[80] Together, contingency and fatality produce a haunting feeling of suspense that goes far toward unifying the highly disparate materials of the work.[81]

The love of Nagel for Dagny Kielland, however it manifests itself, shows every sign of being an all-absorbing passion. A thinker who "never learned how to think" (I: 247), a musician who fills his violin case with dirty laundry, in short, an artist manqué, Nagel in his yellow aesthete's suit seems bent on investing his artistic talent and energies in the business of living. His love is a desperate attempt to give meaning to his life; a metaphysical eros, it is the means whereby he hopes to justify his very existence. That is why its failure brings such disastrous consequences. By the time he starts wooing Martha, he is simply concerned to survive, however meagerly. The pastoral dream of life with Martha that he evokes in chapter sixteen is symptomatic of the psychological regression that Nagel undergoes toward the end of the novel.

Despite the special circumstances of Nagel's attachment to Dagny, his love conforms to a romantic archetype, best exemplified by Goethe's *Sturm und Drang* novel *The Sufferings of Young Werther* (1774). Both Werther and Nagel go into ecstasies in their communion with nature and take a jaundiced view of the societies in which they find themselves; both fall in love with rather ordinary women who have been promised to someone else, and they end by taking their own lives. Though the would-be lovers respect the "injured third parties" whom they seek to supplant, they are powerless to desist from their impassioned wooing. On the contrary, the obstacles in the way of their love, the very impossibility of its fulfillment, seem to act as a stimulus to continued pursuit.[82]

In the working out of the archetype, especially the elements of irrationality and tragic suffering, Hamsun may have drawn upon three German philosophers who were in the forefront of public discussion at the time, Arthur Schopenhauer (1788-1860), Eduard von Hartmann, and Friedrich Nietzsche (1844-1900).[83] To Schopenhauer, love is "the source of little pleasure and much suffering."[84] Hartmann calls it a "demon who ever and again demands his victim," and an "eternally veiled mystery" that wills an infinitude of "longing, joy and sorrow"; it is "eternally incomprehensible, unutterable, ineffable, because never to be grasped by consciousness."[85] As for Nietzsche, his relevance in this context pertains as much to the temper of his thought as to its substance. Nagel possesses a heightened sense of life, a spirit of exuberance, that is very reminiscent of Nietzsche, as is his extolling of "His Eminence Excess" (I: 335). Indeed, it has been suggested that *Mysteries* is an example of tragedy à la Nietzsche, an essay on "agony and ecstasy — with Dionysian strains."[86]

Perhaps the most distinctive feature of *Mysteries* is that the love plot is doubled by a kind of male romance, the bonding between Nagel and Miniman. This relationship operates on two levels, one realistic, the other symbolic. In protest against Edvard Brandes' claim in his review of *Mysteries* that Miniman was "an entirely Russian figure,"[87] Hamsun retorted, in a letter to Philipsen, his publisher, that he was a real person, corresponding in every detail to the character in the novel.[88] However, the manner in which the relationship is developed betrays obvious Dostoyevskian traits. While at the outset Nagel appears as a rescuer, offering protection to one of the "insulted and injured," the subsequent meetings between Nagel and Miniman increasingly assume the character of interrogations, much like the virtual duels between Raskolnikov and the police investigator Porfiry Petrovich in *Crime and Punishment*.[89] Eventually Nagel reveals his long-time suspicion that Miniman had murdered Karlsen. But even after admitting his mistake on that score, Nagel accuses Miniman, with his "mendacious blue eyes," of being "an unclean, unctuous soul," "a cowardly angel of the Lord" who might still infect Martha with his "sanctimonious depravity" (I: 355–56). Here, again, Hamsun's portrayal of Nagel may owe something to Nietzsche, ever suspicious of appearances, especially the mask of humility worn by followers of the so-called slave morality.

The confirmation of Nagel's suspicion on the book's last page, where we are told that Miniman has "come to a bad end" (I: 373), reflects not only on Miniman but on the society of which he is a part. While the townspeople go on with their lives as if nothing had happened, the revelation of Miniman's crime, possibly attempted rape, shows up the moral depravity lurking under the respectable surface. For despite his outsider's status, Miniman's unconscious hypocrisy metonymically involves all the other whited sepulchers of the town.

Nevertheless, it is as Nagel's double that Miniman becomes truly fascinating, adding both complexity and depth to Hamsun's novel and laying bare fateful contradictions in Nagel's psyche. Hamsun himself was fully aware of Miniman's status as Nagel's "alter ego"; therefore, he says, "those mysterious clashes, therefore the dreams, therefore his visions of him when [he] wants to kill himself and so forth."[90] Dostoyevsky tends to use the double to symbolize a central character's moral underground, like Smerdyakov in relation to Ivan Karamazov. By contrast, the difference between Nagel and Miniman is chiefly a matter of class and temperament, not morality, the former being an excessively ebullient member of the middle class, the latter a shy and rather taciturn proletarian. However, it cannot be forgotten that Miniman is physically misshapen, a possible hint at a warped nature. Yet, despite the divide separating them, Hamsun suggests they are united by deep affinities. Thus, in his meetings with Miniman, particularly when in his cups, Nagel sometimes confuses his own persona with that of his interlocutor. Hamsun formulates the situation quite aptly, if somewhat obscurely, in a letter to Erik Skram: "The question is whether he [Nagel] hangs together, hangs together with his alter ego, Miniman, and hangs loosely enough together with himself to almost fall apart."[91]

The deep bonds between these two figures, whose names echo one another—one being called Johan, the other Johannes—are shown most convincingly through Nagel's dreams, in chapter six and twenty-two (I: 189-91; 370-73). Both dreams are agons, the first Miniman's, the second Nagel's; yet, these dreams are important chiefly for what they tell us about the dreamer, Nagel. In the first dream, Nagel is split in two, between the humble, barely human creature struggling to rise out of the primeval jungle and the arrogant intellectual whose taunts prefigure Nagel's semi-sadistic interrogations of his friend. In the second dream—which Hamsun, taking his cue from Dostoyevsky, no doubt, presents as though it were an actual happening—the roles are reversed, Miniman being the potential savior, as well as the voice of reason, Nagel the victim of his own unreason. At this point all certainties have been relativized: moral principle—the categorical imperative or the Christian maxim of doing to your neighbor as you would be done to—is stood on its head as Nagel becomes a victim, rather than a beneficiary, of Miniman's good intentions. The little man who a short time ago turned Nagel's projected suicide into an embarrassing fiasco, once more interferes fatefully in his life, though this time by indirection, in Nagel's dream. Ironically, he enacts in both instances the very principle obeyed by Nagel in saving a young man who jumped overboard on his way to Hamburg. Nagel's world is collapsing; eventually he envisages himself in the role of a clown, dancing in the market place in his stocking feet just like his humble friend. It is as though the transvaluation of all values which underlies his attacks on, and parodies of, received ideas and current ideologies has come home to roost.

The subconscious dialectic revealed in Nagel's dreams of Miniman shows that, however sharply he rejects society, he cannot escape it. Nor is he able to find a satisfactory replacement for it through nature. His rapture in the woods, with its lyrical afflatus, while transporting, is undercut by its associated images. In a state of "perfect contentment," he "perceived music in his blood, sensed a kinship with all of nature, . . . felt enveloped by his own sense of self as it came back to him from trees and tussocks and blades of grass. His soul grew big and rich, like the sound of an organ inside him. . . ."[92] The mystical sense of oneness with creation is accompanied by a self-inflation approaching apotheosis. Nagel even hears someone calling him, a putative divine presence, and he answers the call. The fancy of rocking about "on a heavenly sea, fishing with a silver hook and singing to himself" seems more disinterested, an instance of pure beauty. However, in the midst of his ecstasy he experiences a *Weltschmerz* and a sense of transience so keen as to be soothed only by the thought of "putting an end to it all!" The foetal position Nagel assumes, as he curls up, "hugging his knees and shivering with well-being," similarly associates the experience with a death wish. And the seemingly trivial sight, a moment earlier, of a cat in the arms of a little girl, followed by that of a white pigeon "reeling sideways down the sky" (I: 183–84), presumably shot dead by a hunter, will become a sinister portent of spiritual agony and death.

The ominous undertones of the experience in the woods are confirmed through subsequent events. The forest, the scene of "perfect contentment," later becomes the scene of the abortive suicide. The cat motif, introduced so innocently early on, turns into the gruesome story of a cat "writhing in the most terrible agony," with a fish hook stuck in its throat (I: 351). Two chapters later, in Nagel's delirious monologue, it is Karlsen, with whom Nagel seems to identify, who is choking on a fish hook, and finally Nagel thinks he is himself "lying there with a fish hook in his throat" (369). The romantic image of fishing with a silver hook in a celestial ocean—with a possible allusion to the biblical notion of being "fishers of men"[93]—betrays a sinister reverse of fraudulence as Nagel reflects that everything is "a farce, sheer humbug," that "even the blue of the sky is ozone, poison, insidious poison" (336). Concurrently, the fishing trope turns into the motif of the hunter/hunted. In the end, after Nagel realizes he is no longer wearing the iron ring, the call heard in the woods recurs as a succession of demonic summonses from the sea. Similarly, though discarded by an act of free will, the ring—a pledge of loyalty to the earth—becomes the agency of inexorable fatality.

The "mysterious" aspects of Hamsun's novel are epitomized in some of the inserted stories, in particular Nagel's encounters with a blind girl and with a woman wearing a cross. The first, related on the spur of the moment, is called an *eventyr*, a word that means "adventure" as well as "fairy tale," causing the story to hover on the borderline between dream and reality. It is a kind of fable of eros, charged with beauty, tenderness—and horror. An amateur Freudian reading is irresistible: there is the forbidding father, who yet lures Nagel on; there is the implicit promise of a night of passion, withdrawn when the girl abandons him. Instead, his night is filled with lovely sights and beautiful music: desire has been sublimated into art. However, the grisly denouement the following day, with the blind girl's body shattered on the ground, makes sublimation look like a crucifixion. Though the tale excites Dagny sexually, it presents erotic passion as a blind and ruthless force that wreaks havoc with people's lives. It acts as a foreshadowing of things to come.

The anecdote about the woman with the cross is perceived as an omen of disaster already in the telling, when Nagel visits Dr. Stenersen toward the end of the novel. The woman, whom Nagel had helped out with money in a San Francisco opium den so she could keep her cross, had killed herself the following morning. After her death, he tells the Stenersens and their guests, she once saved his life, but now, having seen her apparition that very morning, he is filled with anxiety. As in the "adventure" with the blind girl, the story's horror is largely conveyed by an image of falling: the blind girl falls to her death from the top of the tower in which she lives, the woman with the cross throws herself into the sea. More importantly, Nagel himself experiences a free fall as his opium trance wears off. While the experience itself, with its musical imagery, recalls his one-time rapture in the woods, his fall into the ocean, which confronts him with the spread-eagled body of the woman with the cross, is an obvious allusion to the crushed body of the young girl. Both stories are uncanny, hinting at the presence of hidden demonic forces. How else to explain the behavior of Nagel's puppy, Jakobsen, who raises his hackles and barks furiously during the second apparition of the woman with the cross?

It has often been said that, toward the end, Nagel suffers a complete psychological disintegration, that, in fact, he becomes insane. Hamsun himself says in a letter that the book deals with a "strange fellow" who "ends up by going quite mad."[94] But it is questionable whether Nagel possesses a core identity to begin with. Not only is he known by more than one name, but in the course of the novel he assumes a gamut of roles, somewhat brashly enumerated by Henry Miller: Nagel plays "the clown, the buffoon, the lover, the con man, the fixer, the patron, the phony detective, the intellectual, the artist, the enchanter,"[95] to which might be added agronomist, globetrotter, collector, do-gooder, friend, heir, self-slanderer, iconoclast, mystery man. The self as portrayed in *Mysteries* is reduced precisely to a collection of roles, played in succession or simultaneously. Nagel even acts out roles in solitude, as in an early scene in his room where he awakens from his mental absorption with a start, "so abrupt that it could have been feigned, as if he had contemplated making this start for a long time, though he was alone in the room" (I: 145). Seen in this light, the novel illustrates the nullity of the self, turning Hamsun into a postmodernist *avant la lettre*, the creator of a "man without qualities." Could the underlying reason for Nagel's love of Dagny, and his dream of a pastoral existence with Martha, be his desire to escape from the curse of a serial personality?

Hamsun's literary technique in this book is equally unorthodox. Much has been written about the angle(s) of narration in *Mysteries*. Though initially we sense the presence of an observer, a townsman perhaps, who tells the story, soon we find ourselves listening to Nagel's thoughts, mostly by way of free indirect discourse or *erlebte Rede*,[96] but also here and there in the form of stream of consciousness. Yet, we do not have to do with an omniscient author, but with a limited omniscience. On the whole, Hamsun treats the handling of point of view rather cavalierly in *Mysteries*. The narrative persona seems to hover above the text like a sort of all-seeing eye, an eye that can feign partial sight at will, if the occasion calls for it. Wolfgang Kayser says that Hamsun's narrator seems to dissolve into "an aura" that "floats around and through the characters."[97] By comparison with *Hunger* and *Pan*, both consistently first-person stories, *Mysteries* is narratologically loose, whether by design or from lack of skill. It looks as though Hamsun's project, that of portraying a strong, complex mind drifting toward crackup, demanded the technical eclecticism that distinguishes this novel from its two classic companions.

Whether one likes the book's narrative strategies or not, Hamsun seems to have achieved considerable success in applying his new aesthetic in a substantial work of fiction. As a whole, *Mysteries* succeeds in creating an intensely immediate sense of the day-by-day, hour-by-hour, stream of thought of the central character, who is poised on the brink of annihilation. The social occasions with their carousing and debates—including Nagel's outrageous sallies at everything under the sun à la Mark Twain and the Dostoyevsky-inspired scenes of scandal—recede in the reader's experience in favor of Nagel's interior monologues. As he experiences one disappointment after another, the devotee of the "higher" or "superior" man who champions the "great terrorist" (I: 172–74)[98] emerges as a sensitive soul at odds with society and, perhaps, with life itself.[99] Withdrawing more and more into the torture chamber of his own subconscious psyche, Nagel is haunted by phantoms and driven to his death by the mysterious forces he so tirelessly defended against the inroads of science and reason, forces now turned destructive.

In *Mysteries* Hamsun shows little concern with some of the most essential elements of the traditional novel: a coherent plot, causality, fullness and consistency of characterization, plausibility, and point of view. Yet, it cannot be called a modernist novel *tout court*. It does, however, display several modernist traits,[100] inevitably so, considering Hamsun's intent: to probe the deepest layers of the psyche, where irrationality reigns and ordinary cause and effect appear to be suspended. This is also the realm of the uncanny, where depth psychology meets the mystery story. The bizarre relationship between everyday reality, dream, and fairy tale in the book borders on the surreal, or on magic realism. All these new elements, grounded in the irrational, forced Hamsun to come up with a novel set of criteria for aesthetic coherence. Perhaps a musical analogy will be helpful. Despite the seeming chaos of Nagel's mind, his story falls into a definite pattern: the repetitions, variations, and recapitulations of situations and motifs that the text reveals generate an aesthetically satisfying rhythm and a sense of completion, while at the same time producing a plausible rendering of a mind at the end of its tether.

Viewed in a different perspective, *Mysteries* can be seen as an absurdist work. Life in society is described as a kind of puppet show, in which the puppets dutifully repeat their lines. Some of the characters have generic names — lawyer, teacher, and occasionally doctor — as in an expressionist play. And in the end Nagel, who considers himself to be above the social comedy, also becomes a puppet as he is drawn to his death by his own subconscious obsessions. But by its very absurdity, Nagel's predicament becomes tragic. The book envisages the human condition as a tragedy of mind: the more highly developed your consciousness, the more acutely you will suffer. The mind of Nagel, which perceives the before and after with a lacerated sensibility, is fraught with existential angst. The loathing instilled by life's humiliations is akin to the nausea felt by Roquentin in Sartre's famous novel *La Nausée* of 1938. However, unlike Roquentin, Nagel has renounced redemption through art.

Mysteries is a very rich novel, and a brief discussion cannot do full justice to it. In any case, the reader will want to work out his or her own interpretation of the book, which, despite its occasional quirks and perversities, presents a bracing challenge to one's critical imagination.

CHAPTER TWO

Satiric Interlude: *Roman à Clef* and Polemical Melodrama

Hamsun's next two novels confront the critic with a riddling question: Why would a writer, having produced two works that were, if not revolutionary, at least novel and innovative, expend considerable energy on projects that, by any standard, fall into the category of traditional fiction? After all, his lectures of 1891 had called for a deep-probing psychological literature, in which conventional plot and character would be replaced by the evocation of the stream of thought, pursued to its innermost springs and displayed in its full range, conscious and subconscious. One feels tempted to quote Hamsun against himself: his radical challenge to conventional portrayal, contained in his stated preference for characters "in whom inconsistency is literally their fundamental trait,"[1] seems to have gone by the board. At this point it is Hamsun, the soi-disant literary innovator, rather than his characters to whom this statement seems to apply.

The novels in question, *Redaktør Lynge* (1893; Editor Lynge) and *Ny Jord* (1893; Shallow Soil, 1914), defy Hamsun's aesthetic program not only by their form but also by an evident didactic strain, especially *Shallow Soil*. In a review of Bjørnson's novel *Paa Guds Veje* (1889; In God's Ways, 1889) that appeared in 1890,[2] Hamsun had scored Bjørnson for his didacticism, and he continued to maintain his antididactic stance. Why, then, did he go on to write two such ideologically committed novels? It looks as though a literary theory, formulated in a fever of creative *élan*, was thwarted by Hamsun's temperament and passionately held convictions.[3] This conflict, which may be compared to that between artist and moralist in the middle and late Tolstoy, will turn up repeatedly in Hamsun's work. Where the convictions win out, the result is an unprepossessing combination of, or alternation between, satire and didacticism. In the present duo, *Editor Lynge* is principally satire, while *Shallow Soil* contains elements of both satire and moral instruction.

Hamsun's motives in writing these books were a mixture of vaulting intellectual ambition and deep-seated emotional antagonisms. In a letter to the Danish author Erik Skram in late 1892, Hamsun objects to his friend's statement that he, Hamsun, was a better poet than thinker, claiming that the exact opposite was true; as his next book would demonstrate, he was, he writes, a "cerebral person."[4] However, as an autodidact, an epithet he repeatedly applies to himself, he is at the same time haunted by a feeling of being intellectually inadequate. Thus, Hamsun's sojourns in Paris during the major portion of the period 1893–95 were clearly intended as a way of making up for his lack of regular schooling. The desire to prove a point in regard to his strength as a "thinker" may certainly have been a factor in the genesis of these two novels. For all that, *Editor Lynge* was chiefly motivated by a desire for revenge upon those who had excoriated him for his lecture series, while *Shallow Soil* looks like an attempt to show up the phoniness of the cultural life of Kristiania, the city that had caused him so much heartache and frustration. Though neither novel is without merit, they do not rise to the level of great fiction.

Hamsun's lectures were denounced by many as being brash and self-boosting as well as uninformed. The previously mentioned attack by his one-time benefactor, Olav Thommessen, was particularly painful. Thommessen's paper, *Verdens Gang*, had featured the Kristiania lectures in a caustic editorial in which Hamsun was accused of "critical-psychological charlatanism."[5] Tore Hamsun says that his father "felt hurt by such a malicious attack by a man whom he valued highly in many ways."[6] One finds a hint of a reaction already in the opening paragraph of *Mysteries*, where Nagel is introduced as an "eccentric charlatan" by the narrative persona (I: 143). In contrast to this brief allusion, *Editor Lynge* looks like a somewhat oversize response, despite its modest length.

Satiric Interlude: Roman à Clef *and Polemical Melodrama*   39

This is not the only link with Hamsun's earlier fiction; intertextuality exists on several levels with *Mysteries* and *Hunger*, as well as with the ill-fated lectures. One suspects that Balzac, whose work Hamsun knew, having lectured about him in America,[7] is behind the appearance of characters already known to the reader, such as Dagny Kielland, now Mrs. Dagny Hansen, Martha Gude, and Øien, a student in *Mysteries*, now mentioned as an author discovered by Lynge, the main character. However, they are noticeably changed, especially Dagny, who is both more worldly and, selectively, more sensitive. Nagel is reduced, in her recollection, to an "out-and-out adventurer . . ., an insignificant dwarf," who had "jumped into the sea head-first and done away with himself without saying a word," and she dismisses the thought of the "poor blue-veined theologian who had fallen so violently in love with her," finding the whole situation just "too ridiculous." She does, however, show remorse for the fate of Nagel, and regret at having turned him down, implying that it had been "touch and go" at their last meeting: "a single word more, another half a prayer on his part, and she would have defied the whole world and thrown herself upon his breast." That he had not uttered this "half prayer" was "her own fault, she had rebuffed him so cruelly a couple of times." The "guilt toward herself," as well as toward him, that she harbors weighs heavily on her, unbeknownst to everybody; for she can "dally and flirt" like a true coquette. Then she will suddenly "grow moody and quiet." Though Dagny leads Lynge on, going to the theater and to political meetings with him, when the chips are down she locks herself in her bedroom, leaving him in the company of Martha, with whom she shares an apartment in the capital. Her grief seems to have softened her, planting a seed of compassion in her heart: thus, to Lynge's plan to expose a pastor who has sexually abused a nine-year-old girl, she responds mentally with, Why did things always have to go wrong? Why couldn't people be happy? (II: 25–26).

My intent in dwelling so long on Dagny, a very minor figure in the book, is to show, first, how Hamsun changes the perspective from one novel to another, second, to demonstrate that, rather than simplifying her character, Hamsun in *Editor Lynge* complicates it, giving it greater depth and emotional resonance. She becomes an example of what Hamsun's raisonneur in the novel, Høibro, calls a "complex soul," in a political speech that features some of the characterological notions Hamsun had expressed in his lectures: "The human soul could only with difficulty be expressed by a whole number, it consisted of nuances, contradictions, of hundreds of fractions, and the more modern a soul was, the more it was composed of nuances" (II: 30). Not many of Hamsun's characters in *Editor Lynge* are "modern" in this sense, as they serve chiefly to show the different facets of the eponymous hero.

At this point in time, and from a non-Norwegian vantage point, the specific political situation at the heart of the novel's plot is of little interest. On a modest scale, the passage of time has effected a transformation of the book comparable to what has happened to a work like *Gulliver's Travels*, now often read as a straight adventure story. To understand what makes Alexander Lynge tick we do not need to know the political circumstances of Norway in the early 1890s, a time when the Liberal Party was divided into a moderate and a radical wing and there was widespread dissatisfaction with the government's policy concerning the union with Sweden. That Hamsun's model for Lynge, Olav Thommessen, failed to pursue a consistently aggressive editorial policy toward Sweden is no longer of interest to readers of Hamsun in English, if it ever was. Meanwhile we can enjoy the incisive portrait given in Hamsun's novel of a highly talented newspaper tycoon, a journalist whose compromises and shenanigans appear like a template for many of our experiences with the contemporary media.[8]

Like so much of Hamsun's fiction, *Editor Lynge* is a novel of disillusionment, for the reader as well as for the characters. It starts with a scene of two young men who hope to make a way for themselves in the world of journalism and politics, respectively. Their fortunes in the course of the novel follow a chiasmic or hourglass pattern: poor, conservative Fredrik Ihlen is employed by Lynge to bestow a patina of gentility to his liberal paper, only to be dismissed when his articles no longer bring in new subscribers; by contrast, the radical Endre Bondesen—whose name means "son of a peasant"—ingratiates himself with Lynge, at the price of compromising his political convictions. Meanwhile Bondesen has succeeded in seducing Fredrik's sister, Charlotte, whom he drops as soon as the affair impinges on his freedom. The standard by which the characters and events are judged is embodied in the above-mentioned Høibro, a thirty-year-old bank clerk whose poverty and shabbiness recall the hero of *Hunger*. Høibro is a mouthpiece for Hamsun's central moral values: "honesty, absolute incorruptibility, contempt for personal gain"; his ideal is summed up by the phrase "nobility of soul," an innate "refinement of the heart" (II: 30).

Alexander Lynge is an excellent portrait of a media trimmer, changing his editorial opinions so as to reap the maximum financial advantage and political clout for his paper.[9] Today, his maneuverings will sound familiar: using sensational news items, such as stories of sexual abuse of minors by the clergy, to sell papers; publicizing needy cases in a show of compassionate concern; enticing public officials to reveal government secrets while promising — on flimsy grounds — that sources are protected; and so forth. Meanwhile, Hamsun enriches his portrait as a public figure by repeated glimpses of his private life. It is the interplay between public and private, political and sexual, which turns Lynge into something more than a mere stereotype of the business world.

In portraying Lynge, Hamsun for the first time provides fragments of a character's past life: from his childhood in the country he bears, tattooed on his hands, some "common, blue peasant letters" which he cannot erase, "however much he had rubbed them for many years" (II: 20). This stigma, which figures as a recurrent motif in the novel, may cast some light on his compulsive womanizing. Although Hamsun's ironic presentation of Lynge, a married man, as a Don Juan — his "spy" bears the name Leporello — may seem farfetched, his womanizing in private life is of a piece with his public quest for power, even the power to tumble governments if the prospects are right. Needless to say, he suffers defeats as well as triumphs in both realms. Aside from a couple of mistresses, one of whom he shows the door in the course of the novel, there is Dagny, who sometimes acts as a kind of muse, and Charlotte Ihlen, for whose sake he gives her conservative brother a job.

Paradoxically, his failings as a human being and as a political schemer redound to his strength as a literary character. Thus, his listening to Dagny's counsel of mercy to support a tottering administration rather than bring it down, while unwise in view of the outcome, shows him to be a man of feeling, acting as much on impulse as on a deliberate strategy. He is easily moved, touched, and can be compassionate as well as revengeful. He also displays a lively sense of humor, as when he erupts on seeing a rival editor during a political crisis: "Oh, behold the lamb of God, which beareth the burdens of the whole world!"[10] In the eyes of the public he is a "great man" (II: 107), while his chief critic, Høibro, sees him as an "inwardly damaged" peasant student, a rootless migrant from the countryside who never grew up but remained a "gifted boyish rogue" (61). These divergent views may confuse those who believe in the existence of a personal essence, but Lynge succeeds as a literary character largely because of them.

By contrast, most of the minor figures are one-dimensional, little more than literary conveniences. Fredrik Ihlen seems a mere device to cast a murky light on Lynge, and Høibro, the raisonneur, is virtue incarnate. The romance subplot involving Bondesen, Charlotte, and Høibro is unconvincing, though the opposition it dramatizes — between Bondesen's caddish behavior and Høibro's highmindedness — is germane to the novel's overarching theme. Hamsun obviously wanted to mitigate the moral shabbiness associated with Lynge and Co. by a story of redemption. For whereas Lynge, true to the satiric genre within which he functions, remains true to his devious, dishonest ways to the very end, Høibro and Charlotte, falling outside Hamsun's satiric intent, undergo a process of change.

The chief trouble is Hamsun's conception of Høibro. Apparently he was envisioned as a fresh version of Nagel, judging by Dagny's reaction to hearing him speak at a political meeting: "There was something about this man that impressed her, the timbre of his voice, his opinions, the metaphor of the orbitless comet; it was as though something of Johan Nagel's voice and turns of phrase were buzzing past her" (II: 32). However, the only similarity between the two is that both tend to disagree with everybody else on practically everything; otherwise they are worlds apart. Despite his thirty years, Høibro betrays the mindset of an adolescent: a poor bank clerk, he forges a document to provide himself with money to buy a bicycle for the girl he secretly loves, Charlotte Ihlen, an act that lays him open to exposure as a criminal. When Charlotte finally gives him her attention, after being "betrayed" by Bondesen, he is horrified to learn that she is no longer "innocent," thinking: "And her he had worshiped every day and hour since the first time he set eyes on her! She would come to him full of experience, . . . would be tender to him as to the others and embrace him with her practiced hands. And then to go through life knowing all the time that it was true! He just couldn't. . . . He would rather do away with himself." A moment later he thinks, "She could have stolen, murdered, only not this" (128).

The subsequent revulsion, causing Høibro to see himself as equally guilty and to turn himself in, despite the fact that he now can redeem the forged paper in the bank, is equally preposterous. His moral contest with Charlotte, who confesses her "fall" when she realizes she loves him (II: 127), seems all too noble; it smacks of didacticism. Though it is not explicitly stated, the reader receives a hint that they are eventually reconciled. Fredrik and his other sister, Sofie, are sent off to America.

Significantly, the language Hamsun expends on his main character markedly exceeds, in vividness and verve, the style he employs in presenting the romance plot. Its distinguishing characteristic is a metaphoric strain of physical violence, including the ultimate punishment: death. Thus, one of the very first images associated with Lynge is "to give the deathblow," in this instance to a faltering government (II: 11). Short of "felling" the unfortunate victim of a story or news item (25), he will use his "whip," which never fails and leaves "weals" behind, by contrast to *The Norwegian*, a despised journalistic rival for the public's favor. Hamsun also draws upon a wide array of other images to evoke Lynge's relentless editorial tactics: animal, hunting, mechanical, elemental, and the like. Conceptually, Hamsun seems to be demonstrating the workings of Social Darwinism, whether he was aware of it or not. As an editor, Lynge "writes with claws, with a pen that gritted its teeth"; not surprisingly, he sees *The Norwegian* as being "toothless" and deserving to die. Like some trained canine, he possesses a "happy knack of . . . nosing about in the narrowest crack for something to put in the paper," and he always "brings to light something rotten" (19–20). The language of the hunt, which Lynge uses with regard to the pastor suspected of child abuse (25), is equally imbued with violence.

In general, these primitive metaphors produce an effect of low burlesque, a well-known satiric device. They are countered by a goodly number of images that, though often equally violent, cast a sheen of heroics upon Lynge's activities. However, these extravagant images prove equally devastating: with their effect of high burlesque, they flash a beam of ridicule upon the editor's self-delusion. His overblown ego is evident throughout. Thus, he sees himself as being engaged in the "vast work of a missionary, filled with the great calling of the press, stern, his indignation and his faith ever fervent" (II: 19–20). Whereas anyone who tries to defy him is cast as a miserable "worm," he appears to himself as someone of "supernatural dimensions" (101). There is a "flame in his heart" (21), his pen "sets things ablaze" (19), he wants his articles to act like "fire and sword" (98). And like a modern engineer he will let "the bomb explode" if he has a particularly sensational news story (23). All of this lofty rhetoric pertains exclusively to Lynge's public life; its chief counterpart in portraying his private life is constituted by the above-mentioned Don Juan motif.

The effect of Hamsun's use of these contrasting image motifs is twofold. On the one hand, the world of publishing is shown up, its *modus operandi* being made to appear like a peculiar mixture of internecine warfare and primitive ritual. On the other hand, the man who is responsible for the shady, near-criminal activities described in the novel sees himself as a hero, carrying out feats of courage and of great moment for his country. The sense of heroism is enhanced by a cluster of images from seafaring: clearing the reefs (II: 87), crowding all sails (99), and so forth. Whenever Lynge runs up against a serious obstacle, these images serve to conjure up the doughty virtues of a salt: "Wasn't he used to riding out the storm?" (93). However, these brave gestures of thought cannot hide Lynge's blatant duplicity, captured to perfection in the following sentence presenting his reaction to being told the sexual abuse story: "Lynge trembled with rapture at this find, this goldmine of wretchedness which now was to be revealed" (22). The oxymoronic phrase "goldmine of wretchedness" brilliantly encapsulates the greed and the delusion of glory that motivate the editor, as well as the vile exploitation that is their inevitable consequence.

When one recalls that *Editor Lynge* is a *roman à clef*, a book—"hot as hate" in Hamsun's own words[11]—generated by a bitter hostility toward a public figure, the wide range of critical opinion it has elicited is no surprise. Arne Garborg, a fellow writer, accused Ham-

Satiric Interlude: Roman à Clef and Polemical Melodrama 45

sun in his review, titled "A Pamphlet," of having written the novel "for the rabble,"[12] and Hamsun himself quotes a remark by Bjørnson to the effect that it was "the most dishonest [book] in Norwegian literature."[13] A subsequent critic goes Bjørnson one better, labeling it "the most malicious, distorted portrait in our literature" and dismissing it as a "nihilistic and impotent grimace, viper's vomit."[14] The young critic Nils Kjær, who wrote an enthusiastic review in *Dagbladet*, appears to have provided the only dissenting voice amid the loud chorus of denunciations.[15] Strangely, Hamsun's next novel, which is if anything artistically inferior to *Editor Lynge*, was well received by the Norwegian critics.

The genesis of that book, *Shallow Soil*, is traceable to a plan for an anti-Bohemian novel that Hamsun was working on already in 1886. He evidently disapproved of the extreme naturalism championed by the leaders of the so-called Bohème movement, Hans Jæger and Christian Krohg (1852–1925), and this attitude seems to have remained unchanged over the years. Thus, he neglected to discuss the Bohème writers in the article he wrote about "The Literary Movement in Norway" for *Revue des Revues* in 1893.[16] Judging by the acid portraits of the Bohème artists in *Shallow Soil*, Hamsun disagreed with them about everything: lifestyle, personal morality, social issues, aesthetics; in particular, he abhorred their frank treatment of sexuality, along with their advocacy of "free love" and women's emancipation. His anti-feminist stand often assumes the form of an uncompromising anti-Ibsenism: Nora, the heroine of *A Doll House*, is a constant presence in *Shallow Soil*, the symbol of a gender liberation that Hamsun vehemently opposes.

The novel focuses on a clique of young Kristiania artists, their friends and cronies, who forgather at the Grand Café and other restaurants frequented by bohemians. Though Paulsberg, a novelist and a married man, seems to enjoy the highest esteem in the group, Irgens, a twenty-four-year old bachelor, is the only character among the artists who plays an important role in the novel's plot. The second milieu that Hamsun depicts is a mercantile one, represented by two young businessmen, Andreas Tidemand and Ole Henriksen, friends who stand by one another in good times and bad, in contrast to the mutual envy and backbiting among the bohemians. Both men allow themselves to be exploited by their bohemian café acquaintances, who represent an artist cult anathema to their creator. Not only are the businessmen expected to pick up the tab whenever they go out together, they are also preyed on for cash. Meanwhile, Irgens is carrying on an affair with Hanka, Mrs. Tidemand, a woman with artistic interests who finds her marriage to be suffocating, and subsequently with Aagot Lynum, Ole Henriksen's eighteen-year-old fiancée, come straight from the country. The novel's structure is shaped by two triangles: Irgens/Hanka/Tidemand and Irgens/Aagot/Henriksen. The hourglass denouement shows Hanka discovering her mistake and returning to the domestic hearth, while Aagot remains a captive of Irgens and appears to be doomed. Ole commits suicide after realizing the fate of the woman he loved.

As noted above, the beginnings of Hamsun's subject belong in the 1880s, when the Bohème movement was at its height. In 1886 he says the novel was to "deal with bohemians" and would be "the tragedy of how people go to the dogs."[17] He worked on the project intermittently, but it was completed only in the fall of 1893 and published in December the same year. Hamsun felt under great pressure to finish it, having meanwhile put *Pan* aside. He now defines his theme as "young Norway,"[18] which seems rather odd considering that he himself was only in his thirty-fourth year at the time. It is also surprising, given the modest artistic milieu of Kristiania and the many allegedly great talents in the clique he portrays, that Hamsun denied having used any "definite living models."[19] He asserts that the picture he has drawn of Norway's "young generation" is "typical of all places."[20] However, his opinion of the work wavers: before publication he feels that, in some ways, he has "scarcely written anything better,"[21] but a few months later, thinking of *Pan* on which he is working, he says: "*Shallow Soil* is just mediocrity to me now, wait until the next one!"[22]

As in the case of *Editor Lynge*, the book shows that Hamsun was capable of writing a traditional novel, though the true nature of that novel seems to have eluded him. Thus, he says that, from the section entitled "Sixty Fold" on, "the characters are drawn toward their destiny by natural necessity,"[23] a statement suggesting that he believed he was writing a novel-tragedy. Moreover, he claims that his book "is full of symbolism," though he hopes it is sufficiently non-Ibsenian to be understandable.[24] Specifically, "Aagot Lynum was supposed to be a personification of the 'shallow soil' woman in our midst, flighty, vacillating, without ardor. . . ."[25] These ambitions are implicit not only in the novel's title, but also in the titles of the three main sections: "Time of Germination" (II: 173), "Ripening" (210), and "Sixty Fold" (248), with their implication that the action is shaped by biological necessity. However, the notion of an inexorable chain of events is a mere pretense, being undermined by the use of essayistic titles for the two remaining sections: "Introduction" and "Conclusion" respectively (139, 284). This kind of formal contradiction, which is replicated in some later novels, betrays Hamsun's difficulty in devising, and following out, a consistent fictional aesthetic.

Hamsun's underlying concept in writing *Shallow Soil* owes a great deal to foreign models. Evidently wanting to emulate the Russians as a critic of the younger generation,[26] he constructed an urban milieu that provided him with convenient targets for his poison pen. The very idea of the novel, summed up in its title, is identical with that of Turgenev's *Nov'*, translated as *Virgin Soil* in English. The content of the epigraph to Turgenev's novel, "Virgin soil should be turned up not by a harrow skimming over the surface, but by a plough biting deep into the earth,"[27] is paralleled, though in a different mode, by Coldevin's complaint about the "shallow soil, pale soil, without much yield, without richness" (II: 295), that condemns the young to mediocrity. In general, Coldevin's excoriation of youth, men and women alike, is reminiscent of Pakhlin's harangue about the cultural and political flakiness of his young Russian contemporaries.[28] When Coldevin says, "Our strength is theoretical, we talk, we intoxicate ourselves with words, we do not act" (290), he echoes Turgenev's heroes.

Strangely enough, in Norway the book was well received. *Verdens Gang*, the paper of Olav Thommessen, whom Hamsun had satirized in *Editor Lynge*, pronounced it to be not only Hamsun's "most important" work, but also "one of the most important works of our literature in the last few years."[29] Just as surprisingly, *Shallow Soil* was the first Hamsun novel to appear in the United States; it was published by Scribner's in 1914. In contrast to the Norwegian reception, as Hamsun complains, the reputable Danish critic Peter Nansen denied him all talent in his review of the book, calling him a self-boosting charlatan.[30]

Another criticism Hamsun attributes to some Danish reviewers, namely, that his businessmen were "angels,"[31] points to the novel's fundamental weakness: the character portrayal is done in terms of black and white. The members of the bohemian clique come across as conceited phonies, Tidemand and Henriksen as moral stalwarts. Irgens is a self-pitying cad, a sponger emotionally as well as financially. Consequently, the two young women whom he seduces come to seem like fools, together with the husband and fiancé who give them a free rein. Evidently, Hamsun came up against the problem of portraying a good man without making him seem like an idiot. Tidemand's generosity toward his estranged wife, Hanka, who does not even recognize the bond of marriage, makes him look absurdly weak; he cannot help realizing what she does with the money she constantly requests from him: passing it on to Irgens, her lover. On the other hand, when she finally gets wise to Irgens' ignoble nature and gives clear signs of wanting to return to the fold, Tidemand appears exceedingly unperceptive or hardhearted. Hanka is no more believable. A twenty-four-year-old wife with two small children, she seeks compensation for the boredom of marriage in the café existence of the clique. Her pretensions and arrogance, along with her subservience to Irgens' fickle moods, produce such a negative image that, when she crawls to the cross in the novel's second part, one finds it difficult to believe in her change of heart. Hamsun's attempt to rewrite Ibsen's *A Doll House* fails to come off. Hanka's gestures as she haunts the house she has left—kissing the door handle and so forth—are simply grotesque.

Though Hamsun tries to differentiate his treatment of the two love triangles, the story of the Irgens/Aagot/Henriksen threesome is no more plausible than the one just discussed. While Tidemand undergoes a severe trial, with financial losses that bring him to the brink of bankruptcy, in the end the couple comes through victorious, both in love and in business. Conversely, Henriksen and his teenage fiancée, who experience no adversity, are destroyed. But again, the characters and events are unconvincing. However honorable and intelligent, Ole Henriksen strikes one as insensitive and unimaginative; if anything, he is even less credible than his colleague. By making his fiancée an innocent country girl of eighteen, the author has stacked the cards against them: if Aagot suffers a more wretched fate than Hanka, it is not, as Hamsun opines, because she is of an inferior "breed" to Mrs. Tidemand.[32] With her tender years she is easy prey for Irgens, the practiced seducer, especially in view of the perfectly chaste behavior of her fiancé. Though the betrothed pair live in the same house, we do not see them exchanging as much as a kiss. Finally, Henriksen's suicide takes the reader by surprise, since he has betrayed no trace of instability before he takes this drastic action. A person who is capable of the kind of righteous rage he exhibits after reading Aagot's parting letter (II: 305) is not a likely suicide. It is melodrama, through and through, both in character portrayal and in the structure of events.

In retrospect, Hamsun realized there was something wrong with his portraits of the businessmen, though his comments appear strange considering the nature of the criticism he had received. He admits that they are "rather insignificant, as they should be, but otherwise just kind-hearted,"[33] and in another letter he says that they are "soft, but what the hell was I to do! Had they been more splendid fellows, the clique couldn't have taken them in so badly in every respect."[34] But the trouble was not that they were weak, but rather their being presented by the author's voice, Coldevin, who looks to the field of business rather than art for his "great talents" (II: 203), as models of perfection. According to him, the only hope of curing the purported cultural malaise is offered by the world of "trade," with its "bustling activity." That is where the "renewal will come from," he declares (296). If this is taken seriously, Hamsun must have intended his merchants to represent a kind of "positive hero," in contrast to the decadent artists and literary men.

Coldevin's presence in the novel serves a double purpose: to keep a snoop's eye on Aagot, his former tutee—with whom he is obviously in love—and to expatiate on the decadence of the young Norwegian artists and intellectuals. As a snoop, his behavior verges on voyeurism, since he manages to show up whenever Aagot finds herself in a compromising situation. It is not a likely role for a forty-year-old, eccentric though he may be. His critique of contemporary mediocrity goes hand in hand with extolling an anarchic ideal, apparently inspired by ancient Norwegian history. This is particularly true of his view of women. He says, among other things: "Our young woman has lost her power, that rich and sweet simplicity, the great passion, the sign of breeding; she has lost her true joy in the one man, her hero, her god, she has become sweet-toothed, sniffing at no matter who and giving everyone the glad eye" (II: 295). It looks as though Hamsun's handling of the plot of his novel was determined by this reactionary ideal.

Hamsun's failure to produce a substantial work of fiction is exposed glaringly when *Shallow Soil* is compared to *Niobe*, a novel by Jonas Lie which appeared in the same month. For whatever reason, Hamsun writes in a letter to his publisher that he had better not show up "simultaneously with Jonas Lie."[35] The subject of Lie's book is also decadence, depicted within the framework of a country doctor's family in which the grown-up children are enticed by the dreams of freedom and achievement offered by the city, in an age when the old values no longer command unquestioning adherence. The book is envisaged as a fictional counterpart to classical tragedy.[36] Not only is *Niobe* superior to *Shallow Soil* in its artistic form and its character portrayal, but also in its evocation of the irrational, which sounds odd in view of Hamsun's declared interest in probing the mysteries of the unconscious mind. In *Shallow Soil*, the principal mystery for the reader is the attractiveness of mediocrity, as symbolized by Irgens, the expert deflowerer of innocents. The difference in quality between the two works stands out sharply if one compares Aagot Lynum—and, to some extent, Hanka—with Minka Baarvig. Minka, a wholesome and innocent country girl, rejects marriage to be a sort of muse, but is drawn masochistically to Varberg, an engineer whose dabbling in spiritualism masks a sadistic drive. Whereas Hamsun's novel is locked into a narrow didactic scheme focused on the idea that a woman can find happiness only as wife and mother, Lie presents a shattering demonstration of the disasters that may befall human beings in a time of cultural upheaval. Hamsun would have done well to study Jonas Lie's type of impressionistic novel, which is not only excellent in its artistic quality but "modern" as well, something that cannot be said of *Shallow Soil*.

Hamsun does succeed in one thing, namely, making the members of "young Norway" look thoroughly contemptible. Hollowed out spiritually, they are shown to be destructive of every human value, of the national ethos, of morality itself, even of true art. But soon the characters begin to seem unreal, first the merchants, afterward the

Satiric Interlude: Roman à Clef *and Polemical Melodrama*   51

others as well. At the end one is left with a few vivid impressions: the bustling activity of the harbor, the preferred haunt of Coldevin, and the regular appearance every morning of the little newsgirl with her dog. A St. Vitus' dance sufferer, "she throws her little body in all directions, jerks her shoulders, . . . rushes along from door to door, clambers up the stairs to the upper stories, rings the bell and hurries on, leaving a paper at each doorstep" (II, 140). The image of the awakening city is evoked with the kind of concrete sensory detail that one associates with the author of *Hunger.*

CHAPTER THREE

Two Lyrical Novels

Pan (1894) and *Victoria* (1898) could scarcely be more different from the two novels Hamsun published in 1893, *Editor Lynge* and *Shallow Soil*. While the latter were polemical, motivated by personal rancor or by distaste for a certain lifestyle, *Pan* and *Victoria*, being love stories, are removed from controversy. Hamsun was fully aware of his change of direction. In a letter of 1893 from Paris, where he spent most of his time from then on until 1895, he writes: "My new book will be so beautiful; it takes place in Nordland, a quiet and red love story. There will be no polemics in it, just people under different skies."[1] Meanwhile, the writing was going very poorly: "[I] get stuck as if I were the most stupid of men. Write today and trash it tomorrow, all the time,"[2] he complains in January 1894. Paris did not seem to provide the right atmosphere for his writing; in a letter to his German publisher of June 5, 1894, he says he was unable to work there.[3] The novel was completed in Kristiansand, Norway, where a bad case of seasickness had made him disembark on his way north. Since his main object was to get "on Norwegian soil and hear the Norwegian language," he decided he might as well settle there for the time being.[4] But while getting back to Norway may have stimulated the process of writing, the quality of the end result was no doubt partly due to the chosen subject and setting, which took the author on a sentimental journey beyond the Arctic Circle, to the region where he had spent his childhood and early youth. *Pan*, called by the contemporary critic Carl Nærup Hamsun's "great triumph,"[5] can be seen as the future Nobel laureate's second, and decisive, breakthrough as a novelist.

Hamsun's intent in writing *Pan* is quite consistent with the literary program he had outlined in his lectures and followed unequivocally in *Hunger* and *Mysteries*: to focus on the characters' psyche and depict the flow of inner experience as closely and vividly as possible. In a letter written after its publication, he says that he wrote *Pan* "for the sake of the changing emotions."[6] According to another letter, Glahn himself is supposed to be "a bundle of changing emotions, soul, rising and sinking moods."[7] To give Albert Langen, his German publisher, an idea of the book, he asks him to "think of J. J. Rousseau" in the region of Nordland—with its Lapps, its "mysteries," its "grand superstitions" and its midnight sun—making the acquaintance of a local girl. He says he is trying to express "some of the nature-worshipping, sensitivity, overnervousness in a Rousseauean soul."[8] In another letter to Langen he writes that "every chapter is a poem. . . ."[9]

Hamsun's description of the novel is quite apt, particularly in calling attention to its poetic qualities. But it is also remarkable for its narrative art, combining as it does a retrospective account—something between a diary, a memoir and a meditation—by the hero, Lieutenant Thomas Glahn, with a much shorter piece, entitled "Glahn's Death," in which the narrator covers up his murder of Glahn by writing that he "died in an accident, killed by an accidental shot while hunting in India" (II: 423). Nevertheless, the interpretive problem introduced by the dual narrators is trivial when compared to the task of analyzing the complexity of the main story, an intricate web of fairly realistic narrative, mythic or legendary tales, and a pervasive strain of prose lyricism. Through the interaction of these compositional elements, the novel's texture acquires a density—dramatic, mythic, lyrical—which imbues the entire work with a poetic character. Hamsun's statement in regard to Lieutenant Glahn's story that "every chapter is a poem" is no mere boast, but articulates the effect of the text, an impression enhanced by the brevity of the chapters, on the average less than three pages long. This brevity is significant, revealing a further characteristic of Hamsun's text, its radical stylization: the narrative is extremely spare, with little or no description of the circumstances surrounding an event. Indeed, in some ways the entire novel reads like a myth, a virtual allegory of desire.[10]

From the reader's point of view, the story begins on a note of wonder, in that the narrator, Lieutenant Glahn, makes several veiled references, in describing his present life, to events which took place two years ago, in 1855. The opening mood, one of mournful reminiscence beneath the pretended gayety, is fraught with suspense, aroused by a number of mystifying remarks by the narrator: about a "pair of bird's feathers" recently received "from far away"; an occasional "touch of rheumatism" in his left foot due to a "gunshot wound that has long since healed"; and his having shot and killed Aesop, his dog. The first item, the bird's feathers, becomes truly intriguing, in that the narrator dwells on it, creating a triad of increasingly intense images — from "a pair of bird's feathers" to "two green feathers," to "those two feathers, so devilishly green." At the same time the sender of the feathers is associated with aristocratic rank, the "sheet of letter paper" in which the feathers were wrapped boasting a coronet (II: 333-34). These allusions to an already transpired sequence of events from the narrator's vantage point will sooner or later turn up as components of the novel's action. The suspense is sustained until the very end of Glahn's narrative, at which point the allusion to the death of Aesop becomes uncannily clear.

In the simplest terms, the novel's plot is one of a tragic love between Lieutenant Glahn, who spends a summer and fall in Nordland, and a young girl, daughter of the local magnate, Mack of Sirilund. Glahn is twenty-eight, Edvarda, the girl, seventeen or twenty, depending on whom to believe. Glahn lives in a hut at the edge of the woods, goes hunting and fishing, and for the rest enjoys the solitude of the forest, or so he says: "only in the woods was all at rest within me, my soul became still and full of power" (II: 334). But the bliss of solitude, a theme we will encounter repeatedly in Hamsun, is short-lived. When Glahn meets Edvarda, they develop an all-absorbing passion for one another, though it stops short of being consummated. Strangely, their ecstatic feelings last only a few weeks, after which the lovers drift apart; when they do meet — at outings, parties, or on the road — the few words they exchange become increasingly cruel and venomous. Meanwhile, Glahn has initiated an affair with Eva, a love slave of Mack's who, unbeknownst to Glahn, is a married woman, the local blacksmith's wife rather than his daughter. Though Edvarda is infuriated when learning of the affair, she still occasionally displays her initial passion for the woodsman.

Glahn's situation and state of mind become more and more precarious, and his behavior borders on hysteria. Suspecting that a middle-aged family friend of the Macks, a freethinking, lame doctor who has been trying to educate Edvarda—taking the young lady "in hand," as he puts it in a conversation with Glahn (II: 372)—is wooing Edvarda, he treats him brutally. Smarting under a taunt by Edvarda, who reacted with "furious impatience" (367) to his suspicious glance at the doctor's stick, left behind after a ball at Sirilund, Glahn insults the doctor when they meet, holding out his gun to him "as if he were a dog" and telling him, "Jump over!" (II: 368). Subsequently, "thrown off balance" by the doctor's conciliatory attitude and recalling Edvarda's words on parting, "You're not lame, no, but even if you were lame, on top of everything, you couldn't hold your own against him" (368), Glahn places his gun against his left foot and pulls the trigger. (Ah, the reader thinks, so that was the explanation of the rheumatism, a self-inflicted wound!) With the arrival of a Swedo-Finnish baron, Mr. Mack's choice of husband for his daughter, Glahn's jealousy is transferred to him, whom he also treats very badly. A greater challenge, however, is presented by Mack himself, on whom Glahn is dependent, living in his hut and needing his indulgence in the matter of hunting rights. Mr. Mack is a more formidable opponent than either Edvarda or her admirers. Having caught the lovers together in Eva's house, Mack avenges Glahn's poaching on his sexual preserve by setting fire to his hut. Seeing Mack afterward, Glahn feels as though he were facing "the world's smartest man" (407).

The gruesome denouement, Eva being "smashed to bits" by a rockfall when Glahn carries out his intention to "blow up a mountain" in salute to the departing baron (II: 403, 399)—an intention that Mack apparently got wind of—is followed by Glahn's final visit, this time in his officer's uniform, to Sirilund, during which Edvarda asks for Aesop as a "remembrance" of him. But before leaving himself, Glahn kills Aesop, the dog, and has the dead body delivered to Edvarda. As described, the killing looks like a vicarious suicide: "I called Aesop, patted him, put our heads together and grabbed my gun. He was already whining for joy, thinking we were going hunting. Again I put our heads together, placed the muzzle of my gun against Aesop's neck and fired" (408).

As a traditional third-person narrative, this story as summarized would appear as undiluted melodrama, or a revenge tragedy in the Senecan style. The presence of a participant narrator who now and again refers to the time of writing, usually at the beginning of a new chapter, asking questions such as these, "Shall I write more?" (II: 339), "How much worse could things be?" (362), and "What more is there for me to write?" (403), sets up a tension between the linear time of happening and the repeated circling back of the time of narration, a tension which slows the pace and moderates the impact of horror and disaster. The various motifs and leitmotifs, emotionally charged focal points of Glahn's involuntary memory, contribute to the same effect. For Glahn as narrator, time "hangs heavy," whereas two years ago, when the events took place, "the summer was gone before I realized it," he notes (333). At the end of his story, a variation on this paradox of temporal experience occurs as he confesses, "And the day goes by, but time stands still" (410). Indeed, the entire last chapter of Glahn's account harks back to the beginning, being mainly a recapitulation of the first chapter, with allusions to Aesop, to the letter with a coronet on it, and — by way of a near-hallucinatory experience — to those green bird's feathers, a "remembrance" given to Edvarda on an island excursion (360). Glahn writes, "A freezing terror runs through me, I turn cold. Two green feathers! I say to myself. . . . And suddenly I seem to see a face and hear a voice, and the voice says, 'Please, Lieutenant, here are your feathers, Sir!'" (410). The story has come full circle, carried back to its origin, a perpetually renewed remorse that refuses to be soothed or repressed.

Three inserted tales further enrich the story's texture, conferring a semi-mythical resonance upon the human events. In each of the tales a correspondence is established with the amorous activity of Glahn. A brief interlude featuring Diderik and Iselin, a pair of legendary characters, is a sort of daydream in which the god Pan also figures. While Diderik, her husband, is watching, Iselin spends an hour with the hunter, that is, Glahn, under the pretext that he is to tie her shoelace. What happens is left vague, but the meaning is clear: when she leaves to go to her "next lover," she is described as "exultant and sinful from top to toe" (II: 346). The realistic counterpart follows immediately afterward, when Glahn picks up a young shepherd girl, Henriette, and spends several hours with her in his hut. Similarly, the tale of Iselin and Dundas, a brief, suspenseful celebration of Iselin's "first night" of love, is linked, and doubly so, with Glahn's sexual situation. For while the motif of the cockcrow announcing morning to the lovers in the tale is echoed in Glahn's "slumber" by a cock crowing at Sirilund (378), the home of Edvarda, on returning to his hut he finds Eva waiting for him. The last tale, "a strange legend from four generations back" about a maiden imprisoned in a tower, is an allegory of undying love, minted on Eva, the slave of love, whose death and burial frame the legend. However, as recalled by Glahn the story also includes an allusion to another woman, whom the "lord" loved "like a slave, like a madman and a beggar" (403), an obvious reminder of Glahn's view of his predicament vis-à-vis Edvarda.

The above summary and discussion should give an inkling of how complex Hamsun's novel is, despite its seeming surface simplicity. At times one may feel that the characters' behavior is excessively wayward and that key incidents are unduly violent; and the narrator hardly ever levels with the reader. Moreover, the concluding section, "Glahn's Death," originally published in the journal *Samtiden* in 1893, presents a challenge to any critic who believes that a work of art should be aesthetically unified. Partly as a result of these problems and idiosyncrasies, *Pan* has elicited a continuous flow of articles as well as two book-length studies,[11] signs of the continuing vitality of Hamsun's Nordland story. For while the interpretations differ, the novel has continued to exercise a magic charm upon readers and critics alike.

In examining the novel, it is necessary to resist that charm, while at the same time doing justice to the remarkable artistic achievement that the novel represents. There are, for example, many telltale signs of an unreliable narrator in *Pan*. Though Glahn writes that, in the two years since the events he is going to relate occurred, he has led what he calls the "merriest of lives," most likely in the capital, and that he has "no regrets," he gets tripped up by contradictions and non sequiturs that belie his words. Claiming to have "quite forgotten" the young woman he met, he refers to what had happened to him as "a little joke, one of those little adventures among many others." His concluding protestations that he is not "weighed down by grief" and that he has been writing purely for his "own amusement," are no more convincing than his initial disclaimer of writing simply "to pass the time" (II: 333, 410).

Early Hamsun critics tended to overlook these signs of an unreliable narrator in *Pan*, envisaging Glahn as a romantic nature worshiper pure and simple and taking his pantheistic feelings and lyrical effusions at their face value. Recent decades have produced a number of new interpretations of Glahn, ranging from psychopath[12] to artist to alienated modern man. In particular, commentators have come to regard Glahn's love of the wilderness as compensation for his social ineptitude and amorous frustrations. Carried to its logical extreme, the older view turned the novel into a paean to nature and eros, whereas the later one has uncovered a far more complex literary structure, permeated with ambiguities and ironies that are compounded by the epilogue, "Glahn's Death," which was largely ignored by the early critics.

In trying to understand Hamsun's *Pan*, it is important to remember that Glahn lives on the edge of the forest, at the point where wild nature and civilization meet. Somewhat of a "superfluous man," like his predecessors in the novels of Turgenev, he can find no meaningful place for himself in bourgeois society, and so he withdraws to the woods, to the state of nature. But so far, despite his "lair" (II: 340), his animal eyes, and his animal clothing, he lacks the natural completion that he so longs for. Interestingly, in his 1888 article on August Strindberg, Hamsun recalls Strindberg's description of himself as "an animal longing for the woods,"[13] before citing examples of modern man's attempt to return to his natural condition. The image of the Rousseauean Swede, who influenced Hamsun as much as anybody, may have been at the back of his mind when conceiving Lieutenant Glahn. While the impulse—whether of Strindberg, Hamsun, or Glahn—may have been authentic enough, Hamsun's hero gives us contradictory signals as to his true nature. Is he simply a disenchanted city man temporarily seeking refuge in the wilds (Glahn as tourist), or is he a self-deceived romantic who compensates for his social and sexual shortcomings and misadventures by a deliberate cult of nature (Glahn the false primitive)?

It is not easy to distinguish between the real and affected traits of Thomas Glahn. Though his "animal eyes" are attested to by several characters (II: 355, 411), in general Glahn gives the impression of being anything but animalistic: when he manages to preserve his self-control he behaves *comme il faut*; one need only note his sense of shock when Edvarda (a more authentic primitive) kisses him "on the lips again and again" during an outing to the cod-drying rocks (351). He repeatedly regrets not having his uniform at hand, hoping it will help him regain Edvarda's favor. In view of these facts, his animal clothing and his "lair" hung with animal skins, together with his idea of being a "son of the forest" (348), become rather suspect. Nor is his feeling for nature that of a true primitive; in fact, it is sometimes so sentimental that it verges on the maudlin, such as licking the blades of grass and getting tears in his eyes from watching a nearly rotten little twig. These are signs of an over-sensitive, nostalgic urban sensibility rather than of a primordial oneness with nature.

Even if one accepts Glahn's feeling for nature as genuine, his invocations and uses of nature prove contradictory. While he clearly enjoys initiating Edvarda into his simple woodsman's life, governed by nature's clock, subsequently nature comes to play an ambiguous role in their relationship. A crucial instance is seen near the end of chapter thirteen, where Edvarda flings her arms around his neck, "breathing audibly," her eyes "quite black." She is obviously offering herself to him. His lack of response becomes a turning point in their relationship: when next they meet, there is not "as much joy in her eyes as before." Glahn's reason—or rationalization—for turning her down is revealing. When she asks him why he got up so quickly, he answers, "Because it's late, Edvarda. . . . Now the white flowers are closing again, the sun is rising, it'll soon be day" (II: 356, 357). Here nature, in the form of the diurnal cycle, is used to justify his evasion of Edvarda's passionate appeal. And during the so-called Iron Nights (chapter 26), by which time he has pretty much given up on Edvarda, he stages a veritable ritual of exorcism, a self-induced mystical union with nature and nature's god that he hopes will liberate him from his passion. Eventually his relationship to nature turns paradoxical: the man capable of a reciprocal feeling of friendship toward a rock in front of his hut eventually causes the death of Eva, a woman he claims to love, by means of a rock fragment released by his farewell salute to his rival, the Baron.[14]

While nature helps Glahn evade human intimacy, it also compensates for the lack of such intimacy. He treats his dog, for example, as if he were a human being: feeling neglected by Edvarda during an outing, he tells the company repeatedly that Aesop, his friend, is waiting for him in the hut. In general, his anthropomorphic attitude toward nature creates a simulacrum of a human society in the midst of the forest, a society that allows his ego to expand to virtual infinity. Thus, immediately before invoking nature to fend off Edvarda's sexual advances, he eroticizes—and therefore humanizes—the very flowers he observes: the flowers "are steeped in an erotic ecstasy" (II: 355).[15] This eroticizing of nature, neatly formulated by Lou Andreas-Salomé when she writes, "The erotic life merges imperceptibly with nature's moods,"[16] cannot but ricochet back on Glahn's consciousness, inflating it so as to embrace the unconscious life of nature itself. The ultimate expression of this relationship is seen in the account of the third Iron Night, where Glahn describes what looks like his sexual union with the moon goddess: ". . . I feel myself lifted out of my sphere, pressed to an invisible breast, my eyes are moist with tears, I tremble. . ." (394). This experience of quasi-apotheosis confers a cosmic dimension upon Glahn's self through mythic identification.

The elements of myth, legend, and dream in Hamsun's *Pan* are central to our understanding of Glahn and of his relationship to the other characters, especially the women. Although the book's title seems to have come to Hamsun by way of a casual impulse in ending a letter to Albert Langen—the letter ends "Pan bless you!"[17]—the ramifications of the Pan myth seem important. They turn up at different levels of the text. On the most superficial level, Pan is present as a figurine on Glahn's powder horn, part and parcel of his gear as a woodsman. We are told that the Doctor "begins to explain" the myth of Pan (II: 340), but we are not provided with his explanation. It seems that Hamsun exploits the paradoxical duality of the goat-god's nature as god and animal in relation to his hero: though Glahn is said to have "animal" eyes, to Edvarda he looks "like a god" (387). More important, Pan combines the attributes of the primitive Arcadian god of fertility with those ascribed to him, by way of etymological confusion, by the Stoics and incorporated in the Orphic Hymn to Pan. According to this interpretation, Pan encompasses "the heavens, the sea, earth, and fire—universal Nature . . ., becoming Supreme Governor or 'soul' of the World."[18]

The Pan that Glahn fantasizes about in chapter eight seems to be the priapic god of the woods, though the way he is imagined as "drinking from his own belly" and shaking with "silent laughter" (II:

345), all the while keeping an eye on Glahn, strongly suggests that Glahn feels uncertain about his own relationship to what the primitive god stands for. During the Iron Nights, however, it is the pantheistic Pan that Glahn communes with, a god "interfusing the world and me," as he puts it (391). The Iron Nights chapter ends with the episode referred to above, where Glahn enacts the role of Pan in relation to the moon goddess, once ravished by the goat-god according to a tradition handed down by Virgil.[19] But again Glahn feels watched by God—by Pan? In any case, Glahn glimpses only what looks like the "back of a spirit wandering soundlessly through the forest" (394), somewhat like Moses, who is vouchsafed to see only Yahweh's "back parts."[20]

While the Pan myth reinforces Glahn's ambivalent relationship to nature,[21] the legend of Iselin conjured up by Glahn immediately after the first "appearance" of Pan adumbrates his ideal of a free, amoral sexuality. But curiously, Iselin's surrender to the hunter occurs only to the detriment of an "injured third party,"[22] her husband Diderik. This archetypal triangle shapes all the love relationships, real or imagined, in the novel: Diderik/Iselin/Glahn; Henriette's sweetheart/Henriette/Glahn; Dundas/Iselin/Glahn; Mack/Eva/Glahn; the Doctor/Edvarda/Glahn; the Baron/Edvarda/Glahn; the narrator of "Glahn's Death"/Maggie, the Tamil half-caste/Glahn. While the use of the Iselin legend may suggest that Glahn desires an absolutely untrammeled, non-binding sexuality—a desire that seems to be fulfilled by his docile partners, Henriette and Eva, after the two installments of the legend are given—his sexuality is no more unequivocal than his relationship to nature. Pure eroticism seems impossible; it invariably entails a power game, whatever its origin, whether in the laws of nature or in those of the society that Glahn flouts. There will always be winners and losers. The anomalous situation in *Pan* is that practically everybody is a loser.

Traditionally, the Glahn/Edvarda relationship has been interpreted in tune with the above: their love falls prey either to a Strindbergian battle between the sexes, or to the natural rhythms of the seasonal cycle. But unlike the amorous attraction that Glahn has for Henriette, the shepherdess, who loses interest in him with the coming of fall, Edvarda's love for Glahn does not die, as shown by her repeated attempts to win him back after their bitter fights,[23] nor does Glahn's love for her. In her second letter, which Glahn receives in India, Edvarda again offers herself to him, though a "married woman" (II: 416), an action testifying to an enduring passion. Though Glahn's response may seem odd, choosing to die, by provoking his jealous hunting companion to kill him, in preference to accepting the offer, his anguish and grief are evident even to the hateful narrator. Glahn's distraught state of mind looks like an exacerbated repetition of the retrospective regret and existential despair betrayed, despite disclaimers, in his own account. Edvarda and Glahn's love is not affected by naturalistic metaphysics; it is a passion love, an arctic variety of the alleged civilized malady examined by Denis de Rougemont in *l'Amour et l'Occident* (1939; *Love in the Western World*, 1957).[24] Comparable to the passion of Tristan for Isolde, Goethe's Werther for Lotte, and Heathcliff for Catherine in *Wuthering Heights*, Glahn's obsession with Edvarda is conditioned by distance,[25] by the impossibility of fulfillment of his "dream of love" (II: 391) — except in death. Significantly, Glahn dresses up like a bridegroom on the last morning of his life: Hamsun ends *Pan* with an extraordinary variation of the love-death motif. Glahn's sexual affairs are trivial by comparison: as he tells Eva, what he loves most is the dream, and that means the complex of transcendent sentiments associated with Edvarda.

Confronted with the archetype of passion love and with Hamsun's emphasis on the unconscious, one comes to feel that a too close analysis of why the characters behave as they do in the novel is pointless; they act as they must, often irrationally and self-destructively. No rational explanation can be found for the undying love of the maiden imprisoned in the tower, or of Eva's steadfast love for Glahn. Nor can we find sufficient reasons for Glahn's eccentric, often self-destructive behavior — breaking his toddy glass at Mack's place, throwing Edvarda's shoe overboard, shooting himself in the foot, expressing pleasure at the idea of being dragged by the hair, spitting in the Baron's ear.[26] The various theories — Dionysian, Freudian, Jungian[27] — cannot quite pluck out the mystery of this book.

Suffice it to cite a deconstructive attempt by a Norwegian critic, Asmund Lien. Having discovered that the text contradicts itself, Professor Lien sees Glahn as a "masked modern intellectual" whose enactment of the role of a Rousseauean "tourist" in a primordial setting leads to disastrous consequences. The text shows, he says, that Glahn "knows" what he does when he triggers the rockfall, that he makes use of Mack's persecution of Eva to kill Eva, thus sacrificing her—as he does Aesop—to Edvarda.[28] Each reader will have to decide whether the work gains or loses by such an approach, namely, interpreting what looks like accidents or gratuitous acts as due to conscious calculation rather than to motives deliberately left obscure by the author.

What type of novel is *Pan*? The question would be more readily answerable if the story ended with Glahn's departure from Nordland. If Hamsun had decided not to include "Glahn's Death," the novel could be seen as a Scandinavian example of what Ralph Freedman has chosen to call the "lyrical novel." Though Freedman does not give us a definition of the genre, he says that it "seeks to combine man and world in a strangely inward, yet aesthetically objective, form."[29] One of the prime examples he offers of this type of novel has already been alluded to, namely, Goethe's *Werther* (1774), with which *Pan* has much in common: an outsider hero to whom the world is largely a reflection of his moods, an ecstatic experience of nature that doesn't stop at mooning over leaves of grass, a sense of eros as an inexorable natural force, and a style that has many of the earmarks of poetry.[30] The "I" persona of the novel is as much lyrical as narrative, producing quasi-musical modulations of pace and rhythm: thus, the mythic and legendary sequences have a timeless quality, as does the evocation of nature in its various phases and moods. Moreover, the circular form, highlighted by the leitmotif of the bird's feathers, has the effect of condensing the elapsed time: while the summer passes quickly and the brief chapters produce a rapid pace, for the narrator—and secondarily the reader—the story contracts to one haunting, eternally recurring moment.

Many critics have been puzzled by Hamsun's decision to add "Glahn's Death" to the novel. Once we realize that it is part and parcel of the text, our understanding of the work as a whole changes radically.[31] For while the lyrical novel is a traditional genre, however recent its critical investigation, the approximation to narrative montage resulting from the juxtaposition of Glahn's story with that of his hate-ridden hunting companion in India marks *Pan* as a distinctly modernistic work. The links between the two parts—the subjectivity of the narrators, the triangle situation, the exotic settings—cannot conceal the drastic change in style and tone: from the near-sentimental to the crass, from nature as a wellspring of sublime, religiously tinged emotions to deadly male rivalry in an arena of killing for sport, from all-consuming passion to tawdry, exploitative one-night stands.

The principal effect of the epilogue is to add another layer of irony to Hamsun's novel. We have seen that Glahn relates his story in such a way as to make him appear as an unreliable narrator; moreover, as an actor in the story he tells he may sometimes strike us as unnecessarily cruel. Yet, we do not therefore deny him our sympathy or compassion, largely because we realize that he is in the grip of utter despair and irremediable suffering. But it is difficult to sympathize with the colonial hunter avid for the kill that we are given in "Glahn's Death," unless we can persuade ourselves that his companion's "inside story" is fatally flawed, based on a murderous jealousy and therefore false. If we begin to suspect that Glahn is slandered, we may even feel like coming to his defense—until, perhaps, we recall that in many respects his own narrative was also rooted in jealousy. The upshot of these reflections is to further problematize the novel, whose meaning, in the final analysis, appears to be undecidable. It will be up to each individual reader to decide who Glahn is, what makes him act as he does, and how to respond to Hamsun's seductive, but perplexing story.

In the period between the publication of *Pan* and *Victoria*, Hamsun wrote mainly plays, despite his low opinion of dramatic literature and the theater. In a letter written August 23, 1898, he says: "I'm tired of the novel, and I've always despised the drama; I've now begun to write verse, the only literature that is not both pretentious and insignificant, but only insignificant."[32] While calling *Victoria* "some sort of 'pendent' (sic) to *Pan*,"[33] he refers to it as "nothing but a little lyricism" and as "full of 'Stimmung'."[34]

The self-demeaning language would be more appropriate if applied to the overall plot of this short fiction, a story of star-crossed lovers whose interest lies less on the surface than in the rather unusual manner in which Hamsun complicates the conventional plot. Thus, despite its title, *Victoria* focuses on Johannes, a young man who, frustrated in love, succeeds in becoming a celebrated author; it is as much an apprenticeship novel as a story of doomed love. The narrative is highly stylized, consisting of selected episodes in Johannes' life from the age of fourteen to his twenties, as far as the reader can make out the vaguely indicated chronology. The opening scene, a teenage excursion to an island on which Johannes serves as oarsman, epitomizes his predicament: as the son of the local miller, he feels upstaged by Otto, a city youngster of wealthy parentage, in his wooing of Victoria, who, as the daughter of the lord of the manor, lives at the "Castle." Though Victoria returns Johannes' affection, they are held apart by the social chasm, but even more, as we learn in a passage of delayed exposition (III: 143–45), by the financial straits of Victoria's father. In due course, Victoria celebrates her engagement to Otto, now a lieutenant, an occasion at which Johannes, who is also present, comes in for a surprise. In a bizarre gesture dictated by a guilt-ridden conscience, Victoria introduces Johannes to Camilla Seier, a young girl he had saved from drowning several years earlier. Johannes gets the message: Camilla is to be a surrogate replacement for the loss of his true love, Victoria, a suggestion confirmed by Camilla's surname, Seier, meaning "victory."

From this point on, events move very quickly. Otto is killed in a hunting accident, setting Victoria free, but by the time she calls on Johannes he has already committed himself to Camilla. The rapturous quasi-monologue in which she releases her long-suppressed passion is met by a curt "I'm engaged" (III: 145). More surprises follow, as the initial triangle of Johannes/Victoria/Otto is superseded by that of Johannes/Camilla/Richmond, the latter previously known as the young gentleman with the "diamond buttons" (134) who honored Johannes with a speech at Victoria's engagement party. Sweet and complaisant, but shallow, very young and immature, Camilla lacks Victoria's intensity; though she keeps protesting that she loves Johannes, her preference for Richmond is unmistakably, and charmingly, manifest in her every word and gesture. These two, she and Richmond, are fortunate, whereas Victoria falls on evil days. The Castle is burned down by its owner, Victoria's father, so that his family can collect the insurance; the arsonist himself perishes in the flames. Victoria falls ill and shortly dies of consumption. Her long ecstatic letter to Johannes that concludes the book—a regular prose hymn to love—reestablishes the novel's emotional balance. The successive triangles that shape Hamsun's rudimentary plot recede in favor of the overarching story of Johannes and Victoria.

If this novel were to be characterized by its plot, the term blatant melodrama would seem appropriate. However, as in *Pan*, the plot is merely a framework within which Hamsun creates a complex web of narrative modes, themes and motifs, the elements that make up the substance of the novel.

Victoria consists of a mosaic of scenes and situations developed according to a basic psychological scheme: dream-like amorous expectation followed by triumph and, subsequently, by bitter disappointment. Sometimes the second stage is missing, causing the narrative to shuttle between the emotional extremes of youthful hope and subsequent disillusion. Yet, the ultimate effect produced by the novel is not one of disillusionment. This may be partly due to a frequently occurring structural pattern in Hamsun's narrative, whereby a flat rendering of an encounter, mostly couched in clipped, constrained dialogue, is amplified by ecstatic recall and, eventually, literary re-creation. Since Johannes and Victoria see each other so rarely, their meetings usually begin very tentatively and awkwardly, but Johannes' pent-up feelings often break through, as happens in chapter three, where they meet in the city. His ardent confession recapitulates the emotional adventures with which his loving memory of Victoria has enriched him. "I always heard or saw something that reminded me of you, all day, at night too," he tells her (III: 109). The scene is rounded off by another dialogue sequence, which ends with her telling him, "You are the one I love" (111).

The first part of chapter four employs the same device on a broader scale, as Johannes recalls the entire experience related in chapter three. Being in a state of semi-delirious happiness after Victoria's declaration of love, he overwhelms an infuriated neighbor, who has protested against his pre-dawn singing, by giving him an ecstatic description of his nocturnal experiences. The story he tells him is a heightened version of the previously noted confession to Victoria; Johannes even uses some of the same expressions. He tells the man that, as he was writing during the night, "the heavens opened, . . . an angel offered me wine, and I drank it; it was an intoxicating wine, I drank it out of a garnet bowl" (III: 112). This possible allusion to the baptism of Jesus also appears in what he related to Victoria the previous day (108).[35] In both instances, the acts of remembrance and literary creativity are indistinguishable. For though Johannes tells the neighbor that he "once more lived through it all" (112), the account he gives him of the meeting with Victoria is a considerably modified version, in some respects quite fanciful. Thus, he says "we met the King, . . . and the King turned around to look at her, at my beloved, because she is so tall and beautiful." He goes on to describe what he wrote as "one long, continuous song to joy, to happiness. . . . It was as though happiness lay naked before me, with a long laughing throat, and wanted to come to me" (113). That Johannes' happiness is dispelled after he runs into Victoria and Otto in the theater, conforms to the larger rhythm of disenchantment.

This sequence of episode, recollection, and creative transformation is only one of several strategies whereby Hamsun complicates the narrative flow of the novel. Having the effect of repetition, it produces a sense of recurring cycles of experience, thereby slowing down the pace of the action and mitigating the melodramatic suddenness of key events. Another strategy, evidenced in the handling of the story's climax, the engagement party, is equally, if not more, decisive to bracketing the novel's conventional plot. The scene of scandal, which Hamsun had picked up from Dostoyevsky and used successfully in previous works, assumes in *Victoria* a particularly outrageous form, since it develops from a celebratory occasion in high society. Again, the opening note, for Johannes, is one of happy anticipation, of which he is cruelly disabused in the course of the party.

In effect, there is a succession of scenes of scandal taking place at the party. Victoria's introduction of Camilla is followed by a series of acrimonious exchanges between her and Johannes reminiscent of the barbed words of Glahn and Edvarda in *Pan*. Johannes is overcome by a "hopeless despair" and turns "deathly pale" (III: 130). Walking around "like an outlaw" (131), he gives and receives refined insults, and when he rises to respond to a toast offered him by Richmond, Johannes suffers a deep humiliation. To the horror of the assembled guests, Victoria repeatedly interrupts his remarks with wild outbursts, "her eyes blazing" (135), forcing Johannes to change course to cover the general embarrassment. Against his will, his speech turns into a fulsome tribute to his past friendship with the Castle children. The image of his childhood that he evokes in this sentimental retrospective is knowingly false; Johannes even implies that his genteel friends—who had consistently looked down on him—had "a huge share" in what he had accomplished as a writer. No wonder Ditlef, Victoria's brother, remarks to his mother, "I never knew that I was, in fact, the one who wrote his books" (136). Obviously upset by the erotic electricity passing between his fiancée and Johannes, the Lieutenant warns Victoria, threatening to go hunting with a neighbor, then pokes Johannes in the eye and leaves in a dudgeon.

In view of these occurrences, which contravene ordinary canons of logic and reason, the death of Otto, whether self-inflicted or accidental, becomes quite acceptable. Similarly, the cruel irony of Victoria being turned down when she is finally free to offer herself to Johannes, an irony that under more normal circumstances might seem manufactured, is quite in tune with an ambience that has lost all contact with decorum and rational order.

Beyond relating a love story, *Victoria* is a celebration of love in all its facets, its ups and downs, its torments and raptures, its capricious twists and turns. It conjures up the charms of adolescent and youthful love, bright and adventurous, or desperately unhappy, as well as the fateful attractions of a besetting passion. While Victoria feels obliged to suppress her love for Johannes, and as a result turns into a prodigy of dissimulation, with occasional bouts of spite and ill-humor, Camilla quickly finds herself in a situation where she simulates a love she does not feel. Here, as in *Pan*, the characters reveal themselves as a cluster of inconsistencies and contradictions: thus, Victoria will tell Johannes, "You're the one I love," embracing and kissing him, while at the same time attempting to palm off Camilla on him (III: 111). A comic sidelight on the vagaries of eros is provided by Victoria's former tutor, who, having chosen bachelorhood after the failure of a youthful romance, ends up marrying a widow. The tutor is a perfect foil to the central characters' sublime passion.

A wider array of perspectives on the irrational, and highly ambiguous, workings of desire is presented in the inserted vignettes or sketches and in the lyrical interludes. The former, mostly depicting typical erotic situations such as adultery, jealousy, and eternal devotion, appear immediately after the scandalous party and its aftermath. Framing the changing Camilla/Johannes relationship, on which they implicitly comment, these anecdotes (chapters 11 and 12) expand the narrative and psychological horizon, taking in anomalous situations that, by themselves, would strike a reader as implausible or absurd. There is, for example, the husband who, having surprised his wife with her lover, asks, "What do you say to putting horns on him—on the one who just left . . .?" (III: 154), a question that elicits a scream from his wife. No less grotesque is the situation of a loving couple who, as they grow old and decrepit, vie with one another in constancy, to the extent that the husband disfigures his face to match his paralyzed wife's "deep furrows of grief" (156).

By contrast, the main lyrical interlude appears early (chapter 3), presented apropos of a poem Johannes has published, "The Labyrinth of Love" (III: 105). While the version that forms part of Hamsun's text is decidedly prose, by dint of its language—carefully structured by anaphora and refrains—it qualifies as a poem in prose. This poem runs the whole gamut of love, from "a yellow phosphorescence in the blood" and a "hot devil's music that sets even the hearts of old men dancing," to a "summer night with stars in the sky and fragrance on the earth" (105). The imagery ranges from the idyllic ("wind rustling among the roses") to the repellent (a garden of "shameless toadstools"), from nocturnal darkness to flashing suns, from heaven to hell. Ultimately, in a pastiche of Genesis, love becomes "God's first word, the first thought that sailed through his brain. When he said, 'Let there be light!' there was love. . . . And love became the world's beginning and the world's ruler; but all its ways are full of flowers and blood, flowers and blood" (106). Love, or desire, has become an all-encompassing metaphysical principle.

Victoria is unquestionably Hamsun's most erotically charged novel; here, more than anywhere else, love is an inexorable cosmic force; it rules not only the human world, but also nature, and Hamsun evokes its omnipresence by a rich array of sensuous images. The "song to joy" of Johannes is duplicated in the forest, by the "wild and passionate music" of the birds as they "sought one another" (III: 99), the mating cry of the blackcock (119), and the sound of the cuckoo (127). Festive music is part of most social occasions, such as the arrival and departure of the packet boat, in Johannes' case fraught with "sensual delight" (*vellyst*, 102) due to his triumph in rescuing Camilla. More intimately, in her post-engagement confession, Victoria tells Johannes that his voice at the party, the only thing that she heard, "was like an organ," which, she says, "captivated me to the point of despair" (144). Significantly, in the postscript to her deathbed letter, Victoria notes that she has "even heard some music" (162). These recurring musical images, together with the images of color — chiefly white, yellow and red[36] — form a counterpoise to the somewhat ominous connotations of "flowers and blood," that ambiguous conclusion to the book's lyric interlude. They mark a borderland where everyman's experience of eros coexists with its sublimated forms, such as a felt kinship with all living creatures and the exaltations of heroism and artistic inspiration.

With all his attention to eros, or desire, as a universal force, Hamsun's major emphasis is nevertheless on individual psychology. As already mentioned, *Victoria* is a kind of apprenticeship story, a book about the artist as a young man. In view of that underlying intent, it is remarkable how vivid the other characters are, expecially Victoria and Camilla. Though they form part of a replicating structure, a kind of round with changing partners, they are nicely individualized: Victoria, a near relation of *Pan*'s Edvarda, is torn apart by conflicting emotions; to her, love approaches a perpetual torment, occasionally interrupted by moments of transcendent rapture. Though the color red is associated with both women, it acquires — together with yellow, the color of joy — a deeper resonance in the case of Victoria: her red hat and parasol, unlikely emblems of passion, are eventually replaced by the red of a hemorrhage (III: 159), the harbinger of a species of love-death. Camilla is appropriately superficial, a bundle of bad faith, but a perfect embodiment of one face of eros, inconstancy, and Victoria's diametrical opposite.

Formally, *Victoria* relates to *Pan* somewhat like *Mysteries* to *Hunger*: a first-person narrative is followed by one in the third person. However, despite the shared overall point of view, there is no profound similarity between *Victoria* and *Mysteries*. The latter is completely dominated by the figure of Nagel; consequently, the other characters, certainly Dagny and Martha, are portrayed largely as seen by him. Victoria, on the other hand, is given the opportunity of expressing herself in a kind of monologue, which endows her with an inwardness that would otherwise remain mere conjecture. Indeed, the long confession of her love in chapter nine and the even longer deathbed letter to Johannes which concludes the book, bring Hamsun's portrayal of Victoria close to that of his male heroes. Hearing Victoria's voice in these monologues contributes to an image of her that is both more nuanced and more sympathetic than it would otherwise be. Edvarda is given no such opportunity in *Pan*; she has to wait until the publication of *Rosa* (1908), a novel in which she appears, before she can give voice to her true feelings.

While these virtual monologues do help to establish a modicum of psychological and aesthetic balance in the story, the center of gravity is nonetheless with Johannes as a developing writer. Already as a child he cuts "letters and signs" into stones found in an old abandoned quarry, which is one of his favorite haunts. Both the quarry, which he envisages as a cave, and the sea, which also gives rise to romantic fantasies, are images of depths to be explored. When he grows up he wants to be a diver, enabling him to descend from the deck of a ship into "strange kingdoms and lands" (III: 91). In a literal sense, his dream is accidentally fulfilled when, at the age of eighteen, he jumps overboard and saves Camilla from drowning. The diving image recurs in an extraordinary dream sequence that will be examined later. These spaces of refuge and exploration are complemented by images of isolation and power: one wish of his was to be a "maker of matches," so that he could command the respect of his comrades (91), another to be the owner of an island guarded by a gunboat. In his chagrin at being condescended to by his social superiors, Johannes even imagines a shipwreck—reminiscent of a scene in Ibsen's narrative poem "Terje Vigen" (1862)—in which he achieves revenge on them, at the same time winning the princess he is dreaming of. These images and fantasies, partly inspired by fairy tales, partly by Johannes' own experiences as a despised member of the underclass, combine the suggestion of literary creativity with human detachment, both of which are realized in the course of the novel's plot.

Johannes' two passions, for Victoria and literary art, are interestingly interrelated in the book. They can scarcely be separated. All his poetry is written for her, and his "big book" (III: 123), completed after years of emotional frustration but before the official engagement of Victoria and Otto, is a transparent reworking of his youthful experiences transposed into the future. We are given his envisioned conclusion to the book, a meeting at an inn between a no longer young graying man and the lady of the castle, easily recognizable as Victoria by her yellow dress. In the emotional scene that ensues, the man sates his pride in a bitter speech, followed by sobs and a prayer for forgiveness. The scene ends with the lady confessing her love; the very words she uses, "I love you; do not misunderstand me, you are the one I love, farewell!" (121), echo Victoria's declaration of love for Johannes in chapter three (111).

We have already seen how such reworkings, though in a different mode, are also found in Johannes' reflections on his past apart from his writing. The following example is somewhat different from those previously cited. It relates an incident in which Johannes tells Camilla how, once, he observed two people, a man and a woman, walking down the road, conversing (III: 141). The scene he describes, however, is not a straight reproduction of a past experience; rather, it fuses two recollected incidents: one in which Victoria, after acting rather unpleasant, brushes Johannes' hand in obvious affection (104), the other an exclamation that her father would never allow her to marry him, dashing the hopes, sealed with a kiss, that Victoria had awakened a couple of days earlier (116). Besides modifying the past, telescoping events, Johannes here introduces himself as an outside observer of what had happened, thus distancing himself from the emotional intensities he had experienced. More generally, the passage shows how *Dichtung*, or imagination, supplements *Wahrheit*, or truth, not only in the books that he writes but even in his own everyday recollections. Whatever the motive, in his life as in his art, Johannes creates an imagined world: experience is always mediated.

The creativity manifest in these activities, whether transforming recollection or artistic production, seems to have an underlying *telos*: to counter, if not to transcend, time's ineluctable passage and, ultimately, death. Passion-love is one way of suspending mutability, and, like Nagel in *Mysteries*, Johannes stakes the meaning of his entire existence on his love. Unlike Nagel, the artist manqué, however, he finds a credible substitute in his writing when love fails.

Victoria's rejection confronts Johannes with existential absurdity, as shown in chapter five (III: 118–20). Isolated in the city after Victoria's departure, he finds himself at point zero, a prey to macabre fantasies of death and dying. Nature itself is dead: "The old poplars outside are stripped of foliage and look like wretched monstrosities;

some knotty branches grind against the wall of the house, producing a creaking sound like a wooden machine, a cracked stamping mill that runs and runs" (119). In this ambience of decrepitude and decay, Johannes is writing about a "green and luxuriant garden near his house, the Castle garden. . . . It's dead now, and covered with snow, yet he's writing about just that, and there isn't winter and snow at all, but spring and fragrance and mild breezes." And Victoria, when she appears, does not sport yellow or red, but is dressed in white; "she looks like a white spirit in the green garden "(119). The reversal of the seasons has a counterpart in his work habits: he writes at night, when most people are asleep. Paradoxically, the whistle of a train around midnight is a wake-up call: "it sounds like a lone cockcrow in the silent night" (120).

The outer limit of Johannes' manipulation of time amounts to outright revolt. In a state of "violent agitation" after being turned down by Victoria, he gives in to an impulse that can only be described by an oxymoron, "happy indignation": tearing a handful of leaves off his calendar, he creates a virtual future moment, which he decides to enjoy to the full smoking his pipe. Unable to locate his pipe cleaner, he "suddenly jerks one hand off the clock in the corner to clean his pipe with" (III: 117). These infractions of temporal order afford him great pleasure. Though the next paragraph begins with the sentence "Time passes," his two-pronged assault on temporality signifies a fundamental aspiration: to create a suspended moment. Just as inspiration or creative activity plays fast and loose with real time, so the literary representation itself aims to concentrate experience in a moment. This is illustrated by the continuation of the garden scene in Johannes' manuscript referred to above. When asked what he wants as he stands there, separated from Victoria by a wall, he answers, "I only want to stand here a moment. It's the last time. I want to get as close to you as possible" (120). The rhetorical question at the beginning of the following paragraph, "What did he have to do with death?," clearly implies that the created moment is a barrier against the inroads of destructive time. Here lies the aesthetic foundation of the novel's unique composition, evidenced most clearly in Hamsun's unconventional handling of plot and diverse narrative discourse.

Despite being a third-person novel, *Victoria* succeeds brilliantly in conveying the inner life of its characters. Its combination of a dialogue technique that could be called behaviorist with free indirect discourse enables Hamsun to render consciousness moment by moment. In the dialogues of Johannes and Victoria, a language of gesture complements the brief verbal exchanges, showing the undercurrent of thought and feeling. This is especially so for Victoria, whose lips, face, eyes, and hands speak when her tongue is tied. Her lips often tremble, she drops her eyes, and her hands touch his, though otherwise she seems cold and unapproachable. The free indirect discourse serves a similar purpose for the portrayal of Johannes, sometimes producing an expressionistic effect. After he says goodbye to Victoria, who warns him not to pursue her, his despondent state of mind is rendered as follows: "The street stretched cold and dead through town, it looked like a belt of sand, an eternal walk" (III: 116). The sights he observes in the street, in particular a withered little boy with "hollow cheeks" and a disfiguring hair disease, are equally imbued with his downcast mood, as evidenced by the following thought: "His soul was also completely withered, perhaps." The lightening of Johannes' mood is signaled by some subsequent observations, as he imagines the little boy watching the other children at play: "Who knows, perhaps he was happy about something, perhaps he had a doll in his small room in the slums, a jumping jack, a whirligig. Perhaps he hadn't lost everything in life, there was hope in his withered soul" (117). The point here is not to describe the life of the streets as much as to show, indirectly, the phases of Johannes' consciousness as he struggles to recover from his grievous disappointment. In contrast, his excitement at being invited to Victoria's party comes through perfectly in the following sentence: "The afternoon was still and warm; the river throbbed its way through the hot landscape, like a pulse" (128).

The technique of free indirect discourse does, however, encompass another horizon beyond that represented by the principal character, namely, that of the implied narrator. Though the narrator's point of view is nearly identical with that of Johannes, there are passages where the narrator and the central character part company. For example, Johannes' writings as exemplified by the scene at the inn referred to above are far less complex than the novel in which they appear; that novel also possesses a greater emotional amplitude. Johannes' literary work is motivated by two diametrically opposed passions: amorous devotion and a lover's revenge; the novel transcends these simplicities. In fact, whereas Johannes the writer shapes experience into ready-made patterns, the novel radically undermines such patterns.

The most convincing example showing that the narrator constitutes an independent entity that transcends the main character's consciousness is Johannes' macabre dream immediately after he has imagined the conclusion to his "big book" (III: 122). At the same time the dream offers the reader some fascinating glimpses into Johannes' subconscious. The writer feels triumphant, his double in the nearly finished book having been reassured of his lady's love. What could possibly be wrong? The dream, which ends with a mocking echo of Johannes' childhood wish to become a diver, an image associated with artistic aspirations, offers some clues. It introduces us to a "deep, dead valley" where an abandoned organ is playing; the organ motif ties in with Victoria's comparison, already mentioned, of Johannes' voice to the sound of an organ during their meeting after Otto's death (144). But as it plays, the organ bleeds. Then the dreamer, Johannes, arrives at a desolate city square, with echoes of recently spoken words in the air, oppressive presences that resist his attempts to dismiss them and return in the form of a group of dismal old men dancing, subsequently discovered to be blind, deaf and—dead. Having come to a mountain, he learns that it is the foot of a trapped giant, who pleads with the dreamer to release him. On his way to the "ends of the earth" where the giant lives, the dreamer comes to a bridge guarded by a man of musk collecting shadows; the dreamer escapes the fate of losing his shadow only through a voice which asks him to turn around. He sees a rolling head smiling at him; it shows him the way, rolling for days and nights, until they arrive at the sea. He wades into the sea and dives in. Standing by a tall gate, he meets a "large barking fish" with a mane, and behind the fish stands Victoria, naked, an echo of an image used in Johannes' account of his nocturnal adventures to his irate neighbor. She smiles at him, he stretches out his hand and calls to her, "he hears his own scream—and awakes" (122).

The dream is sufficiently strange and complex to deserve a brief commentary. In trying to make some sense out of it, one must not lose sight of the context, one of felt artistic accomplishment on the part of the dreamer: with his "big book" he has won "the kingdom" (III: 123), but the princess has eluded him. From this perspective, the dream evokes the complementary negative state to Johannes' literary triumph. His psyche is at a point of stagnancy; it has nourished his art, symbolized by music, words, and dance, with blood and precious time. No wonder the dreamer is anxious. Next, he encounters the captive of the mountain, an allusion to his childhood threat, expressed to Victoria, of going into service with a mountain giant to escape the miseries of life and the torment of unrequited love. The dream, however, suggests that this option is a dead end; in any case, Johannes cannot liberate the giant, who seems to symbolize the state of his creative self. Instead, it looks as though the dreamer may be losing his humanity, a suspicion that is confirmed by his encounter with the shadow-collecting man of musk; we do not know what lies beyond the bridge that he guards, but it instills a "chilling dread" in the dreamer. Rescue comes by way of a smiling skull, a kind of psychopomp—except that it leads Johannes to the sea and Victoria, that is, to life, rather than to the realm of the dead.[37] But however inviting, Victoria is unreachable, defended by a monster, a kind of Nordic Cerberus of the deep that prevents Johannes from enacting his desire (122).

The dream seems almost too complex for the context. It certainly undermines the sense of triumph experienced by Johannes at the completion of his book, though what immediately follows the dream betrays no awareness on his part that he makes anything of it at all. To an outsider, the dream clearly associates the artistic life with a sort of deadness; it also suggests that, in order to be liberated from the death-in-life of artistic production, an arduous journey of the soul is required. However, the journey the dreamer undertakes leads to a nightmarish destination: it looks as though Johannes is incapable of meeting Victoria's challenge, regardless of the wise guide and his own efforts. If the monster is viewed as a part of his own psyche, it becomes an emblem of his sexual fear. This suspicion is confirmed not only by Johannes' calm indifference when confronted with Camilla's fickleness, but also by his failure to seek out Victoria after Otto's death.

One even begins to wonder whether his brutal words, "I'm engaged," were not simply a cover for the cooling of his desire. Now that his passion has been exploited for artistic creation, it no longer seems to exist in its pristine form; once it has been embodied in his work, Johannes attains a condition of emotional stasis. On the one hand, the idea of a poem in which he imagines the earth "seen from above, like a strange, beautiful papal gown," with people walking, "couple after couple," in its folds at the "hour of love," makes him feel as though he could "embrace the earth" (III: 150); but, on the other hand, this general love for humanity goes hand in hand with emotional coldness toward individuals. Meeting Camilla and her family in the street, he thinks, "How little it all concerned him, this carriage, these people, this chatter! An empty and cold feeling took possession of him..." (157). This coldness may be a reason why Hamsun ends the novel with Victoria's uncommented deathbed confession, warm and spontaneous and expressive of a contrarian perspective. In her tragic defeat, Victoria paradoxically looks like a winner.

Victoria could be called a *Künstlerroman*; it is also an example of metafiction, since it problematizes the relationship between lived experience and its artistic representation. That relationship is not a simple one. On the one hand, art is present as an element of everyday life: in our retrospections we reshape the events of our lives in a more expressive and harmonious, though not always truthful, way. Further, much of what is called art often distorts experience, creating compensatory fictional worlds the unstated purpose of which is to magnify our egos. This may lead to spiritual sterility, unless one guards against the emotional indifference—necessary for art but fatal to life—that artistic detachment might produce.

The style of *Victoria* is well suited to its subject. The beginning of the book is written in a fairy-tale manner, describing the world of Johannes as that of a young dreamer who wants to win the princess and half the kingdom. Later, the fairy-tale quality recedes, but not the stylization that the manner of fairy-tale narrative entails. Instead of being described in detail, with circumstantial realism, scenes and situations are rendered sparely, as in legends or myths; thus, places are only vaguely indicated, as is the chronology. In this perspective, what might be considered implausibilities in the plot, such as Otto's sudden death, are hardly noticed; the book instills a reading attitude that does not ask for the reasons why things occur. *Victoria* creates a fictional world in which rigorous notions of time, space, and cause and effect do not obtain. Its success or failure depends on whether it creates a feeling of empathy in the reader, a sense that, however abstract, it renders life, passion, and artistic creation in a manner that is both true and aesthetically satisfying.

A novel like *Victoria*, whose central characters, in their emotional intensity, sometimes appear like emblematic figures, like passions and aspirations incarnate, invites critical hyperbole. Its alternation of everyday scenes with high-pitched speeches is suggestive of the recitatives and arias of an operatic performance. Though ordinary enough, in their pride and vehemence the characters are larger than life, driven by impossible desires. As previously mentioned, eros is expressed by musical motifs, and other images—the cave, the sea, the garden, the creaking poplars—likewise turn up like phrases or leitmotifs in a sonata or symphony. Fittingly, the novel concludes with the organ fugue of Victoria's deathbed farewell.

With one exception, which Hamsun deeply resented, *Victoria* was well received by the critics when it appeared in October 1898. Hamsun, who had married an upperclass divorcée, Bergljot Goepfert, in May of the same year, was criticized by Nils Vogt, editor of the conservative daily *Morgenbladet*, for his "unfamiliarity with" and inability to portray "really fine ladies" and for misrepresenting upperclass Norwegians in general.[38] Subsequent critics have, to my knowledge, found no fault with Hamsun's character portrayal, though more than one have had harsh words for the novel's conventional aspects, using disparaging terms like "innocuous idyll" and "puppet-theatre plot."[39] Edwin Muir, calling *Victoria* one of the "most exquisite" of Hamsun's works, praises the characterization. As a portrayer of women, Hamsun belongs, in Muir's view, in the same class as Thomas Hardy. Though they are merely sketched, he writes, Victoria and Camilla "give that sense of a truth existing in them beyond the reach of observation or analysis which, like the creation of the highest imagination in poetry, has a touch of the occult."[40] John Updike, whose review of the Stallybrass translation of *Victoria* is more mixed, sounds a similar note, describing Hamsun as a "heathen visionary" of "intuitive genius" on the strength of the novel.[41]

Not surprisingly, the book struck a strong emotional chord among critics and readers alike. A Danish critic who published a book about Hamsun in 1929 says that, for his generation, *Victoria* was what

Goethe's *Werther* had been to youth one hundred years earlier.[42] Kurt Wais, the German comparatist, calls *Victoria* a work of unprecedented "emotional resonance," and Thomas Mann, who read the novel as a young man, names both *Victoria* and *Pan* "immortal poems."[43] More dramatically, Martin Nag reports that, according to the wife of Mikhail Bulgakov, author of *The Master and Margarita*, she and her husband found each other through their "shared love of *Victoria*."[44] Such widespread critical acclaim, together with the empathetic response of readers, testifies to the psychological depth of the work. The book's reputation has not waned: George Steiner, in a recent review of *Hunger*, writes that *Victoria* remains, along with *Pan*, a "powerful, even seductive text," and Robert Ferguson deems it one of Hamsun's "four great novels from the 1890s,"[45] a judgment with which I fully concur. Though the tale about Johannes and Victoria is outwardly simple, it encapsulates a dense and diverse texture, with a rich array of themes and motifs—love's predicament in a class-bound society, erotic passion and artistic creativity, ever-renewed hope followed by disillusionment, zest for life and untoward death. The resulting literary structure, complex and many-voiced, testifies to a modernist sensibility and calls for a nuanced response tempering empathy with detachment.

CHAPTER FOUR

Love's Comedy and Sentimental Education

Between 1898 and 1904, Hamsun produced no book-length fiction, though he was otherwise extremely active. Thus, in one year, 1903, he published three titles: *I æventyrland* (*In Wonderland*, 2004), a travel book about his and his newly wedded wife's visit to Russia and the Caucasus in the fall of 1899; *Dronning Tamara* (Queen Tamara), a play; and *Kratskog* (Brushwood), a collection of stories. The remainder of his production during this period was in verse: *Munken Vendt* (1902), a dramatic poem in eight acts, and *Det vilde kor* (1904; The Wild Choir).

Of all these works, *Munken Vendt* best expresses Hamsun's mental and emotional turbulence as he was edging into his forties. In a letter to his Danish publisher of April 1902, he says he has been "going through a crisis,"[1] evidently an allusion to his gambling craze of the preceding fall, with visits to several Belgian casinos, where, among other things, he lost a considerable sum taken from his wife "without her knowledge."[2] Hamsun described *Munken Vendt* as a book "from the north, from the milieu of *Pan*, . . . extremely violent in its language and action."[3] Written with "tempestuous passion," according to Hamsun,[4] it presents the story of a late eighteenth-century adventurer who is in a state of permanent revolt against God and man. Intimations of such an attitude are evident already in *Hunger* and *Mysteries*, but only in *Munken Vendt* is the hero a full-fledged rebel. In view of the more moderate, if not quite resigned, tone of Hamsun's later fiction, the heaven-defying rhetoric, metaphysical pathos, and social revolt of *Munken Vendt* may have brought about a change in his authorial psyche, something in the nature of an imaginative catharsis.

For the next decade or so, Hamsun's fictional output proceeds on two tracks. On the one hand, he turns out three works set in an arctic coastal village of the 1870s or earlier, when Hamsun himself was of a tender age. The focus in these books is on a gifted young man who undergoes a practical and sentimental education and achieves economic as well as amorous success. The other track consists of three first-person novels centered on a middle-aged hero, whose project is to shed the trappings of education and urban sophistication—in short, to reverse time and change so as to retrieve a state of pristine harmony with nature. Though the two sets of novels are fundamentally different, one work in the first set, *Rosa* (1908), is a first-person novel, and both *En vandrer spiller med sordin* (1909) and *Den siste glæde* (1912) of the second set shift the focus from the self-obsessed observer to a domestic or social domain.

Sværmere (1904; *Dreamers*, 1921), which opens the first track, was viewed by Hamsun as a trifling work that could have been considerably better if the contract with the publisher had allowed him greater freedom. The book was commissioned by Gyldendal as a Christmas contribution to its "Nordic Library."[5] Hamsun tells a Finnish friend that he "had to ruin the book on purpose" to ensure its popular appeal.[6] In particular, he regrets not being able to include "a couple of excellent seductions" of the parson's wife. "If I had been given half a hundred pages more, it would have turned into a novel of great worth," he writes.[7] One wonders whether the wildly extravagant language that appears here and there in the text is an attempt, conscious or subconscious, to compensate for the strictures on sexual expression.

Hamsun was obviously right in minimizing the importance of *Dreamers*, which comes across as rather light fare, especially when compared to its predecessors of the 1890s. However, its very lightness makes it Hamsun's happiest book, entertaining, full of humor, and with a story that, however quirky, is not without serious import. Nor are its milieu and characters wholly without precedent in Hamsun's earlier work. The Nordland fishing village in which most of the action takes place is located six miles from Rosengård, a trading center belonging to a brother of Mack of Sirilund, known to the reader from *Pan*. The period could be roughly the same, the late 1850s, judging by an allusion to Russia being at war (chapter 12). Similarly to *Pan*, the time span extends from spring to fall, with white nights made for romance.[8] Even the plot harks back to earlier books. As in *Victoria*, a commoner is in love with an upperclass young lady, and as in both *Pan* and *Victoria* he has to compete with a rival deemed more suitable. And yet, despite these similarities, *Dreamers* is a radically different work: a comedy of love rather than the tragedy or near-tragedy of *Victoria* and *Pan*.[9]

The enactment of the love theme is framed by scenes of village life suggestive of comedy of manners or folk comedy. The rhythm of that life is largely determined by the seasonal fishing and trading and by the presence of Mack's glue factory. Despite the seemingly placid milieu, the villagers are not unacquainted with violence, since local champions like Rolandsen cannot resist getting into fights with sailors on shore leave. Interestingly, these scuffles are experienced as entertainment by the onlookers. Moreover, the glue factory, with its bevy of young female employees, is a hotbed of flirtation; Rolandsen's sexual banter with the girls, spirited creatures capable of giving as good as they get, signalizes a welcome relief from the official repression of eros in this cramped environment.

In other ways, too, the exigencies of desire make themselves felt, regardless of clerical bans: the prevailing sexual mores of the village are extremely relaxed. And wherever an irregularity or scandal occurs, it invariably features Rolandsen as the chief actor. Indeed, irrespective of the broad focus on the community, the novel is most fruitfully viewed as the story of Ove Rolandsen, who is not merely a humble telegraph operator and champion fighter, but also an inventor. His invention of a new type of fish glue might change the entire village economy. He is a genius of sorts, a man possessed by a double dream, namely, to succeed with his invention and to win the heart of Elise Mack. At the outset neither dream seems to have a chance of fulfillment: Rolandsen lacks money to finance his work and he has already been twice rejected by the beautiful Miss Mack.

The composition of *Dreamers*, seemingly quite artless, is rather ingenious. Its action is framed by the arrival and departure of a new parson, who becomes a key player in the life of Rolandsen and others. Sensing rampant sexual immorality in his parish, the parson, who is given no name in the book, supplements his fire-and-brimstone sermons with a letter-writing campaign addressed to the most egregious sinners. When Rolandsen, a thirty-four-year-old free spirit with a big idea brewing in his head and a nagging fiancée on his hands, sees the parson's wife casting admiring glances his way after he has won a fight with a drunken sailor, he decides on a ruse: to win a respite from his fiancée, the formidable Marie van Loos, the parson's housekeeper, with whom he has repeatedly broken up to no avail, he will sing and play his guitar below Marie's window, hoping that the nocturnal disturbance will lead to her dismissal and eventual departure. As it turns out, Rolandsen is caught serenading the parson's wife, who now occupies that room. The incident brings Rolandsen an admonition in writing from the parson, who has long "kept an eye on him for his scandalous way of life" (IV: 153). Worse is to come: broke and desperate to procure money to have his invention tested by the scientific authorities, Rolandsen confesses to an unsolved burglary of $200 committed some time ago against Mr. Mack, the great magnate, so he can pocket the promised reward, $400! In consequence, he loses his job, his fiancée—the latter without regret—and whatever respectability he still enjoyed in the village. But Mack, quite pleased to be able to show off his economic power, pays out the money and forbears having the swindler arrested.

While Rolandsen is exceptional in his intellectual ambition, which enables him eventually to challenge even Mack, his sexual nonconformity is echoed in other characters. It looks as though Hamsun in this novel is a spokesman for the masses oppressed by priestly authority as well as for the untutored genius fighting entrenched power. In any case, he stages a struggle on several levels between an authoritarian pietistic Christianity, with its requirement of conversion or being born again, and the vagaries of human desire, of which Rolandsen, shuttling back and forth between several young women, is the chief embodiment. The story of Levion, who loses his position of trust as the parson's assistant because his sister is living in sin, forms a bizarre parallel to the humiliations of Rolandsen. The parson replaces him with Enoch, who turns out to be a sanctimonious crook. A forest fire on Enoch's property on Midsummer Eve leads to the discovery of the real thief of the $200. This incident, which constitutes a preliminary climax of the novel's action, clears Rolandsen of blame in the matter of the burglary and justifies Levion's long-time suspicion of Enoch, to the discomfiture of the misled parson, who breaks into tears at the revelation of "grievous sin" all around him (chapter 12). The parson's sole accomplishment during his brief tenure consists in making Levion's sister "remember" the name of the man with whom she has been living in sin, the man "who had the duty to marry her" (IV: 181).

But while the parson, the representative of spiritual power in the small community, has been shown up and defeated, the very discovery whereby this defeat occurred makes Rolandsen's situation vis-à-vis Mack quite untenable. Since he has already spent the $400 reward, which he received on false pretenses, he has no choice but to make his getaway. The Crusoe-like existence he leads for several weeks on the small uninhabited island to which he escapes is terminated only after messengers from Mack seek him out and inform him that some "important" telegrams have arrived for him. Back in the village, he is boosted by the financial offers for his invention contained in the telegrams; riding high, he decides to defy Mack, who now wants to see him arrested for making a fool of him. By way of answer, Rolandsen tells the great man, "I'll ruin you" (IV: 180), then changes his threat to an offer of partnership. The ensuing ball at Rosengård, arranged to celebrate Elise Mack's engagement to Mr. Henriksen, a middle-aged ship's captain, brings a surprise ending: at the last moment Elise changes her mind and goes off with Rolandsen.

The combination of luck with intelligence and perseverance bears the mark of myth or fairy tale as much as of realistic human possibility. Unlike Johannes in *Victoria*, who gained the kingdom but lost the princess, Ove Rolandsen in the end realizes the full promise of the age-old story. Though he is not exactly an Ashlad, the Norwegian male version of Cinderella, the pattern of his story, one from humiliation to triumph in both worldly success and love, seems to derive from the folktale.

The novel's stylistic dependence on fairy tale or folk literature is equally apparent. Thus, several characters are associated with simple, folksy, emotively charged images, objects, or events. The parson, referred to at various times as a "sourpuss" (*grinebiter*) and a "gamecock," a kind of hotspur (IV: 141, 133), is broadly comical, his nostrils all "plugged up with whiskers" (127), and Marie van Loos, a "rasp of a woman who had spent all her years until now spiky and sharp" (133), approaches the stereotype of the shrew. Other characters border on the grotesque, such as Enoch, who is epitomized by the ugly kerchief he is wearing around his head: allegedly intended to soothe a permanent earache, in reality it masks a shameful scar, his ear having been ripped off in a scuffle with an outraged Levion. And while the latter is more sinned against than sinning, the impression he projects is no less bizarre, produced by his violation of a social taboo: he carts the body of his dead wife to the cemetery alongside the carcass of a butchered calf sold to Mack. This is a true scene of scandal. Other props or characterizing epithets pale by comparison, such as Mack's red sash worn around his middle for the sake of a stomach ailment—presumably due to his "royal mode of life" (134) and therefore adopted in turn by social climbers all around—and the childish "little head" (139), worn shoes, and total domestic disorder of the parson's wife.

The portrayal of Rolandsen is more nuanced. Though Hamsun has not entirely dispensed with such easy devices in depicting him, they are supplemented by other, more sophisticated methods. Consequently, he is not summed up by whatever descriptive epithets are used about him. Called "big Rolandsen" by the narrator, he also lends himself to other epithets, like "singular," "odd," or even "quaint." But his eccentric appearance and demeanor, such as letting his hair grow all winter, for example, "so that his head became more and more artistic" (IV: 126), do not touch the core of the man. His love of wine, women and song says a good deal about him, but by no means all, though it does make him stand out in the small community. With all these palpable traits, which make him highly visible, on the page as well as in his fictional space, his inner life remains elusive: his exterior offers no clue to the secret ambition he is pursuing or to his longstanding dream of Elise. Altogether, Rolandsen acquires a somewhat enigmatic quality, not unlike other Hamsun heroes. Elise Mack's portrait is equally mysterious, though for a different reason: we learn very little about her. We can only surmise that she has loved Rolandsen all along, but is restrained from showing it due to class pride and psychological uncertainty, a situation that is not new in Hamsun. She can be seen as a Victoria in a lighter mode.

The long-delayed denouement is an inevitable consequence of these two characters' situations and dispositions. With his wounded ego, Rolandsen can soothe his feeling of inferiority only by shuttling back and forth between three women, Marie, Olga—the parish clerk's daughter and the sweetheart of Mack's son—and Elise; he is not an easy man to deal with in matters of love. And Elise is not very helpful. In the end they have managed to tie their lives into a knot which it takes both of them to unravel: Elise is ostensibly celebrating her engagement to Captain Henriksen, and Rolandsen tells her during the engagement party at Rosengård that he is again engaged to Marie van Loos, whom Elise would like to hire as her housekeeper. The situation turns into a duel of hearts as well as of wits; words become inadequate, only the language of gesture and facial expression can release them from their predicament. Elise's declaration of love is a brush of the hand, repeated in the story's last line: "And she again brushed his hand" (IV: 185). Is Hamsun here alluding to the Norwegian folktale "The Princess Whom Nobody Could Silence,"[10] in which Ashlad does, indeed, silence the princess and wins both her and half the kingdom? If so, the twist is very nicely done, with both Elise and Rolandsen losing the use of their clever tongues and resorting to more immediate means of showing their love.

If this appears sentimental, the narrative contains a variety of features that counteract such an effect. There is, for example, the domestic comedy of the young parson and his wife, which functions as a sort of ironic parallel to the future union of Elise and Rolandsen. The parson's marriage, like the union of Ove Rolandsen and Elise Mack, is one of social disparity, the wife being upperclass; hence her total ineptitude as a housekeeper, leading to constant complaints by her husband.[11] In general, Hamsun's style and narrative technique in *Dreamers* maintain a balance between sobriety and sentiment, pathos and irony, inwardness and objectivity. The implied narrator, who seems to express the attitudes of the villagers, is often emotional, even exclamatory; at times, he identifies with Rolandsen, at other times he criticizes him for his impulsiveness and his boastful manner (IV: 146, 151). Other characters are treated less gingerly, such as Mack's son, Fredrik, who is dismissed with subdued irony. A foil to Rolandsen, whose ceaseless activity and grand ambition approach the level of genius, Fredrik finds the key to success in a gospel of mediocrity: "never do too much, rather do a trifle too little of everything, then it comes out exactly right" (165).

It should be noted that, here as elsewhere in Hamsun, the narrator does not pretend to know all there is to know about the characters; as in *Mysteries*, he contents himself with a limited omniscience. Mostly, he lets the main characters portray themselves through free indirect discourse, a favorite Hamsun technique, which allows the reader to share their innermost thoughts. A technique that produces a similar effect, while condensing the narrative, is cutback with subsequent looping, widely used by Joseph Conrad. We will look at two of these, in chapters four and eight.

The former begins with Rolandsen "doing lab work in his room" (IV: 134) and ends with a near repetition of the same words: "And Rolandsen is sitting in his room unable to work" (137). Evidently, the coming of spring is the reason why he cannot concentrate. The pages in between relate what happened the previous evening, when he had a not very agreeable meeting with Elise Mack and then, to make up for his frustration, went to see Olga, whom he courts half seriously, half in jest. Although the sequence, which includes dialogue as well as narration, is not a direct rendering of Rolandsen's stream of thought, it does add a new dimension to his personality, showing him as someone endowed with a complex inner life. The same technique is used to present the infuriated husband's thoughts after the serenade of that "madcap" Rolandsen. The prankster's appearance acts as a trigger, releasing the parson's righteous indignation at the sinfulness of his parishioners, along with a memory sequence that brings back the painful scene of Levion's dismissal and the hiring of Enoch in his place (153–55). Again, while the scenes are presented objectively, though with snatches of free indirect discourse, the parson's consciousness is clearly sensed as a presence throughout.

In conclusion, it must be said that the society depicted by Hamsun in *Dreamers* is not conspicuous for its respect for privacy and inwardness. Both Mack and Rolandsen pay homage to status: Mack is willing to take considerable money losses as long as he does not lose the respect of the villagers; Rolandsen, in his relationships with women, finds it hard to forget how he looks in their eyes. Watchful eyes are everywhere, functioning somewhat like the Sartrean *regard d'autrui*: the pastor, for example, "had the annoying peculiarity of keeping a lookout on one thing and another, even at a distance, even from his office window" (IV: 140), and the book opens with Marie van Loos getting worked up with jealousy as she watches Rolandsen through the kitchen window as he stands talking to Olga down the road (125-26). The pressures of this little community, religious and secular, are formidable, forcing authentic feelings and desires to remain unexpressed, seek unsanctioned modes of fulfillment, or to break through by way of violent, sometimes criminal, modes of behavior.

The complex portrayal of Rolandsen, one of Hamsun's favorite characters, is by far the novel's principal interest. Rolandsen's zest for life, sexual candor, and devil-may-care social attitude eventually come to seem entirely positive values in this purgatorial ambience. The novel's eccentric, somewhat zany style contributes to this impression, producing a carnivalesque tone. For example, spring is said to titillate even "innocent nostrils" with "spicy breezes" (IV: 131); it turns Rolandsen away from the playing of "amusing dirges" (134) and prompts extravagant flatteries of Olga as she cuts his hair: "Ah, your eyes are like twin stars. . . . And your smile bathes me with endless light, like the sun" (136). In this context of metonymies, oxymorons, and hyperbole, there is a place even for flyting. The fight between Rolandsen and the sailor Ulrik is preceded, and accompanied, by picturesque invective; according to the assembled crowd, "both sides had spoken well" (150-51). The freshness, color, and power of this freewheeling language typify the style and manner of *Dreamers*. The novel celebrates joy, exuberance, imagination, freedom; as in *Mysteries*, its tutelary spirit is His Eminence Excess.

The diptych *Benoni* and *Rosa*, both published in 1908, resembles *Dreamers* in focusing on a twofold desire: for worldly success and the fruition of a "higher" love. The ambience, while geographically nearly identical, differs radically through the absence of priestly pietism; the novel's parson, Jacob Barfod, Rosa's father, is an enlightened clergyman whose role, especially in *Rosa*, elicits the reader's sympathy rather than pity or contempt. The mini-society represented in these two novels is decidedly secular, dominated by Mack of Sirilund, the great magnate of *Pan*, who is here seen in the full glory of his economic and sexual power. Whereas in *Pan*, Ferdinand Mack's primary importance pertains to his impact on the novel's plot, being a ruthless, though vulnerable, party to one sexual triangle (Eva/Glahn/Mack) and the class-conscious facilitator of another (Edvarda/Glahn/the Baron), in *Benoni* and *Rosa*, works of greater amplitude, he is shown not only as the source of the community's material well-being but as a consummate master of the game of life. Knowing the ins and outs of both business and pleasure, he uses other people's money to enrich himself, and his workingmen's sweethearts and wives to satisfy his lust.

Mack rules like a feudal lord, a village father in more than one sense. Nurturer and exploiter both, he engenders passionate loyalties and smoldering hatreds. For while a great many people, including a couple of parish paupers, depend on the employment or support that only Mack can provide, his sexual privileges—which he lays claim to as a hallowed family tradition[12]—give rise to much ill feeling among the males in his employ, some of whom must wait until he has impregnated their fiancées before they can marry. To no one's surprise, a brown-eyed baby, trademark of Mack's siring exploits, comes along with the teenage bride.

Hamsun intended *Benoni* and *Rosa* to represent Nordland conditions "about fifty years ago," roughly the period of *Pan*.[13] Writing about *Benoni*, he stresses the novel's "high spirits" and liveliness.[14] While admitting that the book features "an old goat," namely Ferdinand Mack, he qualifies his epithet by calling him a "quite decent" man.[15] Mack's fellow villagers seem to agree. Not only does Mack—that "slippery eel" (V: 21)—get away with his immoral practices, but he is both respected and admired; his Christmas parties are occasions of communal cheer, enjoyed by men and women alike. Amid the general good feeling that reigns at these seasonal celebrations, the memory of bitter rivalries and mortal insults recedes. Thus, when Mack wishes the company a merry Christmas, the blacksmith, the wronged husband of Eva in *Pan*, acts like everybody else, abandoning his vow never to drink a toast with him. After Eva's death, "daily life had gone on as before, and here he was, drinking and celebrating Christmas with Mack. And his eternal hatred was wiped out. . ." (40). As for the women, their feelings are entirely positive, indeed ardent, as they recall intimate moments with the master. The wife of the undermiller "breathed heavily," her mind "filled with memories," and Jakobine, wife of Ole Mensch, another abused member of the underclass, "tossed her curly head full of thoughts." After another drink she "became frisky and extended her toes far under the table." As for Mack, it was impossible to tell by "his calm face that his arms could ever feel good and pleasurable or his eyes look tender" (38). The master of life never betrays his true feelings.

With the crass class differences depicted in these two novels, one cannot help asking oneself what moral norm, if any, underlies the manner in which the characters are portrayed. One soon discovers that the implied narrator, the most likely embodiment of such a norm, is relatively evenhanded; while he can be extremely emotional, his overall attitude is descriptive rather than judgmental: Mack, the elderly exploiter, is treated with no less sympathy than the exploited, young or old. While the present-day reader may bridle at the bitter fate of the blacksmith, the narrator seems blithely to accept the slaps in the face that life delivers to the more humble members of society.

Considering the conflicting interests within the fishing village that forms the setting of the novel, it is remarkable how balanced Hamsun's treatment is. Another writer, more *engagé* and less disinterested, would have turned Benoni and Svend Watchman, both of whom have scores—financial and sexual respectively—to settle with Mack, into real troublemakers, if not outright rebels against the status quo. Such a writer would dramatize the struggle of the poor and disadvantaged to improve their lot and attain a modicum of human dignity. Hamsun made a different choice. Though his storytelling focuses primarily on members of the underclass, neither *Benoni* nor *Rosa* is a proletarian novel, notwithstanding the insurrection that takes place toward the end of *Rosa*, where a party of aggrieved commoners decide to remove and bury Mack's bathtub, the locus of his reputed sexual orgies (V: 264–66). Their attempt to force the voluptuary to abandon his abusive ways ends in fiasco: frightened by the prospect that Mack's health may be endangered, they dig up the offending tub and return it to the owner. Thus, a potential victory for decency and justice, a vindication of a minimum of human rights, changes before our eyes into a hilarious episode of burlesque comedy. The moral issue is dissipated by a sudden shift to an aesthetic perspective, which transforms a worthy cause into a farcical interlude.

The dearth of ethical substance in *Benoni* and *Rosa* underscores the centrality of psychology in Hamsun's conception of fiction. However, psychology no longer signifies interior monologues, surrealist dreams, or a sense of transcendent mysteries. Instead, it serves a realistic purpose, that of portraying average people whose lives are determined as much by others as by their own passions or ambitions. Whatever unity these novels have is largely provided by these characters in the making, first and foremost by Benoni, the eponymous hero of the first novel.

By contrast to Rolandsen in *Dreamers*, who is extremely charming as well as highly intelligent, Benoni seems colorless, a humble fisherman plus mail carrier, called Post-Benoni by his fellow villagers. A cynic would say that, in creating this character, Hamsun has put before us a brilliant parody of the idea of the self-made man. From one point of view he is exactly that, rising from rags to riches in the course of a few years, despite the lack of any particular gifts. In fact, he is quite ridiculous: lacking in self-confidence, easily influenced, vain, ostentatious, and boastful. He is a perfect human illustration of *regard d'autrui*, shaped to a large extent by the way he is perceived by others. Seeing himself as an object, he is able to regard himself with self-respect only through being valued and respected by others. Accordingly, the self-made man is a mirage, concealing the underlying reality of a mediated self, a product of circumstance, imitation, and mythomania.

The crucial episode in young Benoni's life is his encounter with Rosa, the parson's daughter, during which they seek shelter from the rain in a sort of cave. As chance would have it, Gilbert Lapp, a gossipy Sami who passes by, spreads the word in the village. Though at first Benoni denies that anything had happened between them, little by little he adopts his companions' flattering view of him as a dashing Lothario, accepting as true their insinuation that he had made love to Rosa in the cave. However, when he sues for Rosa's hand, he invites disaster. Not only is he refused, but his defeat is made doubly humiliating by the parson's demand that he sign a declaration to the effect that the story he had spread about himself and Rosa was an "outrageous falsehood" (V: 11). What is more, as bailiff it behooves him to read the declaration, along with other official notices, on the church green. Benoni's failure to do so does not save him from disgrace. The following Sunday the sheriff himself reads the signed statement before a large crowd. With the ensuing loss of his job as postman, Benoni feels "good for nothing on God's earth" (13). His rehabilitation, both as a respected member of the community and as a worthy pretender to Rosa's hand, forms the basic narrative of the first section of the diptych.

Benoni is a novel of constantly repeated frustration and ever renewed hopes, a seesaw of a story balancing downturns in love with upswings in worldly success. No sooner has Benoni suffered his amorous humiliation than he acquires a sufficient amount of money through his share in a herring catch to attract the attention of Mack, who encourages him to become a fish trader. Next, having been conned by Mack into buying the latter's raggedy old seine, he makes an extraordinary haul of herring, which turns him into a man of substance overnight. In the meantime Mack, who happens to be Rosa's godfather, has interceded with the parson in Benoni's behalf. In this situation, as in many others, Mack acts as a typical helper, promoting his protegé's sentimental as well as material interests. Soon after Benoni has received the $5,000 for his catch and deposited the money in Mack's business, Rosa begins "to look . . . [him] straight in the face with kind and thoughtful eyes, as if she were wondering about him" (V: 22). When he renews his suit, she tells him, "'Perhaps we could try it, Benoni. My godfather thinks I should do it. But I have to tell you,' she added with a smile, 'that you're not my first love'" (23). Benoni does not mind. His conquest of Rosa is important to him primarily because it validates his upward climb, from humble Benoni to respectable Mr. Hartvigsen; not surprisingly, it further accentuates his less admirable behavioral tics, which, while present from the very beginning, were reinforced by his newfound riches. Bragging and lying, he exhibits the typical symptoms of a showoff and namedropper as the formula "Mack and I" turns into a kind of self-aggrandizing mantra.

The first cycle of humiliation and triumph comes to an end with the return of Rosa's longtime friend Nikolai Arentsen, son of the parish clerk. While Benoni is in Lofoten buying fish for Mack, Nikolai — who by now is a fully trained attorney — succeeds in regaining Rosa's favor. This is not her best moment; she even lets Nikolai, with his malicious wit, read Benoni's helpless letter from Lofoten; what is more, she neglects to mail the breakup letter she has written to Benoni, whose absolute trust in his fiancée is touchingly shown by the ring and the gold crucifix he sent her from Lofoten. When he returns only to discover that he has been replaced in Rosa's affections by another, he regrets, in his frustration and anger, having set his sights so high; in particular, he reproaches himself for the way he had embroidered their first encounter in the cave (V: 72). His increasing dejection, brought to a climax by Rosa's wedding to Nikolai, is aggravated by another discovery, namely, that the mortgage document signed by Mack as security for the $5,000 he deposited with him is worthless, since, according to information received from the sheriff's clerk, Mack's total property is already mortgaged to his brother. As this leaks out—with no detriment to Mack, by the way—Mr. Hartvigsen has come full circle: he is once again stripped down to the nonentity known to everyone as Benoni.

The seesaw continues: a new cycle begins when Benoni's hopes for the future are at their nadir, on June 12, Rosa's wedding day. On that day, after a few drinks at the general store, Benoni wanders out to the rocks by the shore, where he runs across Schøning, the lighthouseman, who advises him to buy the rocks from a financially strapped neighbor because of their silver content. Meanwhile Nikolai Arentsen has been doing rather poorly as a practicing attorney, and his marriage to Rosa is having an unauspicious beginning. In contrast, the purchase of the rocks for one hundred dollars gives Benoni a lift, since it enables him to urge the seller to wind up a foolish lawsuit for which he has been using the services of Nikolai Arentsen. "Ah, how pleasant it was to use one's authority, being a Mack and enjoying people's respect!" Yet, Benoni cannot overcome what he calls "the gloominess in his head" (V: 111). Not until he sells the rocks to an Englishman, Hugh Trevelyan, for $40,000, at the same time as Nikolai's practice utterly fails, does a decisive and permanent change for the better occur in his life. With Nikolai gone—Mack gave the attorney travel money so he could make his getaway—and Rosa being "like a young girl again" (152), Benoni, who has all along maintained a certain loyalty toward the parson's daughter, can finally start hoping he will someday be able to fulfill his desire.

As he prepares to visit the church of Rosa's father at the end of the novel, Benoni is no longer a ridiculous figure, despised by his fellow villagers as a near bankrupt and a spurned suitor. He is in some ways a changed man. Having become manager of Sirilund and Mack's partner as a result of his windfall, he has lost some of his raw sensitivity and got rid of a few rough edges. "He'd gotten in the habit of speaking in a gentle but determined manner—wealth has steadied him, given him more backbone; it has made him dress in more dignified fashion and somewhat changed his language. Ah, the way money could make a human being out of Benoni!" (V: 157). Invited to the parsonage after a service he attends at Reverend Barfod's church during the Christmas holidays, Benoni has the pleasure of hearing Rosa play the piano for him. "He thinks it's lovely, he has never heard the likes, and he feels that she is making a tender gesture toward him by playing like this" (161–62). However, her turning a deaf ear to his hint that she might know where to find a housekeeper for him is a sign that their tug-of-war will continue in the sequel, *Rosa*.

In the preceding, the first part of the diptych has been outlined from the vantage point of the central character, Benoni. But Hamsun does not content himself with telling one story. Thus, one subplot concerns Nikolai and Rosa, another Svend Watchman and Ellen. Moreover, there are several other important relationships, however marginal they may seem, such as that of Mack and his serial bath attendants, Schøning and his wife, Hugh Trevelyan and his Norwegian mistress. The book also includes several genre scenes, including an uncanny slaughtering at Sirilund, and many individual figures whom Hamsun uses to develop specific themes, among others the parish paupers, Mons and Mensa, and Gilbert Lapp. With its broad realistic portrayal of everyday life over a period of several years, the novel depicts the mini-society of Sirilund and environs with impressive detail and verisimilitude. That Hamsun's comprehensive ambition has resulted in a rather sprawling novelistic structure cannot be denied. Whatever unity it has, apart from its central focus on Benoni, is produced by certain recurrent themes and motifs.

One dominant theme in *Benoni* is the centrality of eros in human experience, though it varies enormously, running the gamut from the uncontrolled passion of Svend Watchman for Ellen the maid to Mack's promiscuous sensuality. Love is rarely pure in *Benoni*, nor is it always compatible with marriage. Thus, six months after Svend married Ellen, his ardor wanes; he has stopped singing merrily, as he used to, and walking with a dancing gait. "It no longer occurred to him. Half a year was an endless time now. He had won the one he wanted, fine; but he felt no impatience or suspense anymore. . . . And he woke up every morning to the same condition of having nothing to look forward to, it had been repeated two hundred times on end. . . . And there would no doubt be a few thousand more" (V: 158–59). More important, Nikolai and Rosa's marriage founders on the same rock of monotony: "for more than five hundred days they hadn't been able to avoid each other's faces and hands and hear each other's familiar words. They knew each other so thoroughly that there wasn't the least hope that they would someday manage to surprise each other a bit by varying the day before" (148). To Rosa, Nikolai says, "In the moment love becomes legalized, it becomes dirty. . . . And at the same moment it becomes a habit. But in that very moment *love* has evaporated" (123).[16] The emotional paralysis that attends the married state is even more sharply evident in the Schønings, an elderly couple that no longer communicate on any level with one another. At the Christmas party they "seem to find it hard to be polite to each other" (38). Hearing his wife conversing with Mack, Schøning appears totally indifferent—"oh, how terribly familiar her voice is to him! They have been married for thirty years, they've lived in the same house for eleven thousand days" (41). In this egregiously disenchanting erotic climate, Benoni's romantic interest in Rosa, tainted though it may be by a naive status-seeking, appears praiseworthy by its very constancy.

Interestingly, Nikolai Arentsen formulates a theory that explains the vagaries of love in the novel. His theory is a striking parallel to Freud's concept of "the injured third," developed in the paper entitled "A Special Type of Choice of Object made by Man," which was published in 1910, two years after *Benoni* appeared. For the type of man that Freud examines, the primary precondition for loving is that his love object be a woman "to whom another man, such as her husband, fiancé or friend, can claim the right of possession."[17] Without any reference to Freud,[18] René Girard in *Mensonge romantique et vérité romanesque* (1961) developed a similar theory which he applied to a number of works by some of the greatest masters of the novel: Cervantes, Stendhal, Flaubert, Proust, and Dostoyevsky. The theory is summarized succinctly in a note to the French paperback edition: "Man is incapable of desiring by himself: the object of his desire has to be designated by a third party."[19] As far as the present study is concerned, the interest of both Freud and Girard lies mainly in the fact that Hamsun, by no means an intellectual writer, accommodates within his novel a concept of love that not only elucidates the vicissitudes of desire in *Benoni* and *Rosa*, but reechoes a central European tradition in the fictional treatment of love.

Nikolai Arentsen blames Benoni for his own renewed erotic interest in Rosa: "When Post-Benoni put himself forward, so did I. It is of importance that there be one more, enormously important. An object lying on the ground has no value for you. It's only when someone else comes and tries to pick it up that it acquires value for you, and then you step in" (V: 151). In a previous conversation, the theory is expressed more crassly: ". . . there is no other love except the one that's stolen" (123).

Nikolai's crudely stated theory, while applying first of all to himself, is also relevant to the emotional experience of other characters. Svend Watchman's marital boredom may partly be due to Mack's having found a new favorite, Petrinè, of whom Ellen is fiercely jealous: being no longer valued by Mack, she loses her desirability to Svend as well. It is also worth mentioning that Benoni's desire for Rosa is mediated, since everyone in the village was aware of the longstanding relationship between her and Nikolai. Moreover, as a member of the cultured class, Rosa is a highly valued prize to a plebeian like Benoni, along with the trappings of bourgeois existence that he is slowly and laboriously acquiring. Even Mack's serial choices of love object may be explained by the theory. For one, the young girls and women desired by Mack are usually not unattached; they are either already married or have sweethearts. And the fickleness of Mack, in exchanging one young lover for another, does not invalidate the essential paradigm. Thus, Freud writes that, for the type of man he is discussing in the cited paper, "the love-objects may replace one another so frequently that a *long series of them is formed.*"[20]

Though "the injured third" appears to dominate the novel's erotic landscape, the characters under its sway represent a wide range of different value systems and views of life. At one extreme there is Mack, whose zest for life and appetite for pleasure put their stamp on the novel's ambience. At the other extreme is the Lighthouseman, a cynic who has opted for a minimalist creed: as he tells Benoni, who suggests that he buy the valuable rocks for himself, he needs no more than he already has, poor though he is (V: 95). And yet, contrary to the narrator's explicit description of him as a sort of idiot (40), the taciturn Schøning turns out to be one of the more intelligent characters in the novel, as shown by his true appraisal of the value of the rocks. The same can be said of Nikolai, a cynic of a more sophisticated kind; but he misuses his intelligence both in his court demeanor, arrogant to the point of folly, and in his private life, most flagrantly in his marital squabbles with Rosa. A witty fellow, he knows how to turn a phrase and to play the game of one-upmanship, but he is shallow and weak. Allegedly corrupted by city life, he ends up by using his cynical attitude and verbal nimbleness to gloss over his professional failure. Svend Watchman, a wanderer type, shows traces of classic cynicism in his hand-to-mouth existence, but he is capable of passion and has a gift for song, cheer, and enduring friendship. He is Hamsun's portrait of natural man: simple, candid, spontaneous. In contrast to all these characters, Benoni and Rosa seem not to know themselves: man and woman in the making, they lack, at least initially, an overall view of life or set of values, except those represented by Mack, in Benoni's case, and by her family and social circle in Rosa's.

Though these themes and mentalities are fairly consistently sustained, they do not constitute the broadest perspective from which life and human experience are viewed in *Benoni*. That perspective is provided by the repeated macabre description of the two parish paupers, Mons and Mensa, and by the slaughtering of the pig, one of those genre scenes at which Hamsun excels. Tore Hamsun finds a "reconciling" element of "baroque humor" in the way his father presents his "merciless analysis of human decay."[21] I shall suggest a somewhat different way of making sense of these portrayals. Like the scene of slaughtering, they raise the specter of death, in a novel that seethes with life and eros. What they signify is not only death as finitude or finality, the endpoint of human existence, but as an indwelling part of life, death-in-life: they reek with decrepitude and senility. While most of the novel's characters seem to accept the situation as normal, the narrator appears outraged by the paupers' everlasting presence.

Indeed, it looks as though Hamsun is using these oldsters in an attempt to conjure up a skeleton at the feast, particularly since the main occasions on which they appear are a Christmas party and an Easter dance at Sirilund, the latter taking place in the servants' hall. At the Christmas party the paupers are described as "two dead men from the grave," their fingers having "the slow movements of worms. . . . [T]heir faces smeared with grease, their hands filthy, smelling with age, [they] give rise to immense disgust, a mood of beastliness that spreads along both sides of the table. . . . Only the wife of the undermiller has still sufficient intelligence left to feel embarrassed" (V: 39). Her embarrassment may be due to her being Fredrik Mensa's daughter. At the dance, with everyone joining in the holiday merriment, Mons and Mensa watch from their corner "like lifeless bodies from another world" (56). Our last glimpse of Mensa shows him occupying the same room as Ellen and her brown-eyed baby, with the baby and old Mensa producing a regular antiphony of nonsensical babble. The senile old man has bawled his "idiocy into the ears of the newborn child from its very first day. And the maids who keep bringing him food do not forget to treat him with respect. . ." (153). Though the juxtaposition of the beginning and end of life, the ultimate polarity of human existence, may not be entirely out of place in a novel with so many narrow horizons and mundane desires, the effect it produces borders on the grotesque. Those who find Hamsun's macabre description to be excessive may have a point: in view of the temper and the cultural climate of the period and region depicted, the narrator's evocation of the old men's repellent presence betrays an outsider's tender sensibilities.

On the other hand, one of Hamsun's peculiarities as a novelist is precisely to transcend conventional expectations and convert ordinary occasions and experiences into scenes of horror or scandal. From this perspective, the presence of the paupers at the Christmas celebration is of a piece with Mack's habitual holiday frisking of his own women dependents, with its accompaniment of erotic play and naked lust. The scene of slaughtering, which may seem excessively drawn out—not unlike the ghastly clinical details of extreme old age— acquires relevance from the same perspective: deviating radically from the expected depiction of such a scene, it assumes a decidedly horrifying aspect. Hamsun achieves this effect of horror largely by humanizing the pig, who "grunts as if asking little questions" as he is being led out. Then, listening for a moment, "he blinks his eyes and tries to understand what the people are saying." When the dairymaid dissolves in tears, the pig goes wild and tries to pursue her, screaming as he wonders, "What do these people want with that rope?" Then the long blade sinks in. "At first the pig doesn't understand anything, he lies for a few seconds, trying to think. Ah, then he understands he has been killed and shrieks out his smothered squeals until he has no strength left" (V: 104–06).

Here is another instance of mortality, sudden and violent. Svend Watchman, who takes part in the slaughtering, comments, "It's an easy death to be killed" (V: 106). Not much later, Svend tells Benoni he had tried to kill Ellen; he pulls a butcher's knife from his pocket, the same knife the hired man had used in sticking the pig (113). After Benoni has heard the whole story, he tells Svend, "If it should be true that this has happened . . . and you behaved like a wild beast toward her, . . . I would have to tie you up with a rope" (115). By humanizing the pig and changing Svend Watchman momentarily into an animal, Hamsun manages not only to cast another, quite different, perspective on mortality, but to make a traditional genre scene, however unconventionally presented, resonate with the novel's overarching theme of desire. Indeed, the scene of slaughtering itself is rife with sexual rivalry and innuendo. Thus Bramaputra, a.k.a. Jakobine, tells the hired man in the midst of the tussle with the pig, "You're so angry that I refuse to kiss you. . ." (106).

On close scrutiny, the seemingly random fictional universe of *Benoni* assumes a semblance of order, however unclassical that order may be. The themes that have been discussed, chiefly the polarity of desire and death, are a major constituent of that order, and consequently of the novel's formal design. The ramifications of the eros/thanatos theme provide a structure that encompasses most of the novel's action and makes it possible to see *Benoni* as an aesthetic whole. Nonetheless, it cannot be denied that certain elements fall outside this dialectic. One character in particular, Gilbert Lapp, has no connection with this theme, nor is he related to any figure who does. His recurrent presence is so conspicuous that one cannot help thinking there must be some profound reason for it. Could Hamsun be using him to open up an awareness of wider horizons, beyond the here and now? In particular, is Gilbert there partly to bring out the unpredictable and chance elements in human experience?

Gilbert Lapp turns up at unexpected moments in the lives of three key characters, Benoni, Rosa, and Nikolai; as a result, these moments turn out to be crucial. Thus, he is the prime mover or activator of the Benoni/Rosa plot, in that he sees the two together in the cave and then spreads a rumor about their meeting (V: 9), a rumor that Benoni cannot resist confirming. Gilbert plays a similar role for Nikolai, whom he informs on his arrival that Rosa is engaged to Benoni, a piece of news that made Nikolai's hair stand on end, as he later tells Rosa (50). Moreover, having seen Nikolai and Rosa together one evening when they meet by chance in the Common, he spreads the word that the engagement of Benoni and Rosa is over, *before* Rosa has decided to break with him. In remarking on this meeting with Gilbert, Rosa seems to attribute a special meaning to it, telling Nikolai "thoughtfully": "How strange that I should meet Gilbert Lapp again this evening" (59-60). Though some of the subsequent encounters with Gilbert are less crucial,[22] the last one, occurring at the very end of the novel, as Benoni is returning from the parsonage (165), resonates with an eerie foreboding.

There are several aspects to Hamsun's use of Gilbert. For one, he casts a sidelight on what has been said previously about mediated eros, with the collective instead of an individual serving as the vehicle of mediation. But this effect, chiefly one of gossip, could have been produced without Gilbert. The main reason for his appearance in the novel must be a different one. As an outsider, Gilbert Lapp is a sort of interloper in the society that Hamsun depicts. Belonging to an alien culture, he is enveloped in an aura of mystery, as is clearly felt by Rosa when she remarks upon the strangeness of her second meeting with him. The reader, noting that this outlandish figure turns up again and again, feels that strangeness even more strongly. He or she also realizes that Gilbert's influence is anything but beneficial: his interference in the Benoni/Rosa situation results in much confusion and heartache, and his impact on the relationship between Rosa and Nikolai, which is doomed to fail, is almost equally dubious. Gradually, Gilbert's appearances come to seem ominous, and he himself turns into a bearer of bad luck, a jinx.

If Gilbert is more than a device of foreshadowing and suspense, one may wonder what he is supposed to signify. Perhaps we can arrive at some sort of answer by considering how good fortune, or luck, works in the novel. It soon becomes obvious that Benoni's ultimate success is largely due to a succession of flukes: his initial acquisition of a modest capital, which attracts Mack's attention to him; the huge haul he makes with Mack's old seine; and the purchase and sale of the rocks. One can only conclude that, beyond the drives, motives, and societal pressures that determine a character's action, there exists another realm, one that is exempt from the rules of reason and probability. It is a morally neutral realm, in which good and evil, luck and evil chance are commingled in primeval confusion. Its evocation in *Benoni* lends an aura of irrationality and mystery to human existence as depicted in the novel. However, while in *Mysteries*, Hamsun's most ambitious novel of the 1890s, the locus of the mysterious is to be found in the human soul, in *Benoni* the mystery seems to be rooted in the very nature of the cosmos.

Apart from whatever meaning one discovers in Gilbert's haunting presence in the novel, his appearances do help to give structure to a work whose teeming humanity and profusion of episodes run the risk of generating an *embarras de richesse*. Functioning as a kind of leitmotif, the wily Sami recalls to the reader's mind, as he shows up again and again, the previous contexts in which he appeared, thus helping the reader to better perceive the contours of the narrative. The supporting motifs, such as the repeated instances of good luck mentioned above, also contribute to the novel's form. As the narrative progresses, that form more and more suggests a spiral, the repeated cycles of defeat and triumph ending on an upward curve, despite the allusion to Benoni's ambiguous cave experience as he makes his final exit.

In concluding the novel, Hamsun seems to have had a twofold purpose: to round out his portrait of Benoni and to strengthen the formal coherence of the narrative. The final episode, relating Benoni's visit to the neighboring parish, that of Pastor Barfod, Rosa's father, represents a noteworthy attempt to recapitulate the novel's themes and thus create a sense of an ending, despite the fact that a sequel is announced in the book's last sentence. The landscape that Benoni and Svend Watchman ride through on that Christmas holiday is laden with memories for Benoni; serving as a trigger, it causes him to recall the principal events in his life as related, from the fateful cave incident—"oh, that cave!" (V: 158)—and the ignominious declaration he had to sign, to his engagement with Rosa, the breakup, and Rosa's marriage to Nikolai, together with the reminiscences and sentiments evoked when, just before he leaves, Rosa sits down to play the piano, a symbol of the bourgeois culture he had aspired to for so long (158-62). Unlike the somewhat younger Benoni, who, having bought Mack's old piano, had looked forward to hearing Rosa make music in his own home, the Benoni who listens to Rosa play before taking leave of her is looking backward, overflowing with memories. This memory sequence brings the novel to closure, as far as that is possible where a sequel is announced.

This sequence also demonstrates that Benoni has, indeed, undergone a sentimental education, whereas Rosa has not, or only minimally. On the whole, she comes off rather poorly: neither truthful nor courageous, despite displaying a certain pride, she frequently betrays bad faith, fabricating excuses for her hesitations and capriciousness. She is emotionally confused, shallow, and calculating. And though she is made to suffer for her mistakes, she does not undergo fundamental change, in spite of the chastening experiences she is subjected to. By contrast, Benoni has not only learned to hold his own in the world of business—his demeanor during the sale of the rocks is a gem of shrewd maneuvering (V: 139-43)—but from being an egregious example of inauthentic man, sunk in banality, he has acquired a tinge of everyday heroism. What distinguishes him above all is his steadfast loyalty, if not to Rosa, to his dream of Rosa, however tainted that dream may be by bourgeois materialism. At the end of the book he has attained a point of balance between what he owes to himself and what is owed to the world: inner substance versus outward image.

The change is reflected in a shift of attitude on the part of the implied narrator. As in *Dreamers*, the narrative persona is a volatile presence, at one moment omniscient, at another a mere observer whose knowledge of the characters is limited. He can be quite emotional and is at times prejudiced, as in the way he sums up Nikolai as just a peasant lad who has turned into a "good-for-nothing" by city life (V: 50). He asks questions about the characters that are never answered and expresses wonder and admiration as well as contempt for them. And yet, despite the blatant inconsistencies in the narrative posture, the story holds the reader's attention, partly, perhaps, because of its oral, often vernacular style and the sheer intensity of the narrator's involvement with the world he is conjuring up for us. It is an extremely diverse world, often with a distinctly comic or absurdist tinge to it. Some characters, like Schøning and Nikolai, see through the dreams and illusions—of money, power, or happiness—that ordinary mortals need to sustain their appetite for life. They are keenly aware of life's absurdities, which assume a truly surrealist quality in the grotesque fantasies and witless gestures of the parish paupers. One cannot help admiring the narrator—and indirectly Hamsun—for managing to combine this picture of an arctic vanity fair with a sympathetic treatment of Benoni's quest, quixotic and clumsy though it may be, for an ideal, however imperfect.

While working on *Rosa*, Hamsun seems to have felt it would be superior in some respects to its immediate predecessor. To his German publisher, he writes that it will have "more atmosphere, because Edvarda from *Pan* appears in it."[23] In an earlier letter he says *Rosa* is going to be "good and hot. I have brought Edvarda, an interesting individual, home."[24] He even goes as far as to call the novel "a kind of pendant" to *Pan*.[25] Hamsun is correct in implying that Baroness Edvarda, now a widow and mother of two little girls, plays an important role in the novel; however, if *Rosa* is to be compared to *Pan*, the basis of the comparison ought to lie elsewhere.

Like *Pan*, *Rosa* is a first-person narrative. It is related by a student called Parelius, who records what happened to him fifteen years earlier when he was twenty-two. The subtitle used in the first edition, "From the Papers of Parelius, Student," is a direct echo of *Pan*, which is subtitled "From the Papers of Lieutenant Thomas Glahn." Parelius is, like Glahn, a kind of wanderer; he even carries a gun when he visits Sirilund, and occasionally talks about going hunting, though he admits he "wasn't much of a hunter" (V: 267).[26] Like his predecessor, he falls in love, but contrary to Glahn with a woman seven years his senior, Rosa, who, however indulgent she may be with him, is anything but fancy-free. After a year at Sirilund, Parelius departs, like Glahn before him, and we can return to the occasion for recording his experiences. Here again *Rosa* appears to echo *Pan*; indeed, Parelius' words at the end, "I have taken down all this to pass the time" (301), come as close as nearly possible to being a verbatim crib from Glahn's statement at the beginning of the last chapter of *Pan*: "I have written this to while away the time."[27]

One is tempted to ask, Is Hamsun simply repeating himself, employing a modified, weakened form of a narrative strategy he had successfully used about fifteen years earlier? Or are we to assume that the near identity of the narrative situations in the two novels suggests intentional parody? We have seen Hamsun using parody in regard to other texts than his own; we have also seen him following up a tragic or near-tragic love story, namely *Victoria*, with a comedy of love, *Dreamers*, whose character constellation bears considerable resemblance to that of its tragic predecessor. In view of this tendency to try out different, often opposed points of view, I suggest that, in *Rosa*, Hamsun's use of young Parelius as narrator is an instance of self-parody.

Some of the evidence in favor of this view has already been noted. The similarities between Glahn and Parelius, while obviously real, are undercut by the differences. Parelius carries a gun, but does not hunt; the woods and the sea provide solace and aesthetic pleasure rather than prey. Supposedly a wanderer, he is merely a hiker, someone whose deepest inclination, that of an artist, requires the benefits of civilized life. But the greatest difference pertains to the mental posture of the retrospective narrators: whereas Glahn's recounting of his fateful adventures at Sirilund two years previously is shot through with remorse and mental anguish—emotions that he struggles to hide, with the result that he turns into a very unreliable narrator—Parelius' account of his amorous experiences, made after an interval of fifteen years, seems quite candid and rather tepid, testifying to no profound suffering on his part, despite his repeated lament, "Love is hard." Though he learns at long last to accept his lot as a loser, his quest for love appears imaginary rather than real. And his parting words to the effect that his story, allegedly recorded by someone who is "no good at much of anything," is, for him, "only about one" (V: 301) is contradicted by his very function in the novel, that of narrator of a number of events and stories in which he is little more than a peripheral participant.

The positive aspect of Parelius is that of an *ingenu*, a naive young man, not unlike Voltaire's Candide, who has the ability to describe, with minimal preconception or prejudice, the people and events that come his way. As an observer Parelius comes off very well. Despite his extreme piety—he frequently falls on his knees to pray or give thanks to God—his sensibility is that of an artist, open to all experiences,[28] including a primal scene that may recall the voyeuristic coupling between the landlady and the mate in *Hunger*. Indeed, Parelius' artistic ability, whether as painter or musician, is greatly to his advantage as an observer, whereas it is to his detriment as a potential lover. Thus, Munken Vendt,[29] supposedly a true woodsman and his polar opposite, thinks Edvarda was quite right "about one thing: maybe you aren't a boy!" he tells Parelius. "You play the piano just like a girl, she says." And with a direct reference to sex, he remarks as Parelius prepares to go for a walk, "Yes, you *walk* it off, that's your way out. And then you touch up your pimples with a bit of ointment." Parelius can only respond by thinking, "All right, so I suppose I was just a wee little youth, well-behaved and clever in a small way, created and sent into the world that way by providence. And Munken Vendt was a man" (V: 245). Yet, it is the use of this "sissy" as narrator rather than the presence of Edvarda, as Hamsun claims, that imbues *Rosa* with "more atmosphere" than *Benoni*. The anchoring of the story in the sensibility of a relative innocent, one unschooled in the complexities and ambiguities of adulthood, produces a sense of immediacy that is difficult to match by an omniscient or near-omniscient narrator, despite the personal aura the author might imbue him with.

Though *Rosa* is a sequel to *Benoni*, it is written in such a way as to stand on its own merits, without reference to its predecessor. The change in the angle of narration makes it all new, enabling Hamsun to tell basically the same story over again, though in a different way. On the other hand, anyone reading the two novels in the order in which they were composed and published would expect that Hartvigsen, having undergone so many painful as well as exhilarating experiences in *Benoni*, would carry over some of the lessons learned into the sequel. On the whole, that is not the case. He may have learned something about how to succeed in business, but his behavior remains basically unchanged. As a matter of fact, he acts in a more bizarre manner than ever. Rosa does learn something; at least she discovers a thing or two about herself that she did not previously know, and the reader makes the discovery at the same time. Thus, Hamsun's chosen title for the book, *Rosa*, is fully justified.

Throughout the novel Benoni is working to establish himself as a solid member of the bourgeoisie. Thus, as soon as he finds out that Parelius knows how to draw and paint, he hires him to paint some pictures for the house. Later, he takes him on as "a sort of tutor" (V: 179), producing a situation reminiscent of Molière's *Le Bourgeois gentilhomme*. If it were not for the fact that Hartvigsen possesses, beside his ridiculous proclivities, a healthy store of human, even compassionate, impulses, along with a modicum of cruel ones, one would assume that Hamsun was writing a satire of a typical *nouveau riche* businessman. However, given his rather touching good qualities, as well as an ounce of nastiness, Benoni transcends the comic stereotype. The overall impression produced by him is that of an average sensual man with limited self-knowledge endeavoring to overcome a nagging feeling of inferiority.

The evident overcompensation is sexual as well as material and intellectual. At the same time as he renews his courtship of Rosa, Hartvigsen goes gallivanting in the woods with Edvarda, now a widow with two children acting like a somewhat desperate flirt. His purchase of a Hebrew bible and a diving suit, which he proposes to wear to church in the hope of attracting more attention than the officiating cleric, typifies the bizarre whimsies of Hartvigsen, proud to have been joined with his senior partner under the name "Mack & Hartwich" (V: 198). His purchasing mania goes so far that, according to his own description, his "place is nearly crammed from floor to ceiling with all sorts of things" (251). And Hartvigsen's mind is equally cluttered, if we can trust the narrator: "Bah, what a collection of oddments seemed to occupy that head of his! He would talk about the 'deep sea of life' and give his words the most peculiar wrappings: 'Luther, now, he was truly a champion navigator on the deep sea of life. Well, I don't know much, but this much I can fathom in my innocence" (191–92). His fantasies reach their zenith with the idea of undertaking a pilgrimage to Jerusalem with Edvarda. This project, allegedly a childhood dream of his, possesses all three ego-inflating aspects: sexual, material, and intellectual. Needless to say, nothing comes of it, to the profound chagrin of the Lighthouseman, who helped them map their itinerary.

Hartvigsen's fresh start in outgrowing the comic stereotype must be credited largely to Rosa. An abandoned wife with not only the memory of a failed marriage but of lost opportunities, she develops into a figure of pathos. Her initial prickly manner toward Hartvigsen soon changes, as she notices his apparent interest in Baroness Edvarda, who is prepared to besiege every male in sight in order to relieve her boredom. A new phase of their relationship begins after Rosa is driven to near despair by his nonchalant attitude concerning his "having fun" with Edvarda and by his hesitation when she offers to be his housekeeper, a longstanding wish of his (V: 182). "When she came the third time and threw herself on the ground, Hartvigsen must have been moved; some of his old feelings revived, and doubtless he also felt flattered by being entreated like a master, so he restored her to favor and bade her rise and come into the house with him" (183).

The relationship of Rosa and Hartvigsen follows a very uneven course. Their engagement, after Hartvigsen has "paid off" Rosa's husband to agree to a divorce (V: 184), marks the beginning of a fresh cycle of mental abuse as Hartvigsen chafes at Rosa's past slights. He even waxes jealous of young Parelius, whom he asks to leave, a decision he regrets after discovering that he has been hired by Edvarda to tutor her children. Neither the engagement nor the wedding changes anything fundamentally, contrary to the rosy view of the narrator: "As I left the newlyweds I said quietly to myself that this had begun so warmly, it might still turn out to be a good thing that Rosa had come into this house. Well, there was nothing further to be said about that, happiness had found Rosa" (204). And yet, Hartvigsen soon resumes his rambles with Edvarda, while Rosa must content herself with going fishing with Parelius.

Slowly, changes begin to appear in the spouses' attitudes. Thus, one evening Parelius observes Hartvigsen become "solicitous toward his wife," warning her to put on a shawl on account of the cold (V: 216); somewhat later, at a chance question by Parelius about his "wife," Hartvigsen seems "to make a mental note of the expression. And indeed, from now on he says my wife, my wife, and not Rosa anymore" (241). On her part, Rosa begins to realize her husband's good points. Calling him "incredible," she tells Parelius, "I didn't know anything about it before, but now I see it. They all want to get hold of him, and he helps each and everyone." On the same occasion, as they are watching the return of Svend Watchman's ship from

Bergen, they demonstrate a touching mutual concern, warning each other to guard against the cold. Parelius feels "a stab of displeasure on seeing . . . [Rosa's] tenderness" as she buttons up her husband's jacket (248–49). It is worth noting that these signs of improved relations coincide with Rosa's pregnancy. Later, especially after the baby is born, the prince as Rosa calls him, she acquires a "beneficent power" over her husband. Despite renewed attemps of that siren Edvarda to snare him, Hartvigsen is all "virtuous stubbornness." The narrator even thinks that "Rosa would be sure to wean him from making himself ridiculous with his wealth" (295).

In terms of plot, *Rosa* definitely belongs to the eponymous heroine. This is quite evident from the uses to which Gilbert Lapp is put in the two novels. In *Benoni*, the principal effect of his appearances is to help shape the novel's depiction of human events in general. In *Rosa*, on the other hand, Gilbert acquires meaning chiefly in regard to one character, namely Rosa, who feels that he portends misfortune. The first time he turns up is, not surprisingly, the moment she moves into her future husband's house. Whereas Hartvigsen dismisses the incident "with a little laugh," Rosa responds by saying, "He has brought me bad luck every time." Visibly upset, she tells Parelius, who is present, "It seems so strange. He turns up every time I move. And he turns up every time something happens in my life" (V: 183).

Once she is married for the second time, after being told by Mack and Hartvigsen that Nikolai was dead, Gilbert's appearances are fraught with real menace. From what the wily Sami tells her, namely, that Nikolai's mother, Malenè, has received one hundred dollars in the mail, Rosa infers that Nikolai is still alive. "She spoke about the Lapp with horror, no longer trying to be calm but showing herself to be full of worry" (V: 227). That worry climaxes, along with the suspense, when Nikolai actually turns up one stormy night around the vernal equinox, in a plot development reminiscent of a Gothic tale: a man presumed dead returning from the grave to claim his bride. The final meeting between Rosa and Nikolai, whose return is motivated by the failure of Mack, the intermediary between him and Hartvigsen, to pay him the agreed-upon sum for his consent to a divorce, is the emotional highpoint of the novel; it is a harrowing scene, in which Rosa's mental anguish and a forlorn desire to find "a little bit of shame" in her former husband are set off against Nikolai's cynicism, gallows humor, and devil-may-care cruelty (284).

But though this particular scene has a special resonance, encapsulating the bitter experience of years of intimacy, the emotional predicament it bodies forth is not unique in the novel. Indeed, the fundamental psychological reality of *Rosa* is a congeries of virtual traumas, leaving psychic injuries that are slow to heal. The self-lacerations of Rosa, who even after her marriage to Benoni tells Parelius that she is "not yet quite unmarried to Nikolai" (V: 225), have counterparts in other characters; every one of them has had a painful past experience that must be lived down. Benoni's repeated surliness and show of cruelty toward Rosa are no less a part of his character than his comical traits; betraying the frustrations and suffering he has endured, they imbue him with a tinge of pathos. If this sounds paradoxical, so be it: Hamsun is known for creating contradictory characters. The reader's response is bound to be equally complex, shifting from mockery and outright laughter to pity or compassion.

Baroness Edvarda offers perhaps the most extreme example of self-laceration. Though her actions convey the image of a coquette or vamp, her virtual monologues to Parelius give the impression of a woman whose emotional life is in a state of paralysis due to a besetting youthful memory. The story she tells about Lieutenant Glahn, which contains several fascinating episodes not included in *Pan*, is a strange mixture of reckless abandon, ecstatic happiness, and capricious cruelty. Their love, as she describes it, bears the imprint of a primordial passion, one in which, so to speak, the divine and the animal join to the near exclusion of the human. Though she tells Parelius outright that Glahn "was no god," she also says that he "knew no bounds, none at all"; in her eyes, there was something about him that transcended the human. However, in accord with his portrayal in *Pan*, it is the animal aspect of Lieutenant Glahn that is emphasized: "he was an animal. . . . That's exactly it, he was a wonderful animal" (V: 188). In another speech she conjures up the intense sensations evoked by a shot, a puff of smoke, and the yapping of Aesop, the dog: "'My beloved!' I whisper, and a sound as of a hundred violins streams through me. I take out my breasts and hold them toward him to give him some sweetness in return for the shot he fired for me. My life is his, I cannot see for emotion, the road surges before me, I fall down" (212).

Though the narrator considers her speeches "overwrought," they constitute some of the most vivid writing in the novel, permeated with an intimate nature lyricism. Recalling how she used to put her cheeks "against the blades of grass to caress them," she asks herself, "But what has become of the blades of grass and the paths and everything?" She wonders whether things might have been different: "If I'd married the man I loved and stayed here and walked the woods and the paths, then perhaps I would've held on to my peace, what do you think?" Baroness Edvarda is struggling with the conundrum of an alternative life, also known as the buried life, which she is incapable of resurrecting. Her estimation of what actually happened is dry and disillusioned. "What I developed away from was better than what I received in its place; I entered a rich and cultured home, with no blades of grass and no paths like here. . . ." While other people have remained the same, she feels alienated from what she once was, saying, "I'm a completely different person" (V: 211).

Edvarda's experience of personal discontinuity, a commonplace of modernist fiction, is inseparable from Hamsun's psychology in *Rosa*. It is perceived as a serious problem which the characters attempt to remedy, each in his or her way. Interestingly, it is most acutely felt by the women, Edvarda and Rosa. Edvarda alternates between a religious and a secular solution. She tells Parelius, "I have so much to atone for," and so she decides to go on a pilgrimage to Jerusalem. "I have tried many things here, I've even worshiped strange gods" (V: 221), she says, unaware that Parelius had observed her and Gilbert Lapp bathing in a woodland pond "without a stitch on their bodies." After their swim, Parelius relates, the Lapp "sits down beside her, grabs her suddenly by the throat and overpowers her. Ah, now they are both wild, trembling against each other, merging their arms and legs, doing the unspeakable." This scene, with its animal images, is obviously intended to show Edvarda's desperate attempt to recover the erotic enchantment she experienced with Glahn. Incidentally, it takes place in the presence of a pagan idol. The failure of the attempt seems obvious from the narrator's response to the scene, which produces nothing but a "faint song of squalor. There was a relish of decrepitude and sickness in it, as if the whistling sound came from the stone image itself" (205–06). In effect, it looks as though the circular space around the pond, described in terms of a sacred ground with hovering insects doing a dance, has been desecrated by the savage act of coupling. Edvarda's subsequent hope that Munken Vendt, who attracts her by being a hunter, like Glahn, will meet her standard equally fails. With his brutal manner and down-to-earth approach to love, Munken Vendt appears as an extreme parody of natural man and very unlike Glahn, as Edvarda comes to realize. She tells Parelius, "there is a world of difference" (246).

In the end Edvarda joins her life to that of an English squire, Hugh Trevelyan, a hopeless drunkard who visits Sirilund during the salmon-fishing season; she consoles herself with the thought that, though no hunter, he was a fisherman and, like Glahn, "a lonely and very special soul" (V: 247). Edvarda tells the narrator, "I have a small untapped sum of tenderness in me, and now I can use it up!" (299). To illustrate how far Edvarda has traveled, it suffices to glance at the decadent poem she reads to Parelius and Munken Vendt. Though she passes it off as a "Finnish poem" she has translated, her passionate recital suggests it is her own. A prose poem, it moves between images of eros and death. Here are a couple of representative passages:

> An ax is good-natured and kind, there is no poison in it. An ax is no suicide weapon, it does not split anyone open, it only kisses. A red mouth appears where the ax has kissed, two red lips open where it kisses.
> . . .
> Oh, come to me in the spring, my love, my great one, and bring the ax with you! I take my stand beneath the stars and stretch out my tongue to lick the ax. Such am I.
> Such is life. (V: 244)

Like Edvarda, Rosa is haunted by a youthful love, that for Nikolai, whom she later married. She tells Parelius, "Nikolai I can remember since he was a youth. He was lighthearted and laughter-loving, I can remember many times when he was in love with me. What do I have to remember now? Nothing. I just have more to eat every day, but what good is that to me? I don't have a single innocent memory. But I do have memories of Nikolai" (V: 255). This is a prose counterpart to Edvarda's poetic evocation of her rapturous love of Glahn. Nikolai may have had a point when he used to say, according to Rosa, that she was "an awful bore"; in fact, Rosa herself says, "And I believe he was right" (226).[30] Yet, her feelings seem to run deep. As in Edvarda's case, the fixation on an unresolved youthful love is sufficiently strong to prevent her from forming a new attachment and getting on with her life. Reflecting on her divorce, she tells Parelius that "we never quite free ourselves of the one we have split up with, don't you believe it! Every hour of the day we are reminded of the other one; some feel it more strongly, others less so, but nobody gets off scot-free" (225).

Whereas Edvarda appears to work out her conflict by reliving her past experiences, through relating them to Parelius and actively seeking fresh objects for her love, in Rosa's case the liberating trigger has to come from the outside. For her sentimental bond to the past to be broken, an act of emotional violence is necessary. In the final scene between Rosa and Nikolai, Parelius, who is present, is shocked and impressed by "how needlessly hard this man had been both on himself and on Rosa. If it was to help her that he had behaved like that, then he was no mean person, no, certainly not" (V: 285). As it turns out, the catharsis effected through Nikolai's cynical but benevolent cruelty is so thorough that Parelius subsequently feels called upon to remind her of Nikolai's terrible end in the icy waters of the bay. Her reaction seems almost callous: "I feel as though all that was a long time ago, many years ago. . . . No, that was all over, you heard yourself all he said. I'm only glad it came to an end. Yes, it was a very sad end of course, but still. Now I just have to be as I should toward myself and those who belong to me." Though made possible by her former husband's deliberate mockery of her continuing attachment to what they had shared as young lovers, that is, by a paradoxical act of self-sacrifice that she interprets as sheer cruelty, her emotional liberation is authentic enough. And just as Benoni has learned to think of Rosa as "my wife," Rosa now freely refers to him as "my husband" (290–91).

The redemptive aspect of these stories is countered by fierce rivalries and hostilities that bespeak a naturalistic perspective. Nikolai's version of "the injured third party" is still traceable in the characters' erotic behavior; in fact, the principle has acquired a wider scope, embracing the women as well as the men. Thus, it is Hartvigsen's interest in Edvarda that causes Rosa to change her mind about him. At the welcoming party for Baroness Edvarda, the narrator notes the change: "it looked as though a miracle had happened to her, that she had fallen in love with Hartvigsen" (V: 178). Later, he speaks outright of jealousy as being "to blame" for her turnaround: "her jealousy of the Baroness got the better of her" (185).

Indeed, the erotic dynamics of this novel is largely determined by jealousy.[31] Significantly, Parelius discusses jealousy with Rosa, using a couple of pigeon cocks as his text. "They are jealous of each other," he remarks. She responds, "Well, jealousy may be all right, . . . I guess it's part of love, I don't know. . . . But love cannot live on jealousy, I think, not in the long run" (V: 215). Rosa may not be an intellectual luminary, but in this she is probably correct. It is worthy of note that she eventually overcomes her resentment of Hartvigsen's philandering with Edvarda, who does her best to turn his head: "Rosa let it quietly happen, she was cured of her jealousy and had something else to think about" (260). What is more, she invalidates what we might call Munken Vendt's maxim of "the 'unworthy' third party," which Parelius, modeling himself on his macho friend's theory of seduction, tries out on Rosa. The maxim states that, to turn disappointment in love to triumph, "you just have to rest your eyes for a moment on someone 'unworthy.' Then you will see! Then your beloved will come to you, into your arms, because she can't bear to see you throw yourself away, she will want to save you, drag you up from the depths. A good woman is full of blind hostility toward a bad one." Though Parelius' teasingly suggestive description of his visit to Hugh Trevelyan's sweetheart brings a "scarlet" flush to Rosa's cheeks and makes her exclaim in anger, "Are you completely crazy?," she soon loses interest in the matter, causing him to reflect: "she was no doubt glad at the prospect of getting rid of my irksome passion" (272). Parelius' tryout of his second-hand principle simply demonstrates his callowness as a lover. Jealousy, as Hamsun portrays it in this book, is an overriding passion, not a pawn in a game of seduction.

Hamsun's concept of the human psyche in *Rosa*, a novel which viewed superficially may seem like a simple story of everyday life in a North-Norwegian village on the eve of the modern age, is anything but simple. Conventional notions of good and evil, reason and consistency, tragedy and comedy are too crude to describe the behavior of Hamsun's characters. Thus, the most pious figure in the novel, Parelius, who passes himself off as the best friend of Munken Vendt, leads his friend, as soon as he arrives, into a trap, taking him to the

Love's Comedy and Sentimental Education 115

copse where he discovered the pagan idol. Noticing Vendt's sensitivity to nature, how, for example, "[t]here were some stones he liked better than others, not only to sit on but to have near him," he thinks, "I will show him a stone and see what he thinks about it!" (V: 234). Once they reach the copse, Parelius asks Vendt to take off his gloves, knowing full well that his friend will pick up the stone idol, which he himself was prevented from doing by some mysterious force on his first visit to the copse. Though he experiences remorse when his friend subsequently develops a painful rash, caused by the poison with which Gilbert Lapp has impregnated the idol, one cannot help thinking of Nagel's accusation against Miniman: Parelius's pious exterior may be a blind for a "sanctimonious depravity."[32]

This action by Parelius, a classic case of envy, is paralleled by Edvarda's behavior toward Rosa, ostensibly a good friend, at the end of the novel. Unable to endure Rosa's wedded contentment, she decides to delouse old Fredrik Mensa and spread the vermin in Rosa's house. Parelius, who helps her collect the lice, turns himself into an accomplice by his silence. Although obviously disapproving of her dastardly act, he thinks, "But I appreciated the fact that she had trusted me, uttering not a single word to secure my silence, and accordingly I kept mum." Afterward Edvarda gloats as she walks with Hartvigsen, "What, Rosa isn't enough of a wife to keep the place clear of bugs!" (V: 297). This is the same Edvarda who, a page or two later, falls into a profound grief at the news of Glahn's death in India and then is shown once more to reclaim Hugh Trevelyan from his chronic drunkenness. Whatever reason and consistency can be found in her behavior is perhaps best described by herself, as reported by Munken Vendt, "'I believe in madness by virtue of its necessity,' she said, 'yes, by virtue of its own reason as a balance...'" (237).

The acceptance of extremes in human behavior excludes a truly tragic perspective; consequently, one finds that tragedy, or near tragedy, is in *Rosa* relegated to the periphery, and it is quickly dispatched. One thinks of Ole Mensch, whose wife Jakobine—or Bramaputra, as she is called—was so "kind to strangers that her husband had to snoop on her continually" (V: 196), whether on land or at sea. His jealousy eventually foments a murderous rage against his wife, who is on board during his last voyage. A survivor of the shipwreck in which the brig under Ole Mensch's command went down told "a dark tale: that Bramaputra could have been saved, but that her husband, Ole Mensch, had latched on to her and dragged her down with him.... And Bramaputra had screamed, her eyes round and bursting from their sockets." The narrator wonders, "So maybe Ole Mensch had an object in steering straight at the shoal.... Love is hard" (253–54), hinting at the possibility of suicide as well as murder. Hamsun's choice of a simple, unschooled person for his crime of passion in *Rosa* follows a romantic stereotype: lack of the inhibitions inculcated by a higher culture allows the passions to vent themselves more freely. In *Rosa*, however, the story of Ole Mensch's end remains a mere gruesome vignette.

The suicide of Nikolai Arentsen is presented just as peripherally. Nikolai himself seems to treat it as a joke. "Would you like to learn suicide, boys?" he asks, after greeting the workmen at the dock, whereupon he jumps off the jetty. Judging by what he told the blacksmith, with whom he was staying, "Go down to the dock in an hour or so!," it looks as though he viewed his suicide as a kind of performance or spectacle. By this time he had settled his affairs; in the blacksmith's words, he "provided his mother with a nice bit of cash before he quit this world" (V: 288). Inevitably one thinks of Nagel, who performed several good deeds before he died in exactly the same manner. However, it is even more like the suicide of Svidrigailov, the indefatigable pursuer of Dunya in Dostoyevsky's *Crime and Punishment*, who spends his last evening giving away the remainder of his fortune (Part VI, Chapter 6).

It is difficult to know exactly what to make of Nikolai's suicide, in a novel with relatively happy endings. One may note that the subject of suicide comes up several times, including in a report by Edvarda of a conversation with Glahn in *Pan*. After suggesting that suicide might be "the best" for both of them, she changes her mind and begs off. Glahn, clearly disappointed, says "that it was good that way too," as though one always had the choice between choosing life and choosing death (V: 188). We have also seen Edvarda reciting a poem in praise of the ax. Even Parelius plays with the idea of suicide, aping Nikolai—at least in words—just as he previously aped Munken Vendt on how to win a woman's favor. Asked by Rosa about his future plans, he answers, "Oh, I don't know. I guess the best thing would be to lie in twenty fathoms of water" (291). Suicide as a possible response to failure and loss, whether in love or in the game of life, is very much alive in this period of Hamsun's writing. The sensible people are willing to compromise, to cut their losses and go on with their lives. But, as we know, some of Hamsun's characters are not noted for common sense or reasonableness. For them, the options offered by life are harsh, indeed.

At a more fundamental level, Hamsun depicts a relentless struggle for existence in *Rosa*. Edvarda at one point expresses an idea conveyed in *Benoni* by the scene of slaughtering: "Oh God, how brutal life is, how one devours the other! We chop the head off a chicken and eat it, we use force on a piglet and kill and eat it.... We make the children cry, they rest their eyes on us and cry at us. Oh, how my stomach turns with loathing for life!" (V: 212). The human reality of what she is describing may be hidden most of the time, but certain episodes bring it starkly to the reader's attention. There is, for example, the fight about living space waged by the Hookmaker with Fredrik Mensa, whose room he has to share. The situation becomes acute after Mack passes on Petrinè to him, along with her—and his own—brown-eyed baby. "If I were as strong as you I would kill that cadaver!" the Hookmaker tells Torso, his friend, who answers, "it's worst for the child" (277). Here is a tooth and nail struggle for survival, made even more ruthless by its being a generational conflict.

In a less drastic form this struggle is present throughout *Rosa*, especially if we extend the concept to embrace not mere survival but sexual and ego satisfactions as well. In their different ways, Hamsun's characters are bent upon fulfilling these needs, by hook or by crook. Mack, the feudal lord, is dishonest in business and unscrupulous in his use of women, with whom he is locked in a master/slave relationship. Though Hartvigsen tries to model himself on the master, his basic natural kindness and sense of fairness get in his way. And applied as moral principles, such qualities carry no weight in the real world. Thus, his attempt, together with Edvarda, to put a stop to Mack's traditional holiday "friskings" of his female employees and to his sexual gambols with his teenage maidservants, fails miserably. The return of the monstrous zinc bathtub turns into a celebration of the status quo. Among other things, "Mack ... found an opportunity to thank his daughter for the new maid she had procured for the house: she seemed to be a fine, quiet girl. And this

Mack said without moving a muscle in his face, just as if none of us knew why Petrinè had to leave his service and Margretè had taken her place" (V: 276). Life will go on as before, with the same injustices perpetuating themselves. The man with the "imperial soul" (185) will continue to add brown-eyed babies to those already scattered about the community. "People figured that at the moment Mack had sweethearts in nine families at Sirilund, besides all those in other places both in his house and in the hamlet" (258–59). Hamsun writes as if the society he depicts conforms to immutable laws of nature, whereas they are naked class privileges sanctioned by tradition. The hilarious comedy that results from the rivalries and power struggles he portrays acts like a bromide to make the reader accept the patriarchal concept of life the novel presents.

If there is a raisonneur in the novel, someone who comes close to expressing Hamsun's philosophy of life, it must be Lighthouseman Schøning. A man of few needs and little or no ambition, Schøning is not only thoughtful but possesses a wide experience of life from his years as a sea captain. We meet him first on the beach. Asked by Parelius why he is sitting there, he answers, "I'm sitting here keeping pace with my existence. That's what I'm doing, you bet." He continues, "I said to myself today: come, show me you're beginning to play a part in your own life." However, his subsequent remarks suggest a passive attitude: ". . . life must be treated like a woman. Shouldn't we be chivalrous toward life and let it win against us? We should give in and leave all treasures alone" (V: 170–71). These utterances strike an absurdist note, which is one way of describing the impression Hamsun creates of the so-called human condition in the novel.

However, there is another side to Schøning. Like Pastor Barfod, who gives Parelius a lecture on the balance of nature (V: 267), he is sensitive to the non-human world, warning Parelius not to disturb the birds at nesting time. And the enthusiasm with which he plans Hartvigsen's and Edvarda's itinerary for their contemplated trip to the Holy Land shows him still to be emotionally alive. When he realizes that nothing will come of the trip, he takes it very hard. "It appeared that this man had gone around feeling happy, on other people's behalf, that the world was still open to some at any rate, and that others would have a chance to see it in all its glory" (224). His thirst for life is evident from the very beginning. When the packet boat glides up the bay, with a band playing on board, Parelius observes how "his eyes and nostrils open wide at the gleaming horns and the music" (171).

These two traits of the Lighthouseman make him as contradictory as the rest of Hamsun's characters and, one surmises, as Hamsun himself. In the latter, an unquenchable thirst for life and experience and a rapturous sense of the beauty of nature coexist with stoic indifference and virtual quietism, relieved only by the sublimated pleasures of creativity. Meanwhile, life of the average person follows the laws of the jungle as conceived by a philosophical naturalist.

Both *Benoni* and *Rosa* were well received when they appeared in 1908, and critical opinion continued to be favorable. When a couple of decades later the two novels formed part of a series of illustrated Hamsun works, the well-known critic Paul Gjesdahl called them "masterworks that surpass both the Segelfoss books and *Growth of the Soil*."[33] The reception abroad, while less enthusiastic, was not negative. The reviewer of *Rosa* in the *New York Times Book Review* characterizes the novel as a "tour de force of sustained naiveté," and while finding Benoni "bumptious" and "childish," he calls him an "ingratiating self-made Nordic."[34]

Conversely, most academic critics, seeing the novels as a species of folk comedy like *Dreamers*, have been sparing in their praise. In his biography of Hamsun, John Landquist deems *Benoni* inferior to Strindberg's *Hemsöborna* (1887; *The People of Hemsö*, 1959), a comic novel set in a similar milieu and with comparable situations and characters. The portrait of Benoni, who recalls Carlsson, the wily status seeker in Strindberg's novel, tends to fall apart into a series of "comic effects," according to Landquist, due to Hamsun's allegedly "American" imagination.[35] The Danish author and Hamsun's old friend Sven Lange compares *Benoni* unfavorably to the realistic novels of Alexander Kielland and Jonas Lie, both of whom had been targets of Hamsun's excoriating criticism in 1891. Claiming that *Benoni* has little to do with reality, Lange calls Hamsun an "improvisor" and a "juggler."[36] The literary historian Brian Downs virtually dismisses both *Benoni* and *Rosa*, reducing them to an "undistinguished interlude" within the wanderer trilogy.[37]

Professor Nils M. Knutsen, who has devoted a critical monograph to Hamsun's diptych, finds that such views are "one-sided and unfair." Whereas most critics have dwelled on the broadly comic, even burlesque aspects of Benoni, Professor Knutsen correctly notes his positive qualities: he is honest, faithful, and honorable. Moreover, he claims, Benoni undergoes a "human liberation,"[38] making him a far more complex figure than most critics have been willing to admit. While "liberation" may be a rather strong word, I hope my analysis of the two novels has shown that both central characters undergo significant change. Both endure severe suffering and grow in maturity and self-awareness. Still, the authorial attitude toward Benoni, as Einar Skavlan, a Hamsun biographer, has suggested, seems ambiguous. Benoni, he says, is portrayed with a "benevolent ironic smile."[39]

CHAPTER FIVE

A Counter-Development Triptych: Ironic Pastoral, Rustic Bohemia, Bucolic Fantasy

A series of novels that Hamsun wrote between 1905 and 1912, often referred to as "The Wanderer Trilogy," is difficult to characterize. The concept of a trilogy presupposes a certain continuity of form and substance. The only formal consistency in these three novels, *Under høststjernen* (1906; *Under the Autumn Star*), *En vandrer spiller med sordin* (1909; *A Wanderer Plays on Muted Strings*),[1] and *Den siste glæde* (1912; trans. as *Look Back on Happiness*, 1940; *The Last Joy*, 2003), lies in the angle of narration: they are all first-person novels, with a strong autobiographical element. Thematically, they share a counter-*Bildungsroman* motif, namely, a desire to reverse the normal course of psychological development in order to recover what has allegedly been lost through urban living and bourgeois culture. In terms of narrative technique, one notes the presence of a voyeuristic element, most distinctly so in *A Wanderer*. In other respects, these novels differ greatly from one another. The first, *Under the Autumn Star*, combines a spiritual quest with a couple of abortive romances; the second, *A Wanderer*, shuttles back and forth between marital tragedy and a Swiftian excoriation of small-town life; and the third, *The Last Joy*, is a hybrid of reclusive meditation, vicarious romance, and topical satire. An increasingly didactic tendency becomes noticeable as the individual volumes of the trilogy appear over a period of seven years.

Under the Autumn Star is a short novel about a middle-aged man, Knut Pedersen—Hamsun's original name—who seeks refuge from the distractions of the city in the guise of an itinerant laborer. In the process, he meets his coworker of a generation ago, Grindhusen, with whom he teams up to install running water at the local parsonage. He falls in love with the parson's daughter, Elisabeth, and has several sexual encounters with the parson's wife. Subsequently, he joins a somewhat younger man, Lars Falkberget, in a succession of picaresque episodes, until they are hired to cut timber at Øvrebø, the estate of Captain Falkenberg. Soon the narrator's affections are transferred from Elisabeth to the young and beautiful Mrs. Falkenberg. In his free time, he works on a design for a new type of crosscut saw,[2] an occupation that, together with his skill as a craftsman, raises him above the status of a mere lumberjack in the eyes of his employers. His feelings for Mrs. Falkenberg, whose troubled marriage leaves her emotionally frustrated, are obviously returned, but remain unexpressed until near the end of the novel, when he sends her a brief note, to which she replies, "Do not *write* to me" (IV: 381). Hoping that she might consent to *see* him, he persists in his efforts to meet her when he is back in the city, Kristiania, where she seems to have fled to avoid further contact with him. By now he has dropped his proletarian masquerade and appears in his true identity as a man of culture and somewhat of a celebrity. But despite his continued pursuit of Mrs. Falkenberg, she consistently eludes him, and he ends up by going on a three-week drunken spree.

Under the Autumn Star betrays clear links to Hamsun's previous fiction. In terms of plot, the novel presents a less tragic variant of the Glahn story. Like Glahn, Knut Pedersen escapes from the hustle and bustle of the city, with its sophisticated people and absorbing affairs, to the countryside, only to be drawn into new, complex, and emotionally stressful relationships. His erotic life is divided, like Glahn's, between casual sex and dream-like romantic passion. Both characters are caught in a psychological quandary; however, being older, Knut Pedersen lacks Glahn's impulsiveness, raw nerves, and devil-may-care defiance of fate. The tonal difference between *Pan* and *Under the Autumn Star* is indicated by the endings of the two stories: falling victim to a rival's bullet as against drowning one's sorrow in drink.

Nor is the wandering hero a new phenomenon in Hamsun's fiction. He is found in *Hunger*, where the central figure "wanders" the streets in urban-picaresque fashion, and in *Mysteries*, where Nagel calls himself a "stopped wanderer" (I: 339). He will turn up again, in a more extreme guise, as a vagabond. Already from the outset, "wandering" functions as an epithet to describe a distinct character type, usually an outsider whose past is an enigma and whose name is unknown or questionable, but who is portrayed with obvious empathy. Assuming that the trope of "life as a journey" is the ultimate ground of the outsider hero's meandering course, the journey has in this instance turned into a ramble, with no particular destination in mind: wandering signifies an existence of unconditional freedom, allowing for an endlessly open future whose flip side is a state of ontological homelessness. Thus, when Nagel calls himself a "stopped wanderer," he is saying that, as far as he is concerned, the future is no longer open. In the August trilogy, wandering takes the form of vagabonding, which is equally ambiguous, being associated, on the one hand, with picaresque adventure, on the other with a rootless existence dominated by a jejune, pseudo-Faustian ethos.

Although the wanderer as portrayed in the trilogy, being a lonely, reclusive figure with a flair for the unpredictable, recalls his predecessors, wandering as he engages in it has acquired a somewhat different meaning, psychological and sociocultural. The rationale of Knut Pedersen's entire undertaking, namely, a return to the presumed simplicities of a rustic existence in the guise of a farm worker, is to escape from the perpetual restlessness and irksome constraints of urban civilization. Again, one thinks of Lieutenant Glahn, who exchanges an officer's life for the regressive role of a hunter. During his summer in Sirilund, Glahn abandoned his proper identity as an army lieutenant, appearing in his uniform only toward the end of the book. Similarly, Knut Pedersen returns to his urban persona only at the very end. Finally, neither finds the peace and bliss of solitude for which he yearns, except for brief intervals.[3]

The story that Knut Pedersen tells about his experiences in the country during a few fall months is imbued with the usual Hamsunian charm, with the result that one tends to forget that it is replete with inconsistencies and paradoxes. For example, though there are clear indications of a diary form, such as the first sentence, "The lake was clear as a mirror yesterday and it is clear as a mirror today" (IV: 315), a sentence like "I still remember it" (330), in relation to how the narrator had shown off to Elisabeth, suggests that the story is told retrospectively. Whatever the method, Hamsun's frequent recourse to the present tense undeniably produces a sense of immediacy and authenticity, a desirable effect in a novel based largely on sheer pretense. The very basis of the action is the narrator's assumption of a fictitious personality, Knut Pedersen. The fact that this happens to be the name Hamsun used until around 1880 does not make it any less fictitious. Middle-aged Knut Pedersen is obviously not the young Hamsun, nor is he the author Knut Hamsun of 1906; he is a fictional character like any other. More important, the narrator's assumed role of an itinerant laborer, a role maintained with some difficulty, is a pure literary device used by Hamsun to build a particular kind of story and express a cluster of themes that were important to him. Finally, it is clear from the outset that Knut Pedersen leads a double life: he combines his role as a sort of proletarian with being a well-established and well-known public personage. None of these personae is the biographical Knut Hamsun.

The story is that of a life unlived, of a parallel world that might have been. A simple goodbye to his road construction colleague of a generation ago feels to the narrator like a "summons from my youth," and he decides to join him to dig a well for the parson. From then on, a virtual working-class self is maintained in the presence of others, while in moments of self-communion this self merges with the writing persona. Though it is the impersonated self that arouses the interest of women, the emotional quandaries his ardor generates are described by the supposedly authentic self. In effect, Hamsun has implemented a unique variant on a psychological double, to the point where the two occasionally get in each other's way, as when Knut Pedersen tries to make up for his fellow worker's crudity by addressing Mrs. Falkenberg in French (IV: 341). Furthermore, that fellow worker, Lars Falkberget, who is a true laboring man, is treated as if he were the narrator's social double: for example, they exchange clothes, so that Falkberget, who has the knack of a confidence man, can appear convincing in the role of a piano tuner. He, too, travels under an assumed name, Falkenberg, a name that gives him cachet, in contrast to the common name Falkberget. In addition, it makes him a potential relative of the reputable Falkenberg family.[4]

We recognize the intriguing play with identity used in earlier Hamsun works such as *Hunger* and *Mysteries*. But in *Under the Autumn Star* it has acquired a wider amplitude, infiltrating every aspect of the novel. For one, as a humble proletarian no longer young, Knut Pedersen is a timid lover, overawed by the youthfulness of Elisabeth and by the classy beauty of Mrs. Falkenberg. Under the circumstances he can be little more than a fascinated voyeur. Though he feels tempted to drop the pretense and show himself as a person who has "renounced city life and assumed the guise of a servant" (IV: 327), he prefers his laborer's persona, finding that his working togs suit him better than his dress clothes. In his assumed persona, he backs away whenever he has a chance to get more intimate with Elisabeth; seeing her repeatedly in the cemetery, which he regularly visits, he either withdraws to dream about her or diverts the conversation to neutral territory. When he meets her in the city after abandoning his disguise, the truth comes out: she confesses that she had been in love with him and visited the cemetery to meet him. The abortive romance ends with the narrator, now having resumed his urban incarnation, being used as a pawn to make Elisabeth's young man jealous. This scene, which takes place in Kristiania's Grand Café, rivals Restoration comedy in its playful intrigue.

Though the narrator's feelings for Mrs. Falkenberg run deeper, verging on passion-love, he acts in the same shy, dreamy manner toward her. This is clearly shown in a brief chapter near the end of the novel in which Knut, driving Mrs. Falkenberg back home from a visit to the parsonage, stops at a cottage for a roadside meal. As Mrs. Falkenberg serves the provisions they have brought, the tension rises, all the more so because of the dearth of conversation: it is the subconscious messages that catch one's attention. The entire sequence is steeped in a tremulously repressed eroticism, with signals, more or less subtle—blushes, lowered eyes, heaving bosom—that her companion interprets in his own way, his heart thumping: "No doubt she is uneasy, she is afraid of me, of my saying something, doing something. . . . Don't worry, I think to myself, not a word will pass my wretched lips!" (IV: 364). To all appearances, she is in love with him, and he with her, but it is as if a gleaming sword were placed between them.

The pattern of Knut Pedersen's erotic life in this novel, one alternating between pure sensuality—evident not only in his relations with the pastor's wife but also in a couple of adventures in the bushes at a dance (IV: 351)—and unfulfilled romantic love is reminiscent of what Freud calls "the most common degradation of erotic life."[5] Speaking about the "psychical impotence" of those men who are afflicted with this condition, Freud writes: "The erotic life of such people remains divided between the two tendencies personified in art as heavenly and earthly (or animal) love. Where they love, they do not desire, and where they desire, they cannot love."[6] The assumption that Knut Pedersen fits this description may not be important per se, but it opens up a way of understanding some of the themes and motifs that keep recurring in Hamsun's novel.

Knut Pedersen's rustic retreat can be seen not only as an escape from the commotion of city life, but also as a way of evading the pain and turmoil of sexual passion. The same purpose is implicit in a regressive tendency on the part of the narrator, namely, a desire to revert to the past, whether to childhood, to the childhood of the race, or even further back, to a previous incarnation.

The first regression, to childhood, goes beyond a mere quest for the buried life, the might-have-beens of an alternate existence. It is expressed by way of a Grimm fairy tale, "The Story of the Youth Who Went Forth to Learn What Fear Was."[7] Wanting to retrieve the mystique and sense of horror he once used to associate with the dead, the narrator frequents the nearby cemetery. When he meets Elisabeth there one evening, he tells her there is a reason for his visits: in an allusion to the Grimm story, he says he wants to learn how to "shudder" with fear again. Before leaving the cemetery he picks up a thumbnail that he needs for a fancy pipe bowl he is whittling. Afterward he "waited a little while, staring hither and thither and listening—all was quiet. Nobody called, It's mine!" (IV: 334). He envies his companion, Grindhusen, who shudders at night to think he is lying so close to corpses. "Lucky Grindhusen!" he thinks (327), an exclamation he repeats on discovering that Falkberget, with his eerie feeling about the nail, is also capable of such fear: "Lucky Falkenberg" (339). Subsequently, however, the narrator has two nightmarish dreams in which a woman appears to him, demanding to have her nail returned to her. These dreams, which are quite long, leave him "shivering with fear" and "chilled to the bone with terror," respectively (353, 383). This part of Knut Pedersen's quest succeeds brilliantly, though probably not as expected; still, the Grimm fairy tale, in which the boy finally learns how to "shudder," correctly foreshadowed the course of events.

The sentimental return to childhood signified by the fairy tale motif is paralleled by other aspects of psychological youthfulness. When the narrator realizes that his friend, Falkberget, has also fallen in love with the captain's wife, he thinks to himself, "Oh, what boys we were!" (IV: 344). Indeed, they often behave like juveniles, displaying at once a raw sensitivity and a good-natured readiness to laugh at themselves. Their small disagreements and jealousies usually dissolve in friendly banter: "There was nothing but pleasantry and merriment between us," the narrator comments after a teasing exchange with his companion. Lars's farewell words, to the effect that "he feels only like half a human being now that . . . [they] are to separate" (367), show how close a relationship these two men had developed in the course of a few months. Again, it is not unlike the kind of emotional intimacy known to occur between adolescent boys, short of overt sexuality. But their sharing of everything, including their dreams of women—besides Mrs. Falkenberg, there is Emma the maid, whom they take turns flirting with—seems to indicate a homoerotic element in their relationship. They are certainly the happiest couple in the novel.

The regression to boyhood and the accompanying male camaraderie militate against the breakthrough of the narrator's passion for Mrs. Falkenberg. Significantly, it is only *after* he has parted from Lars Falkberget that he makes his first attempt to contact her. However, the return to childhood is not the only defense against romantic involvement; the very reason given for the narrator's "flight" to the countryside, namely, to "achieve peace at any price" (IV: 315), entails a second line of defense. The longed-for peace is attained in two principal ways: first, by what looks like a deliberate attempt to immerse himself in nature, second, by occupying his mind with creative work, whether invention or craftsmanship.

The novel opens with a set piece of Hamsunian nature description which conjures up a peace so profound that the narrator has recourse to the doctrine of metempsychosis to account for it.[8] The "unearthly joy" that he experiences as he looks out on the "mirrorlike" lake reminds him of a feeling of long ago as he was standing by the Caspian Sea, namely, that he had been there before. He thinks he must have "come there from another time and another country where the forest and the paths were the same. Perhaps," he muses, "I was a flower in the forest, or a beetle making its home in an acacia tree. And now," he writes, "I've come here. I may have flown that long distance and been a bird. Or I may have been a seed in some fruit or other sent by a Persian merchant. . ."(IV: 315). Though the rather fanciful series of possible reincarnations imagined may seem to undercut the seriousness of the passage and to cast doubt on the authenticity of the deep feeling behind it, one impression stands out: that of the depth of time traversed, extending beyond the narrator's personal memory to encompass endless cycles of birth and rebirth in nature and history.

It is as though the narrator's spatial displacement to the countryside is paralleled by another displacement, one in time, as he observes and meditates on the sights and sounds in the forest. While his subsequent nature descriptions are more earthy, one notes how, in a sort of biological egalitarianism, he places himself on the level of the most lowly creatures, often describing their activities in anthropomorphic terms. Sometimes he emphasizes the struggle for existence among them, at other times he is absorbed by the amusing aspects of animal and insect life. His observation of one particular bird gives rise to a regular fairy tale. Though the finch is actually a bird of passage, he writes, "his parents have taught him that it's possible to winter in the North. But . . . he continues to be a wanderer. One day he gathers all his dear ones and takes off, traveling through many parishes to completely different people whom he will then get to know. . . "(IV: 350). Such descriptions have a twofold effect: while raising the birds to the level of humans, they implicitly carry the narrator back through aeons of evolutionary time. The narrator's regressive identification with the finch as a "wanderer"—a nomad in the cultural sense—is quite explicit.

The escape to nature as a path to spiritual peace is supplemented by a pseudo-artistic activity, chiefly the making of the pipe bowl "in the form of a clenched fist; the thumb would form the lid, and," he says, "I would join a nail to it to make it very lifelike." He continues, "With such putterings my head became healthy and quiet" (IV: 326). When he presents the pipe to Captain Falkenberg, the latter calls him "an artist and a master." His first reaction to the captain's praise is, "I think in that moment I could have had Emma" (353). It is worth noting that the narrator uses the same word, "putter," when speaking of his design for the new saw: "Now I began to putter with an invention" (343). And once more Emma is brought into the picture, but in reverse fashion: "What—couldn't I even conquer Emma? Then I became proud and taciturn in the extreme and went my own way, sketching my machine and making little models" (346). The interest in Emma is more feigned than real; moreover, the text clearly shows that Knut's "putterings" are, in effect, sublimations that help keep him clear of erotic entanglements.

Though the narrator maintains his wandering persona until he arrives in the capital in the next to last chapter, the themes are no longer the same during the final period of his stay in the country. Here Knut Pedersen enacts a variation on the mission envisaged by Nagel, namely, to redress the wrongs and injustices of the world. Thus, he intends to give the sewing machine he has bought to the daughters of another family he is staying with, and to donate his bottles of wine to arrange a festive evening before his departure. However, when the girls turn out to be aggressive and greedy, he changes his mind and leaves immediately. Instead, he exercises his beneficence on a poor family he visits next, giving his sewing machine to the daughter, an awkward girl of sixteen, in exchange for a worthless reproduction which he claims to be of great value. One recognizes immediately the borrowing from *Mysteries*, in which Nagel drives up the price of an old chair he wants to acquire from Martha Gude. And like Nagel, who is seen to recoil from the "mission" he has laid down for himself, asking what business it is of his to improve the world, Knut Pedersen makes an about-face when he notices how happy he feels at the good deed he has just performed. He interrupts his snatch of song by a mocking single word: "Neurasthenia" (IV: 378).

It is possible to read *Under the Autumn Star* as an episodic novel of rustic adventure, an abortive romance, or as autobiographical fiction. The book has elements of all three. In preferring to call it an "ironic pastoral," I have accentuated the futility of the "I's" quest for a reclusive life, safe from the encroachment of a besetting passion. The anti-development theme, with regression to boyhood and beyond, eventually recedes in favor of the breakthrough of love, and the sublimation through art and technical ingenuity, while helping the narrator to attain calm of mind temporarily, eventually turns out to be ineffectual. The same is true for the selfless do-goodism seen immediately before the narrator's return to the city and his amorous pursuit. After his failure to meet Mrs. Falkenberg, Knut Pedersen, or whatever the narrator now calls himself, can find an escape only through the loss of his "earthly consciousness" by way of wine and whiskey. He writes, "My fellow neurasthenics: we are poor as humans, and we aren't any good as animals either." He can only envisage a repetition of the cycle already completed: "Then one day it will probably get too boring to be unconscious any longer and I'll once again set out for an island" (IV: 395).

Critical opinion of *Under the Autumn Star* has been extremely diverse, ranging from virtual dismissal—"incoherent narrative," "indistinct characters," and "trivial psychology"[9]—to high praise, the latter coming mainly from Hamsun's countrymen. Carl Nærup, while deploring the absence of the "human values" of earlier Hamsun novels, says that the book's "unified mood" makes us forget to ask whether it is an important work.[10] Helge Krog, the noted dramatist and critic, places *Under the Autumn Star* in the same category as *Pan*, calling it "the most seductive book in Norwegian literature, gay and melancholy, sorrowful and salutary, rich but light and free."[11] In sharp contrast, John Updike, reviewing the 1975 Stallybrass translation, merely praises the "sometimes quite magical lightness of phrase," while finding the materials too "purely atmospheric" and the characters as "evanescent" as the weather and the hero's "whimsical moods."[12] An English reviewer of the same translation says that, though the novel provides evidence of genius, it does not show Hamsun at the "height of his powers."[13] That is a judgment every reader can feel comfortable with.

Like *Under the Autumn Star*, Hamsun's next work, *A Wanderer Plays on Muted Strings*, is a first-person novel related by Knut Pedersen, who returns to Øvrebø after an interval of six years.[14] Nevertheless, it differs considerably, both in literary method and quality, from its predecessor. Whereas *Under the Autumn Star* focuses on the narrator's predicament, *A Wanderer* has a divided focus: the plot centers on the marital drama of Captain Falkenberg and his wife, Lovise, but the narrator, who in the meantime seems to have acquired quite a number of personal biases, makes his presence strongly felt throughout. Some of his comments on the characters appear intrusive, threatening to alienate the reader and jeopardize the novel's artistic integrity.

An attractive couple, the Falkenbergs evoke everyone's sympathetic participation. The captain is a likable individual, friendly and good-natured despite his professional pride; his wife is still beautiful but seems to find no outlet for her passionate nature. As an officer whose duties include military drill, the captain has to spend long periods away from home, a circumstance that, while not given prominence, may help account for their increasing estrangement. The ups and downs of their relationship are conveyed, in near-closeup fashion, by means of a carefully documented sequence of overhearings and observations which, in effect, constitute a secondary drama in the novel. The method is quite successful; besides guaranteeing the authenticity of what is related, it is also conducive to creating suspense, a rather unusual characteristic for a Hamsun novel. The success hinges on Ragnhild, whose credibility as an informant to the principal narrator, Knut Pedersen, is assured by her position as Mrs. Falkenberg's maid. Ragnhild observes or eardrops on intimate scenes between husband and wife, as well as between Mrs. Falkenberg and her future lover.

Contrary to Hamsun's usual practice, the method is applied quite consistently; moreover, it is made acceptable to the reader by being grounded in the narrators' psychology. Knut Pedersen, whose fascination with Mrs. Falkenberg is as alive as ever, cannot help following her with the eyes of an amorous sleuth, and Ragnhild, as Mr. Pedersen eventually discovers, is "only spying on her own account . . ., for the love of the thing" (V: 334). Originally set to keep an eye on her husband by Mrs. Falkenberg, she acquires an increasingly wider role as a source of information to Knut Pedersen. Indeed, her assigned function within the novel's narrative strategy comes to seem quite natural; however extreme the situation, whether the scene is one of emotional or physical intimacy, her presence is made acceptable by a penchant for voyeurism. The importance of other informants, such as Grindhusen, Knut's former fellow worker, a hotel porter in town, and a traveling salesman, is trivial by comparison, serving mainly to document events when the action takes place away from Øvrebø.

A brief summary of the novel may be helpful. Returning to the captain's estate after six years, Knut Pedersen finds that things have gone from bad to worse at Øvrebø. The farm is neglected, the master and mistress avoid each other, life consists of continuous rounds of partying and drinking: bohemia has invaded the countryside. Apparently, both husband and wife are involved in a love affair, but the reader soon realizes that what each of them truly desires is to rekindle a spark of affection in the other. The captain is flirting with Elisabeth, the parson's daughter, now a married woman; Mrs. Falkenberg is being courted assiduously by a certain Hugo Lassen, an aggressive twenty-four-year-old engineer. Mrs. Falkenberg's behavior toward the engineer makes her intentions quite transparent: she is not in love with him, she simply uses him to make her husband jealous. And the captain, on his part, will later tell his wife that Elisabeth "had never been in his thoughts" (V: 378). However, by this time Mrs. Falkenberg has already been seduced by the engineer; what is more, she has lived with him in the nearby town for some time.

It should be noted that Mrs. Falkenberg was under the influence of alcohol when Hugo dragged her into the pavilion at Øvrebø. Hugo's brutal behavior, which was witnessed by both Ragnhild and Knut Pedersen, turns his action, a second try, into rape rather than a seduction. The following scene as related by Knut Pedersen is quite unambiguous in that respect:

> At the pavilion he lets go of her for a moment, slams his shoulder heavily into the door and breaks it down for the second time. One step, and again he is beside her. No one speaks.
> She keeps up her resistance at the door, holding on to the door frame and refusing to let go: "No! I've never been unfaithful to him, I don't want to, I've never, never—"
> He pulls her close and kisses her—one minute, two minutes, hard and without letup; her back gives way, her hand loosens its hold on the door frame. Then she lets go.
> A white fog drifts before my eyes. So—there they are. Now he's unfolding her. He's doing the sweet thing with her—
> . . .
> In the midst of the white fog I see a leaping figure; it's Ragnhild coming out of the bushes. She runs, her tongue hanging out. (V: 337)

In this particular instance, the event related is observed and overheard both by Ragnhild and Knut Pedersen. Mostly Ragnhild reports to the main narrator, or to a group of domestics that he joins. In either case the narrative has the distinctive features of fresh, first-hand information. Where observation stops, as happens at the end of the above passage, fantasy takes over: the sexual act itself comes to us by way of Knut Pedersen's erotic imagination, colored by his own tender feelings for Mrs. Falkenberg.

The psychological suspense is successfully maintained partly because of the deep sympathy which the marital quandary of the captain and his wife elicits from the entire household. It is worth noting, in this connection, that both Ragnhild and Knut Pedersen are participant narrators: they not only report on events but attempt to change their course. Thus, the first time Hugo breaks into the pavilion to have his way with Mrs. Falkenberg, Knut Pedersen frustrates his plan by throwing an empty bottle at the pavilion from his window in the servants' hall. Ragnhild accomplishes a comparable feat: at a moment when her mistress is on the verge of being trapped by her flirtatious behavior for the captain's benefit, she arrives just in time: "they came within an ace of doing it" (V: 327), she tells Knut, who is consumed by jealous impatience as she relates her evening's adventure. She concludes by exclaiming, "Good heavens, what if I hadn't turned up just then! It was a close call!" (329).

Not surprisingly, the "helpers" cannot prevent the adultery, or do much to alleviate its devastating effects on Mrs. Falkenberg. Honest at heart, she cannot adjust to a condition of mental duplicity. From the moment of her lapse onward, she finds herself on a psychological whirligig; or rather, she is caught in an emotional vortex. And the captain, who catches on to what has happened, is in no mood to be forgiving. The "big scene" between the spouses after the guests have departed ends in an agreement to "go their separate ways" (V: 340). Soon we find Mrs. Falkenberg in town, where she is living with the engineer under the pretense of being his cousin. In the meantime, Knut Pedersen has been hired by the engineer, a log driving inspector, to report on log jams in the river. When he gets back to Øvrebø, having been dismissed by Mr. Lassen at the instigation of Mrs. Falkenberg, he starts painting the house, as previously agreed. He overcomes the captain's initial dislike of the color he has chosen by telling him—falsely—that it was suggested by Mrs. Falkenberg. Deeply moved by this thought, the captain soon writes his wife, who, having second thoughts about continuing to live with Mr. Lassen, returns to Øvrebø, to the delight of everyone.

But the tearful reconciliation of the spouses is followed by a number of lacerating scenes, all reported by Ragnhild. It turns out that her mistress is pregnant, and for all their eagerness to believe it is the captain's child she is carrying, they both know better. Besides, Mrs. Falkenberg has lost her peace of mind and behaves quite erratically, repeatedly preparing to leave again and then as quickly changing her mind. She seems unable to commit herself fully to one or the other; thus, as the captain reminds her in one of their long mutual blame sessions, she is still keeping photographs of Hugo on her piano, despite his having "begged" her to remove them any number of times (V: 384). The captain is quite aware of her divided feelings; in any event, he chooses to overlook the not so subtle sexual invitations his wife offers him. As for the photographs, Ragnhild finally burns them, along with other mementos of Hugo, but only after Mrs. Falkenberg has already left Øvrebø—apparently to join the engineer—never to return. The only way Ragnhild can help at this point is to tell the captain a white lie when he asks her about the photographs on the piano, namely, that his wife had removed them: "It was a comfort—it comforted the captain to receive this piece of information!" (408). But by this time his wife is dead.

The dynamics of the novel's action depend almost entirely on the psychology of the major characters, the captain and his wife. Thus, regardless of the attempts of the servants and the main narrator to stem or reverse the course of events, the marital conflict of the protagonists grows increasingly bitter and irreparable. The action assumes the nature of an agon, or a series of agons, with a steady heightening of the dramatic tension. The situation is made to seem even more tragic, ironically so, by a virtual counterpoint between the marital quandary of the Falkenbergs and the great improvements that are simultaneously taking place on the estate, thanks to an exceptionally loyal and hard-working team of hired people: the promise of greater and greater well-being and happiness at Øvrebø throws the deteriorating relationship of the master and mistress into glaring relief. A succession of scenes exposes the psychological impasse husband and wife have reached; there is a sense on the part of both that things have taken a wrong turn. After Mrs. Falkenberg has returned from town, any change for the better in her mood or attitude founders as soon as she recalls her guilt, that of a wife who is carrying the child of someone other than her husband. Her conflicted state of mind displays all the symptoms of a psychological complex, capable of being activated by a single word. And the captain, however understanding he appears to be, has been so deeply wounded by his wife's infidelity and its consequences that a single untoward word of his wife brings to mind the whole shameful situation in which he finds himself.

The following passage, depicting a scene that takes place shortly before Mrs. Falkenberg's final departure from Øvrebø, provides a characteristic glimpse of their predicament:

> When his wife was impulsive once in a while and forgot to be grateful, the captain would look at the floor and, after waiting a moment, pick up his hat and walk out. Every maid knew about this, and I saw it myself several times. Obviously, he would never be able to forget her lapse, no, never, but he could keep quiet about it. But could he also keep quiet about it when she forgot herself and said, "You know I'm unwell, don't you, you know I can't walk as much as before?" — "Hssh, Lovise!" he would answer, knitting his brows. And the battle was joined: "You want to remind me of it again, don't you?" — "No, you are the one who reminds me of it, you've lost your modesty, your fall has made you shameless." — "Oh, why did I come back! I was much happier at home." — "Yes, or with that puppy." — "But you said he helped you once? Yes, God knows I often wish I were back with him. Hugo is much better than you are." (V: 396)

While both spouses invest a good amount of ego in their strife, they are not evenly matched. The captain has the advantage of other outlets for his energies. While the wife has only her grand piano, on which she plays less and less frequently, her husband can compensate for his marital frustration by periodic stints on the drill ground and by devoting more time to the management of his estate. In fact, his interest in the farm activities seems to grow in proportion to the aggravation of his matrimonial malaise. The wife has no such buffers against misfortune; she is depicted as being in thrall to her biological destiny as a woman. Here she is described as she shows Knut Pedersen a postcard from her husband: "Those two sad eyes that were raised and kept gazing at me were laden to the brim with love. She couldn't be quite sane, her glance was pathologically deep, reaching backward and blending with the life she was carrying under her heart" (V: 398). It looks as though Hamsun shaped his story around the idea expressed in Lord Byron's famous lines, "Love is of man's life a thing apart,/It is woman's whole existence."[15] By the time the captain overcomes his officer's pride and appears ready to admit to himself, and to his wife, his continued love for her despite what has happened, it is too late.

However, Mrs. Falkenberg's death in a drowning accident as she crosses the town river to join her lover on the other side—if we are to believe the hotel porter, whose story is based on the engineer's report to the police—bears no meaningful relation to the novel's psychological and moral themes. A more acceptable denouement, in view of Mrs. Falkenberg's distraught state of mind and unpredictable behavior, would be suicide. Such an ending would follow naturally from the story's logic, one of tragic inevitability. In my initial reading of the novel I assumed, as did the distinguished Norwegian critic Carl Nærup in his review of *A Wanderer*, that Mrs. Falkenberg's death was a suicide, an interpretation that Hamsun vehemently rejected.[16] What Nærup's motive was for making this assumption will remain an open question; as for myself, suicide seemed the only plausible resolution of the conflict, once Mrs. Falkenberg had decided to throw herself on the mercy of her half-hearted lover.[17] Hamsun's decision to wind up the story by an accident is a serious blemish on an otherwise quite convincing study of adultery and its consequences.

This is not the only problem with *A Wanderer*. To begin with, the plot, an aspect of fiction to which Hamsun pays scant attention, is obviously manipulated. What are we to make of the choice of a young priapic engineer, a man with an unattractive mouth and an oversized posterior, as Mrs. Falkenberg's seducer, or rather her ravisher? To Nærup's criticism that the captain's wife ran off with "an idiot of an engineer," Hamsun responded that, far from being "an idiot, he is more or less the direct opposite; he is outwardly and inwardly a modern Norwegian sportsman, a Swiss soul in our land."[18] With or without his Swiss baggage, this character is hard to accept as a lover of Mrs. Falkenberg; as a rapist, he becomes even less acceptable, since it turns the woman into a victim and therefore only marginally to blame for her predicament. That, having failed to make it up with her husband, she should return to her victimizer despite his previous refusal to make a serious commitment to her, may be taken on faith, but how can anyone believe in her eagerness to reach her reluctant impregnator on the other side of an only partially iced-over river? Hamsun simply needs a death, and so he lets the river do his dirty work for him. The denouement is not only unbelievable from a realistic perspective, it turns the preceding domestic strife, with its profound suffering and tragic undertones, into a grotesque mockery. The drama lacks a *telos*, being resolved by what one might call a *diabolus ex machina*.

Taking a wider view, one is struck by the fact that *A Wanderer* comes to us both with an "Introduction" and a "Postscript." This raises questions of interpretation that need to be elucidated. Hamsun insisted on the equal importance of both: "You can see," he writes in a letter to his publisher, "that the book has an *introduction*, therefore I would like to have a *postscript* as well. It shall relate to the story, but be of a discursive kind."[19] He could not have been unaware that these additions changed the very nature of the work, transforming it into a sort of oversize exemplum, though the didactic strain is already present in the story itself. This is so particularly toward the end, where Knut Pedersen criticizes both the captain and his wife. Of the latter he writes after her death, "She had no mission, but she had three maids on her farm; she had no children, but she had a grand piano. But she had no children." Along with the needlessly pointed last sentence of the story, "It was a mother and child that went to the bottom" (V: 417), this refrain-like judgment clearly insinuates that the only way a woman can justify her existence is by bringing children into the world. Judging by a letter to his publisher, Hamsun was very pleased with his conclusion, exclaiming, "By God, how good the ending is, and how weighty the *postscript*, take a look at it!"[20]

Apart from a reference to berry-picking and some reflections on old age, the introduction and postscript have little in common. Nor is there any reason why they should, as long as neither was at variance with the main story. However, the introduction conflicts in one crucial respect with the novel proper: a couple of statements imply that the narrator already knows the contents of the story he is going to tell, specifically that it will be a tragic one. Having retold a gruesome tale of revenge related by a Mexican named Rough, a young man who killed the violator of his sweetheart, the narrator comments, "You won't hear of murder from me, but of joys and sufferings and love. And love is just as violent and dangerous as murder" (V: 306). Unless he is a clairvoyant, how can he make such a prediction? There is no indication in the text that the introduction was written *after* the story of the Falkenbergs had been completed. In any event, that story, with its suspenseful action and frequent use of the present tense, points to an immediate relationship between telling and happening; contrary to the strong hints of a retrospective point of view in the introduction, the events of the subsequent narrative are being related as they occur. In view of this, it is odd that Rough's tale of sexual violation, with its bloody resolution, appears as an ironic anticipation of the story of the Falkenbergs, which ends with the captain merely knocking down the violator.

Other aspects of the narrative frame introduce themes that express deep concerns of Hamsun's narrator, Knut Pedersen, but that have at best only a tenuous relation to the story. A pair of characters in the introduction, a one-time quartermaster and a blind boy, represent marginal mental states. In plain terms, the former has lost his mind, though he "flashed with perspicacity the moment insanity closed in on him," the latter never had one. The quartermaster, whose rebellion against his lot assumes the form of a bedlamite's paranoid rage with Knut Pedersen, teaches the latter how difficult it is "to rightly understand people," to know "who is crazy and who is sane." The eighteen-year-old boy, blind since his fourteenth year, is blithely playing on his harmonica and seems "content and happy"; he hopes that a planned operation will enable him to see well enough to walk. To the narrator, the boy appears somewhat of an imbecile: "his submission to his fate was too foolish. Such hopefulness presupposes some stupidity, I thought; for a person to be permanently content with life, even expecting something new and agreeable from it, a certain dearth of mental capacity is required." Yet, admitting that the poor devil "made him wiser," Knut Pedersen decides to "study how to be a peasant again," after being warped by years of refinement (V: 308–09). His itinerant way of life, including his subsequent stint of farm work at Øvrebø, may be seen as an attempt to implement such a decision.

The postscript picks up these reflections in a slightly different vein. Again, the question Knut Pedersen faces is how to come to terms with a human condition that eventually brings physical decline, old age, and untold suffering. The principal link with the introduction is a motif of gratitude for life, for its joys and sorrows: "Life was fun!" (V: 309, 418). By way of a winding self-communion in which reminiscence alternates with rumination, Knut Pedersen has arrived at a position of total acceptance. A pessimist would think as follows: every joy or happiness we experience in life will have to be paid for with subsequent suffering. Knut Pedersen turns this statement around: whatever suffering or unhappiness falls to our lot has already been paid for by previous joy or happiness. Thinking back on the death of Mrs. Falkenberg, who had revealed to him so much beauty and given him so much delight, he reflects: "Then she died. . . . I'm left behind. But her death should not plunge me into grief, since I had been compensated for it in advance by undeservedly being looked at by her pair of eyes. That must be the way it is!" (421). The attitude expressed, a virtual quietism, implies that all is right with the world. It is complemented by a mood of serene joy as Knut Pedersen sits in a cave at the end of the postscript, feeling quite "at home" and seemingly happy just listening to the "soughing of the forest" (422, 423).

Anyone who reads the novel from beginning to end will realize that this viewpoint—whether taken literally or interpreted as a piece of sardonic irony[21]—has little relation to the tragic story of Captain Falkenberg and his wife. It looks as though Hamsun's imagination is traveling in different directions and on two or more separate tracks. Neither the introduction nor the postscript has much relevance to what goes on in-between. The reader knows that, when Knut Pedersen arrives at Øvrebø the second time, he appears under a double disguise, pretending, first, to be a simple laboring man, as he also did in *Under the Autumn Star*, second, to have never set foot on the farm before. While the second disguise is quickly seen through, he tries as best he can to sustain the first. However, though he manages to maintain his naivistic mask, his most substantial accomplishment during this time, namely, to serve as the chief witness and narrator of a sexual drama, goes poorly with his decision to retrace his development and learn to be a peasant. He clearly enjoys the opportunity of observing the worsening crisis between the Falkenbergs, deriving from it a pleasure that many would assign to the refined, if not the decadent, category. One begins to suspect that Knut Pedersen is nothing but an infinitely stretchable, chameleon-like persona, needed by the author for carrying out a series of literary functions. Thus, the same character who, in the postscript, has seemingly arrived at a position of total acceptance, a kind of Carlylean yea to human existence, simultaneously indulges in anonymous parti-pris attacks on the so-called "poets of the home" (Jonas Lie, just deceased?) and on Ibsen, with his "thirty volumes of theatrical poetry about woman." His final cheap shot at Ibsen is directed at *A Doll House*: "In the end he wrote about a woman who abandoned her own children in order to find—the miracle!" (V: 421).

One consequence of this questionable zigzag of opinions and pronouncements worth noting is a kind of inchoate perspectivism in the portrayal of character. Thus, Mrs. Falkenberg, who for most of the story is treated sympathetically by the narrator, toward the end of the novel is seen by him as being "corrupted," indeed, "thoroughly ruined," with her "cabaret eyes." He concludes that life "can afford to let her go to waste" (V: 404), a statement that is repeated at the very end of the novel (417). This callous attitude, with its relish of Darwin and philosophical naturalism, is the polar opposite of the adoration previously shown toward the captain's wife by the narrator. The shift is too extreme to be wholly attributable to a change for the worse in Mrs. Falkenberg's looks or behavior; it is as though hatred or contempt has replaced love or infatuation as the source of the narrator's thoughts about her.[22] A similar oscillation between sympathy and near condemnation colors the portrayal of the captain. In the postscript Knut Pedersen seems to blame the captain, alluding to some words spoken to Lovise, his wife, shortly before her final departure from Øvrebø: "May God grant me his pardon—as he has mine" (399). The passage in the postscript reads, "It is wrong of a captain to ask God to forgive him—just as he has forgiven God. That's just play-acting." Instead, he "assumes the responsibility himself. He puts his shoulder against the turn of fate, that is, he stoops to it" (418). Whatever this means, it entails a moralistic judgment that negates the generally favorable view of the captain as well as the philosophy of acceptance articulated in the postscript.

Sometimes one wonders how serious the story of the captain and his wife is intended to be. Hamsun himself calls his novel a "fine, deep book."[23] That may be so. However, there are many playful aspects to it, which complicate the meaning of the story and one's impression of the characters. Thus, in Chekhovian fashion, Hamsun creates an ironic counterpoint to the love triangle of the captain, Mrs.

Falkenberg, and Hugo, by making Lars, now settled on his own land and married to Emma, insanely jealous of what he sees as Knut Pedersen's philandering with his wife. This absurd little drama among the lower orders, mostly resolved as soon as it occurs, both sharpens and plays down the marital conflict among their betters. As for the love affair between Mrs. Falkenberg and Hugo, it soon takes on the appearance of a farce. Living together in a hotel under the pretense of being cousins, with Knut Pedersen taking turns working for the engineer and deploring what he interprets as Mrs. Falkenberg's increasing brazenness, the pair comes to seem smaller and smaller, and more and more isolated, against the urban background. And the engineer, who, partly because of his youth and energy, has inspired the narrator with respect and admiration, reverts to being a grotesque figure: "This sportsman with the protruding posterior was nothing but a travesty of youth, a weeping Spartan" (V: 358). These changing perspectives, which are also seen in the narrator's repeated questioning of his own motives in describing a character in a certain way, acquire a parodic form in Grindhusen, whose violent shifts of opinion about his employers depend on the size of their tips.

Yet another kind of perspective is used in the description of the town, the environment of Hugo, the engineer, and the ambiance of his affair with Mrs. Falkenberg. One wonders why Hamsun went to the trouble of evoking this town—probably Kongsberg west of Kristiania (now Oslo)[24]—in such minute detail, unless it was intended as part of the delineation of Hugo. The small town is treated with veritably Swiftian satire: everything in it is of diminutive size. The only winged creatures around are "gnats and flies," the railroad cars are so tiny that you cannot sit upright with your hat on, ten men working to disentangle a log jam in the river are "like ten ants to a twig," and the boat hooks used in the process are compared to "harp strings" and a "spider web." The people are equally small, with "little crooked fingers" and "mouse eyes" (V: 348, 350–51). The effect is not one of defamiliarization, making one wonder at the strangeness of the world described, as might be expected, but of a jarring low burlesque denigrating both to the town and to the people in it.

The Lilliputian reduction is fairly general. Thus, a visiting peasant come to sell his cow and do some shopping in town is described in similar terms; he is portrayed as a creature from the nether world, a "gnome" (V: 351). Needless to say, his purchases are equally picayune, as is everything that happens in town. One wonders how Hamsun reconciles this portrait of the peasant with Knut Pedersen's declared intention of learning how to be one.[25] But more important, what possible bearing does the satire of small-town life have on the story of the captain and his wife? For we are not sufficiently interested in Mr. Lassen to want to learn so much about *his* surroundings. While the sketch is quite amusing and skillfully done, it seems out of place. Perhaps better than anything else, it shows how, in writing this novel, Hamsun was acting in obedience to a number of conflicting agendas, with the result that poor Knut Pedersen ends up as a bagful of eccentric behavior and preconceived ideas. And the postscript is an incongruous mixture of self-pity and portentousness. With mordant humor the narrator, at fifty, compares what life still has to offer to the plight of a convict on his way to being executed: "A convict sits in his cart being driven to the scaffold; a nail chafes at his behind, he shifts his position and feels more comfortable" (418).

After these criticisms, what can be said in praise of Hamsun's *A Wanderer*? The Strindbergian drama of man and wife is highly convincing and powerfully evoked, though the occasion of its crisis, the rape, is hard to accept. And the carefully constructed and meticulously sustained narrative technique does justice to the intricacies of the emotional conflict. Mrs. Falkenberg's hesitations, abrupt turnabouts, and torment are conveyed in masterly fashion, so convincingly, in fact, that at times one fears she is losing her mind. As for positive values, Nils the hired man, who may have experienced a tragedy not so very different from that of the captain, is exemplary. He continues doing his job regardless of the apparent indifference of the people he works for. If there is someone in the book who embodies what it means to have the values of a peasant—more properly, those of a yeoman farmer—Nils is the one. By comparison, Knut Pedersen, though a good enough worker, is effete, itching for the emotional titillation afforded by ambiguous erotic situations, which he simultaneously invites and attempts to evade.

A final critical note suggested by the novel's form may be in order. By the rules of aesthetic logic, the fact that the story of the Falkenbergs' failed marriage is framed by the melancholy reflections of an aging narrator, reduces the marital drama to a matter of secondary importance, giving pride of place to the jejune dreams and banal regrets of the narrator. In contrast to the apparent authorial intent, revealed by having the story of the Falkenbergs encapsulated within the context of a mid-life crisis, the reader will most likely foreground the domestic tragedy. If my view is mistaken, my error will be largely due to Hamsun's deficient sense of significant aesthetic form.

Contrary to Hamsun's hope that Carl Nærup, the dean of Norway's practical critics at the time, would be "satisfied" with the book, Nærup reportedly found the novel to be "insignificant."[26] Other criticism has not, on the whole, been very favorable. The *TLS* reviewer calls it a "bad book" which recounts a "matrimonial intrigue without the least moral significance," surrounded by a "confused mass of irrelevant details,"[27] the latter objection a possible reference to the above-discussed framing device. Interestingly, John Updike compares *A Wanderer* favorably to *Under the Autumn Star*, deeming it a "richer, sharper, less muted, and more objective work." But though he admires the way in which Mrs. Falkenberg's tragedy is handled, her fate strikes him as a mere "schematic miming" of that of nineteenth-century adulteresses: "We blink with recognition, but not with tears." The book, in his view, betrays a flagging of creative energy on Hamsun's part; it merely goes through the motions of being a novel. Though this may sound unfair, it is quite understandable that Updike would not find in *A Wanderer* the "intensity of spirit" characteristic of Hamsun's early novels.[28]

The Last Joy (1912) is somewhat of an anomaly in Hamsun's fictional oeuvre. The occasional stridency of its style and its overt didacticism make the moralism of *A Wanderer* seem moderate. Moreover, the novel's shifting focus—from the celebration of a solitary life in the woods to a merciless dissection of middle-class cultural values and attitudes, followed by a vicarious quest for a peasant utopia—leaves little more than the first-person narrator to hold the book together.

The novel's diverse materials and disparate themes may be partly due to the circumstances of its genesis, which extended over a period of years. Its first three chapters were published in a literary journal under the title "Vinterskoge" (Winter Forests) already in 1906,[29] before the appearance of the first novel in the series, *Under the*

Autumn Star. Evidently, Hamsun was working simultaneously on different parts of the wanderer trilogy. The initial three chapters of *The Last Joy*, about one seventh of the whole, hark back to *Pan*. The narrator, whose name is not given, has sought refuge from urban life and a despised humanity in an arctic turf hut.[30] However, unlike *Pan*, which is essentially an attempt at emotional catharsis on the narrator's part, *The Last Joy* is a novel with a broader purpose.

The story is addressed to a city dweller, ostensibly a fellow male, with a "wife and a maid and a hundred expenses" (VII: 8), who is condescendingly referred to as "little friend," an epithet that recurs sporadically throughout and figures prominently in the novel's last, epilogue-like chapter. Here, however, the "little friend" merges with an abstraction, "the new spirit in Norway" (142). A comparison with Boccaccio's *Decameron* is intended both to explain the book's heterogeneous contents and to justify its fiercely critical tone. To his own question why he has "gathered so many different things into one frame," the narrator answers, "Little friend, one of the world's most famous literary works was written during a plague, on account of the plague, that's my answer." He says that he "cannot stop the plague, which by now is beyond control, raging under national protection to the tune of tararaboomdeay. But one day it will surely end. In the meantime I'm doing what I can to oppose it, while you are doing the contrary" (141–42).

The new tone of magisterial critique represents an intensification of the regressive attitude in the postscript to *A Wanderer*. By this time, the mask has been dropped: the narrator of *The Last Joy* is a writer who confesses candidly on the novel's first page, "I've sought the forest for solitude and for the sake of my great irons; I do have some great irons in me starting to glow" (VII: 7). This shedding of the mask creates a more assertive narrative persona, one closer to the author, though by no means identical with him. The allusion to Nietzsche on the novel's first page, while modest and playful, is not without significance. In fact, Hamsun's opening line, "Now I've gone into the forest" (7), sounds like an echo of the first sentence of *Also sprach Zarathustra*: "When Zarathustra was thirty years old, he left his home . . . and went into the mountains."[31] After enjoying his "solitude" for ten years, he descends from the heights to mingle with humankind; Hamsun's narrator makes a similar decision after a brief stay in his

A Counter-Development Triptych 145

primitive hut. The very idea of a wandering hero is, of course, inseparable from Zarathustra's self-appointed mission; in fact, the first chapter of Part Three of Nietzsche's book is called "The Wanderer."[32] And though the two works belong to widely different genres, novel as against a quasi-religious gospel, they do have another thing in common: the text of both is interspersed with poetry. Finally, while Nietzsche's aphoristic style could not be transposed to the novel, Hamsun's narrator does occasionally speak obscurely or portentously, as if addressing his fellow mortals from on high.

Of the novel's three parts, the first, dealing with the narrator's life in the wild, is by far the most interesting, combining a Crusoe-like lesson in self-reliance with a romantic celebration of nature no less fervent than that of Lieutenant Glahn. This particular Crusoe finds that his life in the forest is superior to that of his urban friend: "Waking or sleeping, you are in a race with things," he writes, "never at peace. I am at peace. Keep your bright ideas and books and art and newspapers, keep your cafés too and your whiskey, which only makes me sick every time" (VII: 8). Instead, he prefers the company of the earth and of animals, vhich are viewed from the perspective of the cosmic egalitarianism already found in *Under the Autumn Star*, a conception that occasionally verges on panpsychism. "We are two of us in the hut," he writes, "but if I don't count Madame as a human, I'm alone. Madame is a mouse I live with, I've given her this name to honor her. She eats anything I lay aside in the corners and sits watching me from time to time" (8).

The humor notwithstanding, the humanization of the mouse and other humble creatures is a major trend of thought in the book, along with the transformation of inanimate nature. Not only does the narrator identify with a colony of ants on the move, seeing them as wanderers like himself, he even invests a rock-strewn slope with human meaning: maybe the rocks "wander" too, he muses, expressing his sense of kinship with them. His feeling of oneness with nature is climaxed by a sort of vision that echoes the experience of Glahn.[33] Perceiving a "wave" inside him, the narrator becomes aware of a presence, and a moment later he glimpses a "back disappearing into the forest." The experience is overwhelming: "I feel my whole face flooded with the sight. It was God, I think" (VII: 37). This apotheosis of nature is preceded by a quasi-mystical sense that the mountainside where he finds himself is, in reality, "a bosom, a lap, it's so soft." And he continues, "I climb up slowly, not trampling, not bearing down, I marvel at it: a big mountainside so tender and helpless, long-suffering as a mother, so that an ant can walk on it" (36–37). Rather than the moon, as in *Pan*, it is the earth goddess who commands the worship of the middle-aged narrator of *The Last Joy*.

Admittedly, the language in which the narrator's near-mystical experience of nature is couched lacks the lyrical intensity of Glahn's evocation of the three Iron Nights. This is not surprising: the emphasis has changed. With all his apparent misanthropy, the narrator realizes that he deceived himself when he decided to move still deeper into the forest: "Did I say I was too close to people?" he asks himself. "Worse luck; for several days running I've taken a stroll into the forest, saying good morning and pretending I was in human company" (VII: 18). This discovery on the narrator's part puts a new face on his enthusiasm for birds and beasts and even stones, all of which he tends to transform into images with a semblance of humanity. An excellent example of this transformative power is his changing description of the rock-strewn slope; originally understood geologically—"The glaciers withdraw, the land rises, the land sinks"—it changes in his mind into a town, with "parishes of stone. It's a peaceful community, no big events, no suicides, and there may be a well-formed soul in each of these stones." Then, becoming skeptical, he engages in some drollery at the expense of "the inhabitants of these towns, heh-heh: rolling stones. They can't bark, nor are they of interest to pickpockets, they are only dead weight. Well behaved, to be sure, . . . but there they lie, no one even knows their sex exactly" (37–38). The narrator pokes fun at his own game, to be sure, and yet the very fact that he plays these games, creating a wholly human universe out of the natural world that he ostensibly worships and in the process employing an urban metaphor, betrays a contradiction in the novel's discourse: the narrative logic of the primitivistic theme is undercut by the rhetoric of urbanity with its utopian touches. Other contradictions will become evident in my discussion of the novel's subsequent parts.

The primitivist ethos itself assumes several guises, ranging from a semi-religious worship of the earth to near-glorification of criminality. The latter theme is introduced early on, when a thief seeks shelter in the narrator's hut. Whatever disapproval the narrator expresses concerns merely the pettiness of the thieving. In effect, the portrayal is laced with admiration, as in the following description of the larcenist's reaction to the fear of detection: "In a second he had sized up the door opening and the hole in the roof and decided to meet the danger at the door. He was taut and splendid. . ." (VII: 15). Later on, when the narrator meets him as Eilert, who now runs a kind of lodging house, he bears no grudge against him for the "cock-and-bull story . . . about a sick wife and ailing children" he had told him in the hut. Not only does he have "four fine ragged children by his first wife, who died two years ago, and another by his new wife," but the new wife is "strong and buxom, good with the animals, and pregnant again." He sums up: "I think it's all great—Eilert, his wife, and everything I'm hearing about them" (83). Evidently, in Hamsun's world fecundity effectively palliates anti-social or criminal behavior.

In what I call the novel's second segment (pp. 26–80), where the narrator depicts life at the Tore Peak health resort, Solem, another marginally criminal character, plays a central role.[34] A "footloose laborer" the narrator meets just before leaving his hut for good, he is less interesting in himself than as a catalyst enabling the author to expose the weaknesses of the respectable middle-class tourists who have gathered at the resort for the summer. This coarse, cunning proletarian, a wandering charge of primitive sexual energy, turns into a magnet for all the unfulfilled desires floating around among the young women guests, most of whom are either unmarried or are spending their vacation apart from their hardworking spouses. Described at a dance in town as "tall and with the looks of an Arab" (VII: 104), Solem with his "horse's chin," in the words of a disapproving male guest, is seen by a majority of the women as "the right sort" (38). Even Mrs. Brede, a young merchant's wife with two lovely children, feels the magnetism of his sexual allure, escaping entrapment only by the skin of her teeth.[35]

The principal victim of Solem's predatory sexuality is the "tall and attractive" Ingeborg Torsen (VII: 29), a schoolmistress who has recently been dismissed from her job due to her "eccentric teaching" (31). By befriending Miss Torsen, the narrator elicits from her a sort of professional autobiography, in which she laments "the drudgery during all those years at school"; "we became," she tells him, "stupid with book learning, anemic, unbalanced: sometimes terribly sad about our lot and sometimes hysterically happy and stuck-up about our degrees, our refinement." To judge by her long list of complaints, acquiring her teacher training was not only a waste of valuable time, considering the wretched financial rewards, but also entailed untold sacrifice by "our fathers and mothers and brothers and sisters." Among other "unwholesome effects" of the "pent-up life in school," she mentions the graduates' failure as "homemakers." She concludes her harangue thus: "Oh sure, we had chosen a beautiful vocation, everyone thought so, it was almost like being a missionary. But now I won't go on with this beautiful vocation any longer, if I can find a way to get out. Anything else would be better" (30–31).

Miss Torsen's indictment of the professionalization of women, which is obviously the authorial intent behind her account, is followed up by behavior on her part that the narrator ascribes to a warped sexuality. Though she finds life at the resort to be boring, her decision to leave is reversed by what the narrator calls "a little incident" (VII: 44). By this time, the conversation among the women has begun to focus on Solem. Miss Torsen's initial interest in him appears to be kindled by a desire to thwart his rumored attentions to Mrs. Brede. To forestall this, she invites Solem for a walk one Sunday evening. The narrator finds her behavior "altogether wonderful to watch as she opened a window to her secret. . . . Hadn't she drudged all her youth to get an education and then missed out on the substance?" Already, he is prepared to diagnose her problem: "She had learned grammar but no substance, her *nature* was undernourished. An upright girl, she should have married, she should have been a man's wife, a mother, a blessing to herself." For "nature" we may substitute "sexuality" or "libido." The rule that dictates her action—which makes the narrator exclaim, "How can she bring herself to snatch at a pleasure just to keep others from getting it . . .!"—is given a formulation that is virtually identical with one of Nikolai's sayings in *Rosa*: "A dog is guarding a bone. It waits until another dog has come close. Suddenly it seems to have a fit of ravenous appetite, grabs the bone with its teeth and crushes it. Because the other dog came by" (45–46). When Solem, who must have turned violent during the walk, is cheated of his prey, the narrator comments disapprovingly: "It would be just like her to be unwilling—wanting nothing but sensation, the triumph. . ." (48).

The middle-aged narrator, who is himself in love with Miss Torsen, persists in his campaign against her. Thus, it looks as though she is indirectly to blame for the death of one of the guests, a lawyer with a passion for mountain climbing with whom she spends much time after giving up on Solem. Enraged, Solem lures the lawyer to scale Blue Peak, concocting a story about a rival who might beat him to it. When the lawyer falls to his death, Ingeborg Torsen shows no more emotion than anybody else, and she continues to stay at the resort; she even invites a friend, an effeminate actor, to join her there. The narrator attributes her reluctance to leave to her being sexually fixated on Solem, exclaiming: "How . . . warped this beautiful young woman was!" After the lawyer's death she actually shuns Solem less than before. "Oh, she was so unbalanced," the narrator notes, "a poor soul gone astray. Whenever she got a chance, she would muck around on the sly with tar, and with dung in the field, sniffing at the filth without getting nauseated" (VII: 67). In human terms, "Solem's coarse passion that she herself had kindled, his brutality, his maleness, his grasping hands, the way he looked at her—she sniffed all this and felt something stir inside her. She had been led so astray, been so unnaturally damaged, that her desire was satisfied by the mere thought of this man at a distance." And the narrator concludes, "I suspect that, as she lay in her lonely bed in the evening, the Torsen type was taking delight in the fact that, in an entirely different building, a man lay writhing with lust for her" (68).

In a couple of instances, the narrator becomes an involuntary observer of semi-erotic scenes between Miss Torsen and the actor. With their distinctly voyeuristic quality, these scenes seem to anticipate a central theme developed by the Polish novelist Witold Gombrowicz, namely, that of the young acting for the benefit of, and corrupting, the old.[36] The narrator comes to suspect that "she had nothing against seeing even old men squirm" (VII: 73). "Why did she perform these tricks?" he asks. His silent answer is more pointed than ever: "Your nature is so warped that here you are in your twenty-seventh year and unmarried, barren and unopened" (69). And she is not alone, being routinely called the Torsen type, which is described as follows: "the middle-class child reared on nothing but school books growing up, who has learned about *Artemis cotula* [read 'botany'] but starved her own nature" (66–67).

Nor is sexual denial, here expressed in food imagery as starvation, limited to "unopened" nubile young women. Wives in *The Last Joy* are also kept on rather short sexual rations. Mrs. Molie's husband is a sailor, "a skipper, home only now and then to add to the family. . . . It's howdy and goodbye with him. And here is the wife, for the sake of her health" (VII: 36). And Mrs. Brede is not much better served by her husband, whose time is very precious: his visit lasts a meager three days. Though the merchant is roundly praised as a man of "high spirits and good humor and wealth and all, sweet to his children, everything for his wife," the narrator asks, "Was he also everything *to* his wife?" The answer is quite unambiguous: "He wasted the first evening partying, he wasted time every night snoring. And so the three days passed" (59). One begins to understand why his wife was tempted by Solem.

The Last Joy is as harsh in its treatment of middle-class men as of the educated professional woman. And the narrator's jaundiced view of these men is not limited to Norwegians. Their greatest failing appears to be an uncritical acceptance of what is traditionally seen as a prime mover of progress and human excellence: the spirit of competition. In *The Last Joy* this spirit, as it manifests itself in sport, specifically mountain climbing, brings death and, momentarily, a veritable cult of the abyss and nothingness.

In the discussion among the guests, flat-chested Mrs. Molie is a temptress, subtly egging the men on. "There's supposed to be a blue peak up there somewhere," she says, "that must be next, eh?" A Danish guest is "sorely tempted" to try, and the lawyer boasts that only Miss Torsen's veto has prevented him from scaling it; even the visiting merchant weighs in with a playful hint of having "a go at it" (VII: 57). In persuading the lawyer to make the climb, Solem acts like the biblical serpent, appealing to his vanity: "Everyone says that the first one up Blue Peak will be in the papers," he tells him. The possibility of losing the chance to be the first nearly paralyzes the lawyer: "he looked blank. His little sporting brain snapped" (62). As in Genesis, attempting to rise above ordinary humanity reaps disaster and death.

In fact, subsequent events in the novel establish a direct link between the competitive craze for star status and notoriety, on the one hand, and the thrill of risking self-annihilation, on the other. The lawyer's death leads to an invasion of journalists, who telegraph and write about "Blue Peak and violent death," and of foreign tourists, specifically "Anglo-Saxons," Hamsun's appellation for the English. The description of the latter could scarcely have been more unflattering: "Their perverted sportsman's brains prickled and itched, they had carefully slipped past every insane asylum along their way and come straight here without being apprehended." They are hell-bent on getting to "stand on this fine scene of an accident, this splendid abyss. Some would scale Blue Peak or never know another happy day in their lives, others would just get a sexual thrill from the lawyer's fatal fall; they would send down a yawp and wait for an echo, standing so close to the edge that they stepped on death with their toes" (VII: 64–65). The oxymoron, as in "splendid abyss," is the only figure that can adequately suggest the paradoxical union of ecstatic delight and death. This sexually tinged fascination with self-destruction may be more than just a malicious fantasy on Hamsun's part, considering what happened to European civilization two years later, in 1914. Did Hamsun detect a death wish at the base of the strenuous work of sublimation that was required for modern bourgeois society to perpetuate itself?

Meanwhile, the quasi-mystical worship of nature which dominates the first part of the novel alternates with a prosaic view that sees nature as resource, to be developed and exploited by the farmer. With the rise of the tourist industry, however, agricultural values seem threatened. The narrator brings out the ongoing conflict between traditional and modern ways as he relates the changing fortunes of the Tore Peak resort, which has difficulty reconciling the needs of farming with those of a business enterprise. His bias at this point is that of a champion of the yeoman farmer, whose values are embodied in two women, the owner's wife and Josephine, his younger sister, while the owner himself, Paul, has surrendered to the Zeitgeist. Anyway, he is a drunkard whose habitual binges are known to everybody; his quirky ideas for attracting more tourists — once he thinks acquiring an aquarium might help — are ridiculed as the product of a delirious fancy: "Some see flies, Paul saw goldfish" (VII: 61).

The third and last part of *The Last Joy* is a counter-development story, in which Ingeborg Torsen gradually changes into the image of

Josephine, the young woman whose thrift, diligence, and sheer hard work are epitomized in a recurrent motif: "When she hurries across the yard her feet are a blur below her skirt" (VII: 26).[37] Fearing that Miss Torsen has "backslided since she got back to the city," the narrator resumes his friendship with her; his sole concern for the rest of the story is to promote her marriage to a hulk of a man, Nikolai Palm, a farmer and would-be artisan she met as a fellow passenger on returning from the resort. Having ascertained from Ingeborg where he could find Nikolai, the narrator makes the acquaintance of the young man, whom he describes as built "like a horse, strong and ugly, and horribly closemouthed" (101). Anyone who has read Hamsun's *Growth of the Soil* (1917) will recognize Nikolai's close kinship with Isak, the hero of Hamsun's agrarian novel.

The first glimpse of Ingeborg as a married woman is in the form of a metonymic "rear end" as she kneels "in the doorway, washing the floor." Her dress is "wet and dirty," and "she's so gray," though only a couple of years have passed since she and the narrator saw one another. Yet, "the young mother"—yes, there is a boy, with a second child on the way—"was so happy and so beautiful," her eyes "full of a mysterious tenderness they had never had before." The narrator seems to gloat over the incongruity of her background with her present situation: "Had she ever imagined that her degree would end up here, in the cow barn or with her doing Saturday cleaning?" (VII: 128-29). And there is a missing tooth, which got broken by "buckshot left in a grouse" (130); it has left "a black hole," but she "wouldn't ever" have it replaced, though she feels sorry "for Nikolai's sake." As you get older, she says, children are "the only joy, the last joy." And she goes on, "I want to have more of them, many, oh dear, I want children lined up one after the other like organ pipes, each one taller than the next" (131). One is not surprised to discover that, on Sundays, she reads "the family prayers," though previously she has shown no interest in religion. The narrator comments: "Look, you may not be a believer, no, but if you are nothing else either, what are you? You read the prayers" (133). While founded on solid rural values, the portrayal of Ingeborg as wife and young mother strikes the present reader as the debasement of an educated woman to the level of a household drudge.

The picture of bucolic simplicity created by the author, and promoted by his narrator, is a reactionary fantasy, Hamsun's response to what he considered a national plague, namely, the commercialization of Norwegian culture on the Swiss model.[38] However, the relationship between the narrator and the agricultural ideal that he champions is an ironic one. Far from being a farmer himself, he is a roving writer who seems to feel at home nowhere, unless it be in the woods, where he seeks refuge from time to time. The portrayal of Nikolai and Ingeborg's rustic contentment is the narrator's way of living vicariously. The permutations of the "last joy" motif tell the story. Feeling too old for love, the narrator muses, "But one thing I'll never be done with: withdrawing to sit in the solitude of my room, surrounded by a deep darkness. In spite of all, that's the last joy." Shortly thereafter he plays a variation on this theme: "And there is another thing I'll never be done with: withdrawing to sit in the solitude of the forest, surrounded by a deep darkness. That's the last joy." In the latter instance, he emphasizes the "lofty, religious aspect of solitude and darkness. . . . The mystery is that everything surges toward us from afar, but everything is near, we sit in the midst of an omnipresence. I suppose it's God. I suppose it's one's self as a part of the all" (VII: 69). At the end, the cult of solitude has given way to fecundity, family values in the most elementary sense, an ideal that the narrator, with his self-confessed senility at fifty, can only satisfy vicariously by way of Ingeborg's confession that children are "the last joy."

The vicarious relations between the narrator and his central characters also include a distinctly erotic element. This is a situation we have encountered previously in Hamsun's fiction, specifically in *A Wanderer*, where a scene of rape occurs. In *The Last Joy* such a scene marks the approximate end of the section devoted to life at the resort. As in *A Wanderer*, Hamsun's narrator participates voyeuristically in the scene. One night, returning from the woods, he sees a man, whom he recognizes as Solem under the actor's cloak, enter the building where Miss Torsen is staying. The narrator is extremely agitated by the imminent encounter: "Good heavens, that Solem fellow may be up to something. He may be intent upon something, all right, do her some harm—he could shower her with rape!" (VII: 71). Despite his resolution not to "leave a helpless woman in the lurch," he simply sits there, watching and waiting for several hours, and imagining the worst. "A thorough business that," he reflects, "no trifling in there, for sure; it's now near daybreak. It occurs to me that he may be killing her, that perhaps he has killed her already; growing anxious, I am about to get up — then the key turns again in there and Solem comes out." The next moment he discovers that Solem "had been in the buff in there, under the cloak. Was it possible? Oh well, nothing in the way, no delays, not a stitch" (72).

Behind the righteous horror at the imagined outrage, a note of admiration is evident as well: "Quite a guy, that Solem!" It is as though he has shared the act with the rapist, judging by his apparent fatigue afterward: "I sit and think, collecting myself and trying to regain my strength" (VII: 72). Even after her marriage, the narrator betrays an indubitable sensual awareness of Ingeborg, noticing how, "with her dress clinging to her body, her limbs were clearly outlined under it" (130). And when at the very end, after Solem's visit at the farm, the narrator asks Ingeborg whether Nikolai knows about the rape, she suspects a prurient interest on his part. It does, indeed, look as though the narrator possesses Ingeborg vicariously through Solem's rape and its aftermmath.

Considering the rather pathetic situation of Hamsun's first-person narrator in *The Last Joy*, dependent as he is on the novel's characters for whatever happiness comes his way, it is not surprising that the epilogue (chapter 38) announces his demise. Noting that he has "written about human beings," the narrator continues: "But beneath what is said there is another speech, flowing like the artery under the skin, a story within the story. I have followed an incipient literary septuagenarian step by step, reporting the process of his dissolution" (VII: 141). Marie Hamsun must have welcomed this event. Writing with distaste about having "to go through another I-manuscript," she confesses: "I couldn't look objectively at anything in the book. And with its tone of being finished with life, much in it had a painful effect on me."[39] Indeed, *The Last Joy* was to be Hamsun's last contribution to a type of story which in Russian criticism bears the name *skaz'*, defined by a "narrative manner which focuses on the personal 'tone' of the fictional narrator."[40]

The negative feelings that Mrs. Hamsun perceived may, in effect, have been at the base of Hamsun's creativity in writing the book. It can be plausibly argued that the novel contains the story of its own genesis, thus representing a peculiar variety of metafiction. The old-man, through-with-life syndrome that put off Mrs. Hamsun is compounded in *The Last Joy* by feelings of boredom, emptiness, indefinite longing, and a sense of abandonment,[41] and the story emerges as much from these mostly negative states of mind as from a sense of mission. Indeed, given the narrator's sense of a void, nothingness, his self-appointed mission of rescuing the nation from spiritual blight appears as just another alternative, in addition to vicarious experiences, of filling that void. What saves the narrator from the worst consequences of his malaise is his exhilarating ludic impulse, which generates a series of bizarre situations and zany whims in the first part of the novel, including moods of pure make-believe that carry him back to the "dear, foolish bliss of childhood" (VII: 20), but also stimulates creative activity.

All this being said, one cannot overlook the artistic flaws of *The Last Joy*. Formally, as already mentioned, it consists of three fairly separate stories, linked chiefly by the first-person narrator. True, the wanderer aspect of the narrator is maintained throughout, along with his periodic withdrawal to the woods for communion with nature. However, there is no master plot. And though, as always, Hamsun's characteristic use of present tense narration creates a vivid impression of immediacy, it is slightly confusing to be reminded that, on the whole, the novel is told in retrospect; the one time the narrator mentions that he is writing in the hut, he deletes what he has written.[42]

These rather technical shortcomings pale by comparison with the lack of consistency in the underlying conception of life embodied in the work. Thus, the primitivist ethos is not only contradictory in itself but conflicts with a sporadic humanistic impulse. While animal imagery, for example, has a positive connotation in the narrator's self-description — he surmises he may have an "animal" expression in his eyes (VII: 16) — as well as in the portrayal of Ingeborg and Nikolai, compared to a mare and a horse respectively (133, 136),[43] the same imagery carries a negative meaning when applied to the Sami and to Solem (20, 68). Whereas Nikolai can do no wrong, Solem increasingly assumes the role of a villain. We eventually discover, for example, that Solem also raped or seduced, and impregnated, Miss Palm, Nikolai's sister, at the resort; his sexual power, judged by the narrator as hurtful to his victims, springs from the "aurochs in him" (68). Meanwhile Nikolai, his "macho opposite number, with the strength and spirit of a stallion" (136–37), is idealized. Hamsun preaches a gospel of "back to nature," but at the same time demonstrates the potential evils of such a gospel. The underlying intellectual shallowness is scarcely redeemed by the fact that both Ingeborg and the narrator express their awareness of the need to be "human beings" and not "animals" (137–38).[44] Hamsun's *Weltanschauung* in this novel does not stand up to the most elementary scrutiny.

Worst of all, however, is the often malicious satire voiced by the narrator. The English, which are the prime targets, together with the Swiss, are portrayed as a nation of "runners, coachmen, and depravity which a salutary fate in the guise of Germany will some day chastise unto death" (VII: 35). England, he notes elsewhere, "unsexes its people with sport and fixed ideas: if Germany hadn't kept it in a state of perpetual uneasiness, it would have turned to pederasty in a generation or two" (89). The actual portraits given of English tourists are done in the same spirit of withering contempt. The narrator even hints at bestiality, as he overhears some disturbance in the goatshed caused by two Englishmen. The experience causes him to reflect, "Vice runs in circles, in cycles, just like virtue, . . . nothing is new, everything comes around and repeats itself" (134).

With this crude display of prejudice and xenophobic animus, it is a relief to be able to praise Hamsun's character portrayal in general. Though one would expect to find, in a novel bristling with satire, a collection of stereotypes and caricatures, that does not happen. The lawyer, while lacking a name, is not defined by his profession. He is well versed in business, with a special interest in Switzerland as a premier tourist nation; he is a talented architectural draftsman; and he is an avid sportsman. He obviously also has his weaknesses, considering the success of Solem's ruse, which makes him climb to his death. Mrs. Molie, blue-toothed and with a proclivity toward nastiness, is quite convincing, and her relationship with the high school teacher, Master Høy, is fascinating to watch. Solem and Eilert, cryptocriminals both, are the kind of marginal characters that Hamsun can infuse with a mysterious life even without seeming to try. But honest folk like Josephine and Nikolai come across vividly as well. The main problems arise with Miss Torsen and the narrator. The former is made to serve as the narrator's mouthpiece, especially in her bitter criticism of the teaching profession, while the narrator, as the previous discussion has shown, tends to dissolve into a cluster of personae in response to the disparate agendas Hamsun has burdened him with. In this respect, *The Last Joy* bears a resemblance to its immediate predecessor, *A Wanderer Plays on Muted Strings*.

However flawed, a Hamsun novel usually has some interesting or attractive features. But in the case of *The Last Joy*, critics have found little to admire. Hamsun himself seems to have had doubts about its literary quality. When Sven Lange, his long-time Danish friend, praised the book,[45] Hamsun wrote to his publisher that he does not understand Sven Lange's great "loyalty."[46] Einar Skavlan, Hamsun's future biographer, lauds the "peculiar enchantment" of its style, but writes that, apart from the style, it is only held together by the "temperament stirring rather hazily behind it."[47] In his review of the English translation, Clifton Fadiman finds the book lacking in organization and "unconvincing" in its preachment.[48] Subsequent critics have been no less merciless in their judgments. Robert Ferguson uses the dismissive phrase "one of the worst of Hamsun's books," while a Norwegian critic characterizes it as a "sincere attempt at literary suicide."[49]

CHAPTER SIX

Nostalgic Myth and Critique of Modernity: Novels of Social Change

The two novels dealing with Segelfoss, a Nordland landed estate gradually transformed into a modern community, represent a new development in Hamsun's fiction. With its numerous characters and a decades-long combined time span, this two-part work harks back to the traditional nineteenth-century novel, which Hamsun had so severely, and contemptuously, criticized in his 1891 lectures. Yet, each differs markedly from his ventures in conventional fiction of the 1890s, *The Editor* and *Shallow Soil*. Whereas these can be defined without undue distortion as satirical and didactic fiction respectively, *Børn av tiden* (1913; *Children of the Age*, 1925), the first of these novels, eludes such definition. Even a cursory reading reveals elements of half a dozen novelistic types: novel tragedy, character novel, novel of manners, period novel, generational novel, social satire. The implicit eclecticism has resulted in a fictional form that is *sui generis*; it is considerably looser than anything we have seen so far in the author's production. My initial discussion will focus on some of these aspects of the novel.

Contrary to Hamsun's previous practice, *Children* begins with a genealogical account of the ancestors of his central character, Lieutenant Willatz Holmsen. What immediately follows, however, creates a sense of déjà-vu: the conflicted marriage of a military officer and his German wife, Adelheid, a colonel's daughter. As in *A Wanderer*, the spouses seem incapable of breaking out of their mutual isolation. When the wife, whose upperclass background has fostered a certain independence, signals her desire to resume their intimacy, the Lieutenant responds with a curt, "It's too late, Adelheid" (VI: 87). By adding a child, Hamsun varies the basic situation already thoroughly dissected in *A Wanderer*. But though young Willatz is a source of great joy to both parents, his birth does little to improve a relationship that was troubled before his appearance on the scene. On the contrary, his presence points up his parents' incompatibility: his father calls him by one of his three given names, Willatz, his mother by another, Moritz.

The narrator, who alternates between omniscience and an outsider's ignorance, can only wonder—in a passage where his voice merges with that of the Lieutenant—at the couple's inability to enjoy normal marital relations: "It's all so incomprehensible. What had he done to her? Was she put off by married life as such, the habitude, shame? His long hands, perhaps, his breath?" These questions occur after a scene in which the Lieutenant reminds his wife how many times he has knocked on her bedroom door without being admitted. She tells him she had begged his pardon every time—whereupon she does so once again. His reaction is a combination of absurd laughter and masculine self-assertion. The laughter is described in an unusual way, not very often found in Hamsun: "It is an external sound, the mouth makes an opening, the throat exerts its pressure, and out comes laughter." The effect, that of defamiliarizing a banal reaction, is bizarre, momentarily reducing the proud Lieutenant to a puppet in thrall to irrational tics. And his subsequent behavior, while ordinary enough for a frustrated country squire, may strike the reader as equally absurd: "Then . . . he goes out of the house, across the yard to the stable, gets his horse and vaults into the saddle" (VI: 21). The Lieutenant's robot-like movements make him, as well as the entire marital situation, appear "incomprehensible," indeed.

Like the narrator, the reader is confronted by a mystery. Since the main story begins after the Lieutenant's marriage is several years old and goes on without expository cutbacks, we can only guess at what had happened between the Lieutenant and his wife previous to the onset of the plot. One thing, however, is certain: Adelheid suspects her husband of cheating on her with the maids—another echo of *A Wanderer*—and the reader comes to suspect that *she* has been unfaithful to *him*. But whereas in *A Wanderer* we actually witness the course of an affair and its tragic consequences, here we have to rely on a few ambiguous clues: Mrs. Holmsen's excessive touchiness, her emotional volatility and, shortly before her death by drowning on a visit to Germany, her admission in a letter to her husband of having "done him wrong" (VI: 139). A couple of friends, Fredrik Coldevin and Tobias Holmengrå, were certainly in love with her at one time or another, judging by their reaction to her untoward death. Entering her bedroom after the funeral, Coldevin leaves with a comb that, to him, still gives off the scent of her hair; he muses, "And what if she were suddenly singing up there in the parlor again . . .! Yes, flashing her passion like a fan, letting her hair down. Poor thing!" (160–61). As for Holmengrå, not only is he observed by Holmsen in a situation suggestive of physical intimacy with his wife (126), but the latter's death brings him to the verge of a breakdown. As in *A Wanderer*, the woman pays the price: though the news from Hannover, Adelheid's birthplace, is ambiguous, one can only conclude that she took her own life.

The tragic denouement of the marriage plot is not a matter of chance or circumstance. While the wife's German background may be partly responsible for the couple's difficulties, the chief problem lies in the disparities between two diametrically opposed natures. The Lieutenant, a would-be aristocrat whose mind has supposedly been formed by the humanists and encyclopedists whose works were available "in his father's library" (VI: 12), orders his life by an apotheosis of the will, shown in an exemplary way after his wife's death: "One was not cowed, one was silent and proud, warrior and man of the world, strong by sheer will" (165).[1] In contrast, Adelheid is, beneath her class pride and aristocratic hauteur, an ardent spirit, with a passion for music and a profound need of being loved. If this novel manages to captivate the reader's interest, it is largely because of Hamsun's success in portraying these rather eccentric individuals, as self-contradictory as any figures he ever created, in a manner that carries conviction.

But the author had a broader purpose in mind. With the return to Nordland of Tobias Holmengrå, who had emigrated as a poor youth and made a fortune in Mexico, things start changing at Segelfoss. From here on the novel acquires a wider scope, focusing on the gradual transformation of a near-feudal social order into a modern industrial society.[2] Yet, what captures one's imagination is not so much the social changes that take place as the interplay between the Holmsens and Holmengrå, a character of legend who in time not only gains control of the Lieutenant's estate, but also wins the love of his wife. Furthermore, whatever sense of social change comes across is produced as much by Hamsun's evocation of the shifting power relations between Holmsen and Holmengrå as by general narrative and description. The successive negotiations and financial deals—usually presented in scenic form—whereby Holmengrå little by little acquires real estate and property rights for his expanding entrepreneurial enterprises from the chronically cash-hungry owner of Segelfoss, tell their own story. Eventually the contracting parties turn into symbols of two different social orders, one on the way out, the other emerging.[3]

Here is an example of conveying change descriptively:

> Now things appear to be in free fall. Months pass, years pass, but not the way months and years usually pass, bringing ordinary, soulless trifles, but like an avalanche, large or small. Segelfoss and environs are changed beyond recognition from what they were during the Lieutenant's reign; nothing had really come to an end, but everything had changed its appearance and character, and the changes were still going on, in people and things. (VI: 118)

However, the examples of change that follow—the suspension of visits by members of one's class, the possibility of Segelfoss becoming a parish, the parson's desire to acquire a better ministry in South Norway, the success of a local boy whose theological studies were sponsored by the Lieutenant, the flourishing of the local general store, and Holmengrå's manifold industrial activities—are extremely diverse and lack focus. Besides, page after page of dense prose tends to make one's attention flag. Hamsun's desire to convey the very process of change is understandable, but that process comes across most vividly where individuals are shown in dramatic interaction.

Dr. Muus, a physician and thus a representative of the professional class, has been invited to dinner by Holmengrå. His being portrayed in the novel as an arrogant, class-conscious bourgeois does not invalidate what he has to say about the Lieutenant, on whose prosperity that of so many others depends. In the following exchange Dr. Muus casts doubt not only on Holmsen's character but on his solvency. Responding with skepticism to Holmengrå's statement that Holmsen is a "superior person," he says:

"Really? He is a superior person?"
"That is my impression," Mr. Holmengrå replies.
"I believe your impression is leading you astray," the doctor says.
...
"No, I do believe that the Lieutenant is a superior person," he [Holmengrå] said.
This didn't impress Mr. Muus, because he was upperclass and a man of learning.
"I distinguish between someone who is brought to his knees by misfortune and someone who rushes methodically to his own destruction," he said. "The Lieutenant belongs to the latter. I've heard that you are the one who owns his estate." (VI: 153–54)

One of the more lighthearted features of *Children of the Age* comes about through Hamsun's depiction of the manners of particular groups, or of characters who are representative of a group. At times, these depictions are satirical, but mostly they are sheer comedy. An instance of the latter is seen at the unexpected arrival of Holmengrå, which arouses an unquenchable curiosity among the villagers. Obviously flattered by all the attention they are attracting, the two boatmen who brought him are sparing with their answers to that notorious quidnunc Lars Manuelsen, father of the above-mentioned theological prodigy. The stop-and-go dialogue, which continues for several pages (VI: 27–31), is reminiscent of a duel of wits or a fencing match, with thrust and parry, fresh tacks and feigned surrender. It is a superb mini-comedy of manners, whereby the author succeeds in revealing, beneath the surface of eager questions and reluctant answers, the characteristics of an entire rural manner of life and behavior: aloof, unhurried, and reticent, yet not unwilling to communicate with the outside world as long as its own pace is respected. The excessive curiosity of Lars Manuelsen is a necessary complement to the boatmen's secretiveness; each expresses an important facet of provincial culture, which is at once turned in upon itself and avid for contact with a larger world.

By comparison with the humorous portrayal of folksy types, Hamsun's treatment of professionals like Dr. Muus and Mr. Rasch, an attorney, is distinctly acid, yet with an unmistakable comic tinge to it. Dr. Muus, the more self-important and abrasive of the two, is introduced as a near-grotesque: "A queer little doctor, no doubt well-versed in medicine and certainly sallow enough for dyspepsia, a dried-up face with a large nose, big deformed ears and a sparse growth of beard" (VI: 106). When he calls on the Holmsens, as it happens on the very day when a festive dinner is being given in honor of young Willatz's return to school in England, Dr. Muus flaunts his culture as a member of the educated classes, his connoisseurship of wine, music and painting. After dinner, as the Lieutenant and the doctor find themselves making up the rear on their way to the pier, the following exchange, whose total effect depends on the doctor's name being a homophone of the Norwegian word for "mouse," takes place:

> "What did you say your name was?"
> "My name is Muus."
> "Muus."
> The doctor chews his skimpy beard and says, "And your name is Holmsen?"
> "Yes."
> "Von Holmsen, perhaps?"
> "No, simply Holmsen."
> The two gentlemen were probably about even by now, but unfortunately the doctor started laughing, and the Lieutenant couldn't help looking at him in surprise. (VI: 109)

The mutual contempt of the two men, rooted in a presumed class difference, flares out in their concluding exchange, after the doctor has expressed a desire to meet Martin, the Lieutenant's hired man, because he is "certain to be a cultivated person," a remark that Mr. Holmsen seems to interpret as a slur.

> The Lieutenant slowly turned his head and replied, "Next time you visit Segelfoss, to bid goodbye, let's say, you'll use the entrance of the yellow building in the yard. There you will meet Martin, the hired man."
> "Thanks. If at that time you will have a yellow building and Martin, your hired man." (VI: 110)

The comedy provided by the pretensions of Lars Manuelsen's son, who calls himself L. Lassen after being ordained, is of a cruder sort, approaching burlesque. Exemplifying the Lieutenant's, and Hamsun's, notion of a peasant who has worked his way "down to a parson" (VI: 117), Lassen is portrayed as a nearly schizoid figure: while very conscious of his clerical dignity and rather standoffish before people, turning the question whether to be the first to greet someone into an existential problem, he is exposed as a dirty, guzzling slob in private. Observed through a peephole in the ceiling by Julius, his younger brother, as he feasts on the proverbial fatted calf — actually a goat — he "eats coarsely, blindly, making a mess of himself and dripping fat all around him. And he acted with dispatch, as if bent on putting away as much as possible before he was caught out" (145). His ostentatious piety and scholarly unworldliness are a mere masquerade, necessary attributes of a successful priestly persona that can be dropped at will. Hamsun's characterization of Mr. Lassen amounts to a sort of deconstruction of the very notion of acquired culture. But whether picked up by the individual or passed down in the family, as in the case of Dr. Muus, learning and the associated cultivation of the mind are represented negatively in Hamsun's work;[4] those who have achieved these attainments tend to self-consciously flaunt them, thus inviting a comic nemesis.

Hamsun has located these characters, and the rest of his numerous cast, in a time frame that is only vaguely indicated. There are references to a few historical events, such as the death of the king, Charles XV most likely, and the change of currency from dollars to kroner. We know when these events occurred, in 1872 and 1873 respectively. We also learn that, by the time the story is being related, Willatz Holmsen, who lived until the age of sixty-nine, has been dead for "many years" (VI: 9). Since the novel appeared in 1913, he may have lived until nearly the end of the century. Adelheid was twenty-eight when young Willatz was born, probably around 1870, by which time the Holmsens had been married for a number of years.

Such calculations, which might seem futile, reveal that Hamsun is as indifferent to chronology as ever, though the novel claims to deal with social change. Struggle as he may to find some way of relating the novel's plot to history, the reader has little success; all he learns is that Hamsun intends to depict the transition from an agricultural to a proto-industrial era.[5] And it looks as though the pros and cons of the transformation involved were more important to him than a convincing depiction of it, considering the heated debates between the Holmsens and their visiting friends the Coldevins about how to deal with the Holmengrå phenomenon. *Children of the Age*, therefore, qualifies as a period novel only in a very limited sense of the term, just as its realism is rather spurious. History to Hamsun is essentially a matter of natural cycles, defined by biology: its principal events are the perpetual change of the seasons, people aging, and one generation giving place to another. Archetypal scenes, relating to birth, youthful love, and parent-child relations prevail over period-specific particulars. In terms of narrative, such a predilection gives rise to a sequence of eternal presents, shown by Hamsun's fondness for the adverb "now," a time indicator without any reference to datable occurrences. Events form part of an endless flow of happenings, and the characters are "children of time" rather than "of the age."

Viewed as a single work, *Children of the Age* and *Segelfoss Town* constitute a sort of family chronicle or generational novel, of which Thomas Mann's *Buddenbrooks* (1901) is a well-known example. In a letter written while working on *Segelfoss Town*, Hamsun alludes to the fiction of his countryman Alexander Kielland, who, along with Jonas Lie, had influenced Mann's novel.[6] Noting that *Segelfoss Town* went together with the "previous volume," *Children*, he reminds his publisher that "Kielland, for example, wrote all his books in such a way that he continued with the same characters in volume after volume," though each was an "independent book."[7] The term family chronicle does indeed define fundamental aspects of Hamsun's second novelistic diptych, since it focuses on the changing fortunes of a number of families over several decades, in *Children* mainly the Holmsens and the Holmengrås, while in *Segelfoss Town* families of lower social standing become increasingly important.

One troubling consequence of choosing such a broad, accommodating form was that it allowed Hamsun to indulge in one of his worst aesthetic vices: a tendency to all-inclusiveness, resulting in an overabundance of characters, incidents and thematic strands. In *Children*, for example, the focus often shifts from the Holmsen-Holmengrå relationship to young people, in preparation for *Segelfoss Town*: young Willatz; Holmengrå's daughter, Mariane; Anton Coldevin; Julius Manuelsen, and others. Admittedly, the associated relationships, whether of youthful friendship or young love, are often superbly rendered. However, they have no perceptible relevance to family history, social transformation, or cultural change. Hamsun seems to have been aware of the problem, as shown by a letter to his publisher immediately before the appearance of *Segelfoss Town*. Writing about the latter novel, he says, "I'm not certain that the book is very good, I had to deal with too many people."[8] The same is true, though to a lesser degree, of *Children of the Age*.

The time has come to look more closely at the structure and meaning of *Children of the Age*. Its major plot is by no means simple: Hamsun is faithful to his penchant for self-contradiction. On the one hand, the story recounts the fall of Willatz Holmsen, partly a victim of his own stubborn adherence to the ethos of his class, but mainly overthrown by forces not of his own making. Viewed thus, Hamsun's central character becomes a tragic figure. On the other hand, a rumor of "buried treasure" on the estate opens a possibility for a *deus ex machina* conclusion. Shortly before he dies, having moved out of the main residence into a newly built apartment in an old brick works on the estate, the Lieutenant discovers the family treasure, which will enable his son, Willatz, Jr., to redeem the mortgaged estate. This bitter-sweet denouement sets up a tension between two plot modalities, one characterized by a relentless inevitability, the other tinged with wishful thinking, fantasy. As a motif, the rediscovery of a lost treasure belongs to the novel of adventure, and Hamsun's use of it in a story of presumptive cultural decline can only be explained by his desire for a sequel, one in which the Holmsen family will still play an important role.[9] The solution is anything but elegant: the exigencies of book production obviously prevailed over considerations of verisimilitude and aesthetic form. Instead of an ending, there is the beginning of a new cycle.

While the idea of a continuation is present in the novel, since the Lieutenant hopes that his son will succeed him at Segelfoss, the artistic vocation of Willatz, Jr.—shades of *Buddenbrooks* or of Jonas Lie's *Evil Powers* (1890)?—throws the succession in doubt. On the whole, both the characters and the events are presented in such a way as to suggest an ultimate debacle of the house of Holmsen. The Lieutenant himself, with his Creon-like rigidities, can only break, not bend.[10] The potentiality of disaster is eloquently prefigured by a piece of symbolic action. Until near the end, the Lieutenant is mostly seen on horseback; it is as though he and the horse were one. One day when he is out riding, the horse bolts, frightened by a blasting shot set off by Holmengrå's workmen, and the rider is thrown off balance; he finds himself "hanging lower and lower down the [horse's] flank," until he manages to grab its mane. But the horse stumbles, and the Lieutenant's leg is caught under it (VI: 73). Though he escapes injury and later works with a will to accustom his horse to the explosions, his vulnerability has been exposed, along with the fragility of the social order that he and the horse together represent. Hamsun's handling of this episode evokes the different meanings associated with horsemanship in earlier times, cultural as well as military: the chivalric code is no less important than equestrian skill.

The notion of chivalry relates chiefly to the way in which Lieutenant Holmsen handles his marital relationship. As a married couple, the Holmsens do not correspond to the knight and his lady in any strict sense. Yet, the formality of their behavior toward each other, Adelheid's withholding of her favors, and the Lieutenant's persistent efforts to honor her, produce a situation that invites the comparison. Significantly, the Lieutenant is shown to be vulnerable not only as a horseman but also as a lover, and his inadequacy, and ultimate defeat, is signaled by a reminder of the accident with the horse, transformed into metaphor. On her return from England, where she visited her son at Harrow, the famous public school, Adelheid tells her husband about all the happy married people she had observed on her trip. A snippet of their conversation runs as follows, after the Lieutenant has admitted that she is making him "curious":

> "I am? They were married people. One day they smiled to each other and nodded, they got along so well; they kissed, talked, and wished each other good night."
> "And the next day?"
> "They did the same thing."
> "Strange. What sort of married people could they be?"
> "They were all of them that way."
> Pause. The Lieutenant was caught off his guard, he again seemed to be hanging down his horse's flank. (VI: 85)

Though both the accident and its metaphorization denote circumstances and forces that Mr. Holmsen is unable to control, thus making the reader sympathetic with his plight, Hamsun's portrayal of him could scarcely have been more ambiguous. The narrative voice alternates between hero worship and crass ridicule. True, some of the negative comments about him—that he was a "vain and crazy gentleman" whose "highhandedness went too far" (VI: 9, 19)—are presented as the opinion of C. P. Windfeld, the local pastor, who felt frustrated by a lack of cooperation on the Lieutenant's part in finalizing his donation of a new church to the community. However, the narrator's own comments are sufficiently contradictory to make one wonder about Tore Hamsun's statement that the Lieutenant was a man "after Hamsun's heart."[11] Judging by the details of the Lieutenant's portrayal, the love Hamsun felt for his character must have been a rather unhappy one.

Lieutenant Holmsen is doubtless intended to embody a cultural ideal, one outlined by himself in a discussion with Fredrik Coldevin, an *homme moyen sensuel* who believes one must keep up with the times. In an untypical loquacious moment, the Lieutenant asserts that for the "character which makes a personality of a human being" to develop, there has to be inherited "wealth and luxury for several generations" (VI: 58). From the authorial perspective, the Lieutenant, called a "remarkable personality" (9), seems to fulfill this ideal. However, one may be remarkable because of weaknesses as well as strengths. For a fuller portrait of Mr. Holmsen, one must look more closely not only at the way he is described but at some of his actions.

The main strength of Willatz Holmsen is his unbending character, but that is also his weakness. Burdened with a large inherited debt, he nevertheless strives to fulfill the obligations of his class, assuming the role of benefactor as a matter of course. His attitude is unwavering, whether in good times or bad. Confronted after years and years of unhappiness with the feeling that he has been "cheated and fleeced," that his life has been largely wasted, he can only react by turning against life in a sulk, "obstinate and erect. . . . A revenge on himself? Yes, a revenge on himself, on everything, the whole caboodle, erect" (VI: 165–66). In whatever respect, whether moral or material, he displays a rigidity that makes him an object of ridicule to the narrator. At a time when he is worried about losing the estate, the Lieutenant's inability to change his inherited mindset is burlesqued in terms of the barnyard: "He could have recognized himself in the life of the hens on his farm: when a hen has a mind to do something she cocks her head first to one side, then to the other side, trying to figure out whether the world is just about right for her undertaking. Then she pushes on. . . . Nothing whatever can make her turn her will completely around; she can turn aside, she can walk slantways, but she won't turn around" (123). Nor can the Lieutenant: however poorly adapted to the financial situation at Segelfoss, his attitude remains inflexible, part and parcel of that culture of "wealth and luxury" which he champions. At times the portrayal of Mr. Holmsen turns paradoxical: he is "a spendthrift without riches to spend, a negative genius, with a rare ability to incur expenses. He was the son of his fathers and lived in their shadow" (141). The narrator goes so far as to insinuate, apropos of his timber sales, that he had "acquired a taste for his own self-destruction" (114).

Willatz Holmsen's psychological predicament may be related to his sexuality. Generally, the Lieutenant has difficulty expressing his feelings in words; instead, they show up as muscular contractions like "white knuckles" and "clenched fists," a non-verbal technique Hamsun may have picked up from Tolstoy. He is clearly sexually repressed, as shown in the final encounter with Daverdana, a young girl who was assigned to read passages from the classics to him in the evening. Anticipating her coming, he lies on the sofa with both hands in his trouser pockets, "brutish and wild." When she enters, he jumps up and "remains standing, stiffly, bolt upright" (VI: 44, 165). Then he gives her some money and lets her go: the ego or power drive prevails, but directed inward.

His marriage illustrates a more complex pattern, that of a Strindbergian battle of wills where desire can appear only under the aspect of force or violence.[12] He has, in fact, more than once been tempted to rape his own wife, but has desisted with the reflection that a "human being must surely manage to be a little bigger than his fate" (VI: 88). Again, the power drive is turned inward, as befits the authoritarian personality of the Lieutenant. Meanwhile his tenderness, hardly ever seen in his dealings with his wife, is expended on children, especially young boys. When he makes little Gottfred, a neighbor's boy, a present of an expensive knife, he displays his most tender gesture in the entire novel: "The Lieutenant accepts the hand and nods, he does more, he holds this hand for a while, it was so small, something alive, it moved, a thanking child's hand." The narrator may well exclaim, "What was the matter with the Lieutenant!" (118). His libido appears to be split: affection on one side, desire on the other; moreover, neither finds a natural or spontaneous expression.

Nostalgic Myth and Critique of Modernity 171

The Lieutenant's love for his wife, who according to the narrator had once and for all "taken such absolute possession of his heart and senses" (VI: 88), manifests itself chiefly through sublimation. Thus, his response to her news that she is going to have a baby is to outline a plan for a new church, which he will donate to the parish in his wife's name. Subsequently, he promises to add an organ to this gift, together with a gallery to house it. While other acts of benevolence, such as sponsoring the education of the gifted boy Lars Manuelsen, are an expression of *noblesse oblige*, these religious donations, by a man who refuses to see the pastor on his deathbed, betoken a passion for his wife that can only express itself in sublimated form, as spiritual adoration.

There is, however, a sinister side to the Lieutenant's sexual behavior: through his rigidity and pride, and the associated sexual demeanor, whether repression or sublimation, he eventually brings about both his wife's and his own destruction. In the persistent tug-of-war between the spouses, one's sympathies are with Adelheid, who is more sinned against than sinning. It is quite obvious, though never explicitly stated, that her husband's refusal to change his attitude drove her into the arms of Holmengrå, with fateful consequences. And his extravagant philanthropy, kept up in the same uncompromising spirit as other customs inherited from his ancestors, contributes to the demise of the Lieutenant himself. Whatever Hamsun wanted Willatz Holmsen to represent, he appears to illustrate the workings of *thanatos*, the death instinct: sublimation and repression are carried to such an extreme as to deny the very springs of life, eros itself.

The Lieutenant and the man who supersedes him do have something in common: their names, Holmsen and Holmengrå, share the same syllable: "holm," from *holme*, meaning "islet" or "skerry." Both are loners, isolated from other people. However, their reactions to this isolation are diametrically opposed: whereas Mr. Holmsen's spirits rise when his wife is away, to the extent that this reticent man is even heard humming to himself (VI: 84), Holmengrå, the self-made man, is strangely dependent on company and on people's good opinions. In this latter respect, he echoes a well-known Hamsunian theme, embodied in an exemplary way by Benoni and, in *Children*, by the ridiculous pastor L. Lassen: the upstart's need to "shine" (93, 144), though in Holmengrå it assumes a more sophisticated form. Thus, the narrator impugns Holmengrå's motives for wishing to socialize with the Holmsens, characterizing his behavior vis-à-vis the family as that of a snob. Even his "devotion" to Adelheid is seen as a manifestation of snobbery. "He was a peasant from his cradle. . . . Everything he knew he had learned by listening, he had made all the valuable things suspended in the air among cultured people into a personal possession, their language included. . . . But he was two hundred years younger than the residents of Segelfoss; he had learned to tip his hat, but he did it with a slave's hat" (152).[13]

Even more damaging is Holmengrå's inability to bear adversity alone, as shown by his near breakdown and his indiscreet behavior after Mrs. Holmsen's death: "his balance was gone" (VI: 152), the narrator comments. For a while he loses all self-control, to the point of making sexual advances not only to his own housekeeper but to the Lieutenant's as well. Then, old man that he is, he goes after Daverdana, now engaged to be married, making himself ridiculous by his jealousy and his efforts to impress her. Having impregnated the girl, Holmengrå sets her up with her fiancé, his own dock clerk. While Mr. Mack, the great magnate with the "imperial soul," can get away with such behavior in a Hamsun novel, Holmengrå, the *nouveau riche* representative of modernity, cannot.

Hamsun does, however, offer other perspectives on the "unfathomable King Tobias" (VI: 113), most importantly through Mrs. Holmsen. Not only does she praise his "agreeable demeanor," acquired through a "varied life in the wide world," but she finds him to be "full of tenderness, of delicate reserve" (112). Even the narrator has good things to say about him. Though Holmengrå alone is said to be worth as much as all the rest of the villagers together, he is "just as quiet and thoughtful and considerate for all that" (91). By comparison with the Lieutenant, with his masochistic self-discipline and overblown amour propre, Tobias Holmengrå, with all his faults, gains the reader's sympathy through his sheer humanity. One can only wonder why, after transforming Segelfoss from a landed estate into a thriving community, he is dismissed as a dirty old man: when he leaves the wedding party of Mr. Rasch, the attorney, his housekeeper reflects: "Uh-huh, Marcilie the maid sits waiting at home!" (185).

The most interesting character in *Children of the Age* is Adelheid Holmsen, a misplaced artist who is stifled by the narrow, repressive milieu in which she finds herself. However, unlike her husband she is able to express her sexual feelings through writing, painting, and especially music. After one of those recurrent scenes of mutual recrimination with her husband, for whom she no longer seems to feel any "excessive tenderness," she goes to her diary: "Her hands puttered tenderly with the pages and with the pen." Then she "swoops down upon" her piano, "upon joy," whereupon she rushes to "the nursery, to the boy" (VI: 21-22). The same word, "swoop down" turns up when she plays the piano during supper at Holmengrå's, where a "heavenly Steinway" is waiting to be tried out: "She swooped down upon it like the swan she was, opening up floods of melody. . . . What did she sing? Fire and ashes, longing and love, sonatas, ruffles, chorales—it went on for a long while. . ." (111).

The sexual element in her music-making becomes explicit in another instance of the swan image. In a tête-à-tête with Fredrik Coldevin, he tells her: "Yesterday I heard the swans' mating calls far out, sometimes several swans together, making a choir. It sounded so soft and wild, I couldn't help thinking of you." Even the narrator admits that "when she sang and played for someone she cared about, she . . . let loose a latent passion" (VI: 54). The swan image, occasionally accompanied by that of a cygnet, standing for the Holmsens' musically gifted son, is a leitmotif in the novel. Among the many possible meanings that this image has accumulated, one discussed by Gaston Bachelard seems quite applicable to the situation. Bachelard, focusing on the age-old idea that the swan dies singing, writes: ". . . there is only one desire that sings dying, and dies singing, and that is sexual desire. The song of the swan is, therefore, sexual desire at its climax."[14] Moreover, Adelheid's death is associated with water, the swan's element *par excellence*. Symbolized by the swan, she is an embodiment of eros and thus her husband's antithesis.

It is tempting to draw upon other aspects of swan symbolism as well. In Hamsun's novel, the swan is consistently associated with art and the artist and, by extension, with a style of life and culture in which grace and beauty figure as integral parts. A swan pond is said to have existed in the previous generation, but "now," after the Lieutenant has been dead "for many years," the pond in the park has been filled in (VI: 7, 9). However, we are led to believe that, during his lifetime, there was still something left of the ancient loveliness. The novel is, to a large extent, an exercise in nostalgia. And yet it contains a hope for future continuation of the old life, through the birth of young Willatz on the night of Christmas: "It was almost preternatural" (18). Subsequently, two allusions to this more than natural birth occur, the second referring to him—from his mother's point of view—as "a genius, a child of Christmas night" (129). It is believed that the swan was once a symbol of Virgin Mary.[15] To the Holmsens, in any case, their son appears as a savior figure, capable of maintaining the cultural heritage of his forefathers.

Any attempt at an overall interpretation of *Children of the Age* would seem quixotic. As I have indicated, the book contains elements of half a dozen novelistic types and is narrated by a mercurial persona whose viewpoint constantly changes, occasionally from one sentence to the next. While the central story, dealing with the Lieutenant, Adelheid, and Holmengrå, has something in common with other stories of adultery, such as *Madame Bovary* and *Anna Karenina*, Hamsun focuses on the marriage rather than the affair or affairs, with the result that the husband has a much larger role. Tolstoy's Mr. Karenin, for example, is a minor character. That does not preclude the possibility that Hamsun picked up some hints for the Lieutenant's mannerisms from Tolstoy's portrayal of Karenin, with his habit of cracking his knuckles. In addition to those physical tics already mentioned, the Lieutenant frequently changes his ring from one hand to another.

With his stock of obsessions and his frozen view of the world, Mr. Holmsen comes perilously close to being a caricature. There is a quality of abstraction about this punctilious squire with his aristocratic pretensions; being fully aware of this quality, the narrator makes it explicit through a quaint simile suggestive of the Lieutenant's state of mind shortly before his death. Described as he walks homeward at the crack of dawn, he looks like "a figure in an occult landscape, like a protestation" (VI: 181). He is the symbol of, and the key player in, Hamsun's doleful myth of a doomed preindustrial society, just as Holmengrå is a fairy-tale hero in a story that barely escapes being an anti-fairy tale: at the end, he seems just as disillusioned with life as the Lieutenant. Adelheid Holmsen, the swan-maid—she is a virtual celibate—possesses her own peculiar abstractness, which increases the intensity of the symbolism. She is the one character among the motley crowd of this novel who, with all her failings, displays a pure *joie de vivre* while struggling with the exigencies of an artistic nature.

While *Children of the Age* was generally well received, subsequently Hamsun has been faulted by some critics for his handling of the plot and the major figure, Lieutenant Holmsen. Among those who reviewed the book was Hermann Hesse, who, calling Hamsun "this favorite of my most beautiful years," confesses to experiencing "no disenchantment" after reading it.[16] A Finnish reviewer compares the novel favorably with two earlier works, *Benoni* and *Rosa*, noting its "deeper perspective on the universally human," though he finds the ending, which "evades tragedy," to be "weak and contrived."[17] On the other hand, the *TLS* critic is altogether negative, directing his barbed witticisms at "Lieutenant Lackland" with his "pale cast of thought," summed up as a Lieutenant Glahn from *Pan* "grown older" but "not grown up."[18] Others have also detected weaknesses in the Lieutenant's portrayal, such as Sigurd Hoel, who sees a contradiction between the "ideal" of a patrician he is meant to embody and his behavior: "He is hotheaded and threatening, overbearing, tyrannical, and rude to the local officials—as if he were a typical upstart. . . . His childish family pride and equally childish touchiness can hardly be understood as a sign of old culture, being not so very different from the feverish self-assertion of Rasch, the attorney." Yet, Hoel ends his critique by calling the book a "literary work of note," precisely because the Lieutenant shows heroic courage in meeting misfortune: "*. . . he does not bend in adversity*. He was Hamsun's romantic hero, in disguise. In his helplessness and desolation he showed his true face."[19]

Though *Segelfoss Town* is a sequel to *Children of the Age*, it is a very different kind of novel. A study of small-town life rather than the story of a marriage, its narrative is laid out spatially, time serving less as a medium of action than of displacement. And whereas *Children* has a time span of several decades, that of *Segelfoss Town*, a book that is longer by a third, extends over less than a year, from spring to the following fall. Its scope, in terms of the number of important characters, is much larger, encompassing several families and their complex interrelationships. While it is not a cross-section novel, with systematic cutting back and forth between different social classes and milieus, Hamsun must have intended to produce an encompassing sense of a specific place or historical moment. The portrayals of families as well as individuals clearly aim at offering a global vision-cum-moral critique of a typical Norwegian small town at the beginning of the twentieth century. The time, 1904, is indicated by a reference to the surrender of Port Arthur during the Russo-Japanese War (VI: 305).

Like so many of Hamsun's novels, *Segelfoss Town* is a hybrid work combining elements of several novelistic genres: a period novel as well as a novel of small-town life, it also possesses major characteristics of what the Russians call *bytovoi roman*, the novel of everyday life. To the extent that these elements blend into an aesthetic whole, the cohesive agent is Hamsun's ironic vision of life and human behavior. That vision caused him to depict major developments of the new century—accelerating economic modernization, an ever-expanding capitalism, growing democracy, and a labor movement beginning to flex its muscles—in a spirit of withering satire. However lively and amusing at times, the result can be extremely unfair, with blatantly biased portrayals and an authorial stance influenced by unseemly prejudice.

Life in Segelfoss in 1904 is no longer dominated either by the Holmsens or the Holmengrås. Instead, the foreground is occupied by the families of Lars Manuelsen and Per Shopkeeper. Starting as cotters or poor peasants/fishermen, Lars and Per have risen to a kind of respectability, Lars as the proud father of two successful sons and an eye-catching daughter, Daverdana, Per as the owner of a country store. As Hamsun depicts them, these families may be compared to Faulkner's Poor Whites, the Snopeses. The dominant passion of Lars and Per is greed; acquisitiveness determines their every human relation. This trait is humorously symbolized by a magpie motif, which Hamsun exploits both thematically and structurally. His use of the motif, that of a "noisy bird . . . which often picks up and takes to its nest small bright objects,"[20] is slanted toward the popular notion of the "gazza ladra," the thieving magpie, and influenced by a Sami belief that the magpie avenges itself if wronged: a first offence, as in the case of Lars, who destroys a magpie's nest and kills its young, brings a seven-months-long revenge, a close approximation to the novel's time span.

The magpie is central to Hamsun's evocation of the moral substance of Segelfoss society; however, it is a highly ambiguous or multivalent motif. First associated with Per Shopkeeper (VI: 216), a shortchanging, shortweighting grocer from *Children of the Age* who lingers on as an insufferable domestic tyrant in the sequel, it functions as a quasi-Wagnerian leitmotif in the story of that sanctimonious crook Lars Manuelsen. Whenever Lars appears, the magpies persecute him with their noisy chatter, eventually alerting some villagers to his nefarious activities. Hamsun consistently describes the magpies in anthropomorphic terms; in the opinion of "old Katrina," wife of Bertel, Holmengrå's steadiest worker, they could be an example to people: "God has given the magpie such a cheerful disposition," she used to say, "so that we should look at her and feel contented, too" (245). After Lars has robbed and destroyed the nest near his house, the victims take refuge at Bertel and Katrina's place. Katrina was not the sort of person who would "deny shelter to a traveling pair of magpies . . ., regardless of the pair's nationality" (282), Hamsun writes. The idyllic picture of this kindly couple, whose relationship to their fellow creatures contrasts so sharply with that of Lars Manuelsen, holds out the sweet possibility of peaceful coexistence between humans and the animal creation. When Lars closes out this possibility by going to war against the magpies, on suspicion that they have stolen his eyeglasses, they turn into a flock of avenging Furies.

To understand the complicated nature of magpie justice in Segelfoss, we need to know more about the consequences of Lars Manuelsen's war against his fellow creatures. A storehouse key has been missed for several months at Holmengrå's place. When Lars robs the magpie's nest, he finds, instead of his glasses, a small key, which he "put carefully in his pocket" (VI: 259). Here the magpie is no longer the cheerful harbinger of a happier state; on the contrary, it reveals itself as a petty larcenist. When Lars Manuelsen lets himself into Holmengrå's storehouse with that key one evening, at a time when most of the villagers are attending Mr. Rasch's garden party, he sets the stage for a veritable epidemic of shenanigans and petty crime. Soon the delicacies he has stolen are discovered on the tables at Larsen's Hotel, owned by his son Julius, to the gastronomic delight of the guests. As word of the scandal spreads, Reverend L. Lassen, Lars Manuelsen's famous son, rushes home from the capital to stop the rumor mills. But his intervention is neither needed nor appreciated. His father feels quite safe, confident that his victim, Tobias Holmengrå, will not have him arrested: Holmengrå is still carrying on with Daverdana, Lars's redhaired daughter married to Holmengrå's dock clerk.

It almost looks as though Hamsun had a chart of the seven deadly sins before him as he was writing *Segelfoss Town*; they are all richly represented in the book. However, instead of appearing in their traditional Christian sense as grounds for damnation, they signify the seedy moral reality of a money-grubbing society. Nowhere is this seen more shockingly than in the story of Florina, whose calculating insolence is a worthy rival to Lars Manuelsen's naked cunning. Though she is a mere servant, Mr. Rasch's housemaid, Hamsun uses her to build a web of intrigue that eventually involves a wide segment of Segelfoss society. Seduced by Rasch, she simulates pregnancy, whereupon he presents her with a bank book, ostensibly to make her a good catch and to seal her lips. Meanwhile her sweetheart, a sailor or fisherman called Nils, becomes suspicious, having heard rumors that she had strayed from the strait and narrow during his three-months absence. After a lovers' quarrel, Florina boards the ship of a visiting business colleague of Theodor Shopkeeper, son of Per, a master philanderer called Didriksen who is throwing a party on board. Despite her one-night stand with this playboy, she keeps up the pressure on the attorney, who, accused tearfully of having "picked her flower," adds another sum to her bank account. The narrator comments: "Florina the maid was certainly not helpless, she had developed along with Segelfoss town..." (VI: 251).

One begins to suspect that Hamsun is portraying the morality of the entire town as that of a blackmailing whore, a suspicion that is confirmed by subsequent events. Florina repeats her trick with Didriksen, the womanizing businessman, who is not unwilling to buy her off. At this point Theodor Shopkeeper becomes a party to the intrigue, advising Didriksen to refuse dispensing any money until the child arrives. It is decided that Theodor will hold the money in escrow; in the meantime we see him using, and profiting from, the not insubstantial sum. This arrangement, however, does not suit Florina, who informs Didriksen's fiancée of his philandering. Nevertheless, Didriksen authorizes Theodor to pay Florina the sum of 1,000 kroner. This payment, witnessed by Julius Manuelsen, the hotel keeper, turns the latter into an instant suitor for Florina's hand. The story of Florina ends as follows: "Florina the maid became rich, she had a bank book and oodles of money and finally married Julius" (VI: 446).

The moralistic treatment of casual sex in this novel marks a change from Hamsun's major fiction of the 1890s and the following decade. In *Pan* youthful lust forms part of the novel's tragic action, in *Dreamers, Rosa,* and *Under the Autumn Star,* sexual promiscuity chiefly assumes a comic or burlesque character. Whichever literary mode prevails, casual sex is seen as an integral part of life. In *Segelfoss Town,* on the other hand, it is indicative of moral corruption; a compound motif of sex and money pervades the novel. The corrupting element is obviously money, linked for Hamsun with a repellent and ever-expanding commercialism: in the society that he depicts everything will soon be for sale. Whereas Mack could get away with his serial harem, and Knut Pedersen showed no sign of a bad conscience after his tumble in the hay with the parson's wife, Florina and those involved with her are seen as morally tainted. Sexual escapades like those of old Holmengrå and others are not just described as unseemly in themselves; being associated with blackmail, they turn into negative symbols of a way of life and a form of society for which Hamsun feels a profound dislike, even contempt. Sexual behavior has become a vehicle of moral satire. The only ones who are spared Hamsun's withering criticism are the aristocrats, a few workers and servants who know their place, and that unworldly cynic Bårdsen, Hamsun's raisonneur in *Segelfoss Town.*

A less scandalous shortcoming of Segelfoss culture is an old theme in Hamsun's work: an overriding quest for status. Whereas a blue blood like Lieutenant Holmsen in *Children of the Age* felt secure in his social identity, having found his values within himself or in his ancestral tradition, most of the characters in *Segelfoss Town* look to others for confirmation of who, or what, they are. Even the officials and professionals, such as Dr. Muus and Mr. Rasch, who possess "inherited culture" and are proud of it, are sensitive to any diminution of their presumptive social preeminence. This becomes evident when they bristle at the spreading local custom of displaying the national flag at every possible opportunity. Seeming unaware that as social mobility increases, status symbols are bound to multiply, Rasch complains over wine at Holmengrå's about all the new flags in town, while finding it quite reasonable that he and his peers, who were "born with flags, so to speak" (VI: 304), should be entitled to display them. By way of protest against the democratization of this custom, the doctor has stopped flying his flag.

The *reductio ad absurdum* of the other-directed mentality manifested by Mr. Rasch and Dr. Muus occurs in a passage that ridicules their ambition to combine modernity with their old culture. We are told that "Rasch was by no means simply an inherited entity, period; he and Dr. Muus were also absorbing certain trifles of modernity, as long as they could be reconciled with the faultless taste they were born with." The example given of what they had picked up, a new way of handling one's knife at table observed by Dr. Muus while dining with a traveling salesman on the packet boat, is absurd to the point of fatuity: holding one's knife like a penholder. After some practice the doctor "grew more and more adept at cutting his meat with a penholder." Shortly the attorney learns the trick from Dr. Muus and tries to pass it on to his unteachable wife, formerly Miss Salvesen, Lieutenant Holmsen's one-time housekeeper. The irony of the situation is compounded by Dr. Muus's disappointment when he sees "his art in the hands of the attorney; God only knows whether a man who ate so much and had such thick, stubby fingers could be of good family. When the attorney claimed to have a sensitive stomach, it was doubtless just affectation; Dr. Muus, on the other hand, had a genuinely weak stomach after many generations of refined ancestors" (VI: 358–59).

Mr. Rasch and Dr. Muus are contemptible snobs, guarding their class privileges. Thus, Rasch resents having to compete with Theodor Shopkeeper—Theodor Jensen as he calls himself after his business has begun to flourish—for a leadership role in town. Not that Theodor is without flaws; in fact, he is Hamsun's most egregious example of a status seeker in *Segelfoss Town*. Some of his attempts to impress people are quite ludicrous, such as his ostentatious way of dressing, cultivating a form of speech replete with commercial jargon and foreign phrases, and flashing big bills in front of his customers. Yet, one feels sympathy for the bright, well-meaning young man, who started out in life with no cultural ballast. Theodor is dependent on others for his values and for an ideal by which to shape his behavior. He finds, for example, that his frivolous friend Didriksen possesses some "valuable qualities" simply on the strength of being a "scion of a fine old commercial firm," while he himself had to shed his heritage and "imitate what good he could find in others" (VI: 330). Learning where to find that "good" can be quite difficult. His principal slogan, repeated over and over in the text, runs as follows: we must do things the way they are done in other towns. This applies in particular to his public activities, in which he wants to outshine Mr. Rasch, the attorney. Whether it is a matter of modernizing his business practices, promoting community projects—a dance hall, a local cinema, visits by a traveling theater troupe—or even having fireworks at an island party that he throws, the guiding principle is always one of, to put it crudely, keeping up with the Joneses—those in other towns. The absurdity of Theodor's cardinal rule stands out clearly from the following sentence: when he greets someone, he takes off his hat "just as they do in other towns" (321).

Hamsun concludes the status motif on a macabre note and in a way that involves nearly everyone in Segelfoss. When Theodor puts up a metal cross and a railing on his father's grave, repeating his mantra, modified for the occasion, "Because we must have it the way other cemeteries do," his action leads to "excesses," a veritable "grave cult," an "epidemic." Soon metal is replaced by stone monuments, as the townspeople engage in a "noble rivalry" for the fanciest tombstone (VI: 443–44). Thus, the status motif, so central to the Segelfoss ethos, ends up companioned with death, and death in turn means increased prosperity as Theodor develops a flourishing business in tombstones.

Greed, whether for money or for a flattering self-image, is a hallmark of the new society that Hamsun describes. One character, Per Shopkeeper, the very man whose death leads to the bizarre rash of one-upmanship just discussed, incarnates that greed in an absolutized form: though permanently bedridden, he harbors an unquenchable desire for longevity. Like Swift in his account of the Struldbruggs in *Gulliver's Travels*, Hamsun shows the fatuity of such an ambition. What is more, the description of Per's decaying flesh, in its extreme naturalism reminiscent of Hamsun's nauseating picture of the parish paupers in *Benoni* and *Rosa*, parallels the moral decline that Hamsun traces in Segelfoss society. As in Aldous Huxley's *After Many a Summer Dies the Swan* (1939), whose title is taken from Tennyson's "Tithonus," the dream of eternal life results in devolution: "he [Per] was hastening back to his deep past, to the cave, . . . the roar, and the sudden assault" (VI: 332).

Yet Per is not wholly contemptible; he is "bestial," sure, but he can "roar," and a man who roars cannot be ignored. Hamsun's portrayal of Per is bifocal, alternating between low and high burlesque. While becoming more and more animal-like, Per reacts against his physical helplessness — one side of his body is paralyzed — by gestures of omnipotence, infantile though they may be: he is engaged in "a battle with the impossible" (V: 416), and he "speaks as though . . . to the elements, to the ocean and the thunder" (324). But despite his epic struggle, Per does not elicit our sympathy. Neither comic, pathetic or tragic, he approaches the grotesque. His raucous rebellion against mortality forms a sort of ground bass in the cacophony of Segelfoss life.

One element that is associated with Per Shopkeeper introduces a touch of mystery and a hint of a transcendent perspective. As in *Children of the Age*, swans are present in *Segelfoss Town*, but what they signify is anything but clear. Though the reader may find this frustrating, the presence of the swans does add a not unwelcome enigmatic quality to a work of fiction glutted with the accumulated detritus of ordinary lives. During the short winter days Per would lie "in the dark listening to the song of the swans far away, . . . an uncanny song. . . . It sounded like sheets of iron moving in the wind, church vanes turning, heavy gates swinging on their hinges, whoo! Why the hell do those wild birds have to scream like that?" (VI: 204–05). When Reverend Lassen visits Per to prepare him for communion, the old man complains that the swans "shrieked so terribly and frightened him; they were baneful birds, whoo. . ." (418). The association of the singing swan with dying may by itself explain Per's terror, but Hamsun's usage of the symbol could have been influenced by Norse mythology. Thus the Norns, goddesses of fate, would disguise themselves as swans, and the same applies to the Valkyries; in fact, "in many religions the swan acts as psychopomp, accompanying the souls of the dead . . . to the . . . Other World."[21] The fact that Reverend Lassen refers to swans as "those white God's creatures" and praises the posthumous poem entitled *Swansong*[22] by the eighteenth-century Danish poet Brorson, confirms the religio-mythical meaning of the symbol as here used.

The remaining instances of the swan symbol in *Segelfoss Town* involve Bårdsen, the telegraph manager, Per's diametrical opposite: "Life and death had become of equal value to him, it made him feel light." He tells Nils Shoemaker: you and I "do not sit at the center of the cosmic enigma like two great lights, but like darkness with darkness, at one with it, at home and blessed" (VI: 438). He hears the swans on the evening of Didriksen's party, which he has just left: "It was quiet on the little paths between the houses, the small town had gone to sleep, the swans were singing far away." Bårdsen has just overheard a lovers' quarrel between Florina and her young man; she boards the ship, seemingly in spite. The swan motif reappears after her sweetheart makes a race for the ship but misses it: "The swans are singing far away as before" (227-28). Since the motif is not elaborated, one can only come up with more or less reasonable guesses as to what it might stand for: a world of nature, or even the supernatural, from which the inhabitants of Segelfoss have become alienated? It certainly represents an order that is indifferent to human purposes; this is quite evident from the phrase "as before" in the allusion to the singing swans: individual happiness is of no importance in the grand scheme of things.

The context of Hamsun's last use of the swan motif is Lars Manuelsen's bringing a neighbor to Holmengrå's newly dug cellar, also called a "diamond cave" (VI: 428), after discovering Bårdsen's dead body there. The reader knows that Bårdsen's death was largely self-induced; the two men do not know that. To them, the death presents a riddle to be solved. But they are "big with the news. They talk and talk as they walk along: he was sitting in the cellar, he was dead—everybody gets to know it, they listen, think about it, and move on to their daily tasks. Then there is nothing more. And in the south the swans are singing" (447). It is a haunting conclusion, lifting the reader into another sphere—one of purity, beauty, mystery, and death.

Finally, the swans may, as in *Children*, be Hamsun's last echo of the elegant old life at Segelfoss, before the hustle and bustle of modern life altered everything. For beneath the satire of *Segelfoss Town* runs an undercurrent of nostalgic pathos: the memory of the old order is still very much alive. Thus, young Willatz strongly defends his father's aristocratic values and debunks the so-called "inherited culture" boasted by Rasch and Dr. Muus. According to Willatz, officials or civil servants live on "foreign soil, in other people's houses," and their offspring have their roots torn up, to "trail behind them" whenever their families move to a more attractive district (VI: 308). But however deeply young Willatz admires and tries to embody his father's aristocratic values, the old order is irretrievable. Aware of his ambiguous position in regard to the family tradition, the young man occasionally envisages himself as the last member of a dying breed (307). Not only is he absent from Norway for long periods of time, but when he visits Segelfoss he devotes the time to his music. Anton Coldevin tells his friend and rival: "You are simply administering your father's posthumous grandeur" (345); he accuses him of "aping" the Lieutenant and declares him to be "nothing" by himself (340–41). To this extent Anton is right: if young Willatz will ever fulfill his mission in life, it will not be as an absentee squire, however reverential of his ancestral heritage, but as an artist.

Unlike Lieutenant Holmsen in *Children of the Age*, Tobias Holmengrå lacks the ability to command, and yet he, too, is enveloped in a haze of nostalgia in *Segelfoss Town*. He occupies in this novel a position similar to that of the Lieutenant in *Children of the Age*: he is a leader. At the same time, the varying success of his enterprises invites skepticism, with the result that the very concept of leadership is undermined, deconstructed so to speak. In Hamsun's world, true leadership requires a distinct aura or mystique, deriving either from one's class standing, as in the case of Holmsen, or from assumed fabulous wealth, as in that of "King Tobias," a wealth which, in the popular imagination, is equated with princely or royal status. However, unlike the Lieutenant, whose charisma never abandons him despite an increasing financial dependence on Holmengrå, the latter risks losing his preeminence at a mere hint of business slowdown or other difficulty. His image fluctuates from that of king and fairy-tale hero to a poor old man bent with age, from "miracle man" to a nobody (VI: 273, 238): "Things were fine as long as he was king and a myth . . .; afterwards they went awry. . ." (351). Yet, subsequent to Holmengrå's bankruptcy, it becomes clear to his next-generation successor, Theodor Jensen, that Holmengrå "had sustained everything" at Segelfoss (436).

The irrational basis of leadership is shown even more clearly through Theodor, who consciously strives to create a persona that elicits admiration and public respect, but to no avail. Whatever miracles of newfangled products or entertainments he pulls off, he cannot attain the authority of a Holmsen or Holmengrå's legendary mystery. This character type is not new in Hamsun's work: Theodor is a more extreme version of Hamsun's rags to riches motif, so memorably embodied in Benoni some half a dozen years earlier. Theodor is brighter and more enterprising than Benoni, but he is equally naive. Knowing the poverty and ignorance of his family background, one understands his absurd proclivity to show off and brag, another characteristic of the *nouveau riche* also found in Benoni. Like Benoni, too, Theodor aspires to something higher than mere material wealth, as shown in his enduring fascination with Mariane, Holmengrå's exotic daughter. Again, we are in familiar territory, one that Hamsun never tires of revisiting: a social upstart's dream of transcending his modest status as a money-grubber by means of a classy marriage. But this time it somehow did not suit Hamsun's purpose to award the "princess" to a common man. The reason may be found in a refusal to draw the logical consequences of his own socioeconomic vision.

Hamsun's conception of history in the two Segelfoss novels is a pastiche of secular and Biblical myth. Even a cursory reading of *Children of the Age* and *Segelfoss Town* will reveal, in regional miniature, a pattern of decline, as a basically feudal order succumbs to capitalistic enterprise, followed in turn by a consumerist mass society in which all are "equally small" (VI: 268). The central idea behind this development is not essentially different from Daniel's interpretation of Nebuchadnezzar's dream of the "great image,"[23] or the Ovidian story of the Four Ages. But in the resolution of the novel's love plot, Hamsun contravenes his own pessimistic model of historical change.

That resolution does, indeed, look like a fictional protest against the classic downward spiral. The imminent union of Mariane and Willatz, Jr., at the end of the novel has the appearance of a *ricorso*, a reflux that is denied by the historical reality depicted in the novel.

In any case, the marriage provides romantic solace to those readers who find Hamsun's picture of Segelfoss society to be on the bleak side. This consolatory effect is heightened by the fact that, for a long time, the relationship between the Norwegian blue blood and his beloved, a mestiza, is getting nowhere, while Mariane has a bevy of eager bidders for her hand: beside Theodor, there are the Sheriff, Reverend Lassen, Dr. Muus, and Anton Coldevin. No wonder Willatz feels invaded by a "terrible, restless jealousy," which strangely enough is given a positive role in the development of the young artist. The immediate impression is of a stand-off in their relations, not unlike the strained marital situation of Adelheid and Willatz, Sr., of which the young couple seem to enact a premarital variant, with a lesser charge of passion and commitment. Neither the love nor the art of the younger generation goes beyond the commonplace: to Willatz, Mariane is muse as well as an object of desire; he has been tormented by a "desperate unproductiveness," and when the "wave" of inspiration finally comes, he feels it may be due to his longtime "seething" jealousy of Anton Coldevin (VI: 393, 395).

The linkage of sex and creativity casts doubt on the depth of both. It is worth noting that the "eruption" of Willatz's creative flow is immediately preceded by a dream of sexual power. Observing a rooster in the barnyard, that "glorious warrior bird with a knife on each leg," Willatz reflects: "look, there he gets love and treads his wing and walks sideways. . . . Then he returns to being in command and strides across the yard like a god" (VI: 394). Willatz's macho thinking is transparent; no wonder the meetings of the lovers are permeated with disputes, since Mariane—who is portrayed as a primitive—can stand her ground with anyone. Incidentally, she is associated with time-honored misogynistic symbols: thus, during a lovers' quarrel, a silver fork in her hair is called a "serpent's tongue" (277). One understands the young man's hesitation. His sudden reversal, conveyed through a "forceful and senseless" telegram in which he asks her to "take him as he was," without the opera he is at work on being finished, comes as a surprise.

One can only conclude that Hamsun's heart was neither in the love story nor in his exploration of the creative process. The latter is conveyed far more vividly in a well-known, much shorter passage in Hamsun's first novel, *Hunger*.[24] It looks as though the main purpose served by Willatz and Mariane has little to do with who they are and what they stand for; they are there to provide a happy ending, allowing the genteel past to be repeated: instead of leaving Segelfoss forever, Holmengrå—who by this time must be getting hoary with age—can look forward to returning there to the end of his days as a guest of his daughter, the future mistress of the Castle.

Trying to locate a set of values or point of view that melds the myriad situations, scenes, and characters of *Segelfoss Town* into an artistic unity is not an easy task. The narrator is little help; while not unreliable in the usual sense of the word, he is extremely volatile, at times speaking in his own persona, at other times identifying with a character: to wit, a perfectly normal Hamsunian narrative stance. The closest approximation to an overarching perspective is offered by a character who has already been mentioned in another context, namely Bårdsen, telegraph manager and an amateur cello player, the only member of Segelfoss society with a general philosophy of life.

Bårdsen does have forerunners in Hamsun's fiction, in respect to his *Weltanschauung*, lifestyle, and strange suicide, principally Nagel and Nikolai Arentsen. Like Nagel, he shows compassion for the poor and downtrodden, and like both he acts out his last will before making his exit. He also resembles Nikolai in being a drunkard and a wit: though his view of humanity could scarcely be more disenchanted, he expresses it in a colorful language spiked with mordant irony and cynical bravado. On the other hand, his profound resignation recalls Lighthouseman Schøning in *Rosa*, who tells Parelius that "life must be treated like a woman. Shouldn't we be chivalrous toward life and let it win against us?"[25] Speaking to Nils Shoemaker about the fates of Roman citizens forced to commit suicide, Bårdsen lauds their "noble and courteous conduct vis-à-vis superior power"; to "defend themselves against death—no fear!" Then he adds, "In a hundred years nobody will remember us anyway" (VI: 437–38).[26] His indifference to worldly success and to playing the social game, expressed through his refusal "to make anything of himself" (402), looks forward to another memorable Hamsun hero, Abel Brodersen of *The Ring Is Closed*.

The uniqueness of Bårdsen as compared to the above-mentioned characters, apart from his large frame and shabby appearance, is his wholesale condemnation of modern life, rooted in a spiritual passion that culminates in a deadly hunger strike. "Our life has been derailed," he declares to Didriksen, "it has become ridiculous," an "imitation of living"; "the destiny" of old has been replaced by "the daily wage" (VI: 222). The inauthentic, sham quality Bårdsen ascribes to Segelfoss existence makes his lengthy attacks on the theater assume symbolic meaning: "The so-called art of acting is shamming by formula" (401), he reflects after a meeting with Miss Clara, member of a visiting troupe of actors. Bårdsen himself cultivates detachment and undertakes to teach it to poor Nils Shoemaker, who has been deprived of his livelihood by factory-made shoes. Dismissed from his position as telegraph manager, Bårdsen preaches what looks like a gospel of Oriental quietism. He tells Nils: "the sages of India also starve themselves in order to become white and clear inside, then they see salvation. You may be sure, Nils, that you and I are on the right track" (438). By this time Bårdsen, who was stabbed by Miss Clara when she tried out a switchblade he had given her for a prop, knows it is "all up" with him. But he feels invulnerable: "he had touched bottom. Misfortunes could come, why not, he would cheat them of every triumph" (438–39). Though Bårdsen's death is the result of neglect and abstention from food, in a deeper sense he dies as a victim of the new society. The fact that he is found dead in the "diamond cave," dug in a final mystifying gesture by the initiator of modernity, Holmengrå, confers upon him the status of a *pharmakos*.

It remains to examine a prominent feature of Hamsun's narrative strategy in *Segelfoss Town* and its impact on the novel's structural integrity. What I have in mind in the first instance is mainly the use of visual and auditory motifs that trigger thought or consciousness, thereby allowing the characters to be portrayed indirectly and the story to tell itself, so to speak. This strategy is seen in exemplary fashion in Virginia Woolf's *Mrs. Dalloway* (1925), where a motor car, an airplane, and Big Ben act as springboards of reflection or rumination. In *Segelfoss Town*, two such consciousness triggers stand out: the flag and the magpies.

Nostalgic Myth and Critique of Modernity

I have discussed the flag as a theme with social implications previously. What interests me here is the way Hamsun uses it to help give coherence to his narrative. The novel begins with the question, "A man on the new Flag Hill, what does he want there?" With everyone trying to find the answer, this sentence propels the reader into the midst of everyday life at Segelfoss. It provides a chance to introduce the characters, present expository material, and produce exchanges that delineate the town's mental horizon. At the end of the first chapter the text returns to Flag Hill. But though the identity of the scout is now known — he is Theodor's store clerk — the initial question is not answered, and the same technique is also used in Chapter Two. Before the narrative possibilities of the flag motif are exhausted, over thirty pages of text have been produced. Though the flag never loses its thematic significance, it is shortly replaced by the magpie as a trigger of thought, with hilarious comic-satiric effects that are sustained to the very end of the novel.

At the beginning of my discussion of *Segelfoss Town*, I referred to the novel's loose structure. There is no central plot, nor is a clear pattern of some other kind readily perceptible. The near absence of formal awareness is revealed at almost every transition from one scene to the next, from one character to another: the most tenuous relation — of contiguity, similarity, instrumentality, what not — will do to effect a transition. As a result, there is usually no clear or meaningful aesthetic relationship between incidents and events — things just happen. Apparently Hamsun was largely content to present the phenomena of life in their chaotic flux, without trying to create meaning through the relations of part to whole, or even part to part.[27] His cavalier treatment of time is a case in point, implying an attitude of formal indifference. This attitude is so general that an exception is worth noting. An eloquent instance of explicit simultaneity occurs in the chapter depicting Mr. Rasch's garden party. The chapter, the first part of which consists of some seven pages describing the elegant event, begins with a reference to the noise the magpie is making at Holmengrå's house, then repeats the magpie motif after the burglary at Holmengrå's is discovered (VI: 355, 362). While unstated, the meaning of the juxtaposition, with looping, of these two scenes is quite unambiguous. For though Rasch is clever enough to evade the obloquy of a magpie, his morals are no better than those of Lars Manuelsen, the magpie's sworn enemy.

It is in this context of formal nonchalance that the leitmotifs used in *Segelfoss Town* acquire significance. They provide the novel with a minimal structure, one based on repetition. This structure is reenforced by a pervasive rhythm, one of disillusionment, shaping some of the most important scenes in the novel: the flag scene already discussed; Rasch's garden party; Theodor's island bash; the second, unlucky visit of the actors; and the discovery of Bårdsen's body in the "diamond cave."

The novel opens on a note of great expectation. The hoisted flag evidently announces the imminent arrival of a visitor, a noteworthy event in this isolated town. Though the townspeople are seemingly impressed even after the secret is out, namely, that Theodor is expecting a salesman or agent, the reader senses an ironic intent in Hamsun's handling of the entire situation: one wonders what all the fuss was about. The treatment of Mr. Rasch's party provides clearer cues: however decorous, at least on the surface, its aftermath produces a disillusioning epiphany. Parties, like all ritual events, are expected to go off smoothly, without a hitch. True, no full-scale scene of scandal occurs, yet the party ends in a rather scandalous way: *Segelfoss News* could report that, after the garden festivities, "no fewer than 18 hairpins were found near the shrubberies. . ." (VI: 362). While the sly humor cannot be missed, the news poorly befits the gentility of an "old family of officials" (358). Theodor's party is doubly disillusioning, ending not only with Anton Coldevin's attempted rape of Mariane, who stabs him in the process, but with humiliation for Theodor, the host, when Mariane—the princess whose favor he hoped to gain by the elaborate affair—refuses to accept the expensive handkerchief he offers her in token of his love.

One comes to feel, further, that the rhythm of the entire work is one of profound disillusion. The expectant beginning looks forward to a new coming, an advent; the traveling salesman is the bearer of good tidings, an avatar of total consumer satisfaction. Not surprisingly, Hamsun places a couple of allusions to paradise in the book. One pertains to the "spectacular advertising signs" Theodor has received from the factory; these "made the front of the store look like a paradise on earth" (VI: 320). Such religious echoes are not new in Hamsun; one need only recall the repeated mention of young Willatz as a Christmas child in *Children of the Age*. Finally, the discovery of

Bårdsen's body is a possible allusion to the New Testament, specifically John 20, which relates the visit of Simon Peter and John to the sepulchre. Even details seem to have been reproduced, such as the hesitations of John to enter the sepulchre: frightened by the sight of the dead man, Lars Manuelsen withdraws and only enters the cave again together with Ole Johan. The biblical allusion seems quite justified in view of Bårdsen's spiritual revolt, a revolt that gives him the air of a mock Christ figure. That he is an enemy rather than an emissary of the new business civilization does not nullify the symbolic charge of the novel's conclusion: the discovery of the dead body in a vault, replacing the risen Christ, does not bode well for Theodor Jensen's dream of a "paradise on earth," founded on commerce and consumer satisfaction.

These touches of a presumably intuitive structural imagination are very welcome in a novel as flaccid and discursive as *Segelfoss Town*. That cannot be said about Hamsun's penchant to editorialize, whether by means of his narrator or the characters. In particular, his portrayal of workers and actors leaves ugly stains of meanness and prejudice on a work that often exudes hilarious comedy and fine irony. The "Aslak spirit" (VI: 350), named for a slacker, typifies the attitude of the whole mass of workers as portrayed in this novel: "Their inclination is that of the proletarian, . . . their jaws are always open for more, more" (430). No wonder Holmengrå is hard pressed to handle a work force consisting mainly of Aslaks.

While Hamsun's discriminatory portrayal of the workers is bad enough, his treatment of actors is truly shameful. It is the more so in that the vehicle of his opinions is Bårdsen, whose easygoing disposition could hardly be less suitable for such a task. Max, the most visible actor, is called "abnormal, . . . jealous as a eunuch of everybody" (VI: 403), and Miss Clara is equated with her role in a play the troupe performs, "The Poisonous Snake in Its Cave." Not only does she seduce the infatuated Bårdsen, but through the play with the switchblade she contributes to his physical decline and death. The savage criticism of the acting profession through Bårdsen looks like a throwback to the didactic strain of *Shallow Soil*, with its denunciation of the Bohème movement. Hamsun knew perfectly well what he was doing. He congratulates himself on having given those involved with theater the benefit of his opinions, "which I hope," he says in a letter, "will leave a small mark of my teeth."[28] In another letter he admits that the opinions expressed in the book were "singular."[29] They are also singularly disturbing.

The reviewers do not seem to have been greatly affected by these unfair portrayals. The reception of *Segelfoss Town* was extremely positive. Thus, Carl Nærup's review is rhapsodic, done in the form of hyperboles: he resorts to epithets like a "glorious Noah's ark" and a "Tolstoyan prose epic" to do justice to it. A book "so singularly great and unassuming, so lavishly rich and original, has no peer in what is written in today's Europe."[30] Another Norwegian reviewer named it Hamsun's "richest" and "deepest" book, and Sven Lange, Hamsun's Danish friend, rated it above *Mysteries*.[31] Somewhat surprisingly, another Dane, Poul Levin, who also handed out high praise, found it to be a "firmly constructed work."[32] Edwin Muir is more believable when he calls it comedy "in the grand style. . . . Such abundance of invention, with such sureness of grasp, such soundness, is almost incredible in our literature today."[33]

CHAPTER SEVEN

Growth of the Soil: Primitivist Epic or Utopian Fantasy?

Markens grøde (1917; *Growth of the Soil*, 1920) and *The Last Joy*, published five years earlier, make up volume seven of Hamsun's collected works. Though this violates the chronological order, in that the two Segelfoss novels appeared in between, the publisher's decision is understandable: Hamsun's agricultural novel looks very much like a full-scale version of the concluding section of *The Last Joy*, with its celebration of fecundity and the simple life. Even the main characters are alike. Isak, the central figure of *Growth*, physically resembles the bear-like Nikolai Palm, and harelipped Inger, his wife, recalls Ingeborg with her missing tooth. That the narrative is laced with a good dosage of anti-urban gall also follows the pattern laid down in the earlier work.

Like so many of Hamsun's heroes, Isak comes out of nowhere; we know nothing about his past. This semantic emptiness is useful to Hamsun, allowing him to present him as an avatar of the pioneer, a figure whose story assumes an exemplary character, at least in Hamsun's conception of him. The first few sentences of the novel open up a broad perspective: "That long, long path across the moors, who has trodden it? Man, a human being, the first one who came here. There was no path before him" (VII: 145). Then, in the second paragraph, the individual man, Isak, is seen "walking north," looking for a place that lends itself to farming. This opening note of generality may give a clue to the author's intent: to provide a foundation myth for an agrarian society. That the story to be told is one of epic proportions is evident both from Hamsun's choice of hero and from the literary style. The hero, a hulk of a man whose appearance approaches the grotesque—he is likened to a "log with hands" attached to it and a "horrible water troll" (161, 149)—is a tower of strength who can cope with whatever challenge the wilderness puts in his way. With all his crude physicality, he is also, like Odysseus, a man of many devices, *polymetis*. And Hamsun portrays the life and achievements of his hero, as well as some of the other characters, in a style of equanimity that mixes high and low, the trivial and the tragic, in an all-encompassing synthesis. This is the book at its best. Its shortcomings—and there are many—become manifest once it is subjected to a critical examination.

An extended summary, with commentary, will help prepare the reader for such an examination. The setting is again North Norway, the time period the last several decades of the nineteenth century. The Nordland ambience is easily recognizable by the presence of Sami people; the relatively short distance between the coast and the Swedish border is an equally telltale sign. Beyond being a part of the local milieu, the Sami play a not unimportant role in the story, first as a means of communication, later as a supposedly uncanny influence, not unlike what we have seen in *Benoni* and *Rosa*. For example, when one day a woman turns up, her coming is obviously due to a wandering Sami having spread the word that Isak was in need of a housekeeper. Once Inger finds herself in Isak's rudimentary dwelling, however, nature takes over, but not until they have partaken of a ritual meal: "They entered the hut, ate of her food and drank his goat milk; then they made coffee, which she had brought in a bladder. They had a good time over the coffee before they went to bed. At night he got hungry for her and took her" (VII: 149). Both the action and the style possess an Old Testament simplicity.

The story is one of creating something out of nothing; one is not surprised to see Isak called the "lord of creation" (VII: 153). Isak and Inger—neither has a surname—vie for each other's admiration as Isak builds and works the land, while Inger tends the cattle and a growing family. Their everyday life is full of new experiences; the birth of the first calf is as miraculous as the birth of the first child. Some experiences may be new to the reader as well, such as the wedding ceremony and the baptism of their first-born being part of one and the same occasion. Afterwards everything was "in order, they had even made certain to be wed first, so the child could be legitimate" (162). Such quirky logic, which is not unusual in *Growth*, helps produce a lightness of tone that underscores the comic flavor of Hamsun's novel. The comedy is provided chiefly by Isak, whose mind has preserved some elements of magic thinking; he even believes he can influence the heavens by behaving in a certain way. Thus, during an extended period of drought, when they desperately need rain, Isak deliberately leaves some cut foliage ungarnered, though it was already dry. The authorial voice comments: "[M]aybe he did it on spec, trying to provoke the blue sky at the change of the moon" (164). The novel is studded with such episodes, in which the characters are engaged in a seriocomic battle against superior power.

A break in the even tenor of life at Sellanrå, as the farm is called, occurs with the birth of Inger's third child, a baby girl afflicted with a harelip like the mother. Having followed her usual strategy of sending Isak away so as to be alone at the delivery, Inger strangles the baby: "In the course of ten minutes the child was born and killed" (VII: 175). Shortly the little grave is discovered by Olinè, a remote relation of Inger's who drops by occasionally. With her quaint habit of citing Scripture at every turn, old Olinè, a peculiar blend of good and evil, is the most colorful character in the entire novel: ". . . no one could match her at mixing heaven and earth into a muddle of kindness and spite, chatter and poison" (308). Inger believes that the shock of seeing a hare during her pregnancy was the reason why the baby was born with a physical defect, and she accuses Olinè of being behind the visit of Os-Anders, a Sami, who unwrapped the dead hare to show it to Eleseus, her elder boy. A suspicion that Olinè has nosed out her terrible secret sends Inger into a towering rage, during which she knocks Olinè down and threatens to kill her. The fight is followed by streams of mutual abuse of virtuosic quality and ends with an ironic anticlimax: the prospect that Olinè will take Inger's place in the family after the expected arrest.

Inger's sentence to eight years in prison marks a turning point in the novel. While Isak grapples clumsily with Olinè, who will let no one have the last word, and teaches his two sons their ABC and various bits of folk wisdom—e. g., "that it was harder for a camel to enter heaven than for a human being to thread the eye of a needle" (VII: 200)—Inger receives a real education in the Trondhjem prison. By the time she is released through the intervention of Geissler, Isak's patron, she is quite a different person: trained as a seamstress, she now sees herself as having a "profession" (219) and takes great pride in her handiwork. Moreover, the surgical correction of her lip has greatly boosted her self-esteem. From being a woman whose only chance for fulfillment was to team up with an illiterate toiler like Isak, she has developed into a sophisticated individual with genteel manners, opinions of her own, and a heightened sexual awareness. Instead of simply telling him, "Come and get a bite to eat!" as she used to, she would now say, "Dinner is served, if you please," making Isak wonder whether "things weren't getting a bit too fancy" (216). More important, from a young doctor in Trondhjem she had learned that infanticide was no great crime, and there are hints that she had also picked up some knowledge of contraception. Having been deprived of a normal youth because of her blemish, she has an urge to catch up and is eager for adventure. With a crew of telegraph workers in the area, the opportunity offers. One night, after a dance at which she was hugely popular, being the only woman among some thirty men, she is discovered by Isak having a rendezvous with a young lineman. Later on, her susceptibility to temptation leads to an affair with a Swedish miner, Gustaf, whose departure she briefly mourns.

Ingeborg Torsen in *The Last Joy* undergoes a counter-development, from being an educated young lady to becoming a permanently pregnant farmer's wife. Inger's experience steers her in the opposite direction: curiously, her crime and ensuing imprisonment open up a new world to her, enabling the disadvantaged woman to attain a hitherto never-felt sense of self-worth. However, her sentimental education, which comes about through a change of scene, from country to city, as in a typical nineteenth-century novel, is treated by the authorial voice with scorn, as a process of corruption: she was a "strong and capable woman who had been warped by a long stay in an artificial atmosphere" (VII: 238). Inger's emotional life after the release from prison describes a seesaw, from worldliness to religion and back again, much like that of Edvarda in *Rosa*. It is as though she were expected to behave like a nun, not only sexually but in every other respect as well. For example, her siding with Eleseus, her son, who prefers city life to buying a farm, is seen as "worldliness":

"However it came about, his mother was converted, carried away, oh, she was still so little sure of herself. The world got hold of her so easily. Last winter she had been reading a certain excellent devotional book that she had received when she left the institution in Trondhjem, and now!" (277). But eventually she comes around, letting Isak know how sorry she feels for not having been as she "should" toward him, whereupon she resumes her "devotions" (336-37).

This to-and-fro pattern is supplemented by a metaphor of seasonal change, which ascribes her fling with Gustaf to a flare-up of "autumnal ardor" (VII: 332). Toward the end of the novel, Inger allegedly has no longer any "ardor" to fritter away, "no private wildness to keep under control; winter had cooled her off, what remained of ardor was for household use. . . ." It looks as though she has finally reached an ideal state, judging by these words: ". . . she had begun to be somewhat filled out, handsome, stately" (380-81). Supposedly, she has now attained the rank of a "vestal," which is the final image of Inger left with the reader (397).

The dichotomy of rusticity and citification, of pastoral simplicity and urban sophistication, which in Inger's case causes a painful conflict, is perpetuated in the sons. Sivert, the younger, is a man of the soil like his father, whereas Eleseus, who experienced city living at an early age, finds country life to be dull and confining. The former is treated as a positive hero, but lacking the larger-than-life stature and the amusing oddities of his father, he engages the reader less than Eleseus, who is a conflicted modern man. It is no wonder that Kafka's interest in *Growth of the Soil* was centered on the fate of Eleseus, who in the end fails to find a place for himself in his native country and emigrates to America.[1]

Eleseus' predicament is described in similar terms as his mother's after her release from prison: he was "rather warped and quietly ruined; he wasn't bad but a little spoiled" (VII: 278). The portrait drawn of him shortly before his departure for America differs little from that of the actors in *Segelfoss Town*. Thus, his apparent lack of interest in women after failing to make an impression on Barbro, a local floozy, brings the following comment: "Maybe he never had any sexual drive to speak of, since he is now a regular good-for-nothing." With his "thin clerical hands and a woman's love of finery," any mustache he decided to grow would not be "particularly brutal." As with his mother, the "artificial atmosphere" seems to be blamed, turning him into a "changeling." "Did he become so diligent in the office or the store that all his original nature was lost? Perhaps so" (383). In any case, he is someone to be pitied, if we listen to the voice of the narrator; he is "so frittered away, . . . without initiative, without depth." The young man appears to be "doomed," as though some injury had "permeated his entire being. Perhaps that kind district engineer from the city shouldn't have discovered him when he was a child and taken him into his home to make something of him; the boy had his roots torn, no doubt, and so came to no good" (386-87). One notes the botanical metaphor, which Hamsun finds so appealing, as though human beings are by nature stuck in the ground, like plants.[2]

But whatever fault one may find with Hamsun's works after his mid-fifties, superficiality is not one. There is an almost Jamesian thoroughness in the way he "does" a subject,[3] though admittedly in a highly un-Jamesian manner. I am referring to his doubling of the central theme through the story of a couple belonging to the next generation, Aksel Strøm and that very same Barbro that Eleseus was unable to win. Barbro is the daughter of Brede Olsen, a neighbor whose unfitness for farming and general fecklessness contrast effectively with Isak's drive and quiet endurance. The story of Aksel and Barbro, begun in Part One, occupies nearly half of the somewhat shorter Part Two. Though there are other new settlers in the area, they do not affect the major themes of the novel.

Hamsun's decision to give another turn of the screw, so to speak, showed considerable courage; whether it was a wise decision is questionable. Inger and Isak were not an easy act to follow: their strength, their trials and tribulations, their misfortunes and triumphs would be difficult to match anywhere, the fascination of their singular personalities even more so. Aksel and Barbro are more ordinary. Like Isak, Aksel is a man of the soil and a hard worker, but he lacks color and depth. His treatment of Barbro, who returns from the city to become his housekeeper, shows neither good judgment nor humane feelings. Thus, he thinks of getting the girl pregnant so as to have a hold on her. And once he had obtained that hold, "he began to behave a bit too confidently. . . ." Though he comes to regret his domineering attitude, his thinking has not changed: he would "know how

Growth of the Soil: *Primitivist Epic or Utopian Fantasy?* 199

to lord it over her after they were married, until then he must use his head and give way" (VII: 271). Given Aksel's situation, his practical viewpoint is understandable: he is engaged in a brutal struggle for survival. But his looking forward to playing the master as Barbro's husband contrasts sharply with the relative gender equality practiced by Isak and Inger.

Though Barbro is young and pretty, sings and plays the guitar, besides being a good worker, she, like Inger, is obviously flawed. While Inger was afflicted with a physical defect, Barbro is morally crippled. The reader suspects her secret when, not long after her signing on as Aksel's housekeeper, she reads a news item in the paper about a dead child found floating in the ocean north of Bergen. Aksel does not, though he is surprised at her "careworn" appearance, which she ascribes to the long voyage and the city air she has been breathing (VII: 245). Unlike Inger, Barbro is portrayed as having been corrupted by urban life *before* she takes up with the woman-hungry settler. Her corruption includes having committed infanticide, a crime that will be duplicated after she bears Aksel's child, though she never admits to the murder. She claims that the child was stillborn, or drowned when she gave birth in a brook after falling as she tried to cross. Eventually, in response to Aksel's insistent questioning, she boastfully tells him she had killed her first baby and thrown it overboard traveling north. After Barbro abandons Aksel, allegedly to have her teeth fixed in the nearest town but actually to return to Bergen, the rumor mills are set in motion by old Olinè, who, having been hired to take care of the house, sniffs out the crime. In doing so, she repeats her course of action in helping to bring Inger to justice; combining the roles of pinch-hitting housekeeper and self-appointed sleuth, she is in both capacities motivated by a mixture of malice and shrewd self-interest. Arrested in Bergen, Barbro is brought back, tried and acquitted.

Hamsun's intent in writing *Growth of the Soil* is stated unambiguously in his letters. Writing to his publisher in 1916, he says the novel was supposed to be a "warning to my generation."[4] After the novel's publication, he asserts that he wrote the book "in order to serve a good cause." In the same letter he implies, though in a negative way, what cause, or causes, he had in mind: ". . . I fully understand that it is difficult to get people to till the soil in Norway. They are more willing to kill children."[5] In reaction to a negative review of the book, he expresses the same thoughts with naked sarcasm: "After this piece, of course, the outlook for a work devoted to Norwegian agriculture is very poor; the prospects for the murder of Norwegian babies are much brighter."[6]

No reader of *Growth of the Soil* can miss Hamsun's didactic purpose. To understand why he decided to combine in a novel two subjects that have little in common, we need to know something about what was happening in the world at large as well as in Norway at the time. In 1916 and 1917, Europe was engaged in wholesale slaughter; though Norway was not directly involved, the consequences of the war were severely felt in all areas of life. Thus, Norway's dependence on foreign imports for the most basic articles of food made the situation precarious in a time of naval blockade and submarine warfare. To mitigate the food shortage, any available land, such as parks, was converted to tillage; even Palace Park in Kristiania, as the city of Oslo was still called, was turned up and used to raise crops. Add Hamsun's local patriotism as a child of Nordland who felt that the agricultural resources of North Norway were largely untapped, and his attempt at propagating his back-to-the-soil message in a novel appears less quixotic. As Geissler tells Isak and repeats at the end of the book, "We should have thirty-two thousand fellows like you in this country" (VII: 172, 391).

The background to the infanticide theme is more personal. When Hamsun started work on *Growth of the Soil*, he had recently taken part in a heated newspaper debate about infanticide. Several unsavory instances of the crime had been reported and tried, and public opinion was divided on the issue of how to deal with the perpetrators. Hamsun's view was extremely harsh, to the point of calling for the death penalty. "[H]ang them! . . . Hang both parents, weed them out!" was the recurrent motif of his articles.[7] Thus, the acquittal of Barbro in *Growth of the Soil* must be understood as an ironic commentary not only on the Norwegian system of justice but on the alleged moral and social decline that Hamsun had been so preoccupied with in previous novels. Barbro's eventual return to Aksel, who gratefully welcomes her along with a new baby—not his—on the way, allows Hamsun to present a variant on the theme of a woman's conversion from worldliness and vice to wifely duty and obedience. Like Inger, the chronically wayward Barbro falls in line after her escapades.

While Hamsun's championship of tilling the soil and his continued engagement in the infanticide debate may have pleased the Swedish Academy, satisfying the "idealistic tendency" clause of the requirements for the Nobel Prize in literature,[8] from an aesthetic perspective they are problematic. This is particularly true of Hamsun's handling of infanticide. Granted, *Growth of the Soil* is not a realistic work; however, even a utopian or epic novel, both possible designations for *Growth*, must satisfy a minimal measure of realism. Far from doing so, Hamsun's novel is very unrealistic. To have infanticide repeated in successive generations in a story about a minuscule community would seem sufficiently implausible; its doubling in the second generation, for motives that seem ignoble, violates every canon of the probable. Furthermore, the consequent trivialization of the crime turns Barbro into a moral monster and her and Aksel's story into pure melodrama. The lachrymose scene that follows Barbro's return and Aksel's acceptance of her, though she is pregnant with a stranger's child, could scarcely be more maudlin: "There were more tears and smiles and tenderness. There were only the two of them in the wilderness, no one to fear, open doors, summer warmth, the buzzing of flies. She was so complaisant and affectionate, wanting in everything just what he wanted" (VII: 378).

The problem is not simply the theme of infanticide and the way it skews the portrayal of Barbro and Aksel toward villainy and moral obtuseness respectively; the melodrama also taints Hamsun's depiction of the larger community. Barbro's trial is like a foreign body in Hamsun's narrative of the pioneering life; the participants are treated with his customary condescension toward educated people. A disproportionate role is played by the Sheriff's wife, ridiculed previously for her efforts to help poor women limit the size of their families; when she herself has a child, her situation is gloatingly seen as that of a woman "trapped" by her natural destiny (VII: 275). Her testimony in favor of Barbro, a former maid of whose innocence she is convinced, is made to bristle with feminist animus: "We allow ourselves to think and feel directly counter to men's indictments and prosecutions, we allow ourselves to have our own opinion about things"

(343). And this woman, so "well versed in politics and social questions" (341), turns out to be dead wrong about Barbro, and so do those who decide the latter's fate: the prosecutor tells Geissler, who is present, that he finds Aksel to be "more suspicious" than Barbro (345), and the counsel for the defense sees Barbro as the model of a loving mother whose "tender hands" had swaddled the dead child (349). Meanwhile, the role of the presiding judge, "so human, so clerically mild" (344), is limited to a grumble, a nod, and a sharp glance. At the end the entire trial is referred to as a "play": everything had "gone so nicely" (350). Hamsun has indeed turned the trial into courtroom farce, having Geissler repeatedly interrupt the proceedings and making the jury swallow Barbro's cock-and-bull story about her fall bringing on the labor and the delivery in the little creek.

Hamsun proceeds differently with his major, positive theme. The steady progress at Sellanrå, which is turning into a model farm with its distinctive lifestyle, is placed in relief against the failure of a competing economy and way of life. Through Geissler, acting as a kind of entrepreneur, mining is introduced in the area; suspended and started over again under different management, the operation turns out to be unprofitable and ceases. The off and on nature of the undertaking contrasts negatively with Isak's stubborn loyalty to the land, which in this book is presumed to be the only real value, "the origin of everything, the only source" (VII: 361–62). Accordingly, all who chase after money fare badly. Brede Olsen, whose neglect of his farm is conveyed by the motif of a cart standing "out in the open" summer and winter (212), and who is obsessed with making money in any way he can, goes bankrupt. He and his family have to get by on the pittance his wife's business talent as the hostess of a café and lodging house can bring in.

Curiously enough, the character who embodies the opposite of Sellanrå's slow-paced existence is its most enthusiastic supporter and sponsor. The man is Geissler, a former sheriff fired for embezzlement, who is both hated and loved by the community. Addicted to drink, he is extremely changeable, alternating between furious energy and lethargy, between sober judgment and passionate exhortation.[9] A kind of hybrid of Knut Pedersen in *The Last Joy* and Tobias Holmengrå, with a smidgen of Bårdsen in *Segelfoss Town*, Geissler is a variant on Hamsun's wanderer; he is constantly on the move, shuttling back and forth between Norway and Sweden. As his German name, meaning "flagellator," intimates, he does indeed "whip" people into action whenever he appears, whether the enterprise he sponsors is industrial, like the local copper mines, or agricultural, such as Isak's farming. Geissler seems to be fully aware of his duality, defining himself, in an apparent allusion to a well-known Biblical verse, as a "man who knows what's right but doesn't do it" (VII: 394).[10] He contrasts himself with his son, a "type of the times" who believes in what "the Jew and the Yankee have taught him," yet Geissler himself is very much a wheeler-dealer. As a businessman, he effects big transactions, such as Isak's sale of an ore-rich mountain, which brings the Sellanrå family a tidy sum of money. The difference from his son, equated with "lightning," whereas Geissler sees himself as "fog," is not as great as he suggests, since the word "lightning" (Norwegian *lyn*) is also used to characterize Geissler, specifically his mode of thought (240).

But this complex and divided man exalts the simplicity and harmony of Sellanrå life, its being "at one" with heaven and earth, a life in which "man and nature ... don't compete ... but go together."[11] He tells Sivert: "Be content! You people have everything to live on, everything to live for, everything to believe in; you are born and you produce, you are needful to the earth" (VII: 392–93). In effect, Geissler preaches a message of total acceptance of one's place in the cycle of life: this is "what is meant by eternal life," he says, having noted how each generation brings forth, and is followed by, another. We recognize this as a quasi-religious version of Hamsun's message in *The Last Joy*.

This use of Geissler, namely, to articulate the meaning of the near-inarticulate life of the Sellanrå people, is his most obvious function in the novel. It looks as though Hamsun feared that, without a raisonneur, the intent of his work would not be clear. Without him, *Growth of the Soil* would have approached what Friedrich Schiller called "naive" literature; Geissler's presence brings it into the category of "sentimental" or "reflective" literature.[12] Instead of simply creating a convincing literary embodiment of a life of pristine simplicity, Hamsun supplements this creation with a hermeneutic guide embodying everything that is diametrically opposed to Sellanrå life. Indeed, this is one of the intriguing aspects of Hamsun's novel. Aesthetically, it is clearly an advantage: Geissler's comings and goings break up the even tenor, at times bordering on monotony, of Sellanrå life. His breathless cast of thought and speech brings a fresh rhythm into the narrative, imbuing it with a dynamic impetus. But viewed in its total range of implications, Geissler's involvement with the Sellanrå settlers poses serious problems that must be addressed.

As the stories of Eleseus, Barbro and Inger make quite clear, Hamsun in *Growth of the Soil* expresses intense anti-urban sentiments: city life is steeped in frivolity and moral corruption. Yet, Isak is no technophobe; in fact, he is extremely proud of every new machine that he either acquires or receives from Geissler, as a gift. In general, Geissler's interventions do a great deal to ease the difficulties of the pioneering life: he enables Isak to obtain the land for very little, pays him nicely for his copper-rich mountain, and negotiates for Isak a percentage of what he sells it for. Moreover, he gives Isak valuable advice, saves Isak's crops during a period of drought, and brings about Inger's early release from prison. In effect, he acts like an angel, in the Greek sense of a messenger from another world, not unlike Evgraf, Doctor Zhivago's brother, in Pasternak's famous novel. The latter turns up providentially in moments of distress, as though reassuring everyone, including the reader, that human existence is not wholly subject to blind chance. True, Geissler's intervention carries no such metaphysical message; and yet, one is hard put to deny that he plays a providential role in the novel. Evidently, he is a stand-in for the author, who wishes his favorite characters well and is glad to ease their struggle for existence. The identification of Geissler with the authorial persona, though not necessarily with the real-life Hamsun, is confirmed by a memory that he confides to Sivert at the very end of the novel: "I remember everything. I remember from when I was a year and a half: I stood swaying on the barnbridge at Oppigard Garmo in Lom and noticed a certain smell. I still notice that smell" (VII: 394). That must have been Hamsun's own memory, since the reference is to Hamsun's presumed birthplace.[13]

In attempting to define the special character of this particular novel one comes up against similar problems encountered in discussing earlier works by Hamsun: it does not fall into any pre-existing novelistic category. Geissler's function as interpreted above suggests an epic concept; his participation in the vicissitudes of the Sellanrå farm, which received its name from him, is not unlike that of the gods in the ancient epic, or of Yahweh in certain Old Testament stories, such as those of the patriarchs. Geissler's self-description has the flavor of myth and verges on the preternatural: "I'm . . . the fog, I'm here and there, I swim, at times I'm rain in a dry place" (VII: 393). Further, the hero, Isak, adheres to an epic concept in embodying what, on Hamsun's part, was intended as a national ideal; this is evident from the fact that Geissler holds up Isak as a model to be emulated. Isak's exemplary status is also shown by his being portrayed as an avatar of the *landnåmsmenn*, the early colonizers of Iceland; he is "a figure resurrected from the past who points out the future, a man . . . nine hundred years old and once again the man of the hour" (396). A more special feature of the epic, the single combat, appears in a somewhat unusual form in *Growth of the Soil*; it is nicely exemplified by Isak's stubborn fight with an elusive boulder. That the adversary is part of the natural environment rather than an enemy in the field of battle does not invalidate the comparison; besides, many ancient heroes are shown fighting, and overcoming, some force or element of nature.

An Old Testament paradigm may be equally apropos: the name of the central character points to the Biblical Isaac, whose story is part of what might be called a family saga. Isaac's two sons are as radically different as Eleseus and Sivert of Hamsun's novel. Eleseus, whose name is not totally unlike Esau's, abandons his birthright much like his Biblical counterpart and leaves his native country, while Sivert, whom Isak first thought of calling Jakob (VII: 167), carries on the paternal heritage. And Isak possesses a distinctly patriarchal quality. Thus, he behaves and talks in a way that shows he has a personal relationship with his god, to whom he ascribes very human characteristics, and he goes about his work in the field in the manner of performing a religious ritual: when he sows the grain, for example, he is "religiously bareheaded" (396). He even claims to have "seen God with his own eyes in the woods one night in the fall" (227), an experience that is mockingly echoed by his reported meeting with the devil himself, most likely a moose, one moonlit winter evening (249). On the more trivial side, Inger plays favorites just like Rebekah, the Biblical Isaac's wife, though unlike her she favors the firstborn. That Isak and Inger gave their youngest child the name Rebekka is further evidence of Hamsun's interest in the Old Testament story as a paradigm for his own. Finally, his awareness of the Biblical motif is confirmed by the novel's title, which is taken from a passage of Leviticus that promises all good things, including the earth's "increase" – "markens grøde" in the Norwegian text – to those who "walk in my statutes, and keep my commandments, and do them."[14]

Hamsun's representation of reality, to use Erich Auerbach's term, does indeed possess an epic quality in certain parts of *Growth of the Soil*. In his discussion of the *Odyssey*, Auerbach emphasizes, among other things, the broad inclusiveness and "uniform illumination" of Homer's style.[15] To some degree, Hamsun's style from *Segelfoss Town* on has become increasingly marked by circumstantial realism. This is not, however, what I am referring to. I have in mind a mode of description that joins dissimilars as a matter of course, juxtaposing elements in a way that would ordinarily strike the reader as ironic or humorous. A simple example is offered in a passage about Isak's inability to give his sons "any kind of higher instruction": during Inger's imprisonment "the catechism and the collection of Bible stories rested . . . quietly on the shelf alongside the goat cheese" (VII: 199). Coupling religion with a smelly article of food reveals an aesthetic that deems all aspects of experience to have an equal claim to being represented.

On a broader scale, we see the same juxtaposition of disparate areas of experience in two memorable episodes. In the first, Isak is doing his farm chores and walking his Sunday rounds – tracking down a missing sheep, inspecting the sawmill and grain mill, looking over his fields – while his mind is ceaselessly rankling from the discovery that Inger was having a rendezvous with a lineman in the woods. His inner turmoil, both on this occasion and the following Saturday, is accompanied by everyday objects and mundane gestures – butter and cheese brought to market, a newly ordered harrow, cocking his hat over his ear and scratching his head (VII: 225-27) – that shunt it off center, balancing it against the multifarious cares of everyday life. The situation reminds me of an episode in the *Odyssey* discussed in an essay by Aldous Huxley as an illustration of the Homeric spirit: when the monster Scylla devoured six of Odysseus's men, the survivors gave vent to their grief and "wept for the men" only after they had satisfied their "desire for food and drink."[16]

The "uniform illumination" cited by Auerbach is even better exemplified by Aksel Strøm's accident, particularly its aftermath (VI: 303-10). Caught in a rocky cleft with a felled pine tree on top of him, Aksel knows he may be left to die, but his mind is occupied with everything else, such as Barbro's desertion and the lowing animals that have not been fed. With a storm having sprung up, the growing danger to his life as the daylight wanes is rendered in terms of his eyes and beard getting more and more iced over with freezing snow. His rescue by Olinè, after Brede Olsen passed him by, is described in the same manner: the agonies of the rescued victim, who is after all the central figure, are relatively muted by comparison with the mutual recriminations of Olinè and Brede, who has belatedly offered to help. Olinè's religious imagination bathes the entire scene in a mock-heroic aura: "She would never forget that angel of the Lord who summoned her onto the doorstep. . . . It was as in the days of paradise when they blew the trumpets on the walls of Jericho" (307).

The purpose of the above discussion has not been to demonstrate that *Growth of the Soil* is an epic novel; it would in that case be a rather flawed specimen. But it can scarcely be denied that it contains certain epic qualities—of subject matter, narrative conventions, and style. On the other hand, it could be argued that the book was intended to portray a retrospective utopia. Significantly, Hamsun evokes the Edenic myth more than once in the novel. The allusion to Eleseus and Sivert living in a "paradise of dirt and ignorance" (VII: 199) may be simply a stylistic flourish, but other allusions deserve to be taken seriously. While watching a ram, young Sivert not only feels it is a "relative," but recalls a previous occasion on which he thought: "It's almost as if he stands there looking into the garden of Eden!" (217). When Inger goes berrypicking with Gustaf, they are said to find themselves "in the middle of the wilderness, in Eden" (322). Inger's own awareness of the divine presence is more personal, since she has reason to fear retribution for her sin: "she knew, after all, that God walked around in the evening looking over his whole wilderness and that he had fabulous eyes, he would be sure to find her" (248). Notwithstanding the implicit threat of banishment, Hamsun clearly wishes to suggest an Edenic world, though the reference to wilderness shows that they are living "on the east of Eden."[17]

An allusion to the gardem of Eden does not by itself stamp a work of literature as a retrospective utopia. Nor did Hamsun write such a work. Whether positive or negative, utopian novels tend to have carefully constructed, often scientifically founded plots and a thematic content that stands up to careful scrutiny. This is not the case with *Growth of the Soil*, which is closer to a utopian fantasy than to anything that could be remotely replicated in the real world.

The unreal, fantastic element is evident throughout the novel. I have discussed the role of Geissler from the perspective of the epic. Transposed to a utopian context, he deprives the novel in which he appears of all credibility: homesteaders and settlers do not ordinarily have access to a Geissler who will clear the path to progress and prosperity for them. Nor do most have the iron health of Isak, who never takes off a single day or hour because of illness. Despite the arctic terrain and climate, Isak is able to create a thriving farm in a couple of decades, a truly mind-boggling accomplishment given the technology available at the time.[18]

More subtly, Hamsun's novel is riddled with paradoxes and patent contradictions. In order to have his fantasy succeed, Hamsun needed Geissler with his money and farm machinery, all deriving from that urban civilization that the book derides. Further, the primitivist trend, never far from the surface in a Hamsun novel, is contradicted by the steady economic progress at Sellanrå. Nor does that progress accord very well with an implied exhortation to frugality, a virtue enjoined by a Biblical allusion after Inger has come clean with her husband: "And it was again borne out that godliness with contentment is great gain" (VII: 337).[19] Toward the end, Isak appears under the title "margrave," making his wife a margravine (396–97), titles that betoken neither a primitive simplicity nor pious frugality.

Perhaps the most telling sign that Hamsun was writing an attractive fantasy is his unlikely combination of a pioneering mentality with a near-mystical view of nature. The attitude toward nature of a peasant or farmer, certainly one that settles in the wild, is of necessity utilitarian: he is engaged in the proverbial conquest of nature. It is only after nature has been tamed, and partially destroyed, that less aggressive, more emotionally tinged attitudes toward nature arise. The entire Romantic movement could be cited as evidence of this phenomenon. Broadly, the romantic feeling toward nature is a cultural luxury of the urbanite. It is therefore perfectly legitimate in novels like *Mysteries* and *Pan*, which feature city dwellers as central characters. But to imbue Isak and Inger with a pastoral sensibility, when they are doing their best to change the pristine landscape, seems to violate the canons of verisimilitude. It is hard to believe that Inger "heard a song" made by the small fishes in a tarn near the farm (VII: 247). And Hamsun's description of the "wonders" of the season as observed by the dwellers in the wild is imbued with a refined sense of mystery that may be appropriate to the author but not to his down-to-earth characters. The flight of the greylag geese each spring and fall offers a good example of the allegedly profound, quasi-metaphysical intuitions the latter are capable of: ". . . it was as though the world stood still a moment, until the procession had disappeared. Didn't the people feel a faintness glide through them then? They resumed their work, but they caught their breath first; something had spoken to them from the beyond" (247).

Hamsun may have suspected the falsity of these sensations and feelings; otherwise, why did he attribute two instances of such feelings to young Sivert? Probably because they are more credible in a child than in adults. Besides the above-mentioned sense of oneness he experiences with the ram (VII: 217), there is his "adventure" listening to the antiphonal music of a pair of ducks in the river: "Sivert stands there looking at the birds, looking past them and far into the dream. A sound had sailed through him, a sweetness, he was left with a fine, thin reminiscence of something wild and lovely, something previously experienced but erased" (362). Some of that dreamlike quality of a child's imagination has carried over to Hamsun's entire undertaking in writing *Growth of the Soil*.

Hamsun's strength as a novelist is obviously not to be found in the classic virtues of thematic unity, clear genre definition, and skillful plot construction. His talent is a synthetic one, enabling him to combine genres and styles, while maintaining a tone of oral narration. At his best, he creates works of high literary quality as well as originality. The first half of *Growth of the Soil* meets that standard. The second half is too badly marred by the Barbro story, among other things, to measure up.

It would, however, be unfair to end the discussion of *Growth of the Soil* on a negative note. No one reading the book will come away without an immense admiration for Hamsun's special gifts as a writer. Two of these gifts are his masterful character portrayal and a superb handling of scene. The former attains an uncanny brilliance in the creation of Olinè, called a "Homeric figure" of the most "exuberant vitality" by one reviewer.[20] I shall briefly examine the development of two scenes, the trial run of the mowing machine and Isak's battle with the boulder, while at the same time commenting on how they function as vehicles of characterization.

The first scene is elaborately prepared. The chapter begins with the statement, "Isak returned from the village with a horse" (VII: 273), then continues by relating three pieces of news that he has brought. One is of special interest: the neighbor's farm is up for sale. Next, there follow several pages about Eleseus, including disputes about his future between Inger and Isak: should they buy the farm for him? With regard to the third piece of news, the purchase of a mowing machine, these pages serve as retardation, in tune with Isak's mood of secrecy. He has parked the machine at the edge of the woods to spring a surprise on everybody. The narrator's comment reminds the reader of the chapter's opening sentence: "Naturally, the new horse wouldn't have been picked up just today if it weren't for the mowing machine" (279).

Before trying out the machine, acting as "his own horse," Isak struggles to recall, "with an immensely keen air," the directions for use the dealer had read to him. Of all the intellectual challenges the illiterate man has had to meet, some of which are reviewed as he observes the new machine—"a magpie's nest of steel twigs and hooks and apparatus and a hundred screws" (VII: 279)—this is by far the toughest. Having assured himself that the machine worked, he asks his sons to put away their scythes and to harness the new horse. "He was so big with secrecy and so over-confident that the backs of his knees gave a little at each step, that was how weightily he strode along" (280). Isak's rather pompous, but riddling physicality not only prepares us for the great moment, the revelation of the machine, but also for his comeuppance by his clever son, Eleseus, who knows how to read.

Growth of the Soil: *Primitivist Epic or Utopian Fantasy?* 211

The rest of the scene does two things: it shows Isak using every possible trick to cover his mistakes vis-à-vis his son, and everyone in the family wishing him well. At every error discovered by Eleseus, the father responds with, "Sure, I know that"; "I was just looking for that bolt"; "I don't have my glasses, so I can't see the sketch" (VII: 280–81). Afterward, the glasses fall out of his pocket, but the boys let it pass. Isak is "very proud, sitting at his ease high up, all rigged out in his Sunday best, in a jacket and hat, although the sweat pours off him!" And when he oils the machine he lets everyone know "he is pursuing science." The narrator exclaims, "Happy Isak! Happy people of Sellanrå!" (281).

Ordinarily, the scene would probably be read as a lengthy demonstration of phoniness and bad faith. This is not Hamsun's intent: he obviously loves Isak and understands his need to maintain his preeminence within the family at any cost. Because we perceive the common humanity at the root of Isak's lies and pretenses, we smile indulgently and pass on.

Though there is also some humor in Isak's virtual duel with the boulder, here other elements predominate. While comically absurd in its near-Sisyphean repetitiveness, the scene concludes on a note of profound pathos. In effect, it is a regular drama, comprising the three phases that, according to Francis Fergusson, constitute a dramatic action: purpose, passion, and perception.[21] The scene, which occupies over three pages, is described as a contest between equals, although Isak considers the stone to be "very stupid." After a while, he "began to feel rather teased by the stone," which he wanted to remove so he could use it in building a small house to which he and Inger would one day retire. His purpose is severely thwarted: the stone was "so round and idiotic you couldn't get a hold on it." Whatever tool or ploy he uses, the boulder cannot be moved. When he asks himself, "Had he grown old?" he dismisses the thought out of hand as "ridiculous"; "it was a delusion" (VII: 364). Yet, his struggle is not only frustrating, but fills him more and more with "bitterness" as he suspects he has become weak with age (365). This is the phase of passion, in the sense of suffering. The situation becomes truly embarrassing when Inger turns up and offers her help, to which he just "shakes his head." Even his anger, which makes him think of using the sledgehammer, is no use, though he cherishes the thought of smashing the stubborn stone: "It is only a formality to smash a stone you hate to the death. And what if the stone fought back, if it couldn't be smashed? It was going to find out who would be the survivor of the two of them!" (365). Though he eventually succeeds in raising the boulder together with Inger, whose help he grudgingly accepts after "a moment's consideration," the truth about himself that he has been forced to recognize is a very painful one: "Age had caught up with Isak, he was beginning to get ripe for a pensioner's cottage" (366). This realization causes him to be "depressed" for several days. "They were dark days" (367).[22]

Hamsun had a wonderful ability of portraying simple characters, such as have next to no capacity or desire for articulating their deepest thoughts or feelings. *Growth of the Soil* contains numerous situations in which language masks rather than expresses the characters' feelings; the latter become manifest only by way of non-verbal means. Family occasions of arrival and departure provide distinctive examples of such a situation. Even in portraying Inger, who is fairly articulate after her sojourn in Trondhjem, Hamsun has recourse to physical symptoms and actions to render her feelings. When the two boys run to meet her on her return from prison, she betrays the symptoms of a severe cold, her eyes watering. Then, trying to rationalize what happened to her, she says, "You catch such bad colds on board" (VII: 215). Isak, we know, can be fairly helpless with language. In a discussion with Inger about Eleseus, he says, "'But now I ask you how my own flesh and blood can be disobedient toward—toward my own flesh and blood?' Isak grew silent. He understood it got worse and worse the more he talked" (278). No wonder, then, that a battle with a boulder could serve to elucidate his character more effectively than a more conventional literary device, such as dialogue.

Growth of the Soil leaves one with conflicting feelings. It grew out of a well-meaning project that Hamsun thought was of national importance, a circumstance that may be the clue to both some strong and weak points of the resulting work. While it imbued the novel with a missionary passion, it introduced elements of preconceived opinions and dogmatic perversity that put off the reader who has no hankerings for "the age of the wooden spoon" (VII: 153). What salvages the book is Hamsun's feel for the life of simple folk, whose language and behavior he reproduces with the flair of a true mimic.

Reading this novel provides a welcome relief from the debunking of the cultured, a sport which Hamsun seemed to find it difficult to resist playing.

Though a few critics found Hamsun's gospel of the earth to be fraught with paradox, excessive bias, or unreality,[23] *Growth of the Soil* was exceptionally well received not only in Scandinavia but in other parts of the world as well. And the favorable reception was apparently not a consequence of the award of the Nobel Prize for the book,[24] since the positive reviews appeared *before* the announcement of the prize. The American and English critics, some of whom were well-known writers, were almost uniformly positive, having recourse to phrases like a "great book," a work imbued with "deep poetic feeling," and a "Promethean" achievement demonstrating the "Godlike qualities that belong to the very great."[25] H. G. Wells compares Hamsun's novel to Tolstoy's *War and Peace*, calling them both "books on an almost Biblical scale," dealing with life "so greatly as to come nearest to the idea of a universally inspiring and illuminating literature which underlies the idea of our Canon"; and Thomas Mann dubs it a "masterpiece of European literature."[26]

Subsequent evaluations have varied considerably. While few have followed the critic of *Newsweek*, who in 1967, in a review of Robert Bly's translation of *Hunger*, fairly dismissed *Growth of the Soil*, calling it a "boring romantic saga,"[27] scholar-critics have expended much energy reappraising Hamsun's controversial novel. In an article of 1973, Eberhard Rumbke argued that the novel embodies a regressive, ahistorical social concept, symbolized by a return to the above-mentioned "age of the wooden spoon," which is referred to in the novel (VII: 153).[28] The article provoked several attempts to refute what many critics considered to be an unfair, simplistic reading of Hamsun's Nobel Prize novel. While the interpretive strategies differ, they are all calculated to complicate the meaning of Hamsun's text, whether through the discovery of ambiguity, irony, metafictional elements, or polyphony.

The responses to Rumbke's thesis vary in relevance and plausibility. Thus, Uwe-K. Ketelsen correctly stresses the links between the Sellanrå project and the "bourgeois world," to which one might answer that the project's very dependence on that world demonstrates its unreality. And that is what Ketelsen implies: the settlers' world is not Hamsun's "program" but his "anti-modern dream."[29] Similarly Klaus von See regards Sellanrå as "something like an experiment," a "made-up" program or a "literary fiction," having a "half-playful quality" to it and with Geissler as a sort of stage director of the Sellanrå world.[30] Øystein Rottem claims that the author betrays a "mediated, reflective attitude" toward his own utopia.[31] Geissler, the voice of the novel's utopian endeavor, is an ambiguous figure treated by the author with persistent irony. Moreover, Rottem argues, Geissler's situation mirrors that of the author, thereby enabling Hamsun as writer to elucidate, through him, the "limits and condition of possibility of utopia in an expanding industrial society." Further, the argument goes, the metafictional aspect of Hamsun's utopia, which allegedly "deals with its own origin," marks it as being distinctly "modern."[32] Helge Vidar Holm, while expressing wide agreement with Rottem in a more recent article, suggests a Bakhtinian approach to the novel, which he characterizes as "polyphonic." In this reading, Isak is said to possess his own "voice" as well as a "modern and reflective" view of life.[33]

Despite the differences in approach, all these critical endeavors aim at making Hamsun's work not only more complex and therefore more "modern," but also less hostage to a true believer's atavistic agrarian myth. My own view, as I have indicated, is that the novel is best described as a "utopian fantasy," on the ground that Hamsun's conscious, programmatic intent as stated in his letters is undermined by the nature of its execution. Clearly, a writer who yokes together opposites like Isak and Geissler, supposedly engaged in the same cause, is the victim of a divided mind. To conclude that Hamsun in *Growth of the Soil* deliberately exploits the disparity between the rootedness of Isak and the near vagabondage of Geissler for ambiguity, self-directed irony, or self-referential speculation attributes to Hamsun greater theoretical sophistication than he possessed, and to the novel a modernistic character for which I see no evidence. *Growth of the Soil* is neither a meta-literary nor a polyphonic novel. Suffice it to repeat a point I have already made, namely, that a principal purpose of Geissler is to articulate the meaning of Isak's "project," a meaning that Isak himself is incapable of voicing. Isak has no "voice," in this sense, apart from the one lent to him by Geissler. Moreover, though Geissler is mercurial, displaying a veritably protean changeability that makes him impossible to pin down, his faith in the utopian idea is firm and consistent. His emotional instability and moral failings are irrelevant to what he stands for, being simply Hamsun's way of making him acceptable as the purveyor of an ideal that, championed by a non-problematic voice, would leave the reader cold.

And just as we accept Geissler, warts and all, in reading *Growth of the Soil*, we have to come to terms with its many contradictions and implausibilities, realizing full well, as Harald Næss has noted, that the Hamsun novel for which he was awarded the Nobel Prize is not "his greatest book."[34]

CHAPTER EIGHT

A Universe of Chance: From the Bizarre to the Macabre

Hamsun's next two novels, *Konerne ved vandposten* (1920; *The Women at the Pump*, 1928) and *Siste kapitel* (1923; translated as *Chapter the Last*, 1929), could scarcely be more different from the work that had brought him the Nobel Prize in Literature in 1920. Judging by their length, which exceeds that of *Growth of the Soil* by some thirty and forty pages respectively, these novels, with their savage moods and profound loathing for the human race, must have grown out of a genuine need of the author to air his darkest, most devastating views on modern society and civilization. The personal malaise that they betray is undoubtedly related to the cultural crisis of Europe in the aftermath of World War I. However, underneath the period atmosphere of gloom and disenchantment, one discerns the same themes and characters that are familiar from previous works by Hamsun.

Like *Segelfoss Town*, *The Women at the Pump* is a small-town novel. Though Hamsun runs true to type in being sparing with time and place indications, it soon becomes evident that the town is located fairly close to the capital, much as in the urban sequences of *A Wanderer Plays on Muted Strings*.[1] Moreover, in depicting the life of this town, Hamsun applies the same Lilliputian perspective as in those sequences. Thus, the image of the anthill, a leading motif in Hamsun's description of social life and behavior in *Women at the Pump*, exists *in ovo*, alongside of many other diminutive images, in *A Wanderer*.[2] Yet, the novel's closest cognate, both in terms of character constellation and authorial perspective, is *Segelfoss Town*, which the Danish novelist and Nobel laureate Henrik Pontoppidan (1857–1943) reportedly called a "flea circus," while Carl Nærup's review summed it up as a "Hamsunian anthill world."[3] This image, with its connotations of swarming life viewed impassively and at a distance, is even more apt in describing the human world of *Women at the Pump*. Again, Hamsun has peopled that world with a multitude of rather indifferent characters, including the usual professionals and officials, some of whom play important roles despite being nameless, such as the doctor and the postmaster, as well as an array of figures representative of a wide social spectrum, from the wealthy Consul Johnsen to Olaus, the town bum.

As for structure, Hamsun offers no surprises: the template is that of the family chronicle. However, the portrayal of the two generations whose lives we follow is clearly intended to produce an impression of a collective, a busy coastal town whose life is satirized with near-diabolical cunning, as well as to convey Hamsun's vision of the human condition. Once more, both tasks are carried out dispassionately, so much so that an English reviewer found the book almost "exaggeratedly detached in method," making the author appear "as a watchful but unfeeling god jotting down in short, staccato sentences the feelings, sayings, and doings of the mites that go about their futile business on this earth." In contrast, another English critic, Cyril Connolly, characterizing the book as a "masterly delineation of greed and hypocrisy," says that "gradually a peculiar charm emanates from the author's detachment."[4]

The chief element of novelty in *Women at the Pump* is Hamsun's central character, Oliver Andersen, a sailor whose life was brutally changed by a disastrous accident at sea. True, we have already encountered such a figure in Hamsun's fiction, namely Johannes Grøgård, a.k.a. Miniman, in *Mysteries*. Hamsun's return to this figure, who in *Mysteries* is a sort of adjunct to Nagel, the main character, whose monologues invest him with whatever personality he possesses, is a special case of a literary practice found in earlier novels: inventing a character who represents a heightening of a human predicament already dealt with. While the damage suffered by Miniman has crippled him, the text of *Mysteries* offers no evidence that the accident resulted in emasculation. Oliver Andersen, on the other hand, lost his manhood along with his leg; he is both physically and psychologically on crutches for the rest of his life. And yet, paradoxically, Hamsun casts him as a successful father of a family, a role that Nagel believes Miniman would also have been capable of fulfilling. It looks as though, after nearly three decades had passed, Hamsun decided to improve on his previous creation by presenting a radically different scenario for a victim of personal disaster.

Present in one capacity or other in all but a handful of the book's thirty-some chapters, Oliver Andersen helps provide focus to a novel abounding with characters related in a variety of ways. The narrative begins with a panoramic view of the town, whose citizens are "absorbed by the important people and follow them with interest, . . . thereby in reality looking after their own welfare; they are protected by power and thrive under it, and that is the way it ought to be" (VIII: 7). The first such person to be mentioned is C. A. Johnsen, shipowner and man of business, and one of the pillars of the town's economy. Oliver Andersen, the young sailor, turns up a few pages later as a crew member of Consul Johnsen's *Fia*, the town's only steamship preparing to depart. When the ship returns after a lapse of seven months, Oliver is a mere shadow of his former self, with no job and no prospects. Ironically, instead of receiving compensation from his employer for the damage suffered in the line of duty, he soon finds himself in the position of having to bring up the Consul's offspring, a state of affairs he does his best to exploit.[5] Although Oliver's fiancée, Petra, broke up with him when he returned home as an invalid, she reversed herself once she discovered she was pregnant. The identity of the father remains undisclosed, but the indications—including the baby's brown eyes—point to Consul Johnsen or his son, Scheldrup; Petra has been a maid in the Johnsen family and continues to maintain contact with it. This sort of affair, usually involving lower-class women and an upper-class man, is well known from earlier Hamsun novels, especially *Rosa*, where the eye color of the offspring—brown as in the present case—leaves no doubt as to the children's paternity. In *Women at the Pump* eye color becomes a leitmotif, sustained by Petra's alternate delivery of brown- and blue-eyed babies and by the district doctor's vendetta, in the guise of science, against the Johnsens.[6]

While the theme of illegitimacy, or what could be called sexuality across the social spectrum, is not uncommon in fiction, in Hamsun's case it is a virtual obsession. However, the situation generates neither humanitarian pathos nor moral outrage. As in earlier works by Hamsun, the signals are mixed: whereas the stories of these exploited women evoke the reader's sympathy, the authorial discourse supports the right of the stronger, namely, that of the higher-class males. As Oliver's wife, Petra gives birth to two sons evidently fathered by a Johnsen, followed by a blue-eyed girl, then a brown-eyed one, and finally another with blue eyes. Oliver knows from the beginning that none of the children are his. Curiously, he welcomes the brown-eyed ones, though he himself is "blue-eyed" (VIII: 10), whereas the first blue-eyed girl born throws him into a jealous rage, producing a scene that Thomas Mann thought one of the "oddest and most entertaining" he had ever come across.[7] One can only infer that the thought of his wife being "loved" by a big shot increases her value and makes her even more desirable. Conversely, the sexual attentions of the attorney, Fredriksen, who holds a mortgage on Oliver's house and can only be persuaded to grant deferments in return for sexual favors, is seen by Oliver as a hated intrusion. Petra herself "loathed" the attorney, calling him an "old swine" (214, 240), whereas she clearly has a soft spot for the Johnsens, in this respect acting very much like the maidservants with whom Mack performs his featherbed antics in *Rosa*.

Beyond the psychological and social interest of this bizarre situation, one discerns what might be called a quasi-philosophical or mystical idea. For Petra is not the only woman in the novel to conceive children illicitly. So does also young Mrs. Henriksen, whose husband owns a shipyard but, like his wife, was born in humble circumstances. Before she dies in childbirth, Mrs. Henriksen has given birth to two brown-eyed children; their paternity is quite evident, since Consul Johnsen has betrayed a keen interest in her. A mystery remains: how did Maren Salt, an unmarried woman in her forties or even perhaps fifty years old, happen to become the mother of a brown-eyed boy? True, she herself has brown eyes, but Petra's suspicions have been aroused. Maren's refusal to satisfy her neighbor's jealous curiosity brings the following rejoinder: "'I understand, all right!' Petra says, stiffly and bitterly. 'He is everywhere!'" (VIII: 164). At this point one wonders, Whom could she have in mind except Consul Johnsen?

One is tempted to conclude that, in Hamsun's world, within a societal context of status seeking, hidden rivalries, and engrained animosities, unlicensed eros, with the usual consequences of illegitimate births, is an unqualified good. The favorable description of some key characters involved supports this view: Consul Johnsen is referred to as a "natural force" even as his hair is going gray (VIII: 56); Maren Salt's human worth is determined by her ability to have children "despite her years" (166); and at her fifth pregnancy Petra is exalted for her "blessed fertility" by Oliver: "many years over forty and just as wild!" (230). Indeed, sheer fecundity appears to be the standard whereby a woman's value is measured, regardless of other, specifically human, qualities. Moreover, instead of being held together by laws and institutions, the town—and, by metonymic extension, the world—is largely united by a network of suppressed, unacknowledged sexual bonds,[8] amounting to a species of erotic unanimism: indeed, the novel's subtext is laced with a sexual mystique that legitimizes an untrammeled enactment of desire.

The central character, Oliver, embodies the very opposite of this ideal of fecundity, and he does so in the most palpable way. To his wife he is simply a lump of fat with an unsightly wooden leg, a pair of "watery blue eyes," and a "voice that more and more resembles a woman's voice" (VIII: 62). He is unfavorably compared to Olaus, the bum, Oliver's foil, who lost his hand in an industrial accident. Olaus's face was not "delicate and beardless and womanish, but bony and sharp," whereas Oliver's face was "smooth and round like a baby's bottom, with pendant cheeks and moist lips." He looked "repulsive" (185). The epithets become increasingly demeaning: from being ignominiously paired with the family's "old tomcat," subsequently said to be "useless" (41, 86), Oliver sinks to the level of a jellyfish, "a moniker that supposedly originated with his own merry wife" (274). To retrieve his job in Consul Johnsen's warehouse, he is even prepared to be his employer's "dog, the guardian of his harem" (269); no clearer epiphany of his actual state, that of a eunuch, could be desired.

Before an attempt is made to offer a broader interpretation of Hamsun's central figure in *Women at the Pump*, it is necessary to recapitulate the principal events in his life and his dominant character traits. Actually, nothing much happens to him after the accident, except through Petra, who enables him to play the role of vicarious father to five children. And he is a good father, as evidenced by the children's success, especially that of the two boys, Frank and Abel. Through the school principal's intervention with Consul Johnsen, the latter undertakes to foot the bill for Frank's education, acting on a *noblesse oblige* that replicates Lieutenant Holmsen's benevolence in *Children of the Age*, except that the Consul must be in the know concerning the boy's paternity. Although Frank is ridiculed by the implied narrator for his inclination toward book learning—in contrast to Abel, an adventuresome lad who is early on apprenticed to Carlsen, the blacksmith—his intellectual accomplishment as a philologist redounds to Oliver's credit.

At the end of the book, Frank has become principal of the same school from which he once graduated. Meanwhile, Abel has taken over Carlsen's smithy, where Oliver now spends most of his time, aside from forays at sea. "'My son the master smith,' he says, 'my son the school principal,' he says. He leans on his sons and benefits from their respectability" (VIII: 284). This, too, is a variant on an earlier theme: Lars Manuelsen's publicly displayed pride in his famous son, the Reverend L. Lassen. No one will tell Oliver that he is childless anymore: "His children were only his own fabrication, to be sure, but he does have them; he had been something for them during their entire childhood and adolescence, he and they knew one another, and they called him father among themselves and to others. . ." (283). In fact, on the strength of Frank's obvious preference for him rather than for his mother, Oliver thinks: "the father was the very origin and the child hung on to it, the mother was only the earth it was planted in" (46).

This is only one of a number of self-glorifying mechanisms whereby Oliver prevents a drab, semi-criminal existence from sinking into a psychological slough of despond. His effort to rebuild his life after the unmanning accident at sea describes a seesaw of humiliating reverses and modest triumphs. His moods vary accordingly, from lethargy and mild revolt to one of quiet contentment. His everyday life is at first dominated by squabbles with his mother, a carping widow, and by an absurd feud with his neighbor, Mattis, a carpenter whom he suspects of lusting after Petra. This state of affairs changes one day by sheer luck: on a long excursion in his neighbor's rowboat,

Oliver comes upon a disabled vessel. The salvage money he receives and the praise for his feat of seamanship in the local paper give a big boost to his battered ego. Soon after, Petra's interest in him is revived, and when she proposes marriage to him—"Well, what do you think, Oliver, would you like to have me?"—he can only reply, "Since it is your wish" (VIII: 39). The marriage is no better or worse than any other in a Hamsun novel, despite Petra's constant dissatisfaction and Oliver's periodic attacks of jealousy. This despite the fact that, to him, Petra is essentially a substitute mother: ". . . she belonged to Oliver, she was a nourisher, she had milk in her, he could see her teats" (44). In choosing the word "teat," Hamsun probably wanted to highlight the animal aspect of their relationship and to suggest its parasitic nature.

From a moral perspective, Oliver lives on the margin; many will find him a despicable wretch. Exploiting his handicap, he charges exorbitant prices for the fish he catches and the driftwood he collects on his forays at sea. Sometimes these activities serve as cover for gathering eggs and eiderdown on the skerries, which was illegal. He cheats Mattis, his neighbor and friend, taking back the doors he sold him and shortweighting him in his capacity as Consul Johnsen's warehouseman. He appropriates a boat he finds at sea, and one day he sells his house, mortgaged to Fredriksen, the attorney, a "reckless act" for which he was reported to the police (VIII: 63). Worse yet, his efforts to sell his illegally acquired eiderdown make him an accessory to a dastardly act of burglary, in which a Norwegian officer on an English ship robs his own father, the town's postmaster. Not only does he retain the money he is paid out of the loot of 7,000 or 8,000 kroner, but on a subsequent trip at sea he discovers in some bird's nests that he ransacks for eiderdown a cache of mail with, among other things, unopened registered letters containing money. He concludes that the mail was discarded in haste by the post-office burglar, who showed himself to be "an ass . . ., a bungler, a miserable novice!" To Oliver who, needless to say, holds on to the money, this is a real "adventure" (263), one of several he chances upon during his fishing trips, "nosing around, dreaming and yearning, God knows for what, perhaps for a better life, a new Jerusalem" (132). As a result of receiving the "mail from the sea, mail from heaven," his character "improves, his manner becomes firmer, he acquires a new bearing"

(264). While this scenario of an individual's petty crime may not be remarkable in itself, its generalization resonates with a dark, sardonic intent.

For, strange as it may seem, Oliver's semi-criminal mode of life is not meant to be understood as an exception, but as the rule, among his fellow townspeople. This becomes quite explicit in a passage triggered by his intention to sell the eiderdown he has illegally gathered over a number of years: "Other people weren't a bit better than he; either they lacked the initiative to carry out a prank or they didn't have to do it. They probably also wanted to many a time, . . . but they were in chains, going around like captives of their own honesty and annoyed that they couldn't forget themselves." Then the focus shifts to Oliver: "What, then, could one ask of a man like him, like Oliver, a poor devil of a cripple with a large family? Couldn't he, too, have conducted himself nicely and honestly if he had been able to afford it?" (VIII: 185–86). Though the passage reads in part like a free indirect discourse rendering Oliver's own reflections, certain stylistic features betray the voice of the implied narrator. Besides, Oliver is not temperamentally disposed for a reflectiveness of the kind that the passage displays. If we are still not convinced of the author's grim intent, the novel's next to last paragraph may provide the conclusive evidence: "The life of the town realizes its image in him; it crawls, but it's just as busy for all that" (293).

The word "crawls" points to an important motif mentioned previously, that of the anthill, an emblem of the struggle for existence in the small town portrayed in the novel. It is a reality as well as a metaphor or symbol in the novel. When Abel kills a venomous snake in the woods after getting bitten by it, he dumps the body onto an anthill. The first use of the motif suggests an existence marked by unscrupulous rivalry: "Oh, that little anthill! All the people are occupied with their own things, they cross one another's paths, they elbow each other aside, sometimes they trample one another. It cannot be otherwise, sometimes they trample one another" (VIII: 8). Dostoyevsky used the anthill image in *Notes from Underground* to evoke a dehumanized society of the future; Harald Næss quotes a passage from Rousseau's *Emile*, where the anthill image is used pejoratively about "crowded cities."[9] Hamsun's use of it in *The Women at the Pump* seems to be broader in scope. For though ostensibly applying only to the small Norwegian coastal town where the action is set, the image tends to spill over, imbuing Hamsun's portrayal of life in general with a ruthless naturalism that makes the search for an overarching meaning appear quixotic.

Although *Women* is one of Hamsun's more intellectual works of fiction, as demonstrated by the endless debates between the doctor and the postmaster, the thrust of the authorial voice could scarcely be more anti-intellectual, to say nothing about anti-religious: ". . . the town was that little crawling anthill, and this was no doubt proof that life itself was taking its course in spite of all theories, perhaps mostly in spite of the religious ones" (VIII: 98). In the contest of world views that looms so large in Hamsun's text, those that seek to rationalize, or give a meaning to, human existence get the worst of it. As will be seen, the narrator ridicules the postmaster and the blacksmith, while at the same time they are said to be the only "two righteous ones in the whole town," a sardonic allusion to the Biblical story of Sodom and Gomorrah that equates the town's moral status with that of the infamous "cities of the plain."[10]

The core event that constitutes the thematic center of the novel is a personal misfortune that serves as a test of both character and values: *The Women at the Pump* is another version of the Book of Job. Job loses everything, as do also, though not literally, Carlsen, the postmaster, Consul Johnsen, and Oliver Andersen. Carlsen, the blacksmith, is a very religious man who, whatever happens to him, accepts it as part of God's providence. The postmaster believes he has found the meaning of life through philosophical thinking. His view, which like Carlsen's is predicated on a teleological concept of the world, centers on the idea of reincarnation, whereby the importance of offspring becomes paramount: one's children will continue along the path of ethical self-improvement pursued by the parents, making human perfection possible at some future date. By contrast, Consul Johnsen is an agnostic who feels comfortable dealing with business and politics but is bored by philosophical questions; and Oliver, while occasionally mouthing Christian shibboleths, is religiously indifferent. Two other characters, the doctor and the attorney, Mr. Fredriksen, play important roles, but unlike the above-mentioned figures their convictions are never tested. The doctor, a sybaritic materialist with a bleak view of man's fate, seems to enjoy teasing the deadly serious postmaster with his blue-eyed optimism. Fredriksen, an average sensual man, is a social climber who as a democrat lays claim to a social conscience.

When the horror strikes, as it did for the man from the land of Uz, no convictions, whether religious or philosophical, can provide a shelter from physical or moral collapse. Long before the shattering event, the narrator pokes fun at Carlsen and the postmaster, both of whom he likens to the "women at the pump—oh, they were themselves two women at the pump, just so, only that their gossip was religious, but their soul was full of the same women's naïveté" (VIII: 97). The situation of these men is cruelly ironic: the godfearing blacksmith, three of whose adult children were accomplices in the burglary of the post office, goes into denial, refusing to recognize their delinquency; the postmaster, who evidently recognizes his son in the burglar, suffers a stroke in consequence and lapses into a state of "mental torpor" (198). Though the wreck of Consul Johnsen's ship, the steamship *Fia*, which had apparently been left uninsured, lacks the emotional and moral charge of the blacksmith's and the postmaster's misfortunes, its consequences are farreaching. In fact, the rumored bankruptcy of Consul Johnsen, who was the "focal point of the town's entire well-being," is called an "earthquake," so alarming that the local paper printed "an appeal to people to become religious" (251–52). As for the effect on the Consul himself, the great man "had turned to zero, being gray and wan. . . . If one hadn't known better, one might think that he alone had followed the appeal in the paper and turned religious" (267). That the alarm turned out to be unjustified, because Scheldrup, the Consul's son, had paid the ship's insurance without his father's knowledge, does not invalidate the result of the enacted test of character.

Oliver Andersen's way of dealing with his hard luck constitutes the central theme of Hamsun's novel. His ability to bear up is incomparably greater than that of his fellow townsmen, although his loss was more crushing, the personal disaster more intimate. When the Consul was struck, "a great man collapsed and gave up everything." The postmaster, once that "untried human intellect of his" was subjected to "pressure," became "stupid and dumb from that moment on." And Carlsen, the "decent old blacksmith," couldn't "stand up to wickedness, . . . he became a child, wept, twitched his lips, thanked God for good and evil and waited for death." Oliver was of "a tougher sort, less noble and squeamish, more carefree, and therefore the right human stuff—he could endure life" (VIII: 279-80). After the truth is known about his being a castrato, the gossips at the pump conclude that such a fate would make "everyone else see the error of his ways, seek solitude, seek God; what were chastisements for anyway! But Oliver? No" (275).

The only characters who are even remotely comparable to Oliver in their ability to ride out a wave of misadventure, Mattis, the carpenter, and Olaus, the bum, belong to the common folk, like Oliver. The predicament of Mattis, who "met with a dreadful and absurd trick of fate" when Maren Salt, his housekeeper, gave birth to a child he had no part in, is a comic parallel to Oliver's vicarious fatherhood, since Mattis ends up marrying the woman. Olaus, with his missing arm and a face disfigured by a blasting shot, lives in a state of permanent revolt. A loafer around the docks, he is "an outcast with valuable iron in him"; "he too was a cripple, knocked down by an accident," but he didn't cry, "he merely bridled—ho, he diluted his sorrows with drink and endured them" (VIII: 184). With his rambunctious behavior and shameless chatter, which lays bare the secrets and foibles of the townspeople in the tone of a Greek satyr play, he represents a burlesque variant on the theme of personal calamity. This fellow sufferer of Oliver, while lacking the latter's depth and duplicity, equally demonstrates the value that Hamsun places on animal strength and sheer stamina in meeting life's hazards and uncertainties. Ironically, his seemingly accidental death may have been contrived by Oliver, his fellow sufferer; the information given in the text is ambiguous.

The most fascinating aspect of *The Women at the Pump* is the conception of Oliver Andersen: his identity is not a given but is gradually made up by Oliver himself. The process begins already when, in a conversation with Mattis early on, he boasts that the mutilating accident was caused by a large wave, not by a fall that landed him straddling a "sharp boom," as a former shipmate reminds him (VIII: 61). In his own version of events, the wave hurtled a barrel full of oil into his lap; "it came at me like a cannon ball," he tells Mattis. As he makes the rounds of the stores, he is asked again and again to relate what happened, and as he acquires practice, the story becomes more and more embellished with "interesting additions" (21). In general, he expands and embroiders his past as a sailor and uses every possible opportunity to let people, especially sailors on shore leave, know about it. His marriage to Petra enables him to greatly magnify the role he plays in his own story; apart from acting the part of father to a growing family, he prides himself on having set the two boys, Frank and Abel, on the path of "learning and a useful trade" (155), a sheer fabrication. His shaky relations with Petra, his wife, are at their best when husband and wife engage in a kind of game of mutual deception. Thus, when Oliver bristles on realizing that Petra is pregnant for the fifth time, she forestalls a crisis by going on the attack, relating an alleged rumor that he, Oliver, had fathered Maren Salt's baby. The effect is electric: "At this moment he was perhaps happier than he had been for twenty years, feeling maybe that something had been set right within him, a dignity, a worth, seeing himself rehabilitated by means of a delusion, in the midst of a false light, but rehabilitated." The sacramental images that ensue not only convey the reduced man's euphoria but betoken spiritual rebirth and redemption: "Has he received bread and wine and benediction, have the heavens opened,[11] has a miracle occurred?" (228).

Some readers might feel inclined to dismiss Oliver Andersen as a phony, a grotesque example of Ibsen's "life lie," so memorably dramatized in *The Wild Duck*. One remembers Dr. Relling's often-quoted words in Act V of the play: "Deprive the average man of his life-lie and you've robbed him of happiness as well."[12] But while Hjalmar Ekdal in Ibsen's play is a sentimental weakling, Oliver is strong and, unlike Hjalmar, suffers no disillusionment with deadly consequences. Indeed, it is quite possible to read Hamsun's novel as, on one level, a response to *The Wild Duck* with parodic intent, while acknowledging that Hamsun has presented some positive ideas of his own.

Those ideas, however, are not without ambiguity. Oliver Andersen is such a contradictory cluster of human characteristics that he is difficult to describe, much less define. One wonders, for example, why Hamsun compares him several times to Napoleon, to whom he is said to bear a certain physical resemblance, as well as to other great historical figures, such as Alexander and Hannibal, both of whom were allegedly afflicted with a handicap. And after he becomes warehouse manager and dispenses merchandise to the town, he is compared to Joseph in Egypt (VIII: 72), who was in charge of Pharaoh's storehouses and "sold unto the Egyptians."[13] There is no hint of a mocking or ironic intent in these comparisons; it is as though Oliver, in his day and age, is the counterpart of these great legendary and historical figures. If this parallel has any meaning whatsoever, it hinges on what one might call an existentialist element of self-making, without religious or any other sanction. The text stipulates that the accident deprived Oliver's life of the "content" or meaning that is everyone's birthright, producing a lack, an emptiness "of an unusual flawlessness," and turning the one-time sailor into "something that is nothing" (274). In short, the Oliver we get to know is the product of a *creatio ex nihilo*; with his god-given or innate manhood gone, Oliver has no choice but to build an alternate self by himself, in a never-ending series of small acts that simulate the divine creative fiat. On the strength of this struggle to invest a life without an essence with meaning and direction, Oliver qualifies as an existentialist, though he would not know the meaning of the word, nor care to know. The subjective conversion of brute fact into human meaning is clearly indicated in the following statement: "he invested chance with an exalted dignity and called it destiny" (275).

Another perspective on Oliver's character that the text invites is suggested by a few sentences toward the end of the novel, though it has already been anticipated. A paragraph that enumerates some of the practices that constitute Oliver's mythomania ends as follows: "Nothing but art, then. Nothing but art. But not a poor work of art" (VIII: 275).[14] An earlier passage, just after Oliver was suspected of fathering Maren Salt's baby, presents him as the "creator and sustainer" of an entire "imaginary world," in which he assumes an "increasingly steady position." It is a world that he intends to expand: "after a couple of years he will stand upon a height and look out upon a wide country that is his." The narrator then asks, "And now he'll manage to exist in his world, right? He won't burst into laughter and abandon it, will he? One has to put up with the world one creates, all creators have to" (235). If these enigmatic questions and statements are taken at their face value, they may yield a nugget of insight into Hamsun's concept of the creative process. Is Hamsun with his reference to "all creators" drawing a parallel between the myth-making activity of Oliver, sprung from a mutilating wound, and literary or artistic creativity? If so, the idea exists only *in ovo*, in contrast, for example, to an explicit notion about artistic creativity found in the work of Thomas Mann, expressed by Tonio Kröger in the following words to his friend Lisaveta: "I think we artists are all in rather the same situation as those artificial papal sopranos. . . . Our voices are quite touchingly beautiful."[15] If the sentences from *The Women at the Pump* just quoted are self-referential, the novel can be called a rudimentary example of metafiction.[16] However, I shall leave the further exploration of this possibility to the genetic and psychoanalytic critics.

Another dimension of Oliver's character directs the reader's attention to Hamsun's judgment on the world he was creating in *The Women at the Pump*. We have seen how, in *Segelfoss Town*, Hamsun portrayed the actors and actresses as being sexually inadequate, the men lacking in virility, the women devoid of femininity. Crassly, Max, the leader of the troupe, is called a eunuch. *The Women at the Pump* has a real eunuch as its central character, a man whose entire life is a continuous piece of acting. One sentence reads: "For eighteen years he has played at being human as well as he could, as well as anybody, better than anybody" (VIII: 134). A question comes to mind: Are we to assume that in this respect, too, Oliver provides an image of the "life of the town" (293), just as the actors with their mere simulation of life supposedly do in *Segelfoss Town*? If we are, then the society that Hamsun depicts in the novel comes to resemble the unreal "crowd" flowing over London Bridge in T. S. Eliot's *The Waste Land*, published two years after Hamsun's novel.[17]

As I suggested at the beginning of my discussion, the themes of the two novels with which this chapter deals were no doubt partly determined by the aftermath of World War I. *The Women at the Pump* has more than a similarity of mood in common with such works as *The Waste Land* and Hemingway's *The Sun Also Rises*. All three have an impotent male at its center, Oliver Andersen, the Fisher King and Jake Barnes, and the state of that figure is symptomatic of the perceived spiritual condition of the time when the works appeared. In addition, castration is a key metaphor in the postmaster's tirade against the English immediately before the burglary takes place. Serving here as elsewhere as the author's mouthpiece, the postmaster declares that the English subjugate "people after people, deprive them of their independence, castrate them and make them corpulent and quiet. Then one day the Englishman says, 'Let's now be just according to Scripture!' And so he gives the castrati something that he calls autonomy" (VIII: 190).

Here Hamsun's critique of the postwar cultural malaise blends with his anti-English stance to produce a broadside directed at colonialism, with its penchant for lofty, quasi-missionary pretensions. Still practicing his ethos of suspicion evidenced in earlier works, Hamsun shows that crime and corruption flourish under the cover of religion, as in the case of the young man who burglarizes his own father: the captain of the English ship on which he serves as second mate is said to be religious. But, again, the main charge is delivered by the postmaster, according to whom the English worship a different god, "an English god. . . . Can you otherwise explain," he asks Davidsen, another local consul, "that they are incessantly waging wars of conquest around the globe and then, when they have been victorious, believe they have done a good and noble deed?" (VIII: 190). One seems to hear echoes of Conrad's *Heart of Darkness*, in which foreign exploitation takes place under the cover of a high, semi-religious purpose.

It is difficult to make an overall judgment of a book like *The Women at the Pump*; it is a complex and often puzzling work. I have emphasized what it contains of new themes rather than complaining about how Hamsun repeats himself. And he does, and quite boringly at times; thus, the younger generation is represented by a pair of brothers, Frank and Abel, the first lusting after book learning, the other a down-to-earth soul. We have met these youngsters several times before, with slight variations. While they as well as the other boys we encounter are often vividly portrayed, the detailed report of their pranks and growing-up pains and, in Abel's case, a childish love pursued for years without any apparent success, distracts the reader from the intellectual substance of the novel. Needless to say, Frank is ridiculed, as is Fia, Consul Johnsen's artistic daughter, who is given the same satiric treatment as previous Hamsun female characters whose aims go beyond being able to thread a needle or produce a flock of children.[18] It looks as though the format of the family chronicle was not the best vehicle for doing justice to the book's major themes.

Though the professional types are also recognizable from prior novels, the characterization has become fuller and more nuancé. This is particularly so in the case of the district doctor, whose portrayal, however contradictory, smacks of truth. While unlike Dr. Muus in the Segelfoss novels, he is nameless, we not only come to know his world view, but discover his dark side, that of a permanently frustrated man whose life is joyless and who feels his talents have been wasted in the little town. The implied narrator minces no words in describing him: a "sourpuss, a fool," he is said to be "more than a little feared for his tongue"; he is certainly shown to be a gossip, allegedly motivated by a "sour discontent, bitterness, resentment" (VIII: 170–71). But elsewhere we receive a different picture of the doctor. Though the faith in science that was characteristic of him and his peers garners no praise, the lack of illusions that went with that faith does: his generation "was without cowardice, it could face the futility and hopelessness of life without whining" (266). The doctor's chief interlocutor, the postmaster, comes across nearly as well. What is particularly interesting about the portrayals of these two men is Hamsun's ability to combine convincingly an intellectual profile, including a reasoned philosophy of life, with the ordinary stuff of everyday behavior and experience.[19]

Finally, I would like to make a comment on the novel's title, which has been taken to mean that Hamsun uses a collective angle of narration in *The Women at the Pump*. This is not so. Hamsun's narrative method is the same as in the preceding three novels: limited omniscience and extensive use of free indirect discourse, with frequent questions and comments by the implied narrator. It is a freewheeling method, often frustrating to the reader, who is not always able to distinguish between authorial discourse and a character's stream of thought. The "women at the pump" referred to in the book's title is a sort of narrational leitmotif, the purpose of which must be to suggest that the content of the novel as a whole springs from the town gossip. But as one reads the text one has no awareness of any narrative device or mechanism that bears out this suggestion. If Hamsun simply wants to give the impression that gossip flourishes in the coastal town that frames the story, that is fine. But there is no reason for attributing to his use of the "pump" motif a genuinely novel way of telling a story. Narratively speaking, it is a mere trick, a kind of self-indulgence that, unfortunately, we find all too often in Hamsun's novels.

With a few exceptions, *The Women at the Pump* was unfavorably received by the critics. Here are some phrases culled from the Scandinavian reviews: "one big mess of miniature gossip and of intrigues the size of chicken feathers"; a "tired book," with "no depths, no heights"; a "prodigal waste of writing talent on exceedingly trifling things."[20] Strangely, the foreign reception was more favorable. True, Edwin Muir found the novel to be "almost intolerably boring," while Cyril Connolly sensed a peculiarly "Norwegian long-winded naivety," but on the other side of the Atlantic Clifton Fadiman noted that its "formless and easygoing" narrative makes it easy to overlook "certain beautiful qualities," such as its humor, "as broad and pervasive as it is quiet," and Hamsun's "wonderful gift" of observing simple and even mean people from a point of view which is "at once ironical and sympathetic."[21]

Thomas Mann's more positive 1922 review of Hamsun's "grotesque novel," as he calls it, harbingers less astringent critical reactions. Though Mann does not rate the book as highly as *Growth of the Soil*, its pages, he says, are full of "all the allurements, technical wiles, poetic intensities, and intimate emotions which constitute the secret, the infinitely endearing charm, of Hamsun's art"—an art that combines "the utmost sophistication with the simplicty of ancient epic."[22] Though later criticism cannot compete with this kind of praise, John Updike, reviewing the new translation by Mr. Stallybrass, writes that Hamsun's portrayal of Oliver's "self-deceiving manner" is done with "beautiful tact and believableness." Only the Russians, he says, can match Hamsun's "feel for the inconsistencies of the soul."[23] On a more personal note, an English reviewer, Charles Naughton, testifies to the truthfulness of Hamsun's depiction of small town life: "It is a marvelously profound, ironic, tongue-in-cheek picture of the vipers' nests which is what small villages really are." As for the list of village characters, he continues, the novel "provides a minutely detailed catalogue both of their defects and pretensions and of the mandatory maze of petty intrigue and jealousy which drives them." Judging by the reviewer's comment that the novel's setting "could as easily be the West of Ireland, or Suffolk,"[24] Hamsun has, by his relentlessly sustained and meticulously drawn picture of the manners and morals of a South-Norwegian town, attained a degree of universality.

The Last Chapter (1923)[25] differs from the immediately preceding novels by having a relatively well-defined narrative structure. The main plot, a triangular love story, has a number of suspenseful, even thriller-like moments, a quality not often found in Hamsun's work of this period. But classical purity of genre is not for Hamsun: the romance is interwoven with a piece of detective fiction and a counter-development exemplum of the kind we are familiar with from earlier novels. Though it is not the first time that Hamsun uses serious crime as a plot element, here it occupies a more central position than in, say, *The Women at the Pump*, where it is limited to one episode, the post office burglary. Moreover, the counter-development action in *The Last Chapter* includes an act of murder.

Nevertheless, a reader familiar with Hamsun's previous work will have no difficulty identifying the author. *The Last Chapter* exhibits an unmistakable continuity with already well-known Hamsun milieus, character types and thematic concerns. At first glance, the novel looks like a revised version, set in Central Norway, of *The Last Joy*, set in the North and published eleven years earlier; one notes the near identity of the names given to the localities where most of the action takes place: the Tore Peaks in *The Last Joy*, Torahus (lit. "House of Thunder," IX: 8) in *The Last Chapter*. True, unlike the Tore Peaks resort, which chiefly caters to tourists, Torahus is a sanitarium,[26] but its clientele is a sophisticated middle-class group much like the characters in *The Last Joy*. And though they are nearly all afflicted with some illness, whether physical or psychological, some do use the resort as simply a vacation spot.

As in *The Last Joy*, we are also introduced to an opposing world of rustic simplicity by which the sanitarium culture is judged and found wanting. The center of that world is Daniel, a proud young man who owns the neighboring farm, originally a summer dairy. It is as though Hamsun decided to separate spatially the two elements, "farm" and "resort," that jointly define the Tore Peaks enterprise in *The Last Joy*; as we shall see later, the sanitarium's proximity to the farm will be of great significance for the novel's action. The physically robust Daniel is a variant of Nikolai Palm in *The Last Joy*: though Daniel is a brute and ends up as a criminal, they both serve as Hamsun's vehicles for rescuing two educated women from a supposedly futile existence as office clerk and schoolmistress, respectively. And yet, though the novel begins and ends with what takes place at the Torahus farm—including the conclusion to the counter-development plot in which Julie d'Espard, an urban sophisticate of mixed French and Norwegian parentage who is staying at the resort, ends up as a farmer's wife—its major thrust lies elsewhere.

Death, "the last chapter," is ubiquitous in Hamsun's fiction, either as an event or as a besetting preoccupation, together with aging and the fear of decrepitude. The accent and mode of treatment, however, change in the course of his writing career. Early on, it is associated with suicide, most markedly in *Mysteries*, where Nagel's death is a half tragic, half farcical denouement to his existential despair, or with a kind of accidental murder, as in the gruesome death of Eva in *Pan*, which plays an important role in the novel's plot. Later on, in *Rosa* and the wanderer trilogy, the focus tends to shift toward an obsessive brooding on human mortality, though death as a critical event still turns up, such as Nikolai Arentsen's suicide in *Rosa*, demanded by the need for a happy ending, and the fateful resolution of the marital drama of the Falkenbergs in *The Wanderer Plays on Muted Strings*. The absorption with death continues unabated in *Segelfoss Town*, where two contrary attitudes are depicted: that of Per Shopkeeper, who is in permanent revolt against death, and Bårdsen, who feels relief at the thought of renouncing life. Neither character's death is part of any structure of events that could be characterized as a plot. Rather, both deaths have a purely thematic significance, intensifying Hamsun's scathing portrayal of a greedy, status-seeking society that, underneath its veneer of middle-class respectability, is spiritually dead.

The Last Chapter, as the title suggests, is Hamsun's novel about death. Here he orchestrates the whole spectrum of thematic and dramatic uses of death found in his earlier works. In some instances there is real novelty in the way the theme is handled. Though one main character, Mr. Magnus, for instance, shows an obvious kinship with Nagel in *Mysteries*, his story as well as his behavior are quite different. Called the Suicide, he is a cuckold whose continual delay in killing himself is justified, in his own mind, by the necessity of finding a mode of suicide that is on the level of an act of murder. That marks a distinct difference from Nagel, as well as from other suicides in Hamsun's previous novels. The resolution to Mr. Magnus' predicament is also new, since he chooses to live. The handling of the murder which resolves the principal love plot, that of a tubercular Finn, Mr. Fleming, and Julie d'Espard, is also a new departure for Hamsun. When Mr. Fleming is sought by the police for a bank robbery in his native country, he has to escape, leaving Julie, who discovers she is pregnant, in dire straits; eventually she seduces Daniel, the farmer, so that her child will have a father. When Mr. Fleming, having repaid the "borrowed" money, returns to Torahus and rejoins his lady love, who has by this time given birth to a boy, he is shot and killed by Daniel. This act serves a double purpose: while resolving the love plot in a most unromantic fashion, it gives a decisive fillip to Hamsun's counter-development theme.

Mostly, however, death occurs by other means and plays a different role in *The Last Chapter*. Hamsun's approach to the theme is clearly influenced by a central motif in *The Women at the Pump*: a sudden horror that opens up the abyss, confronting human beings with a meaningless universe and moral chaos. Death strikes without warning, either through a fatal attack of illness, more or less absurd accidents, or through a combination of both. The following characters all come to a sorry end at the Torahus resort: Mr. Ruben, a well-fed businessman, dies of heart failure one night during a short visit to his wife, who may be responsible for his death; a young neurotic girl is gored by Daniel's vicious bull as it breaks loose on being led to slaughter; a maid at the resort falls down the stairs and breaks her neck; the sanitarium's doctor, who goes skating on a mild, foggy winter night, falls into a fishing hole in the ice and dies of pneumonia a few days later; and there are other individual deaths during the novel's relatively short time span. Then, near the end, a raging nocturnal fire destroys the main building of the sanitarium, with many casualties.

Some of these deaths are ambiguous. This is especially true of the final conflagration, whose ostensible fortuitousness is contravened by repeated references in the text to fire, fire insurance, and the like. This fire motif is made to cast ominous shadows upon the future. If we follow this path of reasoning a little further, the destruction of the sanitarium may come to seem foreordained, however counter-intuitive such an idea may be. Other deaths are ironic or simply absurd, like that of the doctor, professionally committed to preventing death but instead falling prey to it through foolish behavior. One death is genuinely tragic, with a sting of irony in it: that of the Suicide's wife, whose room is next to where the fire started. When, reconciled and eagerly looking forward to a new beginning of their life together, they say good night, the husband locks her door from the outside to save her the trouble of getting up to lock the door after he left. For whatever reasons, Hamsun turned his novel into a sort of holocaust.

The text gives several clues as to what those reasons, whether conscious or subconscious, may have been. Following those clues, one can make certain conjectures as to what Hamsun may have intended by having death stalk his characters throughout the novel. The word "stalk" is not an exaggeration: as in the medieval Dance of Death or Danse macabre, the man with the scythe is actually present, though without his fiddle. He is conjured up at the end of the next to last chapter, after the reconciliation of Mr. Magnus and his wife and just before the disastrous fire: "It was the end of an important day. And all could have gone well, but Death stepped in the way" (IX: 291).

A few years earlier, during World War I, this experience of being thwarted by death must have been a commonplace in many European countries. One way of making sense of Hamsun's macabre novel is to read it as a peacetime fable about wartime reality, including the devastating Spanish flu epidemic of 1918. The novel contains several references to war; the most extensive one appears in a long disquisition by the Suicide on the everpresence of death. The occasion, a walk in the moonlight with Miss d'Espard on Christmas Eve, is fiercely ironic: Death, the Suicide says, is not always satisfied by simply doing random pickings; "during war, earthquakes, epidemics he appears as a majesty, his thumb continually turned down, wallowing in lives" (IX: 159). A Biblical allusion to the story of Uriah the Hittite highlights the fortuitousness of human events under conditions of war. During a conversation between the doctor and the lawyer, the resort's manager, after the girl has been gored by Daniel's bull, the manager remarks: "The sword devoureth one as well as another" (74).[27] It looks, indeed, as though Hamsun has imbued peacetime events with the hazardous uncertainties of modern warfare.

Reading *The Last Chapter* in this manner would turn it into a species of allegory, with one world, the one depicted, signifying another that defies description. In the light of such an interpretation, the frequent accidental deaths would appear to be quite realistic, corresponding to what can be expected to happen in times of war and pestilence. Other elements, in particular the devastating fire, suggest a cosmic perspective, whereby human time becomes configured into the meta-historical scheme of Christian eschatology, with evil apocalypse and dark forebodings of the universal end. The Suicide, with his proclivity for reciting or alluding to Scripture, is the vehicle of this somber vision of a destructive end-time. In an exchange with the doctor fraught with despair, he says, "Here we come from east and west, . . . we all look to be healed, but no one is helped, death overtakes us" (IX: 179). The Biblical passage referred to does, indeed, relate a healing, but it contains an ominous prophecy by Jesus, the healer: "And I say unto you, That many shall come from the east and west, and shall sit down with Abraham, and Isaac, and Jacob, in the kingdom of heaven: but the children of the kingdom shall be cast out into outer darkness: there shall be weeping and gnashing of teeth."[28] This is not the only allusion to an evil apocalypse in the novel. The Suicide's response to the death of the doctor at a time when they are celebrating the New Year is to nod knowingly, proclaiming that "the end was not yet!" (194), an allusion to Jesus addressing his disciples on the Mount of Olives. The relevant verse reads: "And ye shall hear of wars and rumors of war: see that ye be not troubled: for all these things must come to pass, but the end is not yet."[29] In view of the fact that Hamsun's novel ends with a great fire, it may not be without interest that, according to Christian eschatology, the world will end in fire: on the day of the Lord, "the heavens shall pass away with a great noise, and the elements shall melt with fervent heat, the earth also and the works that are therein shall be burned up."[30]

Hamsun's use of Christian eschatology, however, is in the nature of a parody: the novel contains too much evidence, both in the events and in the characters' attitudes, that rules out belief in a teleological cosmic order, one that bestows meaning upon human life, individually and collectively. The way things are, if an order existed it would be one presided over by an evil demiurge. The Suicide puts it this way: "Here we are led toward destruction with the rope around our necks, and we follow willingly in the teeth of our best interests. We hear about the wise plan of existence, but to see it, recognize it—no." In the same passage, he refers mockingly to the salvational promise, "For unto you is born this day . . . a Saviour."[31] Given this general outlook, Hamsun's use of premonitory motifs in his novel does not necessarily guarantee a genuine overarching order, whether that of tragedy or divine comedy. What is more, the fact that the implied narrator knew in advance about the events that he relates, since the novel is written in retrospect,[32] tends to reduce foreshadowing to a mere device of suspense, hence without ontological significance.

The conclusion I have arrived at after some reflection is that the apocalyptic aspect of the novel, in particular the burning of the Torahus sanitarium, is *willed* on the author's part.[33] It is the execution of a plan of revenge upon the sickly bourgeois characters who have sought refuge from life there. If we are to believe the description given of these characters, they are a singularly unattractive group of people: "unshapely each in his or her way, some because of scrawniness, others because of fat, deformed barrels on legs, dried-up schoolmarms and ink-spilling office hacks with long thin insect limbs" (IX: 229). In a sarcastic jab at the doctor's concern for the guests, the Suicide refers to the latter as "bedridden victims of life," then goes on to say: "One is requested to be careful with fire and put out lamps and candles so that those half-dead people won't be burned to death!" (179). When the narrator speaks about the guests, a note of contempt creeps into his voice; thus, the first death that takes place is described as "a bomb that exploded in the middle of a flock of weaklings" (63). And if, unlike the neurotic, hand-wringing girl who gets gored, they demonstrate their fitness to live, they are expendable for other reasons.

Mainly, the reason seems to be that they are educated people who savor the refinements of living. Occasionally, a taste for those refinements leads to crime; one of the extraordinary facts about the clientele at Torahus is the number of criminals it includes. And they are not simply anybody, they are international criminals. The English Milady, a former dancer whose presence is used as an advertising ploy, turns out to be a swindler, and Mr. Fleming, who travels in the guise of a Finnish count, unveils himself to Miss d'Espard as an embezzler or bank robber. These are the sort of crimes that have been the object of opprobrium in earlier Hamsun works, whereas grave crimes were treated with respect. Though neither Milady nor Mr. Fleming perishes in the fire, they help create the impression that civilized life, as symbolized by the sanitarium crowd, is morally corrupt and, presumably, ripe for destruction.

Strangely enough, Hamsun has included a character who gives his sinister game away. This is Miss Ellingsen, a telegrapher with literary ambitions. Whenever opportunity offers, Miss Ellingsen will tell or hint at some preposterous story, though she is usually unable to complete it. From her work in the telegraph office, she claims to have knowledge of a great many scandalous secrets, which, however, she is duty bound not to reveal to anyone. Since she is an unwomanly woman, dabbling in literature, Hamsun's narrator does his worst to discredit her. Insinuating that she was probably "conceived under anaesthesia, during a hangover," he finds that her imagination has "gone astray" (IX: 212). Nevertheless, the fact that Miss Ellingsen seems to be the immediate cause of the fire[34] turns her into a vehicle of Hamsun's very own intent, conscious or unconscious, in writing the book.[35]

From the very beginning, she has had an eye on Mr. Bertelsen, a wealthy timber merchant whose capital made the sanitarium possible and who continues to be its principal benefactor. Miss Ellingsen is fiercely jealous of every competitor, but especially of the wealthy Mrs. Ruben, in whom Bertelsen develops an interest after she is widowed, at a time when his business seems to be flagging. During the fateful party at the sanitarium, Miss Ellingsen, who betrayed her revengeful feelings toward Mrs. Ruben as soon as she saw the notice of her engagement to Bertelsen, is chagrined at her rival's contemptuous remark about an incident that she relates and embroiders upon: "Miss Ellingsen looked down, but the lady, otherwise so composed, trembled slightly as she shot her slanted eyes upward from the floor to Mrs. Bertelsen's knees with a narrow flash" (IX: 293). When Bertelsen, who by this time is quite drunk, opens the window, the lamp goes out, leaving a candle as the only source of light in the room. Then Mrs. Bertelsen loses her ring, and Miss Ellingsen fetches the candle to help find it. In the process, "she moved around Mrs. Bertelsen," but in the moment she found the ring, calling, "Here it is!", Mrs. Bertelsen "was ablaze" (294–95). What comes next, "a mixture of screams and fire," echoes the title of Miss Ellingsen's planned collection of stories, "The Scream in the Night" (293).

Admittedly, Miss Ellingsen's sensational imagination is no more than a caricature of Hamsun's own; but that does not exclude the possibility that he uses her to trigger his own revenge upon the Torahus set and the urban culture they represent. In his wrathful reaction to the whole complex of urban life, Hamsun is very much like a Hebrew prophet, such as Amos, whose arch-conservative credentials are self-evident to any reader of his prophecies. And just like half a dozen other Hebrew prophets, Hamsun appears to believe that a so-called "remnant" can be saved from perdition. In *The Last Chapter*, this remnant is represented by Julie d'Espard and Daniel, whose Biblical name guarantees his righteousness despite a brutal act of murder.

The love stories of *The Last Chapter* are driven by a combination of sexual passion and survival, and they are governed by a Zolaesque determinism. The romance of Fleming and d'Espard is inseparable from the former's struggle with his tuberculosis. This is shown by the very spot where their relationship is consummated, a hayshed on the way to Daniel's mountain dairy farm. In a hut on that farm redolent of the stone age, the soi-disant Finnish count finds new strength by drinking curdled milk out of a wooden container and sleeping under Daniel's sheepskin. The nourishing drink has a taste of "childhood and primitivity" (IX: 34). Fleming's and d'Espard's first lovemaking is accompanied by the ironic motif, "Some call it free will" (84), and traced to a "murmur in the blood, necessary stupidity and folly according to the world's oldest model, perhaps also something golden, perhaps love" (103). The vagaries of passion in conjunction with survival are equally evident in Miss d'Espard's relationship with Daniel. As she approaches the hayshed, where she knows she will let him have his way with her, the above motif recurs, "Some call it free will" (143). Subsequently, when she wants to break with Daniel after Mr. Fleming's return, the elemental forces she has set in motion become frighteningly manifest. For Daniel's desire for d'Espard, mother to a child registered as his son, is magnified to a desperate intensity by his need to regain his honor in the community. Having been jilted by Helena, a local girl, after his father lost the farm, he must have Julie to survive socially. His lacerated ego, fired up with lust, makes him turn *olm* (262; vicious), a word usually denoting animal behavior and first used to describe his fierce, murderous bullock (71). And in the moment before he fires the fatal shot that kills Fleming, he is crouched "like a beast of prey about to jump" (264).

One cannot help noticing that the characters who make up the love triangles in *The Last Chapter* have experienced some deep distress or misfortune whose consequences they are trying to live down. Mr. Fleming, who committed a crime to save his life, implies that his act may have sent his "proud parents" to the grave before their time (IX: 263). The rivals for d'Espard's love are not as different from each other as they seem. Fleming, though a bank employee, hails from the countryside; he can understand why Daniel values his reputation in the village as highly as he does. In a less extreme form, we have encountered the same situation in *Rosa*, where Benoni experienced being publicly shamed. There, too, the conflict was only resolved with the death of the first lover. And like Rosa, Julie is sorely tested, though in a different way; her pregnancy and the disputed paternity of the child arouse deeper emotions than Nikolai Arentsen's belated return.

In one respect Hamsun's characters in *The Last Chapter* are like those of Thomas Hardy: victims of forces beyond their understanding, they do not know how to oppose them except by blind maneuverings. Only after some crucial mistake has been made do even the more intelligent among them begin to realize what has happened to them. This is the case with the Suicide, whose story forms a parallel to the Fleming/Julie d'Espard/Daniel triangle, though it does not constitute a full-fledged subplot. We are told the unhappy story of his marriage only late in the novel, when he relates it to Miss d'Espard by indirection, pretending it is someone else's. We gather that here, too, the paternity of the offspring, a girl, is a problem; the affair between his wife and her lover having lasted for several years, the girl's paternity is uncertain. The Suicide, like Daniel, considers having recourse to violence, firing "a shot or two" (IX: 181), but cannot go through with it. Strangely enough, when his wife answers his Christmas card after several months by unexpectedly arriving at the sanitarium, he finds himself in an absurd emotional dilemma and tries to elude her: "Could anything more malicious be thought up: he was hunted by the very thing he desired, was pursued by it and fleeing it!" (279). The sequence of scenes that ensue, in which the Suicide and his wife at long last come to an understanding, brings to mind an Ibsen talkout between long-estranged characters. The amicable resolution of their conflict, brutally nullified by the fire, forms a counterpoint to the violent denouement of the central love plot.

The following two triangles, Daniel/Helena/sheriff's clerk and Bertelsen/Mrs. Ruben/Miss Ellingsen are less in evidence, but equally fraught with potential violence. We learn that Daniel had intended to murder his faithless girlfriend by setting fire to her home; he will never tolerate a repetition of the disgrace he suffered when his girl chose to marry someone else, a young man who will one day be a sheriff. Thus, his behavior when caught up in another erotic triangle is determined by the outcome of the first: letting go of Julie when she wishes to go back to the Finn, whom she obviously loves, would be tantamount to committing moral suicide. Confronted with the exigencies of such inveterate pride, Julie's reasoning and tears are nothing but thin air. When the showdown comes and he catches Fleming with Julie despite her having been warned, his recourse to murder is no surprise. I have already commented on the sinister use that Hamsun makes of the other triangle. Miss Ellingsen, whose passion had supposedly "gone into literature and gossip on the telegraph line, into dreams and delusions" (IX: 109), is early on introduced as a dangerous woman. One day she and Bertelsen come running home from the woods in panic: Bertelsen's cheek had been pierced by her hat pin and was badly swollen. "It looked dangerous, deadly.... 'Oh, it's poisoning!' she wailed" (18). With her Gothic imagination and frustrated sexuality, she is well suited to play the jinx and set the sanitarium ablaze.

This is the human world that Hamsun has created. The large majority of the characters who populate that world have an intuitive sense that their lives are meaningful and that things will get better and better. The slew of disasters that occur at the sanitarium do nothing to change that attitude. As against this Pollyannaish assumption that God is in his heaven and all is right with the world, Hamsun presents a bleak vision of life, one that emphasizes the ruthless struggle for survival and the transience of all things. The principal motifs used to convey this vision echo *The Women at the Pump*, with the anthill as its master symbol. Here is a chapter opening from the anthill perspective: "People crawled and crawled, some here, others there. Sometimes they crawled side by side, sometimes they met and no one would give way. But sometimes they crawled over one another's dead bodies. Could it be any different?" (IX: 174). In the novel's first paragraph, this motif is combined with that of wandering, a frequently used symbol of human time employed by Hamsun: "To be sure, we are tramps here on earth. We wander on paths and in the wilderness, sometimes we crawl, sometimes we walk upright and trample one another." Then Daniel is introduced as someone who "trampled on people and was himself trampled on" (7).

This archetypal wandering motif is found not only in the long meditations on life offered by Mr. Magnus, the Suicide, but also in the general narrative. It looks as though, in this part of his career, Hamsun contented himself with merely figurative "wanderers" or "tramps." Nevertheless, he tries to combine the moral or spiritual connotations of wandering with the actuality, as in the following passage describing Julie d'Espard's reluctant walk toward Daniel's hayshed, where "she knows what awaits her": "There she goes, she too a human being on the earth, a wanderer, a little girl—good grief, a life gone astray..." (IX: 143). These motifs, however trite and savoring of old-time piety, work quite well in a novel like *The Last Chapter*, with its skepticism of progress and foregrounding of the mutability and brevity of human life. For, as the Suicide says, "When we have wandered for a while, we wander for another while, we wander for a day, then for a night, and finally at daybreak the next day the hour has come and we are killed, in earnest and kindness killed. That is the romance of life, with death as the last chapter" (159).

There is another side to these rather lugubrious images, namely, the challenge they pose to an individual to intervene actively in his or her own fate. The Suicide, with his plan to cut his life short, is the source of certain reflections that transcend philosophical naturalism and approach certain ideas of existentialism. When he speaks of an "existence we have been given and not chosen" and a "life that has been forced on us without our slightest wish" (IX: 158), he sounds like Martin Heidegger, approximating the latter's notion of the "thrownness" of Dasein (human existence). Heidegger writes: "As being, Dasein is something that has been thrown; it has been brought into its 'there,' but *not* of its own accord."[36] One might also mention

Heidegger's concept of "Being-towards-the-end" in this connection.[37] In general, Hamsun's sardonic treatment of human temporality and his using it, chiefly through the Suicide, to expose the inauthentic existence of the sanitarium guests, have a Heideggerian ring to them. A remark by Mr. Moss, the Suicide's companion, is reminiscent of another existentialist idea, namely, the contingency of human existence as conceived by Jean-Paul Sartre. He tells Mr. Magnus, "The fact is, you haven't yet discovered your being unnecessary, your being redundant, on this earth" (119). In the famous chestnut tree episode in *Nausea*, Roquentin thinks, ". . . we hadn't the slightest reason to be there," that is, to exist. He also speaks about lives being "superfluous."[38] These quotations are presented simply to give a hint of where Hamsun's reflections were taking him. Granted, the quoted thoughts are those of his characters, but they correspond closely to the overall mood of the novel.

It should be noted that these reflections adumbrate only a few critical existentialist notions, primarily such as negate a Christian or any other universal teleology. By contrast, Hamsun's positive ideas in *The Last Chapter* are closer to the pragmatic conclusion to Voltaire's *Candide* than to the ontological probings of Sartre or Heidegger. When the Suicide visits Miss d'Espard after the fire, she and her maid are taken up with ordinary things, "the earth and the day"; the narrator calls their attitude one of "earthly engagement." The Norwegian phrase (*jordisk optathet*), which is repeated in adjectival form in the book's last paragraph (*jordisk optat*), is almost impossible to translate, because it has at least a triple meaning. Abstractly. it combines secularism with the idea of keeping one's eyes on "earthly" concerns, to the exclusion of speculation about whether life has a meaning or not. Concretely, because of the farm setting, it may also suggest being "occupied with the soil" (IX: 300–01). The closest literary counterpart I can think of is Voltaire's final maxim in his philosophical fable: ". . . il faut cultiver nôtre jardin."[39]

By the end of *The Last Chapter* only two main characters remain at center stage: Julie d'Espard with her boy and Mr. Magnus, badly burned from escaping the sanitarium fire via a downpipe and presumably about to join little Leonora, his daughter. But the Suicide is memorable chiefly because of his companionship with Mr. Moss. This relationship deserves to be looked at a bit more closely, not only because, like Julie, the Suicide undergoes a change, but equally because he and Mr. Moss represent something new in Hamsun's psychological portrayal.

For as long as Mr. Moss stays at the sanitarium, through most of Part One, a peculiar bond exists between him and the Suicide. Both have been "struck down by fate," one through a defacing skin disease at first diagnosed as leprosy, the other through his wife's adultery, which has produced a profound melancholia. Throughout the entire first part—the novel is in two parts—they carry on a mordant exchange of insults and recriminations to relieve their pain and make it bearable: They "kept themselves bitter so as not to whimper, . . . they ground their teeth so as not to burst into tears" (IX: 121). A sort of agreement had developed between them to use each other as punching bags, to fight "in order not to collapse" (120). Their dialogues, which are dominated by the Suicide, abound in quaint abuse and sadistic jokes, with a good sprinkling of black humor. Yet, their relationship, a clear case of codependency, seems touching and mutually supportive. They even help comfort Miss d'Espard at a difficult time, shoring her up "with a certain superior way of thinking and with cheerful speech; at times she couldn't help laughing at them" (114). In a way, they manifest a quiet heroism, a posture that the narrator, along with the author, obviously respects. Eventually, both Mr. Magnus and Miss d'Espard will need a good portion of such heroism to endure their lot.

The situation being played out between Mr. Magnus and Mr. Moss has a strong relish of Strindbergian theater of cruelty, minus the battle of the sexes, mixed with absurdist comedy à la Beckett. The very presence of these two characters in Hamsun's novel demonstrates that even at this late point in his career Hamsun was capable of evoking marginal states of mind and of producing effects associated chiefly with literary modernism.

No less intriguing is the manner in which Hamsun handles the process whereby Mr. Magnus abandons his intention to end his own life. Having suffered a second devastating blow through the death of his wife, who had brought him to the peak of ecstasy and restored his faith in life by returning to him, he feels the time has come to finally carry out his longstanding decision. The turnabout that takes place as he looks for a tree to hang himself from is an excellent example of what the Russian formalist critics called *ostranenie*, estrangement or defamiliarization. His step-by-step preparation for the act—finding the right tree, assuring himself that the branch is strong enough, fastening the rope to the branch and making the noose, followed by his imagining flocks of noisy crows alerting people to his dead body, flushing out a thrush and saying goodbye to everything and to "little Leonora in the city"—this sequential fragmentation of the contemplated act and its aftermath turns the entire undertaking into farce. In a punning echo of the way he had planned to go, the text reads: ". . . since death is nothing one can hang on to, he hangs on to life" (IX: 299).

Not unlike several other Hamsun novels written in mid-career, *The Last Chapter* has strengths and weaknesses. It has a fairly distinct, even occasionally suspenseful plot, and if one can accept the melodrama involved in using murder and fire as vehicles of resolution, it might even be called rather well-constructed. Also, it has several memorable characters. But the novel is baggy, largely because Hamsun cannot resist the temptation to give a full-scale portrayal of every character, however minor. A typical example is the large role given to Frank Oliver, the son of Oliver Andersen in *The Women at the Pump*, whom he had apparently hoped to develop further in the preceding novel. In a letter of 1920 Hamsun complains that he cannot include everything he wants to: "there are, for example, a couple of philologists who must be picked up again in a later work—if I live [to do so]."[40] Frank Oliver is not only a well-known classical scholar but a liberal; among other things, he believes that women are entitled to the same opportunities for higher education as men, a view anathema to Hamsun. The inclusion of Mr. Oliver not only clutters up the novel's action, but his presence—and this is worse—provides Hamsun with a convenient target to take potshots at.[41] It makes little difference that the ridicule of Mr. Oliver is chiefly second-hand, being left to the Suicide, to whom Hamsun has given his own anti-education animus. In effect, it doubles the damage, marring the portrait of the Suicide—who otherwise gives the impression of being a broadminded and intelligent man—as well as blackening an entire profession by a clumsy attempt at the caricature of a pedant. That is, of course, nothing new in Hamsun's fiction; nor are educators, as we know, the only objects of his contempt. His treatment of other professionals is, as before, just as demeaning. Thus, the doctor who went through the ice is summed up as follows: "He had lost his personality reading medical books, there wasn't very much left of him. . . . A boy, a child with a degree" (IX: 192).

What is more, Hamsun's treatment of women in *The Last Chapter* is as benighted as ever. We recall how Ingeborg Torsen in *The Last Joy* had to lose a tooth and acquire some strands of gray in her hair to become worthy of being a farmer's wife. After a while Julie d'Espard comes to seem her near-identical twin—with a split chin, a broken tooth, and a flat chest. In this novel being flat-chested seems to be contagious: it afflicts not only Julie d'Espard but also Mrs. Magnus (IX: 273, 289). One can only conclude that, in a Hamsun novel, it is obligatory for an erring wife or lover, even though she has recently given birth, to be flat-chested. Psychologically, the portrait of Julie, whom we have come to respect as a worldly-wise and courageous young woman, is badly damaged when she betrays the jealousy of a common scold over Daniel's brief business-like meeting with Helena, his one-time fiancée, after the murder. Her apprenticeship to life, as it is called (299), does not come cheaply: beauty, charm, refinement, culture must go by the board; in effect, the world must be renounced.

One feels fairly confident in making these judgments about Hamsun's intent in writing *The Last Chapter*, despite the volatile narrative voice, which has changed very little since the Segelfoss novels. That voice is a protean element, constantly assuming different modalities, at times merging with a character through free indirect discourse, at other times intruding with what can only be taken as authorial commentary. As troubling as the authorial intrusion is the difficulty of deciding whose point of view is being presented, the narrator's or that of an individual character. The circumambient flow of that capricious voice is conducive to a doughy narrative texture that tends to conceal the deeper structures of the work. This has become a permanent problem with Hamsun's fiction. It is aggravated by his seeming inability to represent two or more strands of action in virtual simultaneity. Accordingly, there are long gaps between sequences dealing with a particular character or story, with the result that it requires considerable effort to recall where the previous sequence ended. At times one cannot help wondering whether the author has any technique at all, whether his narrative is not shaped largely by a kind of intuitive incrementalism, by more or less ingenious shots in the dark.

I cannot resist making one final comment. Reading *The Women at the Pump* and *The Last Chapter* made me recall a passage in Aldous Huxley's *Point Counter Point*. Young, forsaken Marjorie Carling has just remarked to old Mrs. Rachel Quarles how "small and insignificant" a certain town seemed when juxtaposed with space: "As though one were looking at it through the wrong end of a pair of field glasses." To which Mrs. Quarles replies: ". . . the wrong end of the telescope is the wrong end. One isn't meant to look at things so that they appear small and insignificant."[42] In both the above-mentioned novels, Hamsun seems to look at people and events through the wrong end of the telescope, though the effect has little to do with cosmic space. But consistently comparing people to crawling insects produces a similar effect. This Olympian perspective has been previously noted by several commentators. Whether the personal point made by Mrs. Quarles also has validity in the realm of literary art is something each reader of Hamsun's novels must decide.

Surprisingly, *The Last Chapter*, which has not by any means been one of Hamsun's most popular novels,[43] was generally well received, not only in Norway but abroad as well. It elicited a particularly strong response in Germany, where it appeared the same year as Thomas Mann's *The Magic Mountain*. Both were "highly successful," one critic reports, but Mann's book seemed tame by comparison with "the eerily adventurous world" of Hamsun, which seemed to have "locked within it all the passions and tragedies of our time."[44] Clifton Fadiman, who also draws a comparison with Mann, says that, while Hamsun's book is much simpler and less ambitious, it is "not less successful." Calling Hamsun a "great writer," he finds in the book a "large humanity, shrewd humor and profound perception," while Percy Hutchison of *The New York Times* extols Hamsun's art, said to be "beyond art," taking on the "simplicity of nature."[45] Robert Ferguson echoes and amplifies this chorus of praise for Hamsun's novel about death, which, he writes, is "undoubtedly the most interesting and thought-provoking of all his late novels as he examines once more the profoundly existential problems which he had first studied in *Mysteries* in 1892."[46]

CHAPTER NINE

Toward a Contrapuntal Novel: Romantic Nostalgia versus Pseudo-Faustian Adventure

Four years passed between the publication of *The Last Chapter* and *Landstrykere* (1927; *Vagabonds*, 1930; *Wayfarers*, 1980). The relative dearth of literary creativity by Hamsun during these years was partly due to what his wife called a "deep and long" absorption with his farm,[1] but mainly to a severe psychological malaise, for which Hamsun eventually decided to seek professional help. From January to June 1926 he stayed in an Oslo hotel while undergoing analysis with Dr. Johannes Irgens Strømme, who according to his own statement of 1918 was at that time the "only physician in Norway" who had been trained in psychoanalysis.[2] The analysis seems to have been successful; in any case, Hamsun was able to resume his writing. According to Marie Hamsun, he "wrote the first part of *Vagabonds* virtually in one breath that summer. He believed he could thank the doctor for that, and he did."[3]

Initially, Hamsun feels uncertain about the scope of his new work, and his opinion of its merits veers from one extreme to another. In July 1926 he writes to his German publisher that the novel he is working on will "hardly be as long" as the last five or six of his books, but in a letter of November the same year he notes that it will be "very long." Indeed, it turned out to be the longest of all Hamsun's novels. His opinions of its worth are equally wavering: whereas in the November letter just cited he says, "I think it will be very good,"[4] less than one year later he writes his Norwegian publisher, "I . . . have for several months been afraid that my book is just tedious and endless old man's chatter." Hamsun uses the same phrase, "old man's chatter," in a subsequent letter to the publisher.[5]

Hamsun's uncertainty as to the novel's worth after completion could be dismissed as a mere postpartum commonplace. On the other hand, it might betray a vague awareness that he was repeating himself, following a personal stereotype which, among other things, included the requirement that a novel had to be of a certain length and to consist of a two-part structure. Starting with *Segelfoss Town*, the first Hamsun novel to comprise two parts of roughly equal length, the scale of his fiction increased considerably. All his remaining novels adhere to this two-part format, as though Hamsun was bent on emulating the Victorian three-decker. A comment on the sequel to *Vagabonds*, entitled *August* (1930; English translation 1931), suggests that, at this point in Hamsun's writing career, to be considered complete a work must comprise so and so many printed pages: there remain, he writes, "some 60 extremely compact pages of the book to do."[6] And a couple of years later, working on the final novel about August, he writes to his wife, "I've reached page 20 in my work, but how far does that go toward 300 pages?"[7] Whatever one thinks about the merit of the individual novels that Hamsun wrote after adopting this length requirement and the two-part format, the quality of his fiction generally suffered when external criteria influenced its design. In particular, his striving to achieve a near symmetry of the two parts has little aesthetic justification and leads to considerable strain. Due to diffuseness, garrulity, or an over-emphasis on minor characters that blurs the narrative perspective, the second part is usually weaker than the first.

A notable characteristic of *Vagabonds* and Hamsun's two subsequent novels, *August* and *Men livet lever* (1933; translated as *The Road Leads On*, 1934), is that they form part of a trilogy, an idiosyncratic roman-fleuve that extends, roughly, from the early 1860s to a decade or two after the turn of the century. The very dimensions of this magnum opus would represent an impressive achievement by any novelist, regardless of literary quality. If we credit Hamsun's own words about *Vagabonds* representing "four years of work,"[8] altogether the trilogy was eleven years in the making. Although a few months before the release of *The Road Leads On* he calls this novel, the last in the trilogy, a "lousy book,"[9] other statements reveal Hamsun's obvious pride in his overall accomplishment after more than a decade-long creative endeavor. When the initial reviews of *The Road Leads On* seemed less positive than he had hoped, he writes to his publisher, "In any case, I know myself what I have put into this volume and into the trilogy as a whole, and some day it will not require anybody's benevolence." The reviewers, he thought, were too narrow in their focus, forgetting to take "time, the future," into consideration.[10]

Hamsun had no reason to worry: the trilogy has done very well both among readers and critics. This is particularly true of *Vagabonds*, which has been the subject of two book-length studies.[11] Generally, this novel has been viewed as a watershed in Hamsun's later production, not only because it evidenced renewed creativity after a dry period but also because the tone was less dark and the narrative persona less obsessed with mortality and corruption than in the two immediately preceding novels. This is a view that must be respected, as long as the continuities of Hamsun's fiction—of character types, themes and form—are acknowledged.

Despite some new departures, one discovers that the central characters and themes have cognates in previous novels. As an injured sailor addicted to mythomania, August recalls Oliver Andersen in *Women at the Pump*, while a deeper kinship relates him to Mr. Geissler in *Growth of the Soil*; like the latter, for example, he is associated with a "fog" image (X: 118). But he is a far more ambiguous figure than Geissler: though starting out as a simple adventurer, he becomes in the course of the trilogy, which follows him from youth to age, a latterday Swiftian projector.[12] In the end his projects, which grow increasingly absurd, come to look like parodies, or travesties, of Geissler's entrepreneurial activities. Both he and his friend, Edevart, are dreamers, but whereas August is in thrall to the Zeitgeist, the spirit of change, and strains restlessly toward an ever-receding future, Edevart falls prey to an incurable nostalgia for an experience of transcendent love that he is unable to recover. Temperamentally, he seems more akin to Scott Fitzgerald's Jay Gatsby than to any previous Hamsun character. His closest relations in Hamsun's fiction must be sought among the outsiders, such as Glahn and Nagel, who come to grief through love. But unlike these predecessors, Edevart is a simple man, the eldest son in a poor family of fishermen/peasants, and his humble circumstances, his insecure sense of self, and his particular emotional quandary—an undying love for another man's wife—suggest a comparison with Benoni in his moments of hurt and frustration. However, Edevart's story, unlike Benoni's, has no happy ending.

Thematically, the trilogy betrays elements previously found in *Segelfoss Town* and *Growth of the Soil*, combining the critique of modernity of the former with the glorification of the soil and those who work it of the latter. As August comes to dominate the trilogy from the second volume on, the critical element expands and intensifies, while the pro-agriculture bias continues. Hamsun was quite aboveboard about his intent. Commenting on the jacket for a new impression of *Growth of the Soil* in a letter to his publisher, he writes: "I want to make the soil attractive to people, I want the same thing in *Vagabonds*." He makes a similar statement of intent five months later.[13] The satire of urbanization and "progress," which reaches a first climax in the Segelfoss novels, is in the trilogy conflated with emigration, a theme already touched on in *Growth of the Soil*. On the whole, Hamsun's fiction continues to explore the themes that came to dominance around 1910 or a few years later, apart from the love theme, which had been present from the outset.

While the form of the first novel in the trilogy, *Vagabonds*, represents a new departure for Hamsun, it is as old as the art of European fiction. A letter to his publisher of 1930, in which he writes that it is "not inappropriate" that the Spanish translation of *August* should be undertaken by Cervantes publishers,[14] suggests that he discerned a certain similarity between his own project and that of the great Spaniard. Hamsun's story, like that of Cervantes in *Don Quixote* (1605), has an episodic structure, contains a sort of quest motif, and follows the fortunes of two contrasting main characters. And because Edevart and August, the central figures, are constantly on the move, the novel portrays a broad social canvas, another Cervantesque trait. The word "picaresque" also comes to mind in trying to characterize the generic qualities of Hamsun's roman-fleuve. August has a distinct *pícaro* side to him: he lives by his wits and, in a pinch, will resort to crime. However, as in most attempts to describe Hamsun's fiction, the categories do not quite fit. Though it may be helpful to pay some attention to typology, Hamsun's art of the novel is *sui generis*.

The travels of Hamsun's young twosome, together or apart, are mainly to places in North Norway and the adjacent Trøndelag counties. Despite their sharply opposed temperaments and attitudes, they become close friends and companions. In their itinerant existence they support themselves by a variety of occupations, ranging from sailor and ship's captain to peddler and shopkeeper, and they run into a gallery of different people, some of whom come to play an important role in their lives. Edevart, the younger, is an average, rather naive youth, not very bright but kind and honest. August, with some years as a seaman behind him at the story's beginning, is worldly-wise, smart and totally amoral. Edevart is a homebody who finds himself leading a kind of life unsuited to him, whereas August is a restless spirit.[15] Their multifarious experiences, partly inspired by Hamsun's own youthful ventures in Nordland, make for a lively narrative. While short on real drama, it is rich in incident; moreover, it gives a vivid picture of the life of common folks and of the regional economy and culture that determine their needs and their values. Though Hamsun introduces a large number of characters, the novel mainly tells the story of Edevart, whose apprenticeship to life it traces from adolescence to his late twenties.

The initial scene of *Vagabonds* embodies a theme of disenchantment that casts long shadows on the future of Edevart Andreassen. At the age of thirteen, Edevart learns that appearance and reality can be quite different things.

A pair of wandering Gypsies turn up in Polden, Edevart's Nordland village. One of them plays a musical medley on a hand organ, while the other passes the hat. Seemingly blind in one eye, the organ grinder stirs the hearts of the bystanders, the more so as he is physically attacked by his companion following a slight disagreement. To the horror of his mother, Edevart intervenes in the squabble and knocks the assailant down, causing him to slink away into the woods. Meantime the victim becomes the beneficiary of whatever generosity the poor villagers can allow themselves, and reciprocates by putting on a puppet show featuring Napoleon and his generals, to the delight of everybody. When the man leaves, after being treated to a meal by Ane Maria, a young wife, Edevart, wishing to be of help against his brutish associate, follows. However, he is angrily rebuffed. Presently the assailant reappears, and Edevart watches in disbelief as the two men act like the best of friends. It dawns on him that he has been fooled. Though he does not immediately "draw any conclusion from his adventure in the woods," a foundation has been laid "which later experiences could build on" (X: 11).

One notes that the con men are wanderers, in keeping with a central theme of *Vagabonds*. In time Edevart himself will be one, with the moral obliquity that usually goes with wandering in a Hamsunian universe. Yet, three years after the initial incident, at sixteen, when he throws in his lot with August, he acts in the same upright and courageous manner. In fact, his friendship with August begins when he stands up for him against Teodor, a good-for-nothing youth who sneers at August for his gold teeth. During his and August's first venture together at the Stokmarknes Fair, where they have gone as skin traders, Edevart recognizes and exposes the two Gypsies who had made him feel such a fool three years ago.

A couple of times Edevart's intervention represents a commoner's equivalent of rescuing a damsel in distress. The following summer, during a barn dance at which August provides the music—he plays the accordion—Edevart fights a battle royal with a skipper he catches in the bushes with Ragna, a girl several years his junior that he is sweet on. Subsequently, when Ragna, in an advanced state of pregnancy, comes to ask for Edevart's help in forcing the alleged father to assume some responsibility for her condition, he realizes that he had arrived too late to prevent the skipper from having his way with the girl. Playing Galahad once again, Edevart undertakes a trip in an open boat to see the skipper, and although he has by this time been told that the child was stillborn, he wangles ten dollars out of him for the girl. To his credit, he hesitates, steeped in "deep ponderings" by the new state of things (X: 121). Going through with his promise to Ragna marks a compromise with his honesty, and it is not the first one.

Edevart, the innocent youth, is a kind of Candide who gradually discovers the world outside his own little village and the unwritten rules whereby it lives. He is several times described as looking over a fence at a way of life and behavior unfamiliar to him. The first time the metaphor is used is when Knoff, a well-to-do merchant, thinks of hiring him. "On his walk through the living room Edevart's eyes had been wide open and quick, he was looking at an unfamiliar splendor: a mirror from floor to ceiling, a sofa with gold on it, a piano with a daughter playing, . . . paintings in gilded frames on the walls." Then his observations are interpreted in terms of the metaphor: "He had an opportunity to peek across the fence to another world, not a very tall fence perhaps, but tall enough for Edevart. . ." (X: 80). The same image appears in connection with his employment by Papst, the watch-peddling Jew he keeps running into off and on. When some customers complain to Papst that Edevart had swindled them by selling defective watches, Papst sees his chance to do some publicity for himself: "You shouldn't buy watches from every Tom, Dick and Harry, you should buy from Papst. He never cheats!" Here the image is picked up again: "Edevart went back to his lodgings and didn't go out again. He had had enough of it. He had again peeked across a fence: there was no large mirror nor any gold things to be seen, it was a world where everybody deceived everyone else" (93). We are reminded of the initial scene, which adumbrates all of Edevart's later disillusioning experiences.

Curiously, this innocent, morally earnest youth admires August, an outrageous liar and unscrupulous conniver with only a rudimentary sense of morality. Perhaps the most damning evidence against August is what he reveals during the companions' voyage to the Stokmarknes Fair. When a severe hailstorm occurs as they cross the hazardous Vestfjord, August—who is courageous on deck but fears being in an open boat—panics as he recalls his past sins and spills his guts: he confesses having participated in the gang rape of an underage black girl in some tropical country; we later discover that the girl was suffocated during the attack. Yet, Edevart persists in his hero worship of the wayward sailor, even after it fell to him, a mere novice at sea, to demonstrate some seamanship and save the day. Eventually Edevart's behavior changes, as his moral scruples weaken. Thus, when August sails "The Seagull" to Bergen after its owner, Skåro, has perished in a notorious quagmire, prey to vengeful Ane Maria, he juggles the accounts for his own benefit and shares the extra winnings with his companion. Though Edevart is perplexed and has qualms about accepting the money, he is swayed by his worshipful attitude toward August to do so: "Surely August had to know..." (X: 54).

This situation becomes paradigmatic for the young man's relationships with other people. When he commands "Hermine" on a fish-buying assignment to the Lofoten fisheries for Knoff, the merchant, Norem, the skipper who commands Knoff's brig, inveigles Edevart into an agreement to "cheat Knoff" by reporting a higher price than the one actually paid. Again, Edevart is in two minds about the proposal, while doing his best to justify himself. "If he reported the plan to the shipping company, he most certainly wouldn't be believed, for Norem was old in the service, and why should Edevart be so much better than the others, why should he stand in his own way?" Still, he knows full well that Norem is a "wily crook who had used friendship . . . to lure others to become crooks as well." The upshot of his reflections is a general judgment on human nature, emphasized by a brief one-sentence paragraph: "That's what people were like" (X: 111). The statement seems to be borne out by what Norem subsequently reveals about Knoff: being in financial straits, he had allegedly ordered Norem to shipwreck the brig. The revelation causes Edevart to regret bitterly his having gone along with this "shameless" man, who "blabbed about his trickeries and boasted of them" (153).

The consequences of Edevart's widening experience resemble, *mutatis mutandis*, those that we see in nineteenth-century novels of young men from the provinces who go to London or Paris or some other metropolis to make their fortune. Edevart may move in different social circles from Rastignac or Pip, of *Père Goriot* and *Great Expectations* respectively, but the effect of his social experience is, as with them, a mixture of good and bad: a degree of self-confidence and worldly wisdom is acquired at the cost of integrity. It is worth noting that the beginnings of intellectual confusion and moral corruption antedate Edevart's initial encounter with Lovise Magrete Doppen, the married woman who will have such a devastating effect on his life. The sexual quandary is one of several destructive forces operating in the novel.

Nevertheless, Edevart's meeting with Lovise Magrete when, on returning Skåro's ship to Bergen, he, August and Teodor stop to take in water in a cove near the Trondhjem Fjord, is the most fateful thing that ever happened to him. As she is described, "barefoot and very scantily clad, with nothing on except a shift and skirt," and with "tears in her eyes" on account of a sheep that has gotten stuck on a rocky ledge, she naturally appeals to the chivalrous disposition of Edevart. Though the sheep is no damsel in distress, its rescue at the risk of Edevart's life arouses deep feelings in the young woman, and when Edevart, for his part, finds out that her husband has been absent for four years, his breast "bled with compassion." He feels a tremor, "perhaps out of humility, perhaps out of love, something sweet" (X: 58). Afterward he shows obvious symptoms of lovesickness: poor appetite, an ashen face, despondency. He can now think about Ragna with complete indifference; he was "overwhelmed by something else and more powerful, it felt like a fit, an attack" (61). On his return from Bergen by the packet boat, he stops at Doppen.

Hamsun not only points up the difference in age and circumstances between them—Edevart is a youth of seventeen or eighteen, she twenty-five or twenty-six and a mother of two—but he also makes it clear from Lovise Magrete's reaction to a letter from her husband that she still loves him. Yet, she enjoys having Edevart around almost as much as he is delighted to be there. During his brief stay at Doppen, a matter of weeks, he makes himself at home, does odd jobs on the little property, and hands out presents to everybody. But his desire to stay with Lovise Magrete, despite his discovery that, contrary to her story, her husband has been in prison for manslaughter, not in America, comes up against insuperable obstacles. However, such obstacles have often been a necessary condition of passion-love. If Hamsun's treatment of this love differs from that of his predecessors, such as Emily Brontë or Tolstoy, the difference is in the aura of Edenic innocence that surrounds it. When Lovise Magrete gives in to Edevart's timid appeals, she seems to act naively and spontaneously, whether "out of motherliness, pity, or love, God knows. She initiated him, and for hours they were in a blissful frenzy, a tumult, completely natural, without any tricks, he continuing to be insatiable and she crying for mercy for nary a moment" (X: 76).

Whatever one thinks of this as a rendering of sexual rapture, one can scarcely miss its programmatic aspect, or the crude throwaway humor: we witness an all-consuming but simple enactment of desire. The remainder of my discussion of Edevart and Lovise Magrete will inevitably come back repeatedly to this *parti pris* of the narrative persona. In his subsequent meetings with Lovise, Edevart perceives her consistently through the bucolic image she presented when he first set eyes on her: a barefoot girl contented with her humble lot. When, next, he sees her at Knoff's general store, where he is a sales clerk, he barely knows her at first because of the way she is dressed: "she seemed a stranger, no longer childlike and sweet; Edevart stared at her and bowed as he did to the other customers before he recognized her" (X: 98). The presence of Håkon, her husband, who behaves in a crass manner toward Edevart, hampers communication. The situation is such that "no secret word" could be exchanged, causing the narrator to exclaim: "He didn't scream, didn't curse, but where was the wonder now? The harsh treatment was so unexpected, it was a cruel, mad experience that turned him from somebody into nobody" (99–100).

Soon after, Edevart suffers a parallel disenchantment with his family when, due to their temporarily improved financial situation, the presents he brings them fail to produce the familiar old gestures of gratitude. His little sisters no longer thank him by hand; only his father, "old-fashioned and uncorrupted," does so. All in all, he "didn't meet the old simplicity, the homey feeling had gone, innocence become rarer, another mentality had taken hold" (X: 117). What the two situations have in common is that Edevart perceives both Lovise Magrete and his family through an idealized past image, one suggestive of a perfect spiritual communion.

Edevart's next meeting with Lovise Magrete takes place the following year in the cuddy of Knoff's sloop, of which Edevart has had the command on a fish-buying expedition to the Lofoten fisheries. The scene, which is a marvel of psychological probing worthy of Ibsen or Strindberg, must be examined at some length. Aware that Lovise and her husband plan to emigrate, Edevart deliberately avoids them by staying on board: "He was lost enough as it was; once he would probably have given his life for her, now he demanded of himself that he act like a grown man. . . . How warped he had become, frittering himself away in foolish whims, roaming restlessly back and forth between Polden and the Fosen country. She didn't mean more to him than a bush back home" (X: 146). Yet, when she comes and asks for his help, he ends by giving her his wallet, with all his money, so that she and her family can pay for their tickets to the New World. Before this happens, he has learned there is now a third child, fathered by him. Moreover, Lovise Magrete's husband, Håkon, has appeared on deck, apologizing humbly for his previous behavior toward Edevart and, without his wife's knowledge, adding his voice to her appeal.

The scene is developed in a manner that reveals the divided feelings of both Edevart and Lovise Magrete. Though Edevart knows that fulfilling Lovise Magrete's wishes, and thus helping her leave the country, "would mean unhappiness and shipwreck for him," he appears resigned, thinking "it was his fate to be destroyed. . ." (X: 150). At the same time he is sexually aroused by Lovise Magrete's physical presence. A cynic might see what happens next as Edevart's attempt to be rewarded for his generosity, but his trying to "unbutton her clothes" can be attributed to a misreading of her passionate expression of gratitude and her fervent kisses. Her behavior is even more ambiguous: instead of welcoming his sexual overtures, she bursts into tears, though she starts undressing, acting "as though she were eager and in the mood for it." With Lovise Magrete crying more and more bitterly, Edevart, "hurt deep down," packs her "brutally" into her clothes and asks her to "take the money and go" (150–51). Before she leaves, however, Hamsun manages to cast a lurid light on the episode.

We discover that Håkon had persuaded his wife to go to Edevart at a time when sexual intimacy would be impossible because she was menstruating. To Edevart's question whether her husband knew she was with him, she answers, "Yes. He asked me himself to go to you. Oh, he's not as bad as you think," to which Edevart replies, "I think he's worse" (X: 148–49). Moreover, just before she leaves, Edevart asks whether she had "arranged it that way" before she came. "'No,' she said, 'I didn't want to, it was Håkon who asked me to arrange it that way. But I'm sorry I did" (151). Not only is Håkon pimping for his wife, but he also sees to it that the designated customer is deprived of his pleasure.

Soon Edevart begins to fear that his wandering style of life has turned him into a *landstryker,* a word that Hamsun uses in a way that has no precise equivalent in English. Approximate renderings are "vagabond," "tramp," "hobo," or "drifter," but the word is also employed pejoratively to mean "emigrant," someone who *stryker av landet,* a phrase meaning to "abandon one's country" which is used repeatedly in the novel (X: 142, 245). Back in Polden, Edevart meditates on his sense of alienation after a "bleak Christmas without festivity." Here an entire congeries of additional connotations of *landstryker* appears. "Was it possible that he had already roamed about too much and had the makings of a vagabond in him? One place had begun to be just as good or just as bad as any other to him, the feeling of home was starting to be blotted out, his roots in the earth were damaged." Becoming specific, he asks, "Did he care about the familiar places in the field anymore, about the hills, the trails, the mountains out there, the sea, Polden, did he even care about those he had known since childhood?" (164).

When Edevart leaves home without saying goodbye at the end of Part One, mentioning America as a possible destination to an old neighbor, he is described as physically strong, but with a divided mind. "Here he sailed off empty and homeless, having gradually come to be from noplace; wherever he roamed he dragged his roots after him" (X: 172). Interestingly, his mental state has a strong resemblance to that of Nagel in *Mysteries*, whose reservation of suicide as an ultimate possibility opens up a field of total contingency and absolute freedom. Edevart's profound indifference manifests itself in a similar way. When Mattea, a former flame of August's whom Edevart meets on the southbound steamer, takes his hand for goodbye after they have cuddled on deck all night, "he lost his footing and said, 'I may as well get off here, too!'" The text continues: "He had no plan, all he had thought was without determination and direction, he abandoned no purpose by following the first impulse that came along" (174–75). On the spur of the moment, he decides to join Mattea and her husband in their peddling venture.

With the return of Lovise Magrete from America some half dozen years later, the cluster of meaning associated with *landstryker* undergoes further expansion. But by now it is Lovise Magrete who exemplifies the corruption that supposedly follows in the wake of breaking away from one's place of origin, whereas Edevart, with his considerable worldly experience and increasing corruption, behaves like a hick who never left home, at least in his relationship with Lovise Magrete. It looks as though, for Hamsun to fulfill his antiemigration agenda, Edevart must be both supremely innocent and not entirely untutored in worldly ways.

Edevart's unspoiled Polden persona is clearly in evidence in the awkwardness that marks his behavior toward Lovise Magrete after her return from America. When the two of them go for a walk at Doppen with Håbjørg, Edevart and Lovise's child, and Lovise asks him, "Which of us do you think she looks like?," Edevart "dropped his eyes; they didn't talk about such things in Polden when the parents were unmarried, he wasn't used to it. . ." (X: 237). Similarly, he is embarrassed at showing affection for the child, blushing when she tells her mother that he kissed her cheek. And although Edevart has had several affairs since they parted, including one with Ragna that resulted in pregnancy, vis-à-vis Lovise Magrete he behaves as though the time in between has stood still. His optics are determined by the retinal imprint of the scantily clad barefoot girl who originally caught his fancy. Again, as in the visit to the store many years ago, her attire—now far more elegant—makes her seem like a stranger, an impression that he represses by recalling "the first kiss, the first embrace" as his heart feels a "renewed love and joy." But even the memory of that first enchantment is poisoned by Edevart's retrospective embarrassment at how "stupid and ignorant" he might have seemed to her at the time (232). The trouble is that, despite the years that have passed, he perceives her with the eyes of the inexperienced youth who began the affair, while his thinking, preconditioned to look beneath appearances, questions Lovise Magrete's every gesture with a suspicion worthy of Hamlet's worst taunts of Ophelia.

Along with his pristine simplicity and yearning for a paradise lost, Edevart displays an uncanny ability to penetrate what he has come to think of as the false front of Lovise Magrete. In his frustration at her inability to make up her mind to share her future with him, now that she is allegedly divorced from her husband, he begins to question her love for him. Recalling that "overwhelming evening" after her return, he finds everything about her to be "beautiful, but it was *contrived*. How could it be otherwise when it didn't last? It was thought out in advance" (X: 246). The difference between his and her values stands out from their attitudes about clothes. When Edevart fondly recalls his first sight of her, she is surprised that he has the heart to "remind her of the bad times, to humble her. 'Yes, I didn't have many clothes in those days,' she said, hurt." And when she tries to show him affection, the invisible narrator vulgarizes it, turning her gestures into a sexual payback for his financial help. Remembering how "kind" Edevart had been to her, shouldn't she "do something for him in return! She became nervously agitated and threw herself upon his breast, crying and laughing, kissed him shamelessly with her mouth and tongue and whispered a promise to be sweet to him tonight" (247).

What we witness in the relationship of Edevart and Lovise can be described as cultural clash, and in his case culture shock. The conflict is so fundamental that it touches every aspect of life and behavior. Apparently, Lovise Magrete, who used to be proud of her weaving, cannot even seat herself at the loom in a natural manner anymore. Now she does so "with both legs together to be genteel. . . . She had learned to be affected, she had learned tricks," blessedly absent from her past way: "One leg at a time, straddling naturally in two flips, one for each leg, the thin skirt drawn tight around her thighs. . . ." Edevart also finds the dinner of "milk and porridge" she had served him when they first met to have been "good food" (X: 248). This opinion is echoed when, after a day of hard work at Doppen following Lovise Magrete's return to the States, Edevart sups contentedly on barley meal porridge with syrup water on the side, "no poor fare for sure, and he thanked God for it" (280). It is worth noting that, aside from espousing a sartorial ideal of no frills and a know-nothing code of sexual behavior, Edevart here is a living example of one of Hamsun's favorite Biblical verses: ". . . godliness with contentment is great gain."[16] Yet, in an exchange with Joakim, his brother, after Lovise Magrete has returned to America, he parrots her contrarian view by saying that Ezra and Hosea, the hardworking counterparts of Isak and Inger of *Growth of the Soil*, are content and happy only because "they don't know anything better" (297, 269).

Vagabondism does, indeed, have much to answer for. In addition to the connotations already discussed, it acquires new ones through Hamsun's handling of the love story, all negative, needless to say. A one sentence paragraph that states, "They had also become vagabonds in love," is preceded by Edevart and Lovise's banter about other possible love interests, an exchange capped by the following authorial judgment: ". . . they felt no shame before one another. Their love lay broken up behind them, and they had nothing firm and steadfast ahead of them." The "ecstasy of bliss" is past, they are both "parceled out, no whole devotion" (X: 261). Telling her how dearly he loved her, "deep down he didn't mind her believing him. Then she would be the executioner and he the victim, a martyr." And she "vied with him in lying" (253-54).

With the anti-emigration charge she has to carry, Lovise Magrete gets the worst of it. After mowing the grass at Doppen, the little farm he was given as security for his "loan," Edevart goes into a fugue of resentment. Though he takes it all back afterward, it has served Hamsun's purpose: to totally destroy any semblance of decency in Lovise Magrete's behavior. Even her "ardor and tenderness" when she gave herself to him were accompanied by "shameless words and outbursts which only coarsened the moment." And how could she be so unconcerned about the possible consequences of their lovemaking? She has obviously "learned some tricks" abroad, he thinks, something he has only heard about and finds offensive. And imagine, she allows herself to sew on Sundays, at a time when the parson is preaching from the pulpit. Oh, she is so "liberated," so gone astray from her "original timid innocence. What place did wantonness have in love?" She can do nothing right. The rather sweet gesture of putting a wildflower in his buttonhole is felt as an embarrassment; it is foolish or affected (X: 279-80).

After this catalogue of solecisms committed by Lovise Magrete, it comes as no surprise that Hamsun finally turns her into a real ninny: thus, after a few years in the States she no longer has complete command of her own language! In his primitivist fervor and stay-at-home zeal Hamsun has falsified the portraits of both figures in the romance plot: with all his virtues, such as kindheartedness and bravery, Edevart turns into a receptacle of narrow views and absurd prejudices, and Lovise Magrete into a mixture of tart and social snob.[17]

Though both August and Edevart are natives of Polden, their stories hew fairly closely to the outsider plot, in which a character appears at the story's inception and disappears at the end. August, the sailor, who returns to Polden early on and leaves shortly before the novel's conclusion, is the archetypal outsider. Edevart's outsider status may seem problematic, since unlike August he does not arrive from somewhere else but is shown in the very first scene to belong to a particular place. His outsider status develops in the course of the narrative; it is emphasized by parallel departures at the end of the novel's two parts, the first time from Lofoten, where he has been fishing, the second time from Polden (X: 170, 334).

Because Edevart and August possess sharply conflicting temperaments, it may look as though Hamsun was writing two novels under one jacket, despite their often shared itineraries. However, a second look at their relationship will serve to correct this impression.

That relationship is quite complex, founded on a shared need to make a living in a harsh environment. August is the mentor, Edevart an admiring, but at the same time skeptical, learner. True, Edevart learns from others as well, especially Norem, the unscrupulous skipper; yet, August's influence is primary. Mostly, of course, what he picks up is not exactly what is best for a young man, though in one instance, at least, he acquires considerable kudos by passing an idea of August's on to Knoff: to build a dock that will make the village accessible to an important steamship company. More common acquisitions are bragging and dishonesty, in which August excels; thus Edevart reports that he hit a burglar at the Stokmarknes Fair with a stone, a blatant steal from an August boast (X: 310, 304). The crucial thing he learns from his association with August is, of course, to be a vagabond, someone who no longer belongs to a particular place but everywhere — or nowhere.

And yet, despite whatever corrupting influence the older friend exerts on the younger, the relationship remains one of abiding contrast. In particular, Hamsun points up their differences by the manner in which they handle their love affairs. August, an absurd caricature of a sailor with a girl in every port, takes love lightly, whereas Edevart's one great love leads to personal ruin: he can never bring himself to utter August's crass "good riddance" when disappointed in love.

The companions' love relationships are described in such a way as to provide reciprocal commentary and critique. While Edevart's mooning over Lovise Magrete may look overly sentimental, August's macho womanizing, accompanied by braggadocio and violence, seems driven by a mechanical lust. The friends' sexual behavior and associated moral norms could scarcely be more different. Yet, certain points of similarity make it possible to view Hamsun's double-barreled narrative in a way that is more nuancé.

Both Edevart and August are extremely generous toward the objects of their love, August ridiculously so: he hands out gold rings and watches to every girl who catches his fancy, often causing the reader to wonder where all the trinkets and watches come from. Edevart's generosity is carried to the point of self-impoverishment. Their erotic inclinations and behaviors are also linked by their shared interest in Mattea, who prefers Edevart to August, the soi-disant fiancé, and in Miss Ellingsen, Knoff's housekeeper, who is a married woman by the time August develops a passion for her. Though Hamsun is vague on specifics, a sophisticated reader will feel confident that Edevart had an affair with Miss Ellingsen. But strangely enough it is August, the incurable philanderer, who in this instance appears as a languishing would-be lover: "When I see her in the morning," he tells Edevart, "I walk around as if befogged till noon, I sup on porridge and think it's meat" (X: 276-77). Here August's situation, one of getting entangled in a sexual triangle, echoes that of Edevart vis-à-vis Lovise Magrete.

Far from invalidating their radical differences, the above coincidences between Edevart's and August's erotic object choice and amorous behavior make those differences all the more apparent: a contrast is meaningful only within a context of similarities. All in all, August's multifarious encounters, real and imagined, constitute a burlesque counterpoint to Edevart's emotional cul-de-sacs. The importance of this interweaving of their stories is chiefly formal: as one follows the permutations of desire in the lives of the young protagonists, the perceived pattern of contrast within similarity helps to give a much needed structure to Hamsun's compendious novel.

But August's role in *Vagabonds* is not simply to provide a comic counterpoint to Edevart's sentimental and social education, with its disenchanting consequences, while he, elusive and mercurial, undergoes no fundamental change. With his assortment of contradictory traits, being described as a "remarkable fellow, able and enterprising, mendacious . . ., well liked by all, loyal and often helpful to his own detriment, but in a pinch unscrupulous to the point of crime" (X: 284-85), August looks like a curious realization of Hamsun's early call for characters "in whom inconsistency is literally their fundamental trait."[18] August's fictional persona is sufficiently broad to accommodate a classic teller of tall tales of the likes of Baron von

Münchhausen (1720–97) as well as a picaresque rogue and impractical dreamer.[19] Whatever consistency August manifests in *Vagabonds* pertains to his constant restlessness and his over-active imagination. To see his innovative spirit in full flower, we shall have to wait until the sequel, *August*.

August's neighbors, however, feel that he has already brought something fundamentally new into their lives. In an unusual discussion with Edevart after August has left Polden, Joakim, Edevart's younger brother, tries to sum up, however ambiguously, the meaning of that new element. Calling August "a kind of emissary," Joakim says that the seeds of their life during the last twelve years had been planted by August: ". . . good and bad, the improvements, the excesses and the uncertainty—all could be traced back to him." Then the metaphor changes to that of an epidemic, for which August is made responsible: "From the day when the circumnavigator emerged from the depths and the darkness, he infected every soul in the village and the surrounding area; he was the source" (X: 326).

In actuality, August has not stirred up very much activity in Polden during the time span encompassed by *Vagabonds*. True, he pioneers fish-drying in the area by stripping the coastal rocks, prods Edevart into building a general store, and does his mite for communication by using the telegraph and putting up a red mailbox on the store. But these are hardly the accomplishments of an innovative spirit worthy of being called an "emissary" or "missionary." Yet, they suffice for Joakim, the most thoughtful member of the Andreassen family, to conclude that their "peace and quiet" (X: 327) are threatened. The near-feudal view of society voiced by Joakim, who believes that people belong where they "have been placed," is clearly those of the author. From that perspective August, an orphan and thus without a home and a place to which he truly belongs, is a stranger in Polden, an undesirable champion of mobility. Significantly, Joakim does not even mention August's leadership in draining the nearby bog, which enabled Ezra, his brother-in-law, to become the foremost and most prosperous local farmer. The underlying assumption of his critique—Hamsun's adaptation of a Rousseauean notion—is that prosperity does not necessarily produce happiness: "We do not become any happier inwardly by coddling ourselves with riches" (328), Joakim says. Then he relates how, by using an overly fat and rich cow dung to fertilize a scrawny aspen, he caused an ugly scab on the tree. We notice once more Hamsun's fondness for vegetal metaphors in dealing with human problems.

One string of incidents in *Vagabonds* exceed the themes that have so far been discussed. Several scenes deal with truly macabre events, matching in ghastliness anything that has been found so far in Hamsun's fiction. The sequence begins with a cold-blooded act of murder: Ane Maria, then a young wife, lures a skipper, Skåro, to a cloudberry bog and leaves him there to die. Somewhat later a cow drowns in the same quagmire, an incident followed by dismay as people begin to hear screams from the bog, grotesquely interpreted as a sign of the skipper's horror at having to share his final resting place with a quadruped. At the initiative of August, subsequently revealed as having masterminded the signals of distress, the bog is drained, the bodies of Skåro and the cow exhumed, and Skåro buried in consecrated ground. However, his decomposing body is not left in peace even now. When August and Skåro met during the Lofoten fisheries, the generous sailor had given him a gold ring, and now, years later, being short of cash, August persuades Edevart to accompany him to the cemetery one night in order to recover the ring. These events, in their absorption with death and dissolution, stand out like an irruption of the uncanny into the everyday routine of Polden life.

Skåro's end conveys something else as well, namely, life's unpredictability and precariousness, a central motif in *The Last Chapter*. His rescue from certain death is only a few feet away, but Ane Maria refuses to help him, and he is too proud to beg her. Ironically, that pride of his was the very reason for her revenge: the merry skipper had not asked her "enough" when he wanted her to go into the bushes with him, as she testified during her trial (X: 156). The suddenness of the incident, its taking place during a barn dance, and the perceived short distance between life and death turn it into a sort of allegory of existential uncertainty. An exemplum of pride that "goeth before destruction,"[20] a doomsday sermon in bog water, the event fairly breaks out of its frame of ordinary village life.

Norem also suffers a ghastly fate, made more ghastly by the way it is related. On the visit that Edevart pays to his former colleague, Norem acts his usual "sinful and satisfied" self, blithely unaware of a "white spot" on his tongue which signifies death (X: 177). We are informed by a cooper's wife whom Edevart befriends of what happened to Norem subsequently, including the clinical details: "They cut and cut in his mouth," the woman reports, "first they took his whole tongue and later they went farther in, but it probably wouldn't have helped if they had cut off his whole head—God forgive" (224).

These scenes, with their graphic descriptions of boundary situations, are more memorable than most of the happenings in Hamsun's novel, especially since they become recurrent motifs.[21] Indeed, such motifs provide crucial elements of structure in a novel that is difficult to see steadily and whole: the Bildungsroman element, while important, applies to Edevart alone;[22] the picaresque aspect is limited; for a family chronicle the net is cast too widely; and for a period novel its focus is too eccentric. It does not even qualify as a regional novel, since it deals with two coastal communities at different levels of socioeconomic development. My best suggestion is to treat it as a novel of everyday life, given a sort of coherence by various types of recurrent elements, whether allusions, characters, or episodes.

Already the book's first episode contains, apart from the itinerant entertainers, two motifs that later appear several times. A button which Ragna, then a little girl, puts into the bowl of the boy in the puppet show is rejected and ends up in the snow. This "bright button in the snow" is alluded to several times after Ragna has reached adulthood. The puppet show features Napoleon, who later turns up in the conversation between Edevart and August as well as through the "Napoleon March," which August plays at the circus during his second visit to the Stokmarknes Fair. The button, associated with Ragna and Edevart, connotes a sense of nostalgia,[23] while the Napoleon image, aspired to by August and continued in the sequel, evokes a quasi-Faustian ambition. Among constantly reappearing minor characters, Papst, the watch-peddling Jew, is as regular as the stars in their courses. Mattea, August's boasted fiancée, also turns up repeatedly. As for recurrent episodes, they form the staple of life both in Polden and the Fosen country.

This pattern of recurrence reflects a concept of life, one determined by the cycles of nature. For despite the fact that *Vagabonds* covers some dozen years, the sense of history is vague: there are very few references to historical events, and except for the Franco-German War of 1870–71, they are not precise enough to date events. Similarly,

Hamsun's handling of the chronology of his characters' lives is, as nearly always, very casual, and at times one is surprised to discover that a character, say Ragna, recently a little girl, is pregnant, and then, after an indeterminate interval, that she has had several children. One is hard put to square the events narrated with the few, usually quite subjective, time indications that are given. For example, while Lovise Magrete speaks about all those years she has been away, in the States, the textual evidence of time having passed elsewhere is negligible. The temporal patterns that regulate the flow of events are those of the diurnal and seasonal cycles; the novel's narrative rhythm is produced by these cycles and, to a lesser extent, by the motifs mentioned above. Life itself, the apparent subject of Hamsun's book, is constituted by these all-encompassing cycles.[24]

Hamsun's treatment of time raises teasing questions. One feels tempted to ask whether the form of his late work is not determined, in part, by a fictional attempt to overcome the sense of transience and mortality which is evident in so many of his novels, including *Vagabonds*. A remark made by Lovise Magrete in an exchange with Edevart betrays a psychological connection between having a permanent place of residence and mortality: "If we settle here, I suppose it can't ever be reversed, and we'll be here until we die," she says (X: 268): to Lovise Magrete, the very direction of time is threatening. While on the level of ideas Hamsun is a champion of rootedness, of living out one's life where one was born, the rhetoric of the organic metaphor savors of inevitable decay, of mortality. Mobility, on the other hand, means endless expectation, constant novelty, an open future. Here we encounter a fascinating paradox: just as mobility in space seems to allay Lovise Magrete's sense of an ending, so the *roman-fleuve*, with its open-ended structure,[25] is at one level an escape from the finitude of human time, a time that is linear rather than cyclical. The previously noted motif structure and the narrative's adherence to a cyclical rhythm may be seen as other means of overcoming the finitude that is inseparable from human temporality. As we move from one novel to another in the trilogy, Hamsun's imagination moves ever closer to August's uninhibited fantasizing, which has little respect for human limitations and human time.

Such a disposition is not conducive to artistic discipline, particularly when, as in the case of Hamsun, it coexists with a penchant for all-inclusiveness. The consequences are quite evident in *Vagabonds*, whose broad canvas often makes it difficult to see where Hamsun is going with his story; one may even wonder what story he is telling. With its multitude of characters and Hamsun's tendency to give everyone his or her due, whether the character concerned is major or minor, the narrative risks losing its focus. Hamsun also devotes a lot of space to quotidian activities of a rather special sort, like tilling the soil and expanding the cowshed, or what not, matters that to most readers are eminently forgettable. The resulting *longueurs*, which often relate to Hamsun's self-imposed mission to be a mentor to his countrymen, inevitably produce tedium. Fortunately, the novel contains, in addition to the central figures, a number of excellent portraits.

The psychological and moral profiles of Hamsun's characters in *Vagabonds* describe a wide gamut, ranging from various degrees of moral obliquity, including abysmal evil, to uprightness, generosity and selflessness. Indeed, as the discussion of August has demonstrated, both moral extremes can coexist in one and the same figure. The most impressive instance of this Hamsunian broadness, which is akin to the Karamazov nature as interpreted by Dostoyevsky,[26] is offered by Ane Maria, the lustful young wife said by her husband to walk about with a "scream between her legs" (X: 129). Described as "wanton in her desires, pleasure-loving, but straightforward and strong," she is a strange mix of good and evil. Once she decided to confess her crime, she "didn't waver, she demanded to be punished"; she "wept as if she were being whipped, but she didn't whine" (156–57). Interestingly, it is a woman who commits the most heinous crime in *Vagabonds*, since August's crimes, including complicity in murder, are merely told, not shown. Another woman, Pauline, Edevart's sister, stands out among a cast of chiefly male characters as a paragon of honesty and common sense.

The portrayals of these two women are untainted by the bias that mars the depiction of Lovise Magrete. For though Hamsun's method has become more objective, in that there are fewer authorial exclamations, comments and special pleadings than in former works, time and again bias skews the course of events and the characters so as to convey his message. For instance, clearing new land is without exception associated with fun, not toil and sweat. Not surprisingly, it is where Hamsun's pet ideas are not in question, as in describing the madness of Karolus, Ane Maria's husband, after his wife's confession;[27] the peculiar blend of deception and honesty in Papst, the watch-peddler; or the deep brotherly affection under a semblance of mutual hostility between Edevart and Joakim—it is where he has no agenda to sell that Hamsun demonstrates his true gifts as a connoisseur of the human soul.

Though, as previously noted, *Vagabonds* was well received, the accolades were not universal. A Danish reviewer complained that Hamsun never tired of "repeating himself."[28] Helge Krog was irritated by Hamsun's "fixed ideas" and "shallow" social views, and found his "smug long-windedness" tiring.[29] Two English-language reviewers show the wide disparities in the critical response to the novel. Focusing on Hamsun's depiction of folk life, Richard Sunne says that eventually "Edevart and his village, and all these people, rounded, breathing, unpsychologized, begin to appear to us in their eternal aspect. The effect, because so unobtrusive, is extraordinarily profound."[30] Conversely, V. F. Calverton faults Hamsun for his lack of selectivity and charges the novel with dullness. "Hamsun," he writes, "takes all of life for his province—and yet reveals less of it than most other authors who focus their vision upon a small but important part of it." Though the characters are "life-like," he says, they are so "ordinary, uninspired," that one doesn't care whether they are real or not. "It is skin-deep realism of the most uninteresting sort." Hamsun, he concludes, has not realized "the potentialities of his materials."[31] In his review of *The Ring Is Closed*, Artur Lundkvist offers a comment that might make it possible to see such divergent views in a positive light. Much of Hamsun's charm, he writes, is that he enables the reader to "read his own meaning, his own inclinations and secrets, into the work of art."[32]

CHAPTER TEN

The Human Comedy: Satiric Fantasy and Mock Apocalypse

The two sequels to *Vagabonds*, *August* and *The Road Leads On*, share settings, themes and characters with previous novels by Hamsun, but introduce artistic devices rarely or never used before by him. Though *August*, for example, takes the reader back to Polden and its inhabitants after an interval of twenty years, the role of the eponymous hero has now acquired an explicitly symbolic dimension. *The Road Leads On*, which continues the story of Segelfoss in the generation subsequent to that portrayed in *Segelfoss Town*, offers no surprises thematically, but except for August, here appearing in yet another incarnation, the characters are new, though cut from familiar cloth. The thematic charge of the two novels differs considerably. While *August* is a satiric fantasy of modernity gone awry, *The Road Leads On* is a celebration of fecundity climaxed by the exorcism of the August spirit.

In *August*, Hamsun's use of the outsider plot is unequivocal: August and Edevart reappear in Polden soon after the novel's beginning, and they both leave at the end. Nobody knows where August has been since he was last seen; Edevart, who is said to have "squandered his inheritance" (XI: 82), is a prodigal son come back from America, to which Lovise Magrete returns, whereas he remains in Polden. As in *Vagabonds*, August and Edevart represent opposing values and attitudes, though Edevart is greatly changed. He is either seen doing heavy physical labor or brooding on his wasted life in a clump of whispering aspens. The opposition between the two characters, which structures *Vagabonds*, is now reduced to that between

August's ceaseless activity and Edevart's virtual quietism. The contrast is epitomized by the manner of their exits, August presumably toward fresh adventures and enterprises, Edevart toward death. Fearing arrest for the attempted murder of Kristofer, a fellow townsman, August leaves Polden, missing the news that he has won a sizable sum in a German lottery, a stroke of luck that ensures his future viability as a fictional character. Ironically, Edevart's death is indirectly due to August's luck: overtaken by a storm when he sets out in an open boat to find August and relate the good news, he is never heard of again. Edevart's last act, one of selfless courage, envelops this star-crossed figure in an aura of profound pathos.

The main focus in *August*, however, is not on the relationship between Edevart and August, but on that of August to the budding town of Polden. August's ability to sway the people of Polden to fall in with his hair-brained schemes makes them all—with a few exceptions—look rather foolish. One cannot help thinking of what happens in Nikolay Gogol's *The Inspector General* (1836), in which a young dandy thought by the townspeople to be a government inspector plays fast and loose with every citizen who has something to hide. In both instances, manipulation is used, more so in Hamsun's case than in Gogol's, since the characters in Gogol's play walk into the trap uninvited. Hamsun may not have had Gogol's work in mind when portraying August's activities in this novel, but one of the latter's enterprises has a decidedly Gogolian side to it: in spearheading a popular appeal to the government for a post office to be opened in Polden, August adds the names of dead people to the signatures of the living, a trick reminiscent of Chichikov in Gogol's *Dead Souls* (1842).[1] There is, of course, little similarity between August and Khlestakov, the false inspector general, though D. S. Mirsky's capsule description of the latter as "meaningless movement and meaningless fermentation incarnate,"[2] sounds intriguingly apt for August as well. Still, the similarity is not one of character as much as of function: the dealings of both with their respective provincial towns expose human vanity, greed, and stupidity and generate an abundance of rueful comedy. A new element in Hamsun's work is its merciless exploration of the herd mentality, ever hankering after miracles and hoping for the appearance of a savior figure.

The Human Comedy: Satiric Fantasy and Mock Apocalypse 277

But while the Poldenites' inability to resist August's mania for innovation does not make them look good in the reader's eyes, August himself comes off no better, being shown up as a phony demagogue and, on a different level, a false Messiah. The following discussion will elaborate on these points.

As soon as he arrives in Polden, August begins his mission to modernize the place. His slogan is the same as that of Theodor Shopkeeper in *Segelfoss Town*: we have to keep up with the rest of the world. In obedience to that slogan and the gospel of progress that it entails, August provides Polden with a post office, a bank, and a herring meal factory; he also engages in the construction of private housing and encourages the local farmers to sell their land for building lots. The necessary capital for the bank and the factory is procured through crude misrepresentation. Thus, to persuade people to invest in the banking project, he pressures Edevart, whose general indifference makes him game for anything, into acting as his proxy, on the understanding that August will cover the fifty shares his friend signs up for. In effect, he uses a con man's tricks, figuring correctly that people are vain and do not wish to be outdone by their neighbors. The bank functions largely as an ego-bolstering toy for the members of the board, except for Pauline, Edevart's sister, who in her capacity as manager keeps track of the deposits and loans. When she gets wise to what is going on, she tells August: "That so-called bank of yours isn't a bank, nor has it been registered with the authorities, and Joakim says it's all illegal" (XI: 203). As for the herring meal factory, it is never completed, largely due to Pauline's intervention: she decides not to dispatch August's orders for the required materials and machinery because the cost will exceed the available funds. In the end, Polden is a kind of ghost town, its situation epitomized by money-hungry Karolus, who, having sold his farmland for building lots and spent the cash accepted for it, has nothing to fall back on. When the chips are down and famine strikes, the man of the hour is Ezra, the only farmer who resisted the lure of August's pipe dream of progress.

The famine at the center of *August* serves several literary purposes. First, it enables Hamsun to portray human behavior at its nadir. Led by the aggressive Kristofer, a group of desperate men burglarize Ezra's cellar, acting on the suspicion that the canny farmer, who has already donated load upon load of provisions to his hard-pressed urban neighbors, still has plenty of produce in his storage bins. Then, finding nothing there, they break into the general store, with similar outcome. These scenes show people at their worst, bearing out a metaphor that Hamsun repeats *ad nauseam*: humankind as a colony of crawling ants. In *August*, Teodor, a good-for-nothing snoop and petty thief, is the prototype of the antlike nature, whereas August is called "an ant with wings" (XI: 212-13). When survival is at stake, human beings crawl over one another, just like ants. This is certainly one of the effects produced by the famine sequence in the novel.

On another level, the famine enables Hamsun to produce a mock-religious allegory of the human need for a savior in times of crisis. A number of details portray August as a Christ figure. More than once, he refers to himself as someone whose time "is not yet come" (XI: 31, 158),[3] and he is repeatedly seen as capable of performing miracles. His promise to order grain abroad telegraphically when the supply at the local store has run out evokes a rhetorical question with decidedly Biblical overtones: "Who could like him still the storm!" (120),[4] and his telling Joakim, "with deep meaning," to go out with the seine (157), at a time when there are no signs of herring in the sea, recalls Jesus' words to Simon in a comparable situation: "Launch out into the deep, and let down your nets for a draught."[5] This last example is particularly striking, since it is preceded by August's quasi-resurrection from the dead after a serious illness. When Joakim takes his advice as a joke, August replies, "When a person has been into the realm of death and eternity as I have, he doesn't joke. Because then he has learned a thing or two" (158). The fact that the herring which alleviates the famine is purchased with Karolus' cash and shows August to have prophesied falsely, does nothing to shake his confidence. He simply takes credit for a subsequent catch, crowing, "What did I say, wasn't there herring in the sea!" (170).

The positive theme that the famine sequence is intended to convey is no news to readers of Hamsun: to score a point in his literary crusade for increasing Norway's tillage and securing the continued viability of a rustic way of life. In terms of character, it brings Ezra, with the name of an Israelite hero, to the forefront. It is quite understandable why Hamsun would resort to such a crisis to promote his agrarian gospel. But, realistically speaking, the famine that

Hamsun describes is not very probable, and in a case such as this one expects to find a realistic basis for events, saturated with fantasy though the novel may be otherwise. Hamsun simply needed the famine to create in Ezra a counter-hero to August, and its implausibility obviously weighed less with him than the use he could make of it.

Hamsun's anti-August campaign does anything but diminish him: in fact, August dominates the novel. One of his fascinating aspects is the astonishing breadth of his personality, partly because Hamsun has drawn upon so many sources, scriptural and secular, in creating him. The false or mock Messiah lives side by side with the notion of an imperial soul, a recurring motif in Hamsun's work. This aspect of August is vividly brought out when he goes courting Pauline, to whom he shows the stiletto in his cane, which he claims had "belonged to an emperor called Napoleon." Going into an ecstasy of utopian reverie, he visualizes a veritable technopolis, complete with the latest inventions and more, such as flying machines. Vowing to "raise Polden up," he anticipates a day when "people would honor him and the district governor come to fetch him driving a carriage and four—." The posture he assumes is distinctly imperial: "August tossed his head, . . . the whole world was his background" (XI: 109–10). One thinks of Ibsen's Peer Gynt as he daydreams of being emperor, seeing himself being received by the King of England.[6]

August and Peer share many other traits as well, such as expatriation and return, financial speculation, a tendency to brag and tell tall stories, even criminality. Thus, Peer pushes the ship's cook into the sea during a wreck,[7] and during his illness, in a confessional mood, August asks Edevart, "If you were clinging to an upturned boat, you wouldn't push your comrade into the sea, would you?" (XI: 145). Both envisage the whole planet as their stage, real or imaginary. Appearing in a number of incarnations, from youth to age, they are mercurial figures, without a personal identity or center. Ibsen's onion parable, which reveals the truth about Peer, could just as well be applied to August.[8] Finally, while Ibsen used his dramatic poem to excoriate what he saw as weaknesses in the Norwegian national character, *August* fulfills a comparable purpose for Hamsun.

Despite being notoriously anti-Ibsen, Hamsun often follows in his footsteps. In *The Last Joy*, he had lashed out at the "new spirit" in Norway, and in *August* the spirit that has invaded Polden, though slightly less new, is considered to be equally harmful. Hamsun never tires of calling August "an expression of the time" (XI: 174), either by way of commentary or through a character who speaks for the author. The role as Hamsun's mouthpiece falls here, as in *Vagabonds*, mainly to Joakim, who is "clever, a bit of a politician." In a concluding discussion, replicating an exchange in the preceding novel, Joakim again describes August as "a sort of agent, an ambassador of the times, of the world," adding for good measure, and rather self-consciously, the epithet "symbol," which he defines as "an allegorical figure or slogan." Though he admits that August had accomplished some good things for Polden, "they were offset by the evils that followed" (255). Working "in the service of desperate negation," August had "raised a town that was without food and a factory without machines. Hadn't he had the best intention? Yes, but this ambassador of mechanics and industry worked fruitlessly" (204).

The phrase "desperate negation" may contain an allusion to another literary masterpiece, namely Goethe's *Faust*, in which Mephistopheles calls himself "ein Teil von jener Kraft,/Die stets das Böse will und stets das Gute schafft."[9] True, in August's case the elements are reversed, in that negation is in the outcome rather than the intention: the possible allusion is steeped in irony. Nevertheless, the most sensible character in Hamsun's novel, Pauline, seems to suspect that August may indeed be evil. On the verge of tears "from anger and helplessness" at his absurd tales and phony schemes, she asks, alluding to scripture: ". . . are you an evil spirit such as we read about, that entered into the herd of swine?" (XI: 169).[10] Pauline's reference to the Gadarene swine will take on catastrophic significance in the last novel of the trilogy, *The Road Leads On*.

Hamsun undermines August and what he represents also by casting aspersions on the nature of his sexuality. There are repeated references to a mysterious disease that forces him to avoid intimate contact with women. It requires little imagination to guess at the reason; in fact, August himself tells Edevart, in the course of a couple of wild tales he concocts to teach his friend how to handle Lovise Magrete, that one of the women he had courted while at sea, a real "bitch," had left him a "remembrance" (XI: 229). During the entire novel, he is under treatment by Dr. Lund, who leaves no doubt what August's health problem is. Moreover, his curious behavior, such as the prurient interest he takes in other people's sex life, together with an attitude toward women that oscillates between aggressiveness and timidity, is indicative of impotence or venereal disease, or both. The text extends the meaning of his handicap beyond the purely sexual: "Already his [August's] first steps on landing in Polden were marked by sterility, a sexual sickness" (204). Indeed, it looks as though Hamsun invites the reader to see August's ceaseless activity, his feverish drive for innovation, as being fueled by a repressed sexuality. Hamsun's psychoanalysis could certainly have provided the necessary impetus for conceiving a character based on such a concept, which, generalized, closely resembles one of the key ideas in Freud's *Civilization and Its Discontents*.[11]

There is another interesting twist to Hamsun's conception of August's psychology. His energy, including his sexual drive, is channeled not only into commercial and industrial activity, but also into quasi-literary creativity. A scene between August and Ane Maria which starts with sexual banter and August's indirect offer of personally remedying her barrenness, develops into a story-telling stint. When he mentioned Turkey and Egypt in a covert brag that he is no eunuch, "his imagination was given a push, and he began to tell about his life experiences; his excitement seemed to calm down and he gave himself over to a tall tale" (XI: 98). Genital sexuality is transformed into orality under our very eyes. Though the Poldenites may not be aware of the source of his compulsive fantasizing, Hamsun very definitely seems to be. They do, however, find it entertaining. As the following apostrophe which the narrator puts into the mouths of August's listeners shows, they not only are wise to his penchant for fabulation but encourage it: "But go on and tell anyway, August, go on and tell! We don't know what is true or false, perhaps you don't always know yourself, but you are nourishment for our dream life. . ." (24).[12] It would not be altogether untrue to say that August provides whatever literary culture Polden possesses. And beside his story-telling gifts, he is a skilled accordionist, although, like Nagel, he no longer plays. All these talents make it possible to see August as a folksy symbol of the artist. In view of Hamsun's description of poets as "vagabond souls," as "restless" individuals "akin to organ grinders,"[13] the reverse may perhaps also be true, namely, that vagabond souls possess a tincture of poetry. In any case, several commentators have noted August's close link with his creator, calling him "a poet in the realm of actuality," Hamsun's "alter ego," or, less flatteringly, a "caricature of a creative writer."[14] In view of Hamsun's low opinion of writers and artists, however, this alleged kinship may be fraught with tension and ambiguity.

Another link between August and his creator is less equivocal. Beneath the satirical surface, where August appears as an abhorrent example of Americanization, there is a subtext endowing him with traits that, in Hamsun's scale of values, were entirely positive. At this level August becomes a bearer of some of Hamsun's most attractive qualities, notably a tender regard for life, especially life that struggles to survive. In *On Overgrown Paths*, which is an autobiographical work, the writer betrays a particular concern for a threatened spruce, and *August* contains a prominent spruce motif. When Hamsun was staying in the Landvik Old People's Home after the Second World War, he noticed that a "little spruce" in the neighboring garden was overshadowed by a "huge poplar" which did not give it "a moment's peace." To rescue it, he writes, "I simply take a quiet little walk on dark fall evenings and cut away leaves and branches so that it will have peace for the night."[15] The spruce motif in *August* emerges from August's desire to beautify the town of Polden. When the plants arrived, August carried them "in his arms like a child" (XI: 120), and when he and Edevart, finding no more buyers for the seedlings, have to dump the remainder in a common grave, they act as though it were a regular funeral. Edevart is ordered to dig a hole. "When the hole was large enough, August got up and put all the plants nicely into the grave together. 'We should act like people toward them,' he said. . . . They, too, have life" (129).

On the novel's last page, the narrator turns August's spruce seedlings into metaphors for the condition of children in a time of want. I shall quote the passage in full:

> The children are like August's spruce plants, the soil isn't the right one for them, they are badly off, droop and are sick. At last the snow goes away, some plants begin to turn a bit light green at the top, oh, such a tiny little bit light green at the top, but what a wonder, how unbelievable, they have all the time had a spark of life in them and have labored with their feeble strength to provide themselves with roots. But some plants die. Some children die. (XI: 261)

Hamsun's love of children is manifest everywhere in his work. Though August is not shown as a particularly child-loving character, the fact that his beloved spruce seedlings are associated with children in a motif of the vulnerability of life looks like the author's declaration of kinship with, and love for, an otherwise highly problematic character.

Hamsun's August as he appears in this novel transcends classical logic, specifically the law of identity, which says that two contradictory predicates cannot be assigned to the same subject. In August's case the logic of either/or must be replaced by the logic of both/and, exemplified by the physical theory of light, in which light can figure both as waves and particles. August is a strange mix of genius and stupidity; though he is competent and knowledgeable, some of his ideas and enterprises are asinine. His endless tales show a vivid imagination, but they are often corny and boring. The motif of lightness that is repeatedly used to describe him seems appropriate: belonging to the element of air, *spiritus*, he often evades his responsibilities by flight, just as he leaves reality for fantasy. But lightweight or not, August does have some first-rate qualities, being generous to a fault and asking little or nothing for himself. He is also, of course, a hopeless megalomaniac, a compulsive liar and a potential, if not actual, murderer. The rhetorical figure that best describes him is the oxymoron, which Hamsun does have recourse to, as in the following sentence about his solicitation of investors in his factory: "He was innocent, he believed in his mission and lied honestly and honorably for its benefit" (XI: 174). It is on the strength of this mind-boggling blend of contradictory qualities that Hamsun's narrator can claim that August symbolizes the spirit of modernity.

In this part of the trilogy, the figure of August is larger than life. If, as some critics have suggested, the novel represents Norway in miniature or is intended as a microcosm of the modern world,[16] August, its central character, assumes a mythic dimension.[17] Indeed, the recourse of commentators to comparisons with Peer Gynt, Don Quixote, and other archetypal figures when describing August betrays a perception of such a dimension. In view of his restless disposition, endless energy, and unflagging activity, August's special quality in a mythical perspective makes him into an embodiment of a Nordic *élan vital* or life force. His creator's ambivalent attitude toward him reflects the inconstancies of Hamsun's *Weltanschauung*, which alternates between virtual nihilism and exuberant yea-saying.

In comparison to August, the rest of the Poldenites are rather simple. In a novel with so many characters, some will inevitably be one-dimensional, barely standing out from a background of common small-town humanity. Even some of the fairly important figures are wholly defined by the recurring motifs associated with them, such as stewardship of the earth with Ezra, "small and gray" (XI: 9), newspapers and books with Joakim, chairman of the community board.[18] More complex is a number of female figures whose behavior is either unwomanly or, as in the case of Lovise Magrete, erratic. Thus, considering Hamsun's antediluvian view of women, Pauline is a marvel of single-woman success. Though she is already "withered and flat-breasted" (8) in her late thirties and called a "dry, bony old maid who didn't care for children" (95), her portrait is a sympathetic study of an independent woman, intelligent, efficient, even witty. She is a far more formidable antagonist to August than her two brothers, Ezra and Joakim, whose views are patently those of the author. And she is not sexless or cold, as shown by her romantic interest in the curate, her touching attempts to wean August of his grand illusions, and the deep affection she demonstrates for Edevart, her near derelict elder brother.

Strange to say, though intended as a horrible example of the alienation caused by so-called vagabondage, Lovise Magrete acquires depth by dint of her moral and psychological perplexity; there is a haunting quality to her spiritual rootlessness. During her brief visit to Polden, she displays the worst possible features of the returned emigrant; pretentious and affected, she comes across as a silly snob, as she also did occasionally in *Vagabonds*. However, in a strange passage that blends Edevart's interior monologue with free indirect discourse and authorial narrative, she is shown from a different perspective. In this passage her restlessness is traced to a never-ending search for her missing husband. "She was driven by a stubborn and terrible delusion. She doesn't mention him, but she whispers his name in her sleep. . . . She didn't spare herself but kept at it, she could have enjoyed quiet days but denied herself. A twenty years' grind" (XI: 84). This Lovise Magrete appears to be a prey to guilt and remorse, with a lacerated psyche for which there is no cure. And her problem

The Human Comedy: Satiric Fantasy and Mock Apocalypse 285

has little to do with emigration and its alleged destructive effects; it is due to the cost of a divided eros, much as in the case of Rosa in Hamsun's earlier novel. The suffering that is here revealed, though seemingly inconsistent with the superficiality and fickleness required by Hamsun's anti-emigration bias, does much to make Lovise Magrete's portrayal acceptable.

Hamsun has a knack for creating characters with a troubled history behind them, one including even serious crime, as long as they are life- and sex-affirming. A splendid example of this is afforded by Ane Maria, the young woman who led Skåro to his death in *Vagabonds*. The success of her portrayal as a middle-aged woman in *August* is partly due to the protean nature of the narrator, who easily shifts from one point of view to another. In an early passage, where the narrator embodies the viewpoint of the villagers, she appears as a "monster, a dissolute woman!" (XI: 11). The Poldenites expect her to give up her pride and walk humbly, as their religion commands. However, Ane Maria has found that religion is not for her: she "had tried to be religious and unworldly, but it didn't last long, she came to a dead stop" (10). In his authorial guise, the narrator approves of Ane Maria's defiant attitude; he is not only indulgent but laudatory, being especially appreciative of her sexual appetite, which gave her husband a lot of trouble trying to "keep her away from himself" (12). Though no longer young, she has her eyes, at different times, on Edevart and August, though to no avail. But August does help her out in one way: he finds two little boys for her to adopt, thus enabling Ane Maria to fulfill her maternal needs, at least temporarily. When, at the end, she has to give up the boys because she and Karolus are destitute, she is shown clearing a potato patch in an outlying field. Nothing daunts her. With all her failings and strengths, she conveys a sense of rich vitality, notwithstanding being called on to make an eleventh-hour plug for the authorial gospel.

A meeting between Ane Maria and Ragna, another morally flawed woman of strong desires, is highly revelatory of both, at the same time as it demonstrates Hamsun's continued ability to use a scenic method for ironic effect. The scene takes place during the famine, when Polden is visited by a kind of religious epidemic; in any case, that is how Hamsun treats the revival. During the famine some people "took to prayers and piety, walking around with grimy streaks of tears on their emaciated faces, and mothers would sit with their little ones on their laps, telling them about all the milk they were going to get when they starved to death and came to heaven" (XI: 134). Ragna, who has one or more children fathered by Edevart and whose marriage to the feckless Teodor is reminiscent of Petra and Oliver in *The Women at the Pump*, has undergone conversion and sets her mind to converting Ane Maria as well. Ironically, her motive is rooted in resentment, a feeling that Ane Maria, who was in charge of the distribution of food supplies from Pauline's store, had not given her a fair share. Ragna being well versed in the Bible, the scene juxtaposes apocalyptic imagery with the most basic human needs. Divine grace and food battle for preeminence, with Ane Maria winning the contest as she offers Ragna a few potatoes and a bit of meat, which the visitor at first turns down as a temptation. When Ragna, though grateful, persists in her self-appointed mission and makes another stab at converting Ane Maria before leaving, the latter, who feels offended by the familiarity of a social inferior, tells her that she knows everything there is to know about conversion. She went through it all "that time in Trondhjem," she says. "I became so converted that I scared both the chaplain and the warden" (137).

Another excellent scene is one in which August serves as a mediator of sorts between Edevart and Lovise Magrete, whose accumulated mutual misunderstandings and rancors are brought to the surface by what may be called literary archeology. Edevart is still fixated on his first glimpse of Lovise Magrete, "barefoot and in a skirt and shift," which to her is a reminder of her one-time poverty and also, now that the "time of the crazy nights" is past, of her vanished youth (XI: 58). Throughout, Lovise Magrete tries to undermine Edevart by appealing to August, whom she sees as a kindred soul. The scene, watched by someone to whom voyeurism is not alien, presents an exemplary battle of the sexes. "She was obviously on the verge of hysteria, . . . her eyes had an unusual brilliance"; meantime Edevart, who has come around to the view that their relationship was doomed from the outset because it began illegally, remains silent. On the other hand, when he makes a friendly gesture and returns the dropped powder puff to Lovise Magrete, "an expression of aversion brushes her face, as if she were afraid he would meet her halfway and patch things up again. 'Keep quiet—throw it down again!' she gasped, bursting into tears" (59). The scene ends with Lovise Magrete shaken by "convulsive sobbing" and with Edevart "laughing to himself perhaps; he wished her joy of her distorted face and didn't feel like saying, or doing, anything consoling and thus spoil her grimaces" (60). The scene is a time capsule of marital—or extramarital—squalor.

The language used in the creation of Polden and its inhabitants is a species of vernacular, with a regional tinge to it as in the whole trilogy, heightened by an evident effort to produce strong effects. It assumes a narrator who is intimately familiar with the milieu he is depicting and who shares its dominant values and attitudes. Often the style has a peasant or folksy flavor, reflecting the ethos of a primitive culture. For example, women are spoken of in animal terms, such as Pauline at the moment of August's proposal: "Pauline was no filly, she didn't whinny..." (XI: 110). The folksiness of the style is also evidenced by the frequent use of hyperbole. More unusual is the resort to litotes, as in the phrase above, "she didn't whinny." A rhetorical figure often found in primitive poetry and epic, as well as in the Norse sagas, litotes entails irony, a hint of things not explicitly stated; however, as used by Hamsun in *August* it approaches hyperbole by the concreteness of the denied predicates. When August wants to sell Pauline some spruce seedlings, the text says that "she took it nicely, she didn't snarl at him or foam at the mouth" (124). Again, the voice with which she questions him about his stabbing of Kristofer is "nothing at all like a harp." The rough humor in these instances arises from a discrepancy between the vehicle and the tenor, the sensory vehicles—"snarl," "foam," and "harp"—being semantically at the opposite end of the intended meaning. Another example of litotes ends in an oxymoron; once more it is applied to Pauline as viewed by August: "She was not a bit pleasantly plump in any place, only bitter, and for the rest with a quite lovable face, but a flower of iron" (220). Though litotes is supposed to be a kind of understatement, in *August* it has a contrary effect, in accord with an overall tendency toward maximal expressiveness in Hamsun's novel.

As already mentioned, the narrative point of view in *August* is a shifting one. That is nothing new, of course, no more than the apostrophes, reflections, and commentaries with which the text abounds, after Hamsun had used a relatively objective narrator in *Vagabonds*. Free indirect discourse is still widespread, but often it coexists with, or veers off into, narrative forms that are truly anomalous. One passage will suffice to illustrate the peculiarity of Hamsun's method. Sitting among his beloved aspens, Edevart reflects on his life in a voice that is neither his nor the narrator's, and the form is not that of free indirect discourse, which is identified by the past tense and third person pronouns. "We don't sit very comfortably, should we get up and lower our butt onto a softer tussock? It has its awkward side, a needless bother, so we'll go home instead. We get up and stagger a few steps, one of our legs has gone to sleep, but it will probably go away, we walk, we stagger." On the surface this sounds like a kind of baby talk, whereby a mother, say, speaks for the child; certainly, the narrative voice is strongly felt: no man in good health would think of himself as staggering. Then, as the sight of Joakim triggers Edevart's stream of thought, the passage shifts to interior monologue. After Edevart has turned down Joakim's invitation to come along to Ezra's place, his thoughts are rendered in free indirect discourse: "To be sure, he had this letter to write and it never came to anything" (XI: 82), after which the narrative voice resumes. In this passage it is fairly easy to sort out the different types of discourse used, but that is not always the case. In consequence, there is a great deal of uncertainty as to how to interpret both the meaning and the tone of Hamsun's text.

The slipperiness of the narrative persona goes hand in hand with a lack of aesthetic form, a criticism of Hamsun's work I have felt obliged to make repeatedly. With such a multitude of characters and episodes, most of which are described in some detail, it is extremely difficult to achieve a unifying impression of the novel's form. For instance, we are presented with a heap of explicit details about agriculture, construction, and business that seem quite irrelevant to the concerns of storytelling, character portrayal, and significant thematic development. The result is a gritty texture without visible design, resulting in taedium and frustration.

In a broader perspective, *August* exhibits a profound tension between a realistic novel and a fantastic tale: fantasy denigrates reality, just as August, from a *Thousand and One Nights* world, demeans the lives of the other characters, who often come to look like a bunch of nincompoops. On the other hand, the circumstantial realism in the depiction of everyday life makes August look like an alien, an absurd clown whose much-advertised modernity shrinks to a preposterous authorial fancy. These effects were clearly not intended by Hamsun; his intent was to glorify agriculture and present a latterday sermon against the American peril, galloping urbanization. Most likely, Hamsun simply let himself go, adding detail upon detail without worrying much about form. It is as though he were describing the life of an entire town by a technique of homegrown pointillism, the result being an assemblage of a myriad interacting particulars that fall short of constituting a structured whole. Life may be chaotic, but art demands form, which Hamsun seems to spurn, except for applying a conventional external division into parts, chapters, and sub-sections. His aesthetic seems to be based on a false concept of mimesis.

August is not a great novel. That does not mean it is lacking in interest. I have attempted a balanced appraisal of the book, praising elements that give insights into contemporary social reality, while criticizing Hamsun's unconscionable self-indulgence and sloppy aesthetic. In view of the stock market crash in October 1929, the novel assumes an aspect of prescient allegory, since it had been conceived well in advance of that date. The Messianic parody in the portrayal of August is also interesting, in view of the call for a strong leader in the decade when the novel was written. The same applies to the hint of a depth-psychological perspective in the depiction of August's mania for development and to the quasi-Marxian showing up of the nature of religious mass movements. Furthermore, the novel contains a considerable number of vividly portrayed characters, at times shown in scenes that probe the underside of the psyche. These are no mean accomplishments. However, they do not by themselves guarantee literary achievement of high quality. That would require the exercise of more formal and stylistic discipline—in short, an aesthetic of significant form in which no absolute distinction could be made between thematic and stylistic aspects of a work. Instead, in *August* as well as in other novels, the themes are stated baldly, whether by a favorite character or by the ever-present narrator. By the same token, Hamsun's style often seems to be an end in itself. His search for uncommon, quaint or shocking turns of phrase leads as often to gaucherie as to verbal felicity. At least this is so in *August*, though space does not permit me to further explore this matter.

By this time the critics had seemingly decided that Hamsun could do no wrong, despite finding fault with some aspects of his work. Thus, Tom Kristensen, while complaining that Hamsun's ideas were getting "more and more barren," concludes his review by declaring he should be awarded the Nobel Prize "a second time."[19] And Ronald Fangen finds *August* to be Hamsun's "most virtuosic opus, brilliantly written, full of ideas," a work of superior art, "without blot or blemish,"[20] though he admits that the presentation is "loose" and that the text gives an impression of being padded. These reviews are fairly typical of the way Hamsun's later novels were received in Scandinavia.

The last work in Hamsun's trilogy, *Men livet lever* (1933; translated as *The Road Leads On*, 1934),[21] looks less like a novel than a journalistic account of the life of a small town. However they are viewed, its contents—social chatter, flirtatious dialogue, family scandals, old legends, bizarre superstitions, folk rituals, grotesque farce, and what not—fail to blend into an aesthetic whole. Judging by the novel's conclusion, the dominant motive of its action, its *telos*, is the destruction of August. For that destruction to seem right, August would have to be portrayed in such a way as to be inevitably headed for a fall. However, no trait or behavior that August displays in Segelfoss, the setting of *The Road Leads On*, justifies such a drastic denouement. Twenty years older now, August keeps a low profile and seems quite harmless, foolish, to be sure, a braggart and a show-off, granted, but generous and kind. No matter what the problem, practical or personal, he is ready to give advice and succor. The name he goes by in Segelfoss, Altmuligmand or, for short, Altmulig, ranges in connotation from wonderworker to jack-of-all-trades; Handyman is a poor English rendering of a cognomen that suits him well, the accent as far as this novel is concerned being on the more modest role. For he is no longer an entrepreneur, as he was to some extent in the immediately preceding volume of the trilogy, *August*, but an employee of Gordon Tidemand, the local magnate. The chief enterprise in which he is involved is Mr. Tidemand's construction of a road up the mountainside to his hunting lodge.

Still, August is not without flaws. With his workaholic mentality, particularly his tendency to oversee too many projects simultaneously, he has difficulty completing them; in this respect, he has not changed from the previous novel, where the herring meal factory was left unfinished. As his boss has made clear to him, the mountain road has to be completed within a certain time frame, so as to be ready for use the moment an English friend of his arrives. The road skirts a deep gully, repeatedly referred to as an "abyss," and requires a guardrail. At the Englishman's arrival, the project is finished except for the rail, but this seemingly minor failure plays a fateful role in August's downfall.

August's other great weakness is a total inability to handle large sums of money. His behavior in this respect seems to be guided by a categorical imperative somewhat like this: the faster money circulates, the better for everyone concerned, whether you gain or lose. As soon as Pauline visits in Part Two and delivers his lottery winnings, August is once more enthralled by the spirit of speculation. Acting on an old idea of his, he begins to purchase sheep in the area, which he puts out to pasture on the mountain plateau. He hires buyers and herders and becomes the owner of a huge flock; only when his herders, Jørn and Valborg, warn him that there is no more pasturage left, does he stop his purchasing. To August, the success of his venture depends on simple arithmetic, as evidenced by the following question to Jørn, "Have you got fifty score sheep?" Since the answer, "fifty-seven score less three," exceeds one thousand, August feels free to round it off; in conversation with others he makes it "over two thousand!" (XII: 255). As we shall see later, this number is not without significance.

In this novel, too, considerable attention is given to August's sexuality. At his age, sexual reciprocity is hard to come by, especially if one's beloved is a young girl. Indeed, buying a bride turns out to be far more problematic than buying sheep. Though the parents of Cornelia, the girl he persistently woos and eventually proposes marriage to, support his suit, grateful for his many gifts, including a horse, Cornelia refuses even to sit on his lap. The situation is grotesquely comic. It ends badly for Cornelia. While August takes on the semblance of a "dirty old man," absurd in his amorous drooling over the girl, Cornelia, who is kicked to death by the skittish gift horse, ends up as a victim of parental greed and senile lust.

Of greater consequence to August, who appears unmoved by Cornelia's death, is the enmity of Åse, a woman in her thirties, "a witch and a Gypsy and Lapp all in one, a wandering horror" (XII: 32), whose sexual advances August spurns. With her clairvoyance and her gifts as a healer, beside her more sinister qualities, Åse is an ambiguous figure. Thus, while helping out Dr. Lund's family—she puts their young son to sleep after he has been in terrible pain for thirty-six hours due to a leg fracture—she rips out the doctor's eye when he tries to hasten her departure. That the victim is a doctor, a man of science who has no patience with alternative methods of healing, indicates one dimension of what Åse stands for: the sacredness of nature. Those people, mainly women and old men, who have begun to "scowl at the Consul's mountain road" invoke some "dark words" by Åse: "'There is no peace for either mouse or sparrow,' Åse had said, 'they hammer and blast in God's mountains'" (108).

The novel's denouement brings together a set of circumstances that look like a conspiracy against August: shots being fired near the hunting lodge by the visiting Englishman; the consequent fright of August's herd of sheep, which stampede down the mountain road, carrying August along with them; Gordon Tidemand's coming uphill in his car on the same road and increasing the animals' panic by his honking; finally, Åse blocking the rest of the roadway and driving the animals over the precipice by her very presence. Anything that Gordon and Åse do to stop them has the opposite of the intended effect. Here is the spectacular finale to the circumnavigator's life:

> The rock wall on one side and the abyss on the other. . . . The stream grows larger, a man is in the middle of the churning vortex, August, seen cracking a smile at the car, thinking he can save himself at the last moment perhaps and reluctant to cause alarm, so he smiles. He cannot save himself. Sheep are sheep, where one rushes off all the rest follow, the stream presses on, an avalanche of animals hurtles into the depths. When August sees that all is lost, he grabs a sheep by its long wool, so it can break his fall perhaps, and holds it up before him, but it wriggles itself free. Then he is carried over the brink.
> "The sailor found his grave in a sea of sheep," says the ballad about August. (XII: 315)

A literary disaster of this magnitude requires, in order to be convincing, a sense of inevitability, whether founded on natural neces-

The Human Comedy: Satiric Fantasy and Mock Apocalypse 293

sity or a moral dialectic. The treatment of August represents a combination of these two modes of explanation or justification, and this creates a quandary. If we view August as an individual character who is to be held responsible only for his own actions, the relevant criteria are those of the moral dialectic. However, judging by the final moments in August's life, he is a victim of circumstances that have little to do with his own activities. The sheep could hardly have brought about the disaster by themselves, and the presence of Åse, whose enmity is at least partly of his own doing, would not suffice, by itself, to force the sheep over the brink. These are the only two elements in the configuration of August's nemesis that can be traced back to his own character. Though he knows that Gordon, who has agreed to pick up his English friend by car at a certain hour, will be coming up the mountain road, this is an extraneous circumstance which, however fateful, entails no culpability on August's part. The same applies, *a fortiori*, to the fired shots which trigger the deadly stampede of the sheep.

What happens is, in other words, out of proportion to whatever defects of character August has displayed. That may be why Hamsun has planted recurrent references to the abyss and the guardrail—missing because August had too many things on his mind. But the device is too tansparently contrived, as are the Friday child motif of bad luck, the ominous crow seen by August before the disaster, and the vague fear that grips him. These techniques, which are calculated to produce an idea of ineluctable fate, instead make one feel that, as far as August the man is concerned, he has been the victim of a miscarriage of justice.[22]

What Hamsun seems to want is to discredit what August represents: his downfall is a kind of evil apocalypse that supposedly spells the end of an era of unrestrained speculation, an era that came to an end with the New York stock exchange crash of 1929. One notes that August has become increasingly abstract in the course of the trilogy, his symbolic aspect acquiring more and more importance. In *The Road Leads On*, that aspect is stressed repeatedly, resulting in much tedious editorializing, as in the following passage in relation to his sheep venture: "He was ignorant and therefore innocent, a champion of human progress even if it ended in senselessness and ruin. . . . The time, the Zeitgeist, caught sight of him and could use him, could use even him. . . . The time turned him into an ambassador. He had the mission of creating development and progress even at the price of destroying the existing order of things" (XII: 115). Though the passage seems to hypostasize "the spirit of the time," with the result that August, as an individual, becomes merely its innocent agent, the ruinous ending treats August as a man possessed, like the Biblical figure "with an unclean spirit" whose name is Legion.

In fact, Hamsun now completes his allusion to the story of the Gadarene swine alluded to by Pauline in the previous novel. That the reader is expected to recall the Biblical story is quite evident from one simple fact: the number of sheep, according to August's rough reckoning, is "over two thousand"; the herd of Gadarene swine numbered "about two thousand." The allusion carries a devastating view of modernity. With the locally more acceptable sheep standing in for the Palestinian swine, we witness how August's "unclean spirit" enters into the flock of sheep, with a result that parallels, and parodies, the Biblical account. Just as the Gadarene swine drowned "in the sea," Hamsun in the novel's last sentence transforms the often mentioned abyss into a sea, in conformity both with the Bible and with August's past as a sailor, vividly recalled in a long passage about a storm shortly before the end (XII: 300–01). One notable difference is, of course, that whereas the possessed man was restored to "his right mind,"[23] August perishes—not altogether tragically, if his attempt to break his fall by riding a sheep is an allusion to Peer Gynt's ride on the reindeer buck over Lake Gjendin.[24]

The symbolic denouement works no better than the literal one, though the finale as drama is very impressive. August is too lightweight, too much of a phony,[25] to represent the modern spirit, which also includes the ethos of democracy, for which Hamsun harbors no sympathy. The absurd predicament into which August's activities have landed him, that of a soi-disant leader being hurtled to destruction by a flock of dumb sheep, alias a mindless mob, does indeed look like a burlesque showing-up of the democratic idea and the concomitant principle of equality. And, indeed, however flaky, August is not without sympathy for the common man. Thus, he makes no distinction between high and low, as is shown in his touching promise to Jørn, the herder, that he will provide him with another job when the sheep are brought home. The trouble is that, with every new symbolic meaning discerned in Hamsun's text, the character of August appears increasingly over-determined, with the consequence that he becomes unbelievable. He is made to carry the burden of every tendency in modern civilization that was anathema to Hamsun, a burden so heavy that he succumbs to it, allowing us to see the poor struggling mortal beneath it. Certainly, his downfall will make no difference to Segelfoss society, where the modern spirit will continue to thrive. Freed of his symbolic burden, August is restored to us as the irresponsible circumnavigator we know from *Vagabonds*, and his end takes on the more modest dimensions of an individual disaster, which he confronts with a a sailor's smile. His fall is a mixture of comedy and tragedy, a sort of comi-tragedy, to coin a word.

The rather thin story of August's vicissitudes does not exhaust whatever meanings can be culled from *The Road Leads On*. If it were not for the fact that August is a serial character, having an important role in each part of the trilogy, the critical parts of the novel would be those dealing with the leading Segelfoss citizens, headed by the Tidemands. Interestingly, a close link is established between Gordon Tidemand and what August stands for. For example, Tidemand did "crazy things out of a sheer desire to be active, like building that mountain road and the hunting lodge. And he did worse things out of pure vanity..." (XII: 107–08). Moreover, his solicitation of August's advice in regard to building an extension to his house to accommodate the local bank is capped by the following comment: "Oh, they were equally disposed toward unproductivity. To build, make deals, realize, as long as they kept their heads above water –." Though the consultation ends with the statement that "he was not only foolishness, he was also a businessman" (265–66), Tidemand – and along with him the good citizens of his class – is as inextricably bound up with the "unclean spirit" of the times as August, who ends up as a scapegoat. However, Hamsun has preferred to view the cultured class from a different perspective.

Segelfoss does not undergo much change during the relatively short time span of *The Road Leads On*. In terms of commercial and industrial development, the difference between the town as depicted in *Segelfoss Town*, Hamsun's 1915 novel, and the one being discussed is minimal.[26] The major difference lies elsewhere, namely, in the ambiguous status of the town's leading family, the Tidemands: while they aspire to gentility and refinement, Gordon's very origin is shrouded in secrecy. Married to Julie Knoff, daughter of the merchant of that name in *Vagabonds*, he occupies the mansion formerly owned by the aristocratic Holmsens. The estate was acquired by Theodor Shopkeeper, whose widow, Lydia, referred to as the "Old Mother," is an important character in the *The Road Leads On*. Gordon, it appears, is the offshoot of an extra-marital affair Lydia had with her husband's dock worker, Otto Alexander, a Gypsy with the "sexual voracity of his race," as the text puts it; the affair was initiated by an act of rape, "but so welcome and unrepented" (XII: 85). The relationship is resumed after Theodor's death and provides material for drama, including an attempt at murder, after Lydia transfers her affection to Konrad Holm, the town pharmacist, whom she eventually marries. Though familiar with the local gossip, Gordon, who was never informed of his true paternity, has all along assumed he is the son of Theodor Shopkeeper.

Hamsun's portrayal of the bourgeois class, which consists of businessmen and professionals, is determined by his nostalgia for the embodiment of nobility provided by Willatz Holmsen, Sr. As the novel's principal bourgeois, Tidemand is depicted as someone who has learned "technical skills, languages and office routines, ... so he knew a great deal, but in reality he had little understanding and poor judgment." Rather oddly, these characteristics are related to his race: "He was what he appeared to be, of mixed race, without distinctive features, not a thoroughbred, only a hybrid, not genuine, a little of everything, good at school subjects, but incapable of anything great" (XII: 34). This is not the only instance of such description. Because of his mixed race, Tidemand can apparently never be "whole" but merely "two halfnesses" (168). A party thrown by the Tidemands early on is described in the same terms, as "a mixture of everything, from good food and several kinds of wine to the showy furniture purchased here and there. Those who lived here were new occupants, the gilt flowers on the walls belonged to other people. Gordon Tidemand didn't brag or show off, but all he knew was acquired, including his reserve." It falls to his wife, Julie, to provide the household with something "more innate"; besides, she wins over everybody "by her natural charm" (26). Given this view of true culture, or breeding, as being congenital, it is dubious whether Gordon's wish to be a "gentleman" (34) can ever be achieved.

By examining, however briefly, three important scenes of *The Road Leads On*, one comes to suspect that Hamsun's critique extends to Segelfoss society at large. Though these scenes—the early party thrown by the Tidemands, a benefit entertainment got up for a recently widowed destitute mother, and an outing to the skerries near the end—may seem conventional, representing the sort of things that the young Hamsun eschewed from fiction, they are all marked by a quality of the unexpected. They may not be scenes of scandal outright, used so effectively in *Victoria* and other works, but they do perform a similar function, namely, to evoke an epiphany of the abject spiritual and cultural state of Segelfoss society.

The Tidemands' party is thrown to disguise a failure: neither of the firm's two seine gangs has made a catch, resulting in a considerable financial setback. In other words, the overriding value stipulated in organizing the event is social status, which must be maintained at any cost. It is worth noting that Gordon's mother finds his idea "incomprehensible" and "outlandish." The outcome is stated baldly at the outset: "The party was nothing much" (XII: 22); the festive mood anticipated did not come about. Disappointed, the host thinks, "Why the hell should one prepare lavish dinners for people anyway! Everyone just sat there, said a few words and then fell silent, nobody seemed impressed" (25). Meanwhile, two of the guests who are long-time adversaries begin wrangling, Dr. Lund relates an uncanny story about shaving a corpse, and the exquisite Tokay wine sits "almost untouched in the glasses" (29). After the guests have left, Gordon tells his wife, "It was an unfortunate idea of mine, I'll never do it again" (30).

It is not easy to decide what precisely is intended by having Tidemand judge the party a failure. Are we to assume that, with his English education, he is alien to Norwegian culture, that the guests, however indifferent they seem to the sumptuous display of food and drink and antique accessories, represent the true Norwegian spirit? Or are they all equally in thrall to what is foreign, in taste and values, but reluctant to seem impressed? Perhaps it does not really matter how one answers these questions. The main point is that neither the host nor the guests enjoy themselves; there is no life to the party. And the reason for that, the text suggests, is the lack of an inborn culture which would allow them all to act naturally and create the desired festive mood. The trouble is that the very motive for the party, to impress the guests with one's wealth and social superiority, preempts the possibility of enjoyment and betrays the cultural vacuum of the bourgeois class.

The entertainment near the beginning of Part Two takes place in the town's movie theater and is attended by virtually everyone. Put together by Messrs. Holm and Vendt, two eccentrics hailing from Bergen, the program is a horrendous mishmash of folk, music hall, and classical numbers, including a cattle call—"a song without text, not a word, but an abundance of tunefulness" (XII: 181)—and ending with a singing race, with "the alphabet as text" (182), between the two organizers, who are by then totally drunk. They have been tippling steadily all along, as well as offering drinks to the performers, some of whom are newly born Christians with religious scruples about taking part in such worldly diversions. Not surprisingly, the evening turns out to be quite different from the planned program: a pianist's stage fright or a guitarist's swollen finger necessitates changes. And the persistent rivalry and mutual envy between the two small-town impresarios are finally dissolved only with the help of liquor. Though their final exploit, the alphabet song, is said to derive from "the same appalling shamelessness in which jazz has its source," strangely enough it is praised at greater length, and more warmly, than any other number: "... here, at least, there was no artfulness, they imitated nothing, they created their song on the spot.... It wasn't playacting, it was sincerity and naturalness" (182).

The fact that a whole chapter is devoted to this absurd affair, the only occasion in which all of Segelfoss participates, suggests that it is not there simply to provoke laughter. A closer look at the organizers, especially Mr. Vendt, the hotel manager, may offer a clue. Both are outsiders, Holm being described as an "oddball" (XII: 67), Vendt, in some detail, as a kind of third sex. "Rather flabby, with nearly no growth of beard, he was left-handed, his voice sounded as if it was still changing, at times being nice and deep, but most often too small for the man's husky build. He could wash, sew and cook.... Several generations ago he had been imbrued with a Dutch Jew, like so many in Bergen...." With all his feminine, or effeminate, qualities, this bachelor in his mid-forties combines an "artistic temperament" (173–74), though he has no great gifts of any kind. The only professional artist on the evening's program was the pianist, Mrs. Postmaster, who will figure prominently in the third representative scene to be discussed.

Vendt's blend of man and woman, Norwegian and Jew, is reminiscent of the portrayal of Gordon Tidemand, also racially mixed, though without the sexual ambiguity. One wonders whether this is to be taken as a hermeneutic sign, offering a clue to the meaning of the inane practical joke that the entertainment turns into. Are we given to understand that, just as Gordon Tidemand, along with his class, is incapable of ever attaining the spiritual wholeness and moral strength of a Lieutenant Holmsen, the touted aristocrat, so the cultural and artistic life of Segelfoss, a mix of high, middle and low in terms of class, is a sham? Oddly enough, the narrator does not seem to mind. In fact, the performances of Gina with her cattle call and of the drunken twosome with their alphabet antics are seen as more authentic than anything else, simply because they are not art, but nature.

The Tidemands' outing to the skerries the day before August's fall confirms the above, at the same time as it gives a new twist to the art theme. The occasion is a kind of replay of the party already discussed, except that the outdoors discourage self-promoting speechifying and nasty backbiting. People tend to be nicer, more unguarded and less on their dignity in the open air. Being on a tiny island surrounded by the ocean on every side evokes a sense of the primeval and sets the stage for drama. In keeping with this mood and the spatial isolation that engenders it, the two events that occur on the island are the breakthrough of a romance and the loss of a life: the Englishman gets together with Marna, Gordon's sister, and the only artist in the group, the postmaster's wife, dies by drowning. We do not learn the details; she is known to have been nearsighted, and her husband explains her disappearance as an accident. It is one of those ambiguous Hamsun situations where artistically gifted women are involved, such as Mrs. Falkenberg in *A Wanderer* and Mrs. Holmsen in *Children of the Age*, whose deaths by drowning are put down to accidents but could just as well, or rather more likely, have been suicides. The following is an attempt to justify the latter reading of the text.

The portrayal of Alfhild, the postmaster's wife, is predicated on the corrupting spirit of modernity, specifically as it manifested itself in bohemia. Unhappy in her marriage, she keeps afloat emotionally through a flirtatious, but not sexual, relationship with Holm, the pharmacist. When Holm throws in his lot with Lydia, the Old Mother, Alfhild tells him she feels "bereaved," whereupon she relates the story of her youth. That story essentially coincides with that of Miss Torsen in *The Last Joy*, with the difference that, whereas the latter went to teachers' college, Alfhild studied music. "We sat in our furnished rooms being artistic," she says, "we played and sang a little, put our pennies together and drank and smoked a little, used risqué language, detested ourselves and loved no one.... We became so washed out." The life they led entailed many misadventures: failed marriages, drunkenness, suicides. Though no details are given about her sexual experiences during those years, we are made to believe that, since then, she has been incapable of love, though being married to an "excellent" man who loves her, because she failed to "become something. I was warped" (XII: 276).

In a previous conversation with Holm she tells him, "We are both so empty" (XII: 160), this despite the fact that she has studied abroad and is an accomplished pianist; she plays in public as well as at private parties and has several students. Nevertheless she feels she is a nobody. Her flirtatious routine with the pharmacist is apparently a means of forgetting her emptiness, at least temporarily. "It was this that I missed when you didn't come yesterday," she tells him, "that's how warped I am, I missed your risqué rubbish—excuse the expression! I hadn't heard it for many years when I met you here, I got used to it when I didn't get to be anything, it kept me alive anyway, I existed" (277). Strangely, this woman, whose unexpected death anticipates that of August by just one day, seems to share something fairly important with him: when he is not absorbed in his feverish activity he experiences a sense of emptiness (299). Walking in the mountains toward the end of the novel, he interprets the silence all around him as an emptiness, but what he feels is obviously his own inner void, which he then projects into the landscape.[27] To Hamsun, art and bohemia bring disaster and death in their wake, in this respect paralleling the consequences of August's modernizing zeal. Both August and Alfhild, who have little else in common, represent aspects of contemporary life that Hamsun loathed, and he had no qualms about burdening his novel with his precious insight.

Instead of culture, artistic and intellectual, and the comforts of civilized living, what Hamsun celebrates in *The Road Leads On* is fecundity, which is found everywhere, among rich and poor, young and not so young. And it goes together with a relatively high degree of marital happiness, an unusual phenomenon in a Hamsun novel: Gordon and Julie, Dr. Lund and Ester, Lydia and Holm not only follow the Biblical injunction to be fruitful and multiply, but seem to experience the joys of sex. Ordinarily, Hamsun coyly abstains from describing sexual activity, usually contenting himself with using animal metaphors, like "spirited," "filly" and "wild" for a sexy wife (XII: 8, 15). In *The Road Leads On* he gets slightly more real, while still using general words whose erotic flavor is reduced through humor. Thus, Ester was "proficient in the kitchen, the living room and the cellar, and she was proficient in the bedroom. Ester? Blind and sweet and wild in the bedroom" (247). Julie, "supple as a snake," was "housewife, mistress, and mother, attractive and ardent, all woman" (16, 38). The prize, however, goes to Lydia, who after her stormy relationship with the Gypsy is united with Holm and, like Maren Salt in *Women at the Pump*, finds herself pregnant at an advanced age. What is more, she is convinced, she tells August, that the child was conceived on her wedding night (280). To evoke the romance of conception, in another instance the narrator has recourse to nothing less than the Annunciation, as Julie Tidemand is called "blessed among women" (252) at the delivery of her fifth child.[28]

Another prominent thematic strain in *The Road Leads On* is associated with nature and with a rich residue of legends, superstition, and pagan ritual. These cultural relics from a remote past are preserved by the humble peasants of the area, among whom belief in "trolls and forerunners and denizens of the nether world" is common (XII: 18). Old people tell countless stories about the hill folk, who live in the mountains with their cattle and their farming, "rich and peaceable creatures when they were left in peace" (108). But if disturbed, as has been mentioned earlier in connection with Åse, they will cause trouble and perhaps move to another mountain, depriving the people of the protection they supposedly provide. These chthonic powers work in mysterious ways, which could be called magical, and they foreshadow what will come to pass through dreams, omens and other signs. The bad luck of Solmund, who "was taken by the Segelfoss waterfall" along with his horse, is believed to be the doing of Åse, who became offended at his refusal to "have her" and allegedly caused the horse to become "skittish from that day on" (19). Åse acts as a sort of sibyl or priestess, a role for which she seems suited by her sexual ambiguity, being likened to a "castrated girl" (20). She is almost universally feared, and simple folk try to placate her so as not to get jinxed.

The depth of what today passes for superstition among the populace is shown in particular by an elaborate ritual performed by two youths in the novel. A friend of Benjamin's, Cornelia's twentyish sweetheart, suggests that the two of them go on a quest for the *hulder*, or wood nymph, thought to bring good luck to any mortal who catches sight of her. They prepare as for an ordeal: after going to communion, they make sure to stay away from girls and give up tobacco; and, following the "learning of the old," they wear their shirts "inside out, carried no knives, and had each three juniper berries in their pockets" (XII: 138). The situation is exploited for considerable humor, Benjamin having to fend off Cornelia, in tears because she suspects him of having forsaken her for someone else. Though the wood nymph fails to appear, they do see something: the attempted rape of Marna by Adolf, one of August's workmen. Their experience, while not what the boys bargained for, dramatizes sexuality as a natural force symbolized by the animal-like *hulder*.

Much of the folklore in *The Road Leads On* serves no detectable literary purpose; it seems to be there for its own sake, as though Hamsun were engaged in a project of cultural recuperation. This applies not only to legends and superstitions, but also to customs and practices, such as mutual assistance among the poor. The novel pays much attention to poor people, especially the women, who are portrayed with considerable sympathy: they "slandered and helped one another, they were all people with a little good and a little bad in them." While envy flourishes among them, Hamsun's description of a group of women in the general store betrays a deep empathy with their quiet endurance of a humble lot: "They knew one another and talked together; almost all were mothers, their sod roofs leaked and food wasn't always easy to get at—just so. But they knew of nothing else and they didn't suffer privation" (XII: 309). Poor people, having remained largely unaffected by social change, are depositories of values that Hamsun deems important.

I have enlarged on the timeless pursuits and ancient beliefs and customs described in *The Road Leads On* because of their incongruity with the very concept of a trilogy, a species of fiction expected to pay serious attention to history. With his nonchalance about chronology, Hamsun is ill suited to trace social and economic developments over time. After studying the three novels of the trilogy, one becomes painfully aware of how similar the social conditions and major characters are in all of them: the crucial change taking place is one from agriculture to commerce and industry, with an added refinement or two, such as a petit bourgeois like Theodor Jensen being succeeded by Gordon Tidemand, a bourgeois with a pretension to gentility and elegance.

Hamsun's lack of historical stringency is glaringly revealed by the contradictory chronological data that emerge from the few time indications that he offers. This applies in particular to the trilogy in relation to *Segelfoss Town*. If we assume, as seems reasonable, that Theodor Jensen of the latter novel is twenty years old in 1904, a date that can be inferred from the fall of Port Arthur in the Russo-Japanese War (VI: 305), Gordon must have been born around 1925, since Theodor was over forty at the time of his birth (XII: 9). Further, assuming that Gordon is at least twenty, a very conservative estimate, when the action of *The Road Leads On* begins, one realizes that he would reach that age only in 1945, twelve years after the novel was published. Moreover, Romeo Knoff, whom Gordon befriends as a young man in London and whose sister, Julie, he marries, is a grownup already in *Vagabonds*, whose action extends over some dozen years, from the early 1860s to the mid-seventies. If, say, Romeo was eighteen in 1875, he would be eighty-eight in 1945. Finally, Mariane, Holmengrå's daughter, who is enjoying her honeymoon with Willatz Holmsen, Jr., at the end of *Segelfoss Town* (VI: 439), is in *The Road Leads On* said to be unmarried and working as a housekeeper in Tromsø (XII: 8).

Hamsun's evident contempt for historical chronology and his failure to coordinate the time periods covered in the trilogy and *Segelfoss Town* confirms my view, which has been stated more than once, that his concept of society is based on memory and myth,[29] not on factual knowledge of actual change. The great emphasis on old tales, legends, and superstition in *The Road Leads On* is consonant with such a view, as is the anachronistic thinking and behavior of many of the novel's characters. To judge by the few time indications in the text as well as the allusion to jazz (XII: 182), the action takes place around 1920 or a few years later. But it is quite unbelievable that people in the 1920s, however poor and uneducated, should harbor the rampant superstitions that are described in the novel, which even August is affected by. While the educated characters are acceptable as belonging to the early decades of the twentieth century, most others are not, seeming to belong to a far older world, a period not far removed from that of Knut Pedersen's youth in North Norway.[30] In historical terms, therefore, *The Road Leads On* makes little sense, since as a whole it portrays no particular period, but mingles a modern mentality with ancient ways of thought. In his disgust with modernity, Hamsun has largely regressed to a time that enabled him to stage the battle between the old and the new as forcefully as possible, while celebrating as usual ever-resurgent life and the recurrent cycles of nature.

Hamsun's own opinion of *The Road Leads On* as a "trashy book," expressed in a letter to an old friend,[31] was most likely not meant to be taken seriously. He expressed similarly disillusioned views about other novels. In a letter to his publisher, he gives a more nuanced opinion: "Something good and some rubbish, as in all books."[32] In my view, the best way of summing it up is this: a work that is less than the sum of its parts. The reverse is also true: the sum of its parts is larger than the whole. Like so many of Hamsun's novels, it has magnificent scenes and life-like characters; it also contains excellent comic passages, richly ironic humor, and pungent satire.

The above qualities produce a lively texture in a loosely structured work. Hamsun's knack for ironic humor and satire is evident throughout. It is brilliantly displayed in his depiction of the religious revivals taking place in Segelfoss when the town is visited by a pair of evangelists, one of whom is an Anabaptist who immerses the sinners in the Segelfoss waterfall, despite the warnings of the district doctor: ". . . no one took notice of Dr. Lund in religious questions" (XII: 57). Nor did they pay much attention to the parish pastor, a tolerant man whose congregation is torn by "dissension and strife and hatred" as a result of the revival. The dispute among the parishioners even leads to fights, the bone of contention being the Holy Ghost. "Never before had this more hidden god in God been so popular. . . ." In the debate, the less radical revivalist has the advantage of wit, the other of drama. The former claims that the Anabaptist "'jeers and sneers at the Holy Ghost, no holds barred. But it's bad manners to jeer and sneer at—someone not present!' he said stingingly" (121). On the other hand, rebaptism "in running water" (57) is surrounded with an air of excitement and even provides entertainment. Thus, an acquaintance of August tells him that one woman, Mons-Karina, "entered the water with a plug of chewing tobacco in her mouth and couldn't help spitting, ha-ha, spitting into the baptismal water!" (59). Hamsun's irony ranges from near-slapstick, as in the above instance, to shades of the bizarre and grotesque. Dr. Lund's loss of his eye through Åse transforms a man chronically dissatisfied with his lower-class wife into a loving husband, "jealous as a youth. . . . A new life dawned, embraces, insane wedding nights, laughter in the house. . . . Åse be blessed!" (116). And the picture of August as a seventy-year-old wooer singing a sentimental ballad in the presence of Cornelia and Hendrik, her boyfriend, his "drooping mustache trembling helplessly" (259), epitomizes the grotesqueness of the January and May situation that Hamsun here has evoked.

As long as the narrator's attitudes are objectified in action or concrete images, they do not preclude the minimal suspension of disbelief necessary for any fictional narrative to be convincing. On the other hand, when the narrator steps out of hiding and addresses his own characters, the reader cannot help being puzzled. In *The Road Leads On*, the narrative persona is not only more protean than usual, he is also excessively obtrusive, turning a mere voice into a speaker, that is, a character in the text. One instance will suffice. After the pharmacist has married Lydia, Marna's mother, he feels nervous about meeting the daughter, whom he had previously courted to no avail. But the meeting runs smoothly, supposedly because Marna is rather phlegmatic. The text continues: "Besides, Miss Marna shouldn't be astonished by anything whatever, she'd better not be, she herself having followed a workman to the hospital in Bodø, as was well known. Pardon, Miss Marna, a pharmacist has married your mother—so what?" (XII: 275). The first sentence seems to be a comment by the narrator. But who utters the next sentence, with the question? Regardless how one reads it, as the voice of a cruel and cynical public, or as a tease answered dismissively by Marna, the speaker is no longer a mere narrator but a character in the novel, on a par with the rest. The narrator's inability to stay in hiding or, if that is too much to expect, to limit himself to the task of narration, is here, as so often, an annoyance to the reader of a Hamsun novel.

The critical opinions of *The Road Leads On* span a wide range, from the highest praise to virtual dismissal. Ronald Fangen says it "fully measures up to the best" that Hamsun has written. Describing it as an "exuberantly humorous book," he pronounces August "more splendid than ever."[33] In contrast, Nordahl Grieg sums it up as "two volumes of eventlessness."[34] The Danish critic Christian Rimestad found it "extremely uninteresting," though he, too, applauds the portrayal of August.[35] Again, an American reviewer considers it one of the author's "major achievements," demonstrating the ability to give to local people the "timeless traits of human nature" and yet to keep the characters "differentiated."[36] Conversely, the *TLS* reviewer says that the "sayings and doings" of the inhabitants of Segelfoss threaten to be as boring to the reader as they would be in life. The reviewer admits, however, that August, called a "rolling stone," is portrayed with "exceptional humor and sympathy."[37] A recent opinion is more merciless than any of those cited. Robert Ferguson characterizes *The Road Leads On* as "one of the worst" of Hamsun's novels: it is lacking in "genuine inspiration," and its narrative technique is marred by "windy mannerisms."[38] Clearly, this is a novel about whose merits readers and critics will have to agree to disagree.

CHAPTER ELEVEN

Absurdism Revisited

The action of Hamsun's last novel, *Ringen sluttet* (1936; *The Ring Is Closed*, 1937), is, like that of *The Women at the Pump*, set in a small coastal town in South Norway and extends over nearly two decades; the time is roughly contemporary. Like Oliver in *The Women*, Abel Brodersen, the central character, starts out as a sailor and afterward lives mostly on the margins of society, leading like his predecessor a semi-criminal existence, though for different reasons. Psychologically, his situation appears to be a variant on that of Edevart Andreassen, whose life is derailed by a youthful passion. There are many other echoes of Hamsun's earlier themes, such as marital conflicts, moral corruption, and crime. Though Abel Brodersen is an out-and-out antihero who comes to reject the bourgeois values of his fellow townsmen, his life is closely linked to that of the town, whether as a respectable citizen or as the town bum, a role that he periodically occupies.

Difficult to describe in genre terms, like so many of Hamsun's novels, *The Ring Is Closed* has been called an "unlikely *Bildungsroman*" and, by a witty Dane, a "virtual *Missbildungs-roman*,"[1] a reverse development novel. As far as the main character is concerned, the novel does, indeed, relate a process of shedding whatever values and attitudes he grew up with, but contrary to earlier Hamsun characters who have undergone such a change, Abel replaces them with a minimalist creed that many would define as point zero. Oddly enough, however, his supreme indifference does not make him immune to disillusionment. For despite his increasing detachment from a conventional way of life, Abel's emotional life is largely ruled by members of the very society whose values he has rejected. The question of the novel's typology is further complicated by the ancillary task of social critic that Hamsun has imposed on himself. While the small-town community is richly deserving of satiric treatment, the divided focus distracts the attention from the novel's main purpose, to portray the life of Abel Brodersen.

The son of a former sea captain turned lighthouse keeper, Abel grows up on an islet and is from childhood on isolated from his peers. He is further set apart from his middle-class comrades by the family circumstances, having a tightwad for a father and a mother who is a tuberculous alcoholic. His early youth resembles that of Johannes, the miller's son in *Victoria*. Like Johannes, Abel is eager to show the children who live in town, including Olga, whom he admires, the wonders of his own little secluded world. But the trip to the island is disappointing, marking a pattern of disillusion that runs through the entire novel. The several instances in the book's first two chapters of a terse one-sentence paragraph, "He fell silent" (XIII: 8, 11, 18), indicate Abel's bewilderment at his failure to achieve reciprocity, whether from Olga, who rejects his love, or his father, who seems incapable of affection. In this, the father recalls Schøning, the cynical lighthouse keeper in *Rosa*, though lacking his concern for the environment. With such a background, it is no wonder that the young man became alienated from his place of origin. When he returns from his two periods at sea, the only thing he looks forward to is seeing Olga again, though by the second time, when he is twenty-six, she has been married for several years.

The course of Abel's life from this point on, until he returns to the States for good on the novel's last page, is a seesaw of ups and downs. Lolla, his young stepmother, only six years his senior, wants him to study and make good, but whatever he tries soon ceases to interest him. Thus, his efforts to acquire a deck officer's certificate end in failure, and he goes on to lead an aimless existence. Lolla makes another attempt to put him on a straight course when she acquires a majority of shares in the private shipping company that operates "The Sparrow," a local steamer. She rigs him out with a captain's uniform, and for about a year he serves as captain, she as stewardess, on the ship. By that time Abel no longer experiences a "red joy" at the thought of life on board (XIII: 144), gets increasingly bored and wants to quit. "It was different at the beginning—all beginnings are different. . . . He put his heart and soul into it, talked to the passengers, sent empty milk cans ashore and took full milk cans on board, made the run in forty-eight hours, came back and moored at the quay. It was all in keeping with his abilities." But once it becomes routine, the job bores him. "Nothing happened to him on the trip, no danger of shipwreck with people calling on God, except that now and then he had to take care not to ram a fishing smack drifting indifferently before the bow. . ."(145). The thought of escape gives him a "flicker" of joy (172), and as soon as he has the money for the voyage to the States, he tells Lolla he wants to go there again; among other things, he must visit a grave.

The grave relates to a series of events that took place during his second period of absence, after which he is said to be "changed through and through." We are filled in gradually on what had happened. Already during his first turn as a seaman, between fourteen and eighteen, Abel was living on the edge; having jumped ship in America, he found employment on shore and learned to work in wood and metal, while at the same time managing to fall into "the clutches of the police" for theft: accompanied by a girl, he made off with a barge (XIII: 14). This behavior was quite consistent with his previous ways, such as stealing a gold bracelet for Olga at fourteen, "from Jesus in the church" (11), a piece of sacrilege that he undoes when Olga refuses to accept it: he filches the key to the church at the parish clerk's and lets himself in, while Olga keeps watch outside. A friendship struck up during his first American sojourn with an expatriot Irishman whose fiancée had married someone else, becomes decisive; Abel obviously admires Lawrence, and during the brief interval he spends at home at eighteen he brags to his peers à la August about their exploits together, including criminal acts.

In his second turn at sea, which lasts for eight years and takes him around the globe, Abel again meets Lawrence, this time in Kentucky. The critical event takes place when Abel catches his friend with Angèle, his wife, whom Lawrence had known and presumably been intimate with before Abel met her. In relating his last encounter with Angèle and Lawrence to Olga near the end of the novel, Abel says it was Lawrence who shot and killed his wife, but a slip of the tongue shows that *he* was the killer. However, Lawrence accepted responsibility for the murder. When he visited the States the previous year,

Abel tells her, he discovered that his friend had died in the electric chair "many years ago." He calls it a "double murder: my wife and the child. With him, that makes three lives" (XIII: 216). Later he indicates he had intended to kill Lawrence, not Angèle.

Since Hamsun has used a method of incremental exposition in relating the story of Abel Brodersen, the meaning of that story changes as we proceed; in effect, there is no central meaning, but a cluster of possible ones, or a series of perspectives on the mystery at the core of the central character. Given the initial impression of Abel as a neglected boy who feels compelled to play pranks and display derring-do to attract attention and admiration, it is not surprising that he comes to savor a life of excitement and danger. He and Olga share much wickedness as children; among other things, they kill a tomcat together, throw it into a sack and sink it in the bay. I have mentioned above the theft and return of the bracelet. The prankster in him is still alive when he returns home at the age of twenty-six. After Olga refuses the bracelet he has bought for her, which he feels he owes her after what happened twelve years earlier, he sneaks into the belfry at the conclusion of the Pentecost service and stays there until the church is empty. Then, thinking "Jesus will get a new bracelet," he puts it in place, "arranges it nicely, gives it the once-over and steps down again." Recalling his teenage exploit, he feels sorry for himself as a boy, "so small and so chillingly scared of ghosts all through the night." He still seems to identify with that boy. As it dawns on him that Olga could have accepted the bracelet he offered her despite wearing a wristwatch, since after all she had two arms, he reflects, "It almost looked like he was still a child, not a grown man!" (XIII: 51–52).

This is one way of reading Abel's story, namely, as that of a young man who never grows up, an eternal adolescent.[2] What he desires most of all is excitement, the sense of living dangerously. Hence, in the long run life on board "The Sparrow" becomes unbearable to him, a "daily idiocy [that], once established, continued without change. . . . How could anyone endure it? The absence of danger everywhere on the ship, the contrived safety on all sides and in every direction irritated him, porcelain nameplates over every door so you won't lose your way, buttons to press, cushions everywhere, cushions." Then there is a qualification: "Not that he sought danger and death, . . . but some change would be a delight" (XIII: 173).

Paradoxically, Abel's juvenile need of change coexists with virtual ataraxia, stoical indifference, a state of mind considered desirable by certain Greek philosophers. "He had a god's indifference about how things turned out. That was something. He could endure, could be without" (XIII: 173-74). Speaking to Lolla about his time together with Angèle, he praises their hand-to-mouth existence, dependent on luck and petty thievery, while denigrating a goal-oriented life. They were "blissfully happy together, like wild animals," he tells her. "Now and then," he relates, "I made her happy with a chicken from the farmer. He was so stingy and kept watch. Once he fired a shot at me and afterward I didn't dare go. It didn't matter, there was fish in the streamlet, and in the fall there was fruit everywhere" (49). Not only does Abel find this return to a primitive mode of life to be satisfying, he uses it as a standard whereby civilized life is judged. The fact that the idyll exists "as a form of nostalgia," as one critic has noted, "does not necessarily reduce its value."[3]

In a late conversation with Olga, the terms that average mortals would use about Abel's way of life are stood on their heads. What Olga sees as total failure, Abel views as success. Though he uses negative terms in describing his own situation—"I'm nothing, I'm annihilated and nameless"—he finds it to be preferable to hers: whereas he claims to be "at peace," he sees her as "perplexed," trapped in a childless marriage to an impotent husband, after a first marriage in which she refused to have children. "Why should we become something?" he asks her. "All the others become something and yet are not happy. . . . Their peace is gone, their nerves are frayed, some drink to cope and just get worse . . .; I, who live in a shed, pity them." What to her is degrading, he sees as mature. By a mysterious higher logic, negatives turn into positives. "It began," he tells her, "in childhood. I was so without every opportunity, that's how it began. Then I became rootless in foreign lands, and that ripened me. Then I got married to Angèle, and that liberated me completely, thank God" (XIII: 210-11).

What Olga sees as lack of will on his part, he views as a talent. Referring to what he had seen in the tropics, he waxes lyrical over the millions who live "from day to day, from hand to mouth, live on next to nothing and on sunshine. . . .[T]hey don't think in terms of money and livelihood and furniture, they lead simple lives, using flowers for ornaments." Abel even manages to support his argument with a reference to the Sermon on the Mount, asking Olga what it benefits a person "to gather into barns" (XIII: 211-12).[4] In contrast to Olga, Clemens, her husband at the time, seems to find Abel's singularity admirable, telling Lolla, "The rest of us become the little we become because we are so ordinary. He is from a borderland that is unknown to us" (109). Hamsun's use of this aperçu, credited to "Young Clemens" (208), as an epigraph to a subsequent chapter of the novel, shows how seriously Abel's gospel of simplicity is intended.

The patina of idealism with which Abel graces his life as an international outcast agrees well with a statement Hamsun made in a letter to a Danish author after the book had been published. Here Hamsun says: "My intention with the central character was to show a mentality not entirely different from the one that you describe in your profound and fine feature article about the Arabs. I know no Arab personally; what I have written is the result of some reading and also some thinking and experience during a long life." A note explains that the author, who lived in Tangier, Morocco, relates "how the Arabs live for the present and for eternity—'that is the great difference between them and the Europeans, who almost always live and work for the day tomorrow.'"[5] But if Hamsun's intent was what he says it was, why did he make both Abel and what he represents so ambiguous?

To Abel, the most intense and worthwhile life is inseparable from a willingness to go to ruin. This applies in particular to his view of love. In Kentucky, he and Angèle "lived on the rocks," though allegedly in a state of perfect bliss (XIII: 49). On his return to Norway, he soon gets involved with a married woman, Lili, with whom he has several children, though she lacks what it takes to be his soul mate: "She could only be his temporal lover." On the other hand, he thinks that Lolla had the right temperament. "Lolla could have been good to shiver through life with, but first she was his stepmother, second she had become a lady. But she might at one time have had the wild abandon necessary to throw herself away" (60). He uses the same self-destructive language in conversation, telling her, "you could have been good to have for myself to go to the dogs with" (65). After he beds Olga, who uses him to get impregnated, he suggests a similar possibility to her: "You are gloriously reckless, Olga. And if you were poor and forsaken and down-and-out, you would be ready to go out into the world with me, eh?" (222). These associations of passion-love with a willingness to go to rack and ruin look like Hamsun's attempt to make amends for the defeat of Edevart Andreassen in *August*. By contrast with Edevart, who turns into a kind of zombie after his erotic misadventure with Lovise Magrete, Abel Brodersen accepts ruin, which he ostensibly sees as the price of ecstasy.

There is one more turn of the screw: in the moment Abel makes his slip of the tongue and betrays the truth about the death of his wife and unborn child, a new perspective on his life and on the novel as a whole opens up. Once it becomes clear that the young man who returned home at the age of twenty-six was a murderer, his behavior is seen in a different light. At this point, all the rationalizations, his persistent critique of bourgeois society and his refusal to find a place within it, appear like cover-ups of a deep-seated sense of guilt that can only be expiated by returning one last time to the States to answer for his crime. Contacted by the police and informed that Lawrence's family want to rehabilitate him, Abel leaves once more for Kentucky, supposedly to turn himself in. Before his departure, he pays his debt at a photographic studio and sends a promised children's bike to Lili's house. Though his decision to return and face possible execution for murder may seem praiseworthy, now that we know what has been weighing on his conscience all these years, his past behavior becomes understandable as the subconscious expression of a death wish. In any case, Hamsun's incremental exposition, giving the American part of his story piecemeal, serves him well, but puts great demands on the reader, who at the conclusion of the novel has to go back and reconsider his or her previous responses to the text.

The shifting perspectives on the central character of *The Ring Is Closed* are complemented by thematic uncertainty. For example, in previous novels Hamsun has expressed a dogmatic view in favor of so-called rootedness and against a wandering type of existence. Though his last novel contains a more extensive discussion of the topic than any previous one, the result is by no means clear. The champion of *hjemmekjærhet*, "love of home," is Clemens, Olga's first husband, a kindly lawyer who marries Lolla after his divorce. Talking to Abel aboard his ship, "The Sparrow," Clemens calls "love of home" the "voice of the blood." He continues: "With all the confusion and incomprehensibility amid which we humans wander, life has here expressed a will and a meaning: life itself has established love of home, it's not invented." Clemens argues, for example, that even God is not the same at home as he is abroad. In his view, people are connected by an irrefragable bond to their place of origin; indeed, he believes this applies to the entire animal kingdom. He gives numerous examples to support his view, citing salmon and trout seeking out the spawning grounds "where they belonged" and migratory birds which nest "where they were born" (XIII: 166-67). All this is alien to Abel, the captain, who changes the topic when Clemens suggests that he may have gotten "some roots torn." Noting the falling snow, Abel remarks that "now the sun is shining warmly in Kentucky!" (168).

The context of the discussion, together with Abel's decision to leave Norway for good, casts a skeptical light on Clemens's notion of an absolute sense of belonging. The discussion is preceded by a sort of animal fable, about a cow, recently sold to a butcher, which had "broken loose and opened the door and run home again" (XIII: 166). In Hamsunian fashion, the animal is anthropomorphized throughout, and the whole episode has a decidedly humorous effect, which tends to qualify Clemens's claim. In any case, the conflict in Abel's mind between home and away from home is in the end resolved in favor of the latter: the pull of a grave, and of the triple deaths he considers himself guilty of, wins out over any residual sense of belonging where he was born. Perhaps the question to be asked is this: What determines where your home is? Is "home" definable simply in terms of geographical origin, or is the decisive factor the depth of experience associated with one place or another? Hamsun's last novel enters new territory in leaving the question unresolved on the discursive level: Clemens's argument is just too sweeping and ends up seeming sentimental.[6]

What tips the scale in favor of Kentucky is the cruel disillusion Abel suffers in his relations with Olga. The novel's conclusion is steeped in mordant irony: when his lifetime dream of Olga is finally fulfilled and she gives herself to him in his ramshackle shed, he discovers it was the sensation she "was after." At the end of her second visit, she says, "her eyes glistening, 'I have twice slept with a murderer. That's something anyway!'" Abel appears stunned: "He paled, his lower lip fell, he looked foolish. 'Was that why—?'" She says, "Don't be angry with me. It was exciting. I know I'm a bitch" (XIII: 223). When they meet after their intimacy, Olga barely knows him. The last time he sees her, he notices that she is pregnant: she has achieved her object. Soon after he leaves for the States.

Notwithstanding the lack of an unchanging perspective in relating Abel's story, the treatment of other characters and their relationships is informed by values that Abel stands for. Most of these values assume a negative form: indifference to money, class, and social status, with material demands at a minimum; calm of mind, concentration on the present moment, lack of concern for the future; an Edenic sexual euphoria, predicated on a relationship of perfect harmony. Not surprisingly, most of the characters in *The Ring Is Closed* exemplify the exact opposite of these values. Still, they are judged, together with the life styles they practice, whether middle- or lower-class, by a bum's ethos, which serves as a touchstone of their human worth. This is seen, first of all, in Hamsun's handling of Abel's relationships with Lolla, Olga, and Lili, the three Norwegian women who are important in his life.

Neither Lolla nor Olga understands Abel's indifference to social status; his lack of ambition and refusal to make something of himself remain a mystery to them. However, the impression created by the manner in which they are portrayed could scarcely be more different. Whereas Lolla comes across as someone who is fighting for her very survival, materially and psychologically, Olga is a child of privilege; she divorces her first husband, Clemens, because he can no longer afford to give her the required pin money, and marries a businessman, Gulliksen. In contrast, Lolla's motive for marrying old Brodersen was not a selfish one; she did it to prevent her father from being exposed as a crook: he had forged Brodersen's signature on an IOU and then skipped town. The situation is worthy of Dostoyevsky: a young girl in her mid-twenties has to marry a man in his sixties, a near dotard. True, old Brodersen's death soon after sets her up as a well-heeled widow, but Lolla considers that the money she has inherited is as much Abel's as hers. A passionate woman, to judge by her "wild nostrils which went in and out" (XIII: 18), she possesses the sensuality required for a female character to pass muster in a Hamsun novel. The fact that her nocturnal visits to a boy friend had given rise to gossip does not diminish the narrator's sympathy. She and Abel are obviously attracted to each other, but he shies away from physical intimacy with her.

When Lolla is subsequently wooed by Clemens, the son of a judge, after Olga has dropped him for Gulliksen, Hamsun brings together the two most sympathetic characters in the novel. This turn of events, with its implicit disdain for class distinctions, accords well with Abel's spirit of indifference to rank and status. Clemens's decision costs him dearly: his parents refuse to accept the new wife. But having followed convention in his first choice of a wife, suppressing his long-time love for Lolla to avoid the scandal of a misalliance, Clemens has learned his lesson. Though one sometimes feels impatient with Hamsun's tendency to signalize a happy marriage by the birth of a child, in this case it seems appropriate. The event is handled very much like the birth of "the prince" in *Rosa*: only with the advent of "the wonder" does Clemens, who has been annoyed by reminders of his wife's past, become a full partner in the marriage. Moreover, the birth acquires archetypal significance: "Strange how everything had changed, it was not only in Bethlehem that a child was born" (XIII: 231). Of the many marriages depicted in *The Ring Is Closed*, that of Clemens and Lolla is the only happy one in town. And this is so despite the fact that Lolla, a career woman and an independent person, represents the epitome of upward mobility.

In contrast, Olga is portrayed as a parasite, financial and emotional. For one, her expensive taste forced Clemens to embezzle money from the office, which he shared with his father. The threat of imminent inspection throws her into a frenzy. Though she, like Lolla in a similar situation, is aware of the potential scandal to the family, her reaction, one of virtual hysteria, appears excessive, especially when juxtaposed with the cool equanimity of Abel, who finds that her need of two thousand kroner, half a year's average income, is nothing to "make such a fuss about! . . . If only you could take everything as the trifle it is," he tells her. "That's what I do" (XIII: 92-93). The fact that Olga's immodest request is preceded by her getting Abel to retrieve from the church the gold bracelet she had once refused to accept, casts an even darker shadow on her. Nor is it to her credit that she pays back only half the loan, forcing Clemens, to his "great shame" (238), to visit Abel in his shed before his final departure and repay the rest, apologizing profusely for the delay.

Superior to Lolla socially, overall Olga cannot hold a candle to the woman who once was her maid. They could hardly be more different from one another. Spoiled and vain, Olga depends on men for her very identity. And according to Abel, who compares her to electric light, to "a fire that is created for the eyes alone, to be seen," she is lacking in passion or ardor. "I suppose there is also some warmth in it," he tells her, "but it's not like an oven" (XIII: 154). Yet, her portrayal is not entirely negative. Indeed, one cannot help admiring Hamsun's fairness in portraying the two women. For all her virtues, Lolla did, after all, exploit old Brodersen, and for all her nastiness and leeching, Olga's suffering is real enough. By holding out the prospect of a baby for her as well, Hamsun may have wished to demonstrate a modicum of sympathy for the self-styled bitch.

While Lolla and Olga, a happily married career woman and a chronically frustrated wife and sexual predator respectively, represent newcomers to Hamsun's character repertoire as a novelist, Lili is a familiar type, a variant on Petra in *The Women at the Pump* and Ragna in *Vagabonds*. However, having someone like Abel to exploit, she comes across as meaner than both her predecessors. Marginally working-class, she and her husband, Alex, are a pair of feckless spongers beholden to Abel for the very roof over their heads. Once a relationship has been initiated, with children being born to Abel as well as to her husband, Lili has a hold on him and keeps pestering him for money. Threatened with losing their house, she and Alex are even prepared to take possession of Abel's shed. Hamsun's portrayal of this shabby pair, whose conjugal life alternates between mutual deception and collusion, is remarkably gentle, possibly because Lili transcends class by her zestful and unashamed erotic life. The one and only girl who showed Abel some kindness in childhood, Lili had remained dormant sexually until she met him again. Considering that she could only be his "temporal" love, Abel must have known how to do something right. "The gentle Lili had been awakened; after all these years in a faithful marriage, she'd only now been awakened to a true erotic experience" (XIII: 71).

This is one of many marriages depicted in *The Ring Is Closed*. Most of them are a dismal failure as a source of human happiness. The novel encapsulates a virtual marriage test, for which the Edenic bliss of Abel and Angèle in the midst of extreme poverty serves as standard. The triggering situation, the bankruptcy of the sawmill, may be less drastic than the famine in *August*, but its consequences are severe, focused this time on the marital repercussions of the failure. The ruinous effects, described with humorous hyperbole, cut across the whole spectrum of the work force, from manager to common laborer. The manager and his wife "stuck together out of common decency and for the sake of the children, but they were without joy." The wife becomes aware of the less attractive aspects of her husband's physiognomy, thinking lately "that he had a repulsively turned-up nose, and what's more, he was beginning to grow a potbelly. She argued with him off and on till evening and didn't say a word to him at the table. . . ." The workers' reactions to their quandary are more violent, their homes ringing with "quarrels and bangings of the table"; there is even a threat of suicide by a sorely tried husband. He and his wife, a woman with a sluttish past, "had had nothing against each other at the outset, oh no. They had even agreed to be a little religious. But when the sawmill stopped and the week's pay was not forthcoming, many things went to pieces; she became quite insufferable, and he became the same to her" (XIII: 70). Whether bourgeois or working-class, the marriages scrutinized in the novel are fraught with discord. By contrast, if we are to believe Abel, his life with Angèle, with whom he shared a hand-to-mouth existence, was one of perfect harmony.

The Ring Is Closed derives much of its interest from the interdependence that exists between Abel as an outsider and those who live within the conventions. This interdependence functions as the novel's overall compositional principle. In addition to the already noted themes of love and marriage that connect Abel and the stay-at-homes, the book contains numerous plot elements, in particular sexual triangles, which help provide a modicum of structure to a sprawling text. The analysis of these parallel developments will not only reveal consistent patterns of action, but also cast new light on the predicament of the central character, Abel Brodersen.

Abel tells Olga that he was "liberated" by his marriage to Angèle (XIII: 211); he says nothing much about the effect of Angèle's death. I have previously raised the possibility that his entire behavior after returning from abroad is motivated by a deep-seated guilt left by the traumatic event. What remains to be discussed is a seeming dynamics of recurrence, whereby Abel repeats the event with a new triangular cast. Whether parody or not, a hostile encounter between Abel and Alex leads to a near reenactment of the Abel/Angèle/Lawrence confrontation. Ironically, Abel now assumes the position of Lawrence in the triangle, the man he wanted to kill for sleeping with his wife, while Alex who, using the revolver he has snitched from his friend, wounds Abel with one of the two shots he fires, is the cuckolded husband. The circumstances repeat those of the Kentucky affair, in that the lovers are caught *in flagrante* by the husband. The parodic aspect emerges through Abel's cold-blooded indiffeence to Axel's threats: he simply continues to put on his shoes. Subsequently, as captain of "The Sparrow," Abel thinks back to this moment with pride: "When Alex some time ago shot him, he was tying his shoelaces — and he finished tying them. He would've acted the same today. . ." (174). Nevertheless, nonchalance cannot hide the fact that Abel is reenacting, in an ironically reversed constellation, his one-time trauma.

The other triangles in which Abel becomes involved, though less fraught with danger, are both psychologically and structurally significant. In his relations with Olga, Abel is by turns in competition with Clemens and with Gulliksen. Though the Olga/Clemens/Abel triangle exposes Abel to considerable emotional turmoil and shapes a good amount of the novel's action, the Olga/Gulliksen/Abel group is in retrospect more important, since it is as a trapped member of this group that Abel's relationship with Olga is fulfilled in a supremely disenchanting and sardonic manner. Abel's triangular relationship with Lolla is, in a way, even more fateful, since in this triangle Abel is the rival of his own deceased father, representing the incest taboo. In the end, death itself steps into the triangle, after hovering in the background throughout the novel. In that regard, one may wonder what Hamsun meant by the title he chose for his book, whether it refers, among other things, to the pattern of fateful recurrence which determines Abel's life. Hamsun's explanation of the title is so obvious as to seem opaque: "What is meant is that the last link in the chain joins the first link."[7] With Abel's return to the scene of the crime at the end of the novel, with a likely death sentence to follow, he circles back to the onset of his sexual tragedy.

One particular device in *The Ring Is Closed* confirms this hypothesis of a *ricorso*, namely, the repeated appearance of a blind, or professedly blind, organ grinder. He is part of the brief initial scene, a sort of preamble, and dies near the end, at which time the huge sum of 12,000 kroner is found "under his shirt, tucked away on his naked body.... Now this large sum of money was to be divided among relations he had never seen and didn't know about, the newspaper wrote," after which the narrator comments, "Life's queer paradox" (XIII: 232). Possibly a reminiscence from Hamsun's reading of Flaubert's *Madame Bovary*, where a scar-faced blind street singer is heard singing a love song in the moment of Emma's death, the organ grinder not only punctuates the narrative with his comings and goings, but acts as Olga's messenger at a crucial juncture in her life. Along with a portrait of her, he brings Abel a note in which she makes an assignation with him for that evening. Thus, the organ grinder is used to harbinger the continually suspended climactic moment of their relationship. Being blind, or supposedly so, he is an appropriate choice to carry a message of what used to be called illicit love. Since no one takes him seriously, this enigmatic figure is privy to the townspeople's secret lives, and his recurrent presence hints at the dark undertow of those lives. A figure of fate, he is also a symbol of a society in which appearance and reality, as in *Vagabonds*, do not necessarily meet. That he should himself be overtaken by an ironic fate, in having his accumulated wealth scattered among relatives he never knew, may be part of the "queer paradox" we are alerted to at his death.

From mid-career on, Hamsun's fiction has been marked by a certain excess—an excess of minutiae, minor characters, tendentiousness, authorial intrusiveness, and so forth. *The Ring Is Closed* is conservative in these respects. Even so, for a novel with a central character as distinctive as Abel Brodersen, *The Ring Is Closed* does appear rather diffuse. Its broad canvas can only be explained by assuming that what Hamsun intended to produce was a comprehensive representation of life *tout court*, along with his distinctive perspective on it, within the framework of a small-town milieu.

That milieu is not exactly what one might expect to find. One striking feature of the society depicted in *The Ring Is Closed* is how permeated with crime it is, mainly such as has to do with money. During one of her visits to his shed, Lili tells Abel the local news: "A young girl robbed in the town woods last night. . . . Robertsen, the customs officer, had been shot and lay in the hospital. . . . Then there were burglaries, thefts and car accidents—" (XIII: 217). Robertsen, who was shot while pursuing a band of smugglers, appears early on as a forger. Even Fredriksen, with his country house, is called a "scum in his stinginess and greed" (223). The atmosphere engendered by these corrupt pillars of society makes a character like Ulrik Fredriksen, the black sheep of the family, quite understandable. With his twenty-year-old dream of a married woman he fell in love with in Natal, South Africa, an English violinist with "sex all over her body," this "aging roué" (83) is not unlike Abel, the great dreamer.

In depicting the social dynamics of the little town, Hamsun makes excellent use of the ship motif, specifically the local steamer, "The Sparrow," whose function recalls that of the sanitarium in *The Last Chapter*. First, with its hierarchy of officers and crew and the three classes of passengers, life on board acquires a striking resemblance to life in town, except that it is more transparent. In effect, "The Sparrow" constitutes a microcosm, a society in miniature. As stewardess, in charge not only of the restaurant but of allotting cabins as well, Lolla strictly inforces the unwritten laws of a class society. These laws are never forgotten, since they are constantly being broken by Abel, who cares little for rank and blurs his public image by acting as he sees fit. A leitmotif that constantly turns up is his inability to keep his officer's uniform clean, just as the new suits of clothes that Lolla keeps buying for him soon take on a shabby look. In this society, where external appearance is so important, clothes do indeed make the man.

A less obvious use of the mini-society aboard "The Sparrow" is to probe beneath the clothes, the ship ambience serving as an alibi for opening up. A subtle game of playacting takes place which, while aiming to conceal the truth, cannot help but reveal hurt and failure. There is, for example, the engineer, ruined when the sawmill went bankrupt. A regular passenger, he always travels with a "hefty briefcase" under his arm (XIII: 85), a pure pretense. He and Ulrik Fredriksen, captain of "The Sparrow" at the time, indulge in a game somewhat like that of Old Ekdal in Ibsen's *The Wild Duck*, though without losing contact with reality. The situation resembles that of an expressionistic play, in which characters reenact what they once were or dream of what might have been. Ulrik, as I have indicated, is in thrall to his dream of the English musician. The showing-forth of the "[u]nrest under the surface" (165) even implicates Olga, who reminds Abel of what she had once told him, that when he got himself a "big ship," she would leave with him. But, of course, she adds, "you've forgotten that I wanted to run away with you" (156). The regrets, dreams and velleities that are glimpsed in these unguarded moments add a welcome depth dimension to Hamsun's portrayal of the citizens of a starchy town.

Eventually, Hamsun's use of "The Sparrow" becomes allegorical, evoking the idea of a "ship of fools."[8] With Abel's departure and the death of the mate, Gregersen, the ship is left without officers. The crew of three run it successfully for a while, though not through any virtue of their own, according to the text: ". . . God led their first trip and the next and the later trips without visiting misfortune upon them." When a crisis occurs, the resulting disaster is also attributed to intervention by the Almighty: "He who is standing, let him see to it that he does not fall! God probably thought and permitted something to happen." Then the human agent is identified: "It was Alex, that vain peacock, who caused it" (XIII: 197). When he begins to strut about in the former mate's cap, left behind on the steamer with other apparel, his two fellow crew members make a protestation, which Alex flouts, proclaiming, "I'm a proletarian" (198). The ensuing scuffle, during which the ship runs aground on an underwater reef, does more than discredit the folly and vanity of Alex; it exposes what Hamsun saw as the hazardous arrogation of power by the underclass. But beyond creating a political fable demonstrating the futility of an egalitarian, non-class society and of political democracy, Hamsun here also adumbrates a mock-theology, whereby the failure of the experiment is seen as a reenactment of the Fall of Man.

Other characters and scenes betray Hamsun's ambition to create a global vision of life. Thus, the scenes early on in which Old Brodersen meets with his cronies add the category of the aged to a fictional population consisting mainly of the young and middle-aged. These scenes, like so many others, are excellently done. The impression of creeping senility, with mutual raillery yielding to spells of dozing, is less fierce than in previous works, being tinged with humor. The emotional dynamics, which resembles that between Magnus and Moss in *The Last Chapter*, is indicated in the following comment: "On the way back home they quarrel, thereby bolstering one another a little bit" (XIII: 25).

Hamsun's portrayal of his *memento mori*, Mr. Gregersen, mate on "The Sparrow," serves more than one purpose. On the one hand, the situation of the mate expresses a permanent element of Hamsun's sensibility, a veritably Calvinistic awareness of death, an awareness shared by Abel and given voice by him. After Gregersen's death, Abel meets Olga's argument about his lack of ambition by recalling the mate, who "wanted desperately to rise, . . . to own the ship," then dies (XIII: 213). On the other hand, by refusing to seek treatment for his throat cancer, Gregersen becomes an emblematic figure who virtually dies on his feet. Shortly before he leaves the ship for good, he tells Lolla, "I can neither sit nor lie, I can only stand. I'll stand until I fall dead" (195). Forced upon him or not, his posture while waiting for death cannot help evoke admiration. Whatever its source, whether Stoic philosophy or the Viking ethos, this symbol of dying courageously must have been dear to Hamsun. It appears already in *Hunger*, in a passage showing the hero's desperate struggle with exhaustion: "Bursting into sobs of rage, I fought my distress with my innermost soul, bravely holding my own so as not to fall down: I had no intention of collapsing, I would die on my feet" (I: 133).[9]

Though the narrative voice used in *The Ring Is Closed* is, on the whole, less garrulous than in the trilogy, it does occasionally obtrude on the narrative through uncalled-for apostrophes, ejaculations, addresses to the fictional characters, and so forth. Some of the interventions are so bizarre that one suspects Hamsun felt hampered by the realistic conventions to which his fiction basically conforms and was tentatively playing with the possibility of breaking into a new form. In this novel he violates literary realism more openly than before, having recourse to devices and rhetorical figures that bring to mind Laurence Sterne's *Tristram Shandy* (1760–67).

A trivial example is offered by the narrator mimicking the reader's surprise—"What—?" (XIII: 218)—at the news that Lolla has been presented with a canary. More eye-popping are the narrator's apostrophes to the characters within the fiction. After Lolla has let herself into the house one day soon after her marriage to Clemens, a paragraph begins with this sentence: "How strange for you, Lolla, to belong here and take part in things!" (192). Then the text continues with past tense narration. Another apostrophe, this time to Abel but concerning Lolla, runs, "But Abel, you should have seen her when she used to steam to town in your motorboat at night!" (48). A truly mind-boggling speech is addressed to "The Sparrow" during the fight among the crew which causes the shipwreck. The episode is related in a quasi-rhapsodic style, with the ship as well as the offending reef being personified as they engage in mortal combat. Here is the passage: "'The Sparrow' went by itself. There certainly is nothing sickly or dreamy about you, little sparrow of mine, you're surely not going about in a daze, you're making the run you have in your body. I bet you'll find the way home by yourself!" (199). The most distinctly Sternean element, however, is the already cited epigraph to chapter twenty-six, a quotation from Clemens where he offers Lolla his opinion of Abel: "The rest of us become the little we become because we are so ordinary. He is from a borderland that is unknown to us. Young Clemens" (109, 208). The violation of realistic norms is here so radical as to erase the ontological distinction between the reality of the writer and that of his characters.

By comparison with these touches of a quaint experimentalism, Hamsun's customary authorial intrusions, while commonplace, can be damaging. Thus, the very portrayal of Abel betrays an inconsistency that may be due to a latent desire by the author to appropriate him for his own purposes: though Abel has little education and, supposedly, only a "mediocre intelligence" (XIII: 174), he occasionally speaks like a book.[10] While this can be passed over as a mere aesthetic shortcoming, for the author to use Abel as a mouthpiece for his own crass antifeminism is tantamount to a moral violation of his own fictional creation. At a time when Abel is annoyed at being made the object of women's do-goodism, he is given a coarse mental harangue in free indirect discourse which sounds totally wrong:

> Those hens, now they were at their wit's end how to do good, and he was to suffer! They didn't see themselves how repulsive they were, but he held his nose before them. They were at an age when they were sexually played out, so they took up religion, good deeds, and politics, cackling together but no

longer laying eggs; they even tried to crow but couldn't learn how to. Those hens, those pitiful hens of the human world, what was left for them to do? Engage in religion, good deeds, and politics. If only he, at least, could steer clear of them! (XIII: 233)[11]

If Hamsun had expressed such sentiments on his own account, through the narrative voice alone, we would have found it to be in poor taste and the barnyard language unseemly. Represented as Abel Brodersen's thoughts, they falsify the psychology of the novel's central character and mar the text. With his bum's purity, without calculation or ulterior motives, Abel exerts a powerful attraction on women. This is clearly demonstrated at the very end by the attentions of Mrs. Fredriksen, a fifty-year-old widow who offers him a job as her personal chauffeur, with a clear hint of possible intimacy. Abel treats her with courtesy, as he has done in every case where women were concerned. For Hamsun to use Abel's annoyance at a few undesired attentions from female well-wishers as a springboard for trumpeting his own prejudices is not only inartistic but morally shabby.

It is heartening that, in the midst of such crudities, one also comes upon some subtlety. Notably, Hamsun's title, *The Ring Is Closed*, appears to be self-referential, adding a metafictional dimension to the novel. Beyond a figurative announcement of laying down his pen, the title may contain an allusion to the real start of his writing career, namely *Hunger*. In effect, his last novel circles back to connect with his first significant work, thus rounding out his career as a creative writer.

The heroes of these two novels conform to the same archetype, being modern variants of the Cain figure. The association with brotherhood implicit in the patronymic Brodersen is a teasing suggestion that Abel may, indeed, be a Cain in Abel's clothing, or he is intended as a conflation of the two sons of Adam. In my discussion of *Hunger* I have alluded to the kinship of Hamsun's first hero with what I call the "Biblical outcast."[12] The heroes of *Hunger* and *The Ring Is Closed* are cut from the same cloth. The former is a cosmic outsider engaged on a quest, the latter a social outsider in pursuit of a dream. Both experience disillusionment: Ylajali merges with the blaspheming whore, and Olga demeans herself and Abel by using him as a stud. They are both absurdist heroes, upholding certain basic values in the midst of a meaningless world, such as honesty, human dignity, and the courage to make a constantly new beginning, despite setbacks. Even their daily life is often similar, in that Abel Brodersen also endures periods of hunger. But chiefly they are both chasing illusions, one as an artist and lover, the other as a knight-errant of romance. The illusion to which Abel gives his life is more precious, to him, than any reality. Both lose out, but are not defeated.

In the Christmas Catalogue of Gyldendal Publishers for 1936, Hamsun says: "*The Ring Is Closed* is both as fantasy and as thought the best I have done."[13] The critics did not agree. And no wonder: how could a reader or critic of the mid-1930s accept the favorable portrayal of a character who has been called the "first true hippie!"[14] He could also have been called an existentialist *avant la lettre*. Hamsun's Abel Brodersen antedates both Camus' Meursault in *The Stranger* (1942) and Roquentin in Sartre's *Nausea* (1938), two works that brought the absurd hero to the forefront of critical attention. That Hamsun had conceived him nearly five decades earlier, when he wrote *Hunger* and *Mysteries*, only heightens one's sense of wonder: a few years short of eighty, Hamsun was able to recapture the mood of his literary beginnings, while investing the absurdism with a positive, though not unambiguous, ethical content. Abel's recognition of life's meaninglessness does not entail moral nihilism.

Oddly enough, some English-language reviewers were less censorious than their Norwegian colleagues. Whereas Alf Larsen, for example, called Abel "almost an animal," a "half-rotten cadaver," and Nordahl Grieg says the book shows Hamsun to be a "shadow of his former self,"[15] Stanley Young of *The Nation* praises the "brilliant portrait" of Abel Brodersen, who, he says, possesses "all the features" of the early Hamsun heroes.[16] And Michael Sayers of *The New Republic* speaks of the almost "hallucinatory vividness" of Hamsun's text, finding in Abel "all the simplicity without the saintliness" of Dostoyevsky's Idiot.[17] Several recent critics discern essential qualities of Hamsun's early work, hailed as the beginning of fictional modernism, in Hamsun's last novel. In that vein, a comment by Henry Miller, that great Hamsun enthusiast, seems apropos: Abel is "the stuff of which much modern literature is made." [18]

Summary Evaluation

To evaluate Knut Hamsun's overall achievement as a novelist is a daunting, if not impossible, task. The difficulty is not his notorious Nazi sympathies, which led to his support of the Germans during the occupation of Norway in World War II; these were ugly blots on his escutcheon as a man and citizen, but did not directly affect his art. Rather, the problem lies in the absence of an all-encompassing *logos*, or *telos*, to his novelistic production. Indeed, the twenty-one novels included in his collected works do not constitute an organically developed whole, an oeuvre whose diversity is balanced by commonalities of intent, manner, or mode. Nor was artistic mastery, once it had been achieved, followed by a consistently high level of literary accomplishment. As we know, Hamsun tried his hand at several genres or types of fiction, with various degrees of success; and, oddly, his first novel, *Hunger*, is by many considered to be his best book. This raises the counter-intuitive possibility that Hamsun's evolution as a novelist was, from the very beginning, haunted by the specter of decline.[1]

Even if we disregard Hamsun's forays as a playwright and poet, both lyrical and dramatic, there are plenty of turns and twists to his writing career. Who would have expected that, after *Hunger* and *Mysteries*, both innovative novels, he would spend his time writing such arch-conventional works as *Editor Lynge* and *Shallow Soil*, which are unworthy of his demonstrated talent, especially *Shallow Soil*? These literary choices seem erratic, if not perverse, a piece of self-indulgence to settle a score or act as a self-appointed scourge. A mere three years after the publication of *Hunger*, these books mark the beginning of an unfortunate tendency on Hamsun's part, namely, to allow patent subjectivity, whether in a satirical or didactic vein, to determine the thrust of his fiction.

The two-track pattern which characterizes what could be called Hamsun's middle period, from about 1900 to 1912, marks another bifurcation in his creative ethos, one track focusing on stories of folk life (*folkelivsskildring*), the other on the quandaries of the wanderer hero, now middle-aged and enacting the role of a septuagenarian. In terms of genre, *Dreamers*, *Benoni*, and *Rosa* hark back to the early novels of Jonas Lie, one of Hamsun's despised elders, with the addition of a strain of self-parody: the love plots now have a happy ending, as though Hamsun, whose sensibility, in such previous novels as *Pan* and *Victoria*, is distinctly tragic, has suddenly been converted to seeing life and love from the vantage point of comedy.[2] The change in literary mode is accompanied by increased objectivity of representation; that is true even for *Rosa*, despite the use of first-person narration. By contrast, the second track is marked by a more and more extreme subjectivity, shown in its least attractive form in the prejudiced portrayals and implausible denouements of *A Wanderer* and *The Last Joy*. Both tracks gave rise to idiosyncratic rather than great fiction: a species of arctic success story in the case of *Dreamers* and the Benoni diptych, a trilogy of vicarious, resignedly middle-aged love in the wanderer novels.

One would be hard pressed to discover significant formal similarities between these six novels and Hamsun's four important works of the 1890s. At most, one discerns a temperamental likeness, a perceptible flair for the bizarre and macabre along with a whiff of decadence. The same can be said about the nine novels Hamsun was yet to write. These basically realistic works present broad pictures of life, mostly in the North, but their realism is laced with social and moral satire rooted in an agrarian, quasi-feudal value system. If there is a link to his past production, it is certainly not a formal one. While one notes the continuing blend of subjectivity and representation of reality, these elements assume such different aspects in successive periods that they do not properly define Hamsun's creative imagination in general. But again one cannot miss the peculiar, often bizarre, character of his work, whether he engages in utopian fantasy, as in *Growth*, or reminiscence in the guise of historical reconstruction, as in the August trilogy. The question arises whether this peculiarity is sufficient to hold his total novelistic production together.

In my opinion, it is not. The best we can do is to conceive of that production as consisting of several clusters, or sets, of works, each of which is formally and materially different from the other sets or clusters. What holds them all together, apart from the eccentric element referred to above, is chiefly the fact that they have sprung from the same author, Knut Hamsun. One feels tempted to suggest, contrary to the organicist maxim, that in Hamsun's case the whole is smaller than the sum of the parts.

Though Hamsun's countrymen will no doubt continue to read and admire the entire gamut of his creations, from *Hunger* to *The Ring Is Closed*, to international readers and critics Hamsun's artistic achievement will most likely be defined, more and more, by his startlingly innovative output of the 1890s—*Hunger*, *Mysteries*, *Pan*, and *Victoria*—while much of his later fiction will increasingly assume an exotic character. Alex Bolckmans says that only these novels represent "an achievement of the first order."[3] In terms of form, *Hunger* is the most original of the group, but all four are remarkable in one aspect or another and expressive of a modernist or proto-modernist sensibility. And whatever Hamsun may owe to Dostoyevsky, Strindberg, Nietzsche and others, it has been seamlessly assimilated to his own creative élan.

Hamsun himself openly admitted his susceptibility to influence. In a 1929 letter in response to an article by his German biographer, Walter Berendsohn, he writes, "There is perhaps no one who is more influenced than I, I'm no man of stone. I'm impressionable, highstrung, hysterical, if you like; I may have learned from all the authors I've read, what do I know!" Then he goes on, "But in my younger days, nobody made as great an impression on me as Dostoyevsky, Nietzsche, and Strindberg."[4] Seven years earlier, Thomas Mann had stressed Hamsun's link with the first two members of this trio in a spirit of the highest praise: "I came early on to feel that neither Nietzsche nor Dostoyevsky had left a disciple of this rank in his own country."[5] On the other hand, both Hamsun and his critics recognized that these writers were kindred spirits, so that whatever effect the elders exerted upon the "disciple" was essentially to stimulate his own creative power. Thus, in the same letter about Berendsohn's article, Hamsun writes in regard to his literary relationship to Dostoyevsky: "For me Dostoyevsky was in the air even before I knew his name; I suppose I had a little of his temperament if not of his ability."[6] Affinities are also seen with other writers, from whom he supposedly learned something. Thus, Krøger Johansen, an American friend who attended his literary lectures in Minneapolis during Hamsun's second American sojourn, says that "[m]ost independent, most distinctive" was his discussion of J. P. Jacobsen and August Strindberg. "There was something of them both in his own temperament; he was moved by the color-saturated aspect of one, by the rebellious and paradoxical aspect of the other."[7]

This judgment suggests, curiously enough, that Hamsun was most original when he was stimulated by the work of others; moreover, it matters little whether the stimulus was acknowledged or not. For example, while his lectures on America contain faint praise of both Whitman and Emerson, the former's poetry being referred to as "a wild carnival of words" and the latter being dismissed as a moralist with an underdeveloped psychological sense,[8] he absorbed important impulses from both, as several critics have noted. Martin Nag contends that "Whitman's style, the flowing, repetitive, seemingly uncontrolled catalog style, is the model of his own style. He reduced the loose Whitman style to a system, disciplined it and turned it into his own original invention."[9] In a more sober vein, Hamsun's friend Christian Gierløff, says that, to the mature Hamsun, Whitman was an "attractive" figure, "in some ways even a near kinsman."[10] As for Emerson, Harald Næss finds it strange that Hamsun failed to recognize his own thoughts in the New Englander's work: the attraction of the Orient, his mystical experience of nature, contempt for the masses and admiration of great men.[11] Of even greater importance to Hamsun, perhaps, was Emerson's concept of language, in which "[e]very word which is used to express a moral or intellectual fact, if traced back to its root, is found to be borrowed from some material appearance."[12] In view of his frequent use of concrete, image-forming words to convey states of mind in his fiction, Hamsun—who excepted Emerson's handling of language from his censure[13]—must have found the latter's endeavor to return to abstract words, such as those denoting mental phenomena, their original metaphoric aura or symbolic power a very attractive project.

Hamsun was, indeed, impressionable, and his books were much the better for it. Being self-educated, he found the seeds of his art wherever he could, in Sweden and Germany, Russia and America, but what came to fruition was decidedly his own; and, at its best, what he brought forth belongs to Europe and to the world rather than to a single country. According to Thomas Mann, that broad reach was in no small degree due to the author's having nurtured his imagination on a diversity of literary cultures. Hamsun's art, Mann writes, would not have become a "Europan possession" if it had not drawn its "nourishment" from both East and West.[14]

Yet, the roots of that art were profoundly personal, along with the values it embodies. One Norwegian critic has suggested that the nature of Hamsun's "sense of life and poetic creativity had its deepest sources in the passion and impressionability of puberty."[15] However that may be, much of his literary work is an unequivocal celebration of desire, inspired by the primitivist dream of a lost paradise that can still be recovered. Fundamentally Rousseauean, the idea is based on a pantheistic concept of nature. Such a concept is affirmed by Hamsun in the draft of a letter of 1916: "*God in everything* — to avoid becoming a pantheist is an impossibility. God is in everything. Or there is God in everything."[16] Though Hamsun abstains from preaching pantheism, implicit trust in a god-informed nature and in unadulterated natural desire is evident throughout his oeuvre. The perfect incarnation of Hamsun's dream of a pristine sexuality, one without both the moral-psychological constraints and the corruption of civilized sexual behavior, is the coupling of Isak and Inger in *Growth of the Soil*, epitomized in the following sentence: "At night he got hungry for her and took her" (VII: 149).

Hamsun's cult of unlicensed eros, in some novels carried to the point of sexual unanimism, is conditioned by an acute awareness of death. As in Gide's *The Immoralist*, the exuberance and *joie de vivre* in a Hamsun novel are experienced against the ever-present thought of death and dying. This association of death and eros almost certainly stems from the death sentence pronounced on Hamsun by his American doctor in 1884, causing the young man, not yet twenty-five, to return to Norway, apparently resigned to die. The letter to Erik Skram at Christmas 1888 cited in Chapter One clearly demonstrates the association, which left a permanent mark on Hamsun's attitude toward sexuality. For one, it imbued desire with the cosmic dimension of an *élan vital*, a life force, and secondly, it conferred upon sexual experience an intense, but vulnerable, seize-the-day quality. These properties tend to become valorized, figuring as norms whereby the worth of individual characters and relationships is gauged. For example, in Hamsun's last novel, *The Ring Is Closed*, it is the simple, animal-like sexual bliss of Abel and Angèle, whose existence could scarcely be more precarious, which constitutes the standard of matrimonial happiness. Like D. H. Lawrence, who in *Lady Chatterley's Lover* (1928) portrayed an upperclass woman in a state of cultivated, civilized sterility finding sexual fulfillment in a union with a primitive gamekeeper, Hamsun could be called a life worshiper; indeed, before Lawrence, he had in several novels dramatized similar situations, though sheer fecundity becomes increasingly important, acquiring a preponderant value to the detriment of sensual joy.

To us, Hamsun's ideal may appear unattractively atavistic. Apart from its implicit naturalizing of man, it demeans woman, turning her at best into a sexual mate and, eventually, into a mere producer of offspring. To Hamsun, this is the natural order of things. If, however, lust or desire lose their simplicity and take the form of passion-love, Hamsun projects bitter disillusion or tragedy, seen at its most shattering in *Mysteries*, *Pan*, and *Victoria*. Contrary to simple desire, which turns tragic only by accident or untoward fate, passion-love is tragic in itself; furthermore, it assumes the semblance of a modern malady. This is fully in accord with Hamsun's view of civilization: intellectual culture and emotional refinement threaten the natural relationship between men and women. One of the best examples of the destructive consequences of passion-love is the permanent stand-off of husband and wife in *Children of the Age*: the quasi-medieval self-image of Lieutenant Holmsen, with his courtly manner and stoic sense of life, destroys all natural feeling in the way man and wife relate to one another. If, as Tore Hamsun says, the Lieutenant is "a man after Hamsun's heart,"[17] the author has in this book betrayed his celebration of desire.

Whereas passion-love is treated as a bitter fruit of civilization in general, so-called corrupt or perverted manifestations of eros are linked in Hamsun's works with specifically urban, commercial and industrial civilization. As my discussion of the individual novels has shown, Hamsun uses prostitution, impotence, and venereal disease as symbols of the moral corruption and spiritual malaise of the modern age. Usually he incorporates these conditions in a character, who then comes to symbolize the moral makeup of the society of which he or she is a part. Thus, the calculating one-night stands of Florina in *Segelfoss Town* are a metonymical revelation of the moral condition of an increasingly acquisitive society, and Oliver Andersen, the eunuch in *Women at the Pump*, is Hamsun's repellent symbol of the sterility of Europe in the wake of World War I. But of all the characters invested with a symbolic dimension, the most reprobate, and at the same time the most intriguing, is August, whose quandaries, whether sexual sickness or senility, reflect back on the spirit of modernity he supposedly represents. Effeminacy and hints of homosexuality serve similar functions in Hamsun's fiction, within the narrower confines of a group or a profession, such as actors.

The reliance on sexuality in one form or another for creating all these effects—paeans to joy, tragedy, and social satire—indicates a view of life that, despite Hamsun's confessed pantheism, is steeped in philosophical naturalism. Without an otherworldly dimension, that view could be summed up by a saying of Nietzsche's Zarathustra: *"be faithful to the earth (bleibt der Erde treu)*.[18] However, faithfulness to the earth, while rich in possibilities, leaves a bleak landscape once life has passed the zenith. In the words of Nordahl Grieg, "There exist no reserves, Hamsun has no ethical values to fall back on; when the *sparkle* is gone, things go downhill. . . . It is the brief, wonderful, irretrievable now of earthly life which Hamsun has increased."[19] Life as such, however, is seen by him as being ultimately meaningless, a perception that accounts both for the unmistakable pessimism and the distinct sense of the absurd found in so many of Hamsun's novels.

In depicting life as he saw it, Hamsun pulls no punches. His two darkest novels, *The Women at the Pump* and *The Last Chapter*—sardonic exposés of the vulnerabilities, horrors, and cruel ironies of human existence—bear witness to a terrifying, disillusioned honesty. The impact of these novels would most likely have been less strong if Hamsun had found a place for higher values, whether moral, intellectual or cultural, in his *Weltanschauung*. Nevertheless, one cannot help deploring, as Nordahl Grieg does, the dearth of these elements in Hamsun's fiction, as well as the fact that, starting with *The Last Joy*, characters with a modicum of intellectual ambition or aspirations are exposed to ridicule. Meanwhile, the novels' idea content deteriorates into primitivist cliché, shown at an egregious extreme in the above-mentioned final work in the wanderer trilogy. True ideas, such as permeate a novel's substance and determine its shape and form, are increasingly scarce, a phenomenon that has been noted as a weakness of the later fiction.[20] In regard to form, Walter Berendsohn discerns little "intellectual architecture" in Hamsun's books, and Peter de Mendelssohn, perhaps Hamsun most merciless critic, asserts that Hamsun contributed nothing to the novel as an "artistic form."[21]

While deficient in intellectual values and formal stringency, Hamsun's fiction abounds in memorable portrayals; indeed, if one were asked to single out one of Hamsun's talents for special praise, it would have to be his knack of creating a gallery of remarkable, often eccentric, but true-to-life characters. The author himself was duly proud of his accomplishment in this regard, as shown by his response to Professor Gabriel Langfeldt when asked, during his psychiatric examination after World War II, to delineate his own character traits: "I haven't analyzed myself other than by having created in my books several hundred different characters—every one of them spun from myself." Affirming in his eighty-seventh year his youthful championship of a "nuanced psychology," in contrast to the naturalists' alleged adherence to a "dominant trait," Hamsun claims that one cannot find a single instance of the latter in his production. His creations, he says, "are all without so-called 'character,' they are divided and fragmented, neither good nor bad, but both, nuanced and changing in their disposition and in their actions."[22]

Old Hamsun's claim was obviously overstated, yet his achievement as a portrayer of character remains unchallenged. One is particularly struck by the economy of means used in evoking a sense of a complex living person—Ylajali's response to a bit of dead hair on a man's shoulder; Glahn reacting to Edvarda's impulsive embrace by changing the subject, and her puzzlement at his sudden aloofness; Victoria's admiring attention to Johannes' wrist after objecting to his gaze; Elise Mack confessing her love of Rolandsen by the touch of a hand. These are trivial examples, but they serve to illustrate Hamsun's incremental method: basically impressionist, that method relies predominantly upon indirect means of portrayal; formal portraits are virtually non-existent in his novels, the most successful of which adhere to what could be called a behaviorist aesthetic. Where he employs this basically objective method, which was part of the common literary repertoire of the time, Hamsun succeeds in creating interesting and believable characters.

As my discussion of the individual novels has shown, however, Hamsun did not always practice what he preached, particularly from about 1910 onward. In fact, most of his bourgeois figures—and there is a lot of them—are distinctly social or professional types, and since they are mostly satirized, they are reduced precisely to a "dominant trait": Dr. Muus in *Children of the Age* to the vanity of the well-born professional; Hugo Lassen, the priapic engineer in *A Wanderer*, to mechanical lust; Dr. Oliver in *The Last Chapter* to pedantry. Where the stake is high and the character appears as a mouthpiece for the author's pet ideas, the stereotyping is even more blatant: Ezra in the August trilogy is the epitome of the earthbound farmer; Edevart is the eternal adolescent, traumatized by the modern age; and Lovise Magrete turns into an anti-emigration, anti-American icon. It looks as though Hamsun's ideas—in the main, stubbornly held preconceptions—served him ill as an artist: inveterately conservative, even reactionary, they blurred his vision, disturbed his artistic tact, and forced many of his important figures to carry an ideological load they would have been better without.

Hamsun is at his best when he writes about the common people, except for eccentrics or for "imperial souls" like Ferdinand Mack. He obviously loves the poor and the uneducated, especially if they show no signs of trying to improve their lot. From this perspective, Abel Brodersen in *The Ring Is Closed* is a young man after Hamsun's heart. While this seems wildly ironic, in view of Hamsun's real-life status as a gentleman of the gentry, it accords with his background and early experience, since as a young man he had periodically been forced to support himself as a common laborer. If it were not for the contempt of labor as a political force, seen at its most extreme in the depiction of some of Holmengrå's workers, Hamsun could easily pass for a proletarian writer. He certainly shows an uncanny aptitude for evoking the mentality and ways of life of the lower classes, and he is exceptionally good at portraying marginal types. One thinks of Eilert, the small-time thief in *The Last Joy*; Oliver Andersen in *Women at the Pump*; and August of the trilogy, with a set of gold teeth in his mouth but without an honest bone in his body. In these instances, Hamsun's intuitive sensibility has enabled him to shape convincing, visually realized specimens of common humanity, however queer or grotesque, whatever satirical or ideological purpose may lurk in the background.

The oral flavor of Hamsun's style, frequently mentioned in the previous discussion, is consistent with this common touch. However, as I have indicated, Hamsun's language also manifests a straining for maximal expressivity, a tendency which militates against a simple, oral style. I can think of no better description of this aspect of Hamsun's language than that given by Francis Bull. According to Professor Bull, Hamsun did not choose "the plain and simple words, . . . the austere beauty of naked form." Hamsun, he claims, "liked an unnatural, ornamental language and a rich and decorative style"; he "liked to turn a phrase, spruced things up with sound and color, and let his sentences wind along smoothly and supply, with lighthearted whims and playful charm."[23] In the interest of expressiveness or originality, Hamsun would even violate the rules of grammar. When Arild, his younger son, expressed an interest in becoming a writer, Hamsun's advice was, "To hell with grammar, I write grammar to smithereens."[24] To some extent, Hamsun did exactly that, as exemplified by what has been called his "free noun clauses,"[25] in which he employs an incongruous blend of direct and indirect speech. The following sentence from *Rosa*, as rendered literally, gives an idea of the infraction involved: "Hartvigsen was very anxious about the Baroness and wished in a loud voice *that if only* the tub were safely indoors!" (V: 275; my italics).[26] Though the syntactical irregularity derives from oral usages, ordinarily associated with folksy simplicity, Hamsun's recourse to it manifests a desire to stand out and be different, to fashion a way of writing uniquely his own. To achieve that end, Hamsun drew upon a variety of means. One was hard work, a conscious striving for the *mot juste*; another was a kind of serendipity, which enabled him to enrich his prose with what he referred to in a review article as "linguistic finds or stylistic flukes."[27]

A noted Danish scholar-critic, Sven Møller Kristensen, finds that Hamsun has been "overrated," being "too much of a wordsmith [*ordkunstner*] and too little of a thinker."[28] Others, perceiving a decline in creative power in the middle and late Hamsun, have expressed nostalgia about what might have been had he chosen a different path.

Summary Evaluation

Thus, a 1967 reviewer writes that, if Hamsun had gone on in the vein of *Hunger*, "he would have become one of the great progenitors of the modern novel."[29] Hamsun's own self-evaluations were quite sober, as shown by his stated opinion of *The Road Leads On*—"[s]ome good things and some rubbish as in all books."[30] That sounds a bit too easy; a more precise and balanced judgment of the quality of his work should be possible. Though it is up to his readers to decide for themselves what is good and what, if anything, is rubbish, I hope my discussion will help spur fresh appraisals of Hamsun's achievement as a novelist.

Notes

Foreword

1. See James Wood, "Knut Hamsun's Christian Perversions," in *The Broken Estate: Essays on Literature and Belief* (New York: Random House, 1999), p. 77.
2. For comparisons with Dickens, see Tom Kristensen, "Knut Hamsuns nye roman [*August*]," *Tilskueren* 47.1 (1930): 251; Ronald Fangen, "Hamsuns to siste romaner," in *Dagen og veien* (Oslo, 1934), p. 231; and Robert Ferguson, *Enigma: The Life of Knut Hamsun* (New York: Farrar, Straus & Giroux, 1987), p. 227. Ferguson writes that, starting with *Children of the Age*, all Hamsun's novels are "conventional in form, one might almost say Dickensian." As for Lawrence and Hamsun, James W. McFarlane's pioneering article "The Whisper of the Blood: A Study of Knut Hamsun's Early Novels," *PMLA* 71 (1956): 563–94, notes a considerable number of parallel ideas in the work of the two authors. A German critic, Heinrich Fischer, also mentions Hamsun's resemblance to Lawrence ("The Case of Knut Hamsun," trans. David Maurice Graham," *The New Writing and Daylight* 6 (1945): 90. One scholar, Akos Doma, discovered sufficient affinities to justify a full-scale comparative study: *Die andere Moderne: Knut Hamsun, D. H. Lawrence und die lebensphilosophische Strömung des literarischen Modernismus* (Bonn: Bouvier Verlag, 1995).
3. Knut Hamsun, "På gjengrodde stier," *Samlede verker* (Oslo: Gyldendal, 1992), XV: 241. Subsequent references to this publication, Hamsun's Collected Works (*SV*), will appear in the text, with omission of the volume number where it is evident from the context. See also Knut Hamsun, *On Overgrown Paths*, trans. Sverre Lyngstad (København & Los Angeles: Green Integer, 1999), p. 10.
4. Leo Löwenthal, "Knut Hamsun. Zur Vorgeschichte der autoritären Ideologie," *Zeitschrift für Sozialforschung* 6 (1937), Heft 2: 295–345; Leo Lowenthal, "Knut Hamsun," in *Literature and the Image of Man* (Boston: Beacon Press, 1957), pp. 190–220.
5. Aasmund Brynildsen, *Svermeren og hans demon: Fire essays om Knut Hamsun 1952–1972* (Oslo: Dreyer, 1973).
6. See, for example, Inge Eidsvåg, "Mellom fascinasjon og fordømmelse. Mitt møte med Knut Hamsuns liv og diktning," *Bokvennen* 11.4 (1999): 40.
7. *Enigma: The Life of Knut Hamsun*.
8. Hanna Astrup Larsen, *Knut Hamsun* (New York: Knopf, 1922); Harald Næss, *Knut Hamsun* (Boston: Twayne Publishers, 1984); Martin Humpál, *The Roots of*

Modernist Narrative: Knut Hamsun's Novels "Hunger," "Mysteries," and "Pan" (Oslo: Solum, 1998).

Chapter One

1. "Knut Hamsuns *Sult,*" in *Søkelys på Knut Hamsuns 90-årsdiktning*, ed. Øystein Rottem (Oslo: Universitetsforlaget, 1979), p. 39.
2. "Knut Hamsun," in *Skildringer og stemninger fra den yngre litteratur* (Kristiania, 1897), p. 15.
3. The traditional place of birth has been reported as Garmotrædet, Lom, in the neighboring township, but Lars Frode Larsen has documented that, though the boy was baptized in Garmo, Lom, where the family had lived, he had been born in Vågå (*Den unge Hamsun* [Oslo: Schibsted, 1998], p. 29).
4. Hamsun describes this part of his childhood experience in the travel book *I æventyrland* (1903; *In Wonderland*, trans. with Introduction and Notes by Sverre Lyngstad [Brooklyn, N. Y.: Ig Publishing, 2004]), *SV*, III: 233-34.
5. Lars Frode Larsen, *Den unge Hamsun*, p. 84.
6. Letter to Svend Tveraas of Feb. 29, 1884, in *Knut Hamsuns brev*, ed. Harald S. Næss, 7 vols. (Oslo: Gyldendal, 1994-2001), I: 42; *Knut Hamsun: Selected Letters*, ed. Harald Næss & James McFarlane, 2 vols. (Norwich, England: Norvik Press, 1990, 1998), I: 42. Hereafter referred to as *Brev* and *Letters*, respectively. The translations of letters not in the English edition are my own.
7. Harald Næss, *Knut Hamsun*, pp. 12-13.
8. Letter to Nikolai Frøsland of Jan. 19, 1886, *Brev*, I: 63.
9. Hamsun had used the spelling without a "d" in correspondence before the Mark Twain article appeared. See letter to Nikolai Frøsland of January 8, 1885, *Brev*, I: 57 and note 6; *Letters*, I: 52, 254.
10. Letter to Erik Frydenlund of Sept. 4, 1886, *Brev*, I: 69; *Letters*, I: 58.
11. Letter to Bolette and Ole Larsen of November 1894, *Brev*, I: 431; *Letters*, I: 214.
12. As quoted by Tore Hamsun in *Knut Hamsun – min far*, 4th ed. (Oslo:Gyldendal, 1992), pp. 102-03. — In a note on a Hamsun letter to Edvard Brandes (*Brev*, I: 81; *Letters*, I: 258), Harald Næss quotes what the author many years afterward told Harald Grieg: "I exaggerated my 'rescue' through Edvard Brandes. He lent me the first time 2 – two – kroner. Later he lent me by mail, without my asking, 20 – twenty – kroner. It was all repaid rather promptly."
13. Letter to Johan Sørensen of Dec. 2, 1888, *Brev*, I: 87; *Letters*, I: 71.
14. Letter to Johan Sørensen of Dec. 8, 1888, *Brev*, I: 91-92; *Letters*, I: 75-76.
15. See letter to Erik Frydenlund of Sept. 20, 1886, *Brev*, I: 73. In *Letters* (I: 61), *rådstue* is mistakenly rendered as "doss house" instead of "jail."
16. *Brev*, I: 98; *Letters*, I: 81.
17. *Brev*, I: 99; *Letters*, I: 82. For commentary, see Dolores Buttry, "A Thirst for Intimacy: Knut Hamsun's Pyromania," *Scandinavica* 26 (1987): 129-39.
18. Letter to Erik Skram of Dec. 26, 1888, in *Brev*, I: 99; *Letters*, I: 82.
19. Saul Maloff, "The Edible World," *Newsweek*, July 31, 1967, p. 76; George Steiner, *The Observer Review*, January 26, 1997, p. 17.
20. Letter to Gustaf af Geijerstam in May or June 1890, *Brev*, I: 160; *Letters*, I: 118.

21. Letter to Georg Brandes of May/June? 1890, *Brev*, I: 161; *Letters*, I: 114.
22. Letter to Geijerstam, loc. cit.—According to a recent American review, Hamsun accomplished precisely that. J. Peder Zane writes: "Introspective but not analytic, the action in *Hunger* pivots on the whirligig fluctuations of the narrator's mind: suicidal one moment, joyful the next, angry, heartbroken, proud, malicious, pretentious, polite, petty, perplexed, generous, hilarious, warped, inspired . . . seemingly all at once" (*The News & Observer* [Raleigh, N. C.], June 6, 1999, p. 4G).
23. Letter to Geijerstam, loc. cit.
24. *Six Plays of Strindberg*, trans. Elizabeth Sprigge (Garden City, N. Y., 1955), p. 64.—Hamsun could have found the same idea in Dostoyevsky's *Notes from Underground* (1864), whose narrator, having confessed to possessing a swarm of "contradictory elements" inside him, goes on to say that "an intelligent man in the nineteenth century must be . . . a characterless creature" (*Notes from Underground*, trans. & ed. Michael R. Katz [New York & London, 1989], p. 4). As for Hamsun's relationship to Strindberg, whom he greatly admired, one finds a token of his indebtedness to him in *Hunger*. A room of a café frequented by the hero, the Oplandske Café, is named after a restaurant, The Red Room, in Strindberg's *The Red Room* (1879), "the first truly modern Swedish novel" according to Eric O. Johannesson (*The Novels of August Strindberg: A Study in Theme and Structure* [Berkeley & Los Angeles: California UP, 1968], p. 45). While Hamsun's novel differs radically from that of Strindberg, a traditionally realistic work, the latter contains a great many motifs, themes, and situations that Hamsun responded to and used, however differently, in his own novel. Thus, Strindberg's Arvid Falk, a flâneur turned littérateur, lives in a garret, wanders aimlessly about the streets of Stockholm, and considers taking hire on a ship. He also experiences hunger.
25. Letter to Yngvar Laws of Aug.-Nov.? 1888, in *Brev*, I: 82; *Letters*, I: 88.—Rolf Nyboe Nettum believes that Hamsun derived the concept of "fractional" feelings from the French psychologist Théodule Ribot (1839-1916), who introduced it in an attempt to define the most delicate nuances of mental life ("Fra Hamsun til Falkberget," in *Norges litteraturhistorie*, ed. Edvard Beyer, IV [Oslo, 1975]: 35).
26. "Kristofer Janson," *Ny Jord* II (July-December, 1888): 385.
27. Letter of May-June? 1890, in *Brev*, I: 161; *Letters*, I: 114.—Martin Nag suggests that Hamsun was competing with Dostoyevsky on this point in *Hunger*. See "Forbrytelse og straff i norsk litteratur," in *Dostojevskijs roman om Raskolnikov*, ed. Geir Kjetsaa (Oslo, 1973), p. 160.
28. Marlow states: "The mind of man is capable of anything—because everything is in it, all the past as well as all the future" (*The Portable Conrad*, ed. Morton Dauwen Zabel [New York, 1952], p. 540). The following statement by Gide's Michel sounds like an echo of Conrad: "Everything is within Man" (*The Immoralist*, tr. Richard Howard [New York, 1970], p. 157).
29. There are several references to the "broadness" of human nature in Dostoyevsky's last novel. See *The Brothers Karamazov*, tr. Richard Pevear & Larissa Volokhonsky (New York: Vintage Books, 1991), pp. 108 & 733.
30. Gide wrote a highly appreciative preface to Georges Sautreau's translation of *Hunger*. See Knut Hamsun, *La Faim* (Paris, 1961), pp. v-vii.

31. See, for example, Exodus 8:19 and Psalms 8:3.
32. The Russian writer Aleksandr Kuprin (1870-1938) was deeply impressed by this scene, the handling of which generated, in his words, "some of the most awesome pages in all of world literature" ("O Knute Gamsune," in *Sobranie sochinenii v 6 tomakh*, VI [1958]: 594).
33. Kuprin also admired Hamsun's treatment of the novel's "love" scene, calling it "profound." He can be "drunk, a bit crazy perhaps, a thief or a murderer" — that wouldn't prevent her from giving herself to him; "but when she learns that he is *only* hungry, desire gives way to disgust, pity and horror" (ibid., pp. 594-95).
34. Martin Nag has suggested that the hero of *Hunger* is a "suffering Christ figure" ("*Sult*—en Messias-roman?" *Kirke og kultur* 70 [1965]: 299-304). Though the suffering is unquestionable, the allusions to Christ, along with other references to religion in the novel, have an ironic accent and produce the effect of parody. With that qualification the Christ-identification seems acceptable.
35. Letter to Edvard Brandes of Sept. 17, 1888, in *Brev*, I: 81; *Letters*, I: 70.
36. These quoted phrases, which did not appear in the first edition of *Hunger*, were added in the edition of 1907. Their effect alerts the reader to the hero's divided mind, creates a distance to the highly emotional experiences that are related, and strengthens the impression that the hero is able to view his predicament with a touch of irony.
37. See *Crime and Punishment*, tr. Michael Scammell (New York: Washington Square Press, 1963), p. 15.
38. This idea of "dying on one's feet" may be an echo of the next-to-last sentence of *Niels Lyhne* (1880), a naturalistic novel of disillusionment by the Danish writer Jens Peter Jacobsen (1847-85), one of young Hamsun's favorite authors.
39. A different approach to the absurd in *Hunger* is offered by Einar Eggen's article "Menneskene og tingene: Hamsuns *Sult* og den nye roman" (in *Søkelys på Knut Hamsuns 90-årsdiktning*, pp. 55-76). Taking his cue from Sartre's *Nausea* and the French new novel, Eggen sees *Hunger* as a study in alienation of broad relevance, far transcending the individual case. While the novel reveals "a gaping distance between the I and the world," the hero is in constant danger of being reduced to an object through what Eggen calls "the demonism of things" (p. 75).
40. For a discussion of Hamsun's treatment of time in *Hunger*, see Martin Humpál, "Hamsuns merkverdige klokkeslett," in *Norsk litterær årbok 1994* (Oslo), pp. 125-28.
41. See, for example, Paul Auster, "The Art of Hunger," in *The Art of Hunger* (Los Angeles: Sun & Moon Press, 1991), pp. 9-20.
42. Thomas Fechner-Smarsly, *Die wiederkehrenden Zeichen. Eine psychoanalytische Studie zu Knut Hamsuns "Hunger."* Texte und Untersuchungen zur Germanistik und Skandinavistik 25 (Frankfurt am Main: Peter Lang, 1991).
43. "Modern Fiction," in *The Common Reader* (New York, c1925), p. 154.
44. *Luft, vind, ingenting. Hamsuns desillusjonsromanar frå "Sult" til "Ringen sluttet"* (Oslo: Gyldendal, 1984).
45. See Eduard Hitschmann, "Ein Gespenst aus der Kindheit Knut Hamsuns," *Imago* (Vienna) 12 (1924): 336-60; rpt. in *Auf alten und neuen Pfaden: Eine*

Dokumentation zur Hamsun-Forschung, ed. Heiko Uecker (Frankfurt am Main: Peter Lang, 1983), I: 1–29; Gregory Stragnell, "A Psychopathological Study of Knut Hamsun's *Hunger,*" *The Psychoanalytic Review* 9 (1922): 198–217; and Trygve Braatøy, *Livets cirkel. Bidrag til analyse av Knut Hamsuns diktning* (Oslo: Cappelen, 1929).

46. Per Mæling, "Fysiognomier. Kommentar til kroppen som skriftens scene. Lesning av Knut Hamsuns *Sult,*" *Edda,* 1994, pp. 120–33. Mæling suggests that the rhythms of the novel's discourse are determined by the phases of bulimia.

47. See *The Cultural Life of Modern America,* trans. Barbara Gordon Morgridge (Cambridge, MA: Harvard UP, 1969).

48. One critic, Knut Brynhildsvoll, has developed a substantial argument to the effect that *Hunger* is a basically expressionist work, akin to Edvard Munch's paintings of the 1890s and Strindberg's late plays. Dealing with universal experiences—eros, anxiety, death—the novel, Brynhildsvoll suggests, can be read, contrary to Hamsun's own psychological bias, "in a parable-like, mythic-allegorical manner." He ends by saying that it is "quite reasonable to understand *Hunger* as perhaps the most decisive initial text of the just emerging literary expressionism" ("Knut Hamsuns *Hunger*—Ein frühes Dokument expressionistischen Schreibens?" in *Sult, sprell og Altmulig: Alte und neue Studien zu Knut Hamsuns antipsychologischer Romankunst.* Texte und Untersuchungen zur Germanistik und Skandinavistik 42 [Frankfurt am Main: Peter Lang, 1998]: 55–89).

49. As quoted by Martin Nag in *Verdens Gang (VG)* of August 19, 1996, p. 38, from the same paper of October 15, 1891.

50. In regard to rootlessness, statements in the first edition of *Mysteries* echo Hamsun's letters of the time. In a passage subsequently deleted, Nagel reflects nostalgically, "One ought to . . . get on, have a house, a wife, and a dog" (*Mysterier* [København, 1892], p. 56; *Mysteries,* trans. Sverre Lyngstad [New York: Penguin, 2001], p. 294, note 50). In a letter to Bolette and Ole Johan Larsen of March 7, 1892, Hamsun says, ". . . one shouldn't write for people, one should . . . settle down in a forest, acquire a house, a wife, and a dog" (*Brev,* I: 247). Nevertheless, Hamsun refused to be identified with Nagel, as shown in a letter to Erik Skram of November 5, 1892, where he says he cannot be responsible for "all of Nagel's opinions" (*Brev,* I: 284; *Letters,* I: 163–64).

51. Aslaug Groven Michaelsen refers to Hamsun's "astounding naiveté" in assuming that he had "discovered" the unconscious life of the mind. What was new, she notes, was Hamsun's "passionate, almost religious, delight at the discovery" (*Kjetterier om diktning og sannsynlighet* [Oslo, 1969], pp. 42–43).

52. "Psykologisk literatur," in *Paa Turné: Tre foredrag om litteratur,* ed. Tore Hamsun (Oslo: Gyldendal, 1960), p. 51.

53. Ibid., p. 66.

54. Ibid., pp. 70–71.

55. "Fra det ubevidste Sjæleliv," in Knut Hamsun, *Artikler,* ed. Francis Bull (Oslo: Gyldendal, 1939), p. 60.—In his article "'Et dyb af mimoser, hvori vinden puster': Om hvordan Knut Hamsun oppdaget Nathalie Sarrautes tropismer en natt i Lillesand," *Vinduet* 46.3–4 (1992): 97–101, Pål Norheim claims to find striking similarities betweeen what Hamsun means by the mimosa metaphor

in describing his aesthetic program and the meaning of tropisms in Nathalie Sarraute's literary work.

56. "Fra det ubevidste Sjæleliv," p. 61.
57. See "The Unconscious in the Aesthetic Judgment and in Artistic Production," in Eduard von Hartmann, *Philosophy of the Unconscious*, trans. W. C. Coupland, with a Preface by C. K. Ogden (London & New York, 1931), I: 276ff.
58. For a sampling, see Knut Hamsun, *Mysteries* (2001), pp. 291–313.
59. The opening sentence has a striking resemblance to the beginnings of two Dostoyevsky novels which Hamsun knew, *The Demons* and *The Insulted and the Injured*, both of which refer to some "very strange events" or "adventure" about to be related.
60. According to a German critic, Heinrich Fischer, the scene shows that Hamsun knew the "abysses of petit bourgeois bestiality" and prefigured the SS mentality long before Hitler ("Die Welt Knut Hamsuns," *Neue Schweizer Rundschau*, N. F. 18.2 [June, 1950]: 93; rpt. in *Auf alten und neuen Pfaden*, I: 109–21).
61. Both the substance and the manner of Nagel's polemics against contemporary culture and its avatars show a kinship with the vehement outpourings of the splenetic hero of Dostoyevsky's *Notes from Underground*. In particular, the two characters share an intense dislike for rationalism, especially as represented by science. In Dostoyevsky's story, the derided "conclusions of natural science and mathematics" are denoted by the motif "two times two makes four"; further, the underground man finds that consciousness is "infinitely higher than two times two" and that "two times two makes five is sometimes also a very charming little thing" (op. cit., pp. 9–10, 24). While Hamsun switches the formula to addition, using "two and two is four" as shorthand for a philistine criterion of "truth," the underlying intent is the same. Nagel's chosen example of epistemological pharisaism is the much-revered William Gladstone, to whose "pedestrian rightness" Nagel opposes his "blood's subjective logic." Doing a variant on Dostoyevsky's motif of "two times two makes five" he declares: "Seventeen times twenty-three is three hundred ninety-*seven*," instead of three hundred ninety-one, the correct answer (I: 173, 199). Indeed, the expression of Nagel's irrationalism owes a great deal to the underground man.
62. In a letter Hamsun comments on how he wrote most of this chapter, number nineteen, at one sitting, between five in the afternoon and three in the morning, in the "most blissful burst of inspiration" he had yet experienced in Copenhagen (letter to Caroline Neeraas of June 12, 1891, *Brev*, I: 260). Interestingly, the date of the month, June 12, matches that of Nagel's arrival in the small town.
63. This image is anticipated at the beginning of chapter eight, where the town appears "like a weird, splayed giant insect, a fabulous creature that had thrown itself flat on its belly, extending arms and horns and feelers in all directions" (I: 210). Hamsun's description of this monstrous creature brings to mind Ippolit's "Explanation" in *The Idiot*, in which, during a spell of possible delirium, nature appears to him in the guise of an "immense, merciless, dumb beast," or "a huge and loathsome spider" (*The Idiot*, trans. Constance Garnett [New York: The Modern Library, 1935], p. 389). In both instances, the context is one of suicide, potential or actual.

64. A biographical sidelight on Nagel's ring is offered by Arthur Holitscher, who reports that, when he met Hamsun, the latter was wearing an "iron ring" on his right hand (*Lebensgeschichte eines Rebellen* [Berlin, 1924], p. 142).
65. Hamsun was familiar with suicide as a means of denouement from the death of Stavrogin in Dostoyevsky's *The Demons*. He may also have known Strindberg's novel *I havsbandet* (1890; *By the Open Sea*, 1913), though in a letter written shortly after *Mysteries* was published he claims never to have read it (letter to Karl Birger Mörner of October? 8, 1892, *Brev*, I: 283). Axel Borg, Strindberg's "superman" hero, exhibits many resemblances to Hamsun's Nagel, and his suicide is linked to the sea. Nor was Hamsun unfamiliar with suicide in his own life and experience. In 1890 Charles Douzette, one of his anarchist friends in Minneapolis, took his own life (see letter to Marie Herzfeld of June 25, 1892, *Brev*, I: 267, note 5; *Letters*, I: 273), and Hamsun had himself contemplated suicide as a way out after being diagnosed with "galloping consumption" in 1884 (see Næss, pp. 12–13).
66. Gregory Nybø, *Knut Hamsuns 'Mysterier'* (Oslo: Gyldendal, 1969).
67. "Den moderne norske literatur" (1896), in *Norsk skrivekunst*, ed. Erling Nielsen (Oslo, 1958), p. 17; "Knut Hamsun," in Carl Nærup, *Skildringer og stemninger fra den yngre litteratur* (Kristiania, 1897), p. 28; and Carl Nærup, *Illustreret norsk litteraturhistorie. Siste tidsrum, 1890–1904* (Kristiania, 1905), p. 100.
68. Kristofer Randers in *Aftenposten*, September 25, 1892, as quoted in *Norsk litteratur i tusen år. Teksthistoriske linjer*, ed. Bjarne Fidjestøl et al. (Oslo, 1994), p. 365.
69. See "Sidste kapitel og det første: Hamsuns og Kincks sidste bøker," in *Norsk national kunst* (København, 1924), p. 147; *Hamsun som modernist* (København, 1975), p. 197; and Arne Falck, "Storm mot *Mysterier*," in *Ni artikler om Knut Hamsun*, ed. Arild Hamsun (Arendal, 1976), as quoted from Faldbakken's article in *Dagbladet*, August 6, 1973.
70. *Enigma*, p. 132.
71. See Henry Miller, *The Books in My Life* (London, 1952), p. 40, and Updike's review of Gerry Bothmer's translation of *Mysteries* in *The New York Times Boook Review* (*NYTBR*), August 22, 1971, pp. 1, 30.
72. Reinhard H. Friederich, "Kafka and Hamsun's *Mysteries*," *Comparative Literature* 28.1 (Winter 1976): 34.
73. Nico Rost, "Aantekeningen bij het lezen van Knut Hamsun," *De nieuwe Gids* 37 (1922): 40.
74. See "Heart of Darkness," in *The Portable Conrad*, p. 561.
75. Janko Lavrin, "The Return of Pan (On Knut Hamsun)," in *Aspects of Modernism* (Freeport, New York, 1968), p. 95.
76. Matthew 6:4.
77. Myshkin even hopes that his jealous rival, the fiery Rogozhin, will eventually become Nastasya Filippovna's "providence." See *Polnoe sobranie sochinenii v tridtsati tomakh* VIII (Leningrad,1973): 192; *The Idiot*, p. 218.
78. *Polnoe sobranie sochinenii v tridtsati tomakh* XIV (Leningrad, 1976): 214–15, 223, 239; *The Brothers Karamazov*, trans. Richard Pevear and Larissa Volokhonsky (New York: Vintage Books, 1991), pp. 235–36, 245, 263.

79. A reviewer of the first English translation of *Mysteries* already noted the paradoxical blend of qualities in Nagel, part Myshkin, part Stavrogin (*Times Literary Supplement* [*TLS*] 26 [August 18, 1927]: 560).
80. Hamsun's use of clairvoyance in *Mysteries* recalls *The Visionary* (1870) by Jonas Lie, who also grew up in Northern Norway, known for its uncanny tales of the supernatural. Walter McFarlane believes it evidences Hamsun's reliance, to some extent, on the ideas of Eduard von Hartmann, who was aware of both the advantages and the dangers of possessing "mystical" gifts ("Knut Hamsun," in *Ibsen and the Temper of Norwegian Literature* [London: Oxford UP, 1960], p. 135).
81. Gregory Nybø's study of *Mysteries* analyzes the work in terms of psychological detective fiction. His assertion that such a critical approach helps to bring out the organizing structures of the story (*Knut Hamsuns 'Mysterier,'* p. 16) is no doubt valid. However, the strategies of detective fiction do not by themselves unify the work. Nagel's self-appointed exercise as a detective, in an apparent attempt to clear up the puzzling circumstances surrounding Karlsen's death, shows up only sporadically and is abandoned well before the end of the novel.
82. The close kinship between the two heroes is suggested by several shared motifs: Nagel's description of himself as a "stranger on earth" seems to echo Werther's self-definition as a "wanderer, a pilgrim on earth"; Werther, like Nagel, fantasizes about meeting his beloved in the beyond; he is also associated with the color yellow, wearing a yellow vest (*The Sufferings of Young Werther*, trans. Harry Steinhauer [New York, 1970], pp. 57, 90, 96).— For further discussion, see Frank Thiess, "Das Werther-Thema in Hamsuns Mysterien," in *Heimat und Weltgeist: Jahrbuch der Knut Hamsun-Gesellschaft*, ed. Hilde Fürstenberg (Mölln, Lauenburg, 1960), pp. 133–52. The classic study of the history of passion love is Denis de Rougemont's book *L'Amour et l'Occident* (1939; *Love in the Western World*, 1957).
83. Hamsun had close contacts with the circle associated with the Copenhagen journal *Ny Jord*, which published the fragment of *Hunger* in 1888. Its first three volumes, 1888–1889, featured selections from Schopenhauer's most popular book, *Parerga and Paralipomena*, as well as critical discussion of his philosophy, and from Nietzsche's *Thus Spake Zarathustra*. Georg Brandes' study of Nietzsche appeared in another Danish journal during the same period: "Aristokratisk Radikalisme: En Afhandling om Friedrich Nietzsche," *Tilskueren* 6 (1889): 565–613; *Friedrich Nietzsche: An Essay on Aristocratic Radicalism*, trans. A. G. Chater (New York, n. d.). In general, Hamsun's knowledge of Nietzsche, many of whose ideas appear in Nagel's debates and monologues, may have been mediated mainly by Strindberg. According to Harald Næss, Hamsun probably acquired what Georg Brandes called his "touching blind faith in Eduard von Hartmann's profundity" from Strindberg (*Brev*, I: 135 & 136, note 1). In an 1889 article on Strindberg, Hamsun describes Hartmann as a "subtle, aristocratic author whose . . . refined thoughts delight in . . . losing themselves in a drunken orgy of suffering" (Hamsun, *Artikler*, p. 41).
84. "On the Sufferings of the World," in *Parerga and Paralipomena*, trans. T. Bailey Saunders, in K. Francke & W. G. Howard, eds., *The German Classics* XV (New York, 1914): 84.
85. *Philosophy of the Unconscious*, I: 229–30.

86. E. C. Barksdale & Daniel Popp, "Hamsun and Pasternak: The Development of Dionysian Tragedy," *Edda* 76 (1976): 343.—For an illuminating discussion of Hamsun's relationship to Nietzsche, see Øystein Rottem, "'*Humbug*, cela aussi, rien que *humbug*, *humbug* de décadence moderne . . .'—Nietzsche, Hamsun et la grande illusion," trans. Régis Boyer, in *Présence de Knut Hamsun*, ed. Régis Boyer & Jean-Marie Paul (Nancy, 1994), pp. 15-35.
87. Brandes' review of *Mysteries* appeared in *Politiken*, September 21, 1892.
88. Letter of September? 1892, *Brev*, I: 280. A story entitled "Small Town Life" (*SV*, IV: 96-109) has a similar social setting to *Mysteries*. Based in all likelihood on Hamsun's stay in Lillesand during the summer of 1890, the story contains a trenchant exposé of small town life. Tønnes Olai, a rather mysterious figure in the story, recalls Miniman by assuming the paternity of an illegitimate child, a proposition that the latter turned down.
89. Apart from the cat and mouse aspect of the Nagel-Miniman relationship, *Mysteries* contains several other echoes of Dostoyevsky's novel, including a kind of laughing tic—heh-heh-heh—that Nagel shares with Porfiry Petrovich and, as Walter Baumgartner has argued with respect to both *Hunger* and *Mysteries*, a frequently repeated motif of the great role played in life by trifles, on which the heroes "founder with perfect regularity" ("Intertextuelle Mysterien: Hamsun, Brandes und Dostojewski," in Annegret Heitmann & Karin Hoff, eds., *Ästhetik der skandinavischen Moderne: Beiträge zur Skandinavistik* 14 [Frankfurt am Main: Peter Lang, 1998]: 309).
90. Letter to Gustav Philipsen, *Brev*, I: 280.
91. Letter of November? 5, 1892, *Brev*, I: 284; *Letters*, I: 164.
92. The account that Nagel gives of his blissful experience to some acquaintances he meets at the steamship landing in the evening of the same day, which happens to be Midsummer Eve, June 23, echoes Ippolit's "Explanation" in Dostoyevsky's *The Idiot*. Dostoyevsky's motif of "the fly in the warm sunshine" is a symbol of universal harmony: even the "tiny fly, buzzing in the sunlight beside me," Ippolit says, "has its share in the banquet and the chorus, knows its place, loves it and is happy; and I alone am an outcast" (pp. 402, 393). Nagel relates, "It began this morning while I was still in bed. I heard a fly buzzing . . .; then I saw the sunlight filtering in through a hole in the curtain, and at one stroke a delicate, light mood sprang up within me. I had a sensation of summer in my soul" (I: 187). Like Ippolit, Nagel seems to find in the coincidence of the "*single* ray of sunlight" and the buzzing fly a promise of some great natural harmony, one that, unlike Ippolit, he does not feel excluded from.
93. Matthew 4:19.
94. Letter to the Larsens of May 13, 1892, *Brev*, I: 250; *Letters*, I: 150.
95. Review of *Mysteries* (trans. Gerry Bothmer) in the *NYTBR*, August 22, 1971, pp. 1, 30.
96. Formally, third person, past tense authorial narration, *erlebte Rede* or free indirect discourse converts in the act of reading to a first person, present tense mode, producing the impression of a direct rendering of speech or thought. Thus, it foregrounds the voice or consciousness of the fictional character being portrayed, though without eliminating the reader's awareness of the hovering presence of a narrative persona. The chief merit of this type of discourse, which

is perceived as figural presentation with, often, the effect of interior monologue, is its aptness for combining authorial distance with presentational immediacy.

97. *Entstehung und Krise des modernen Romans*, 4th ed. (Stuttgart, 1963), p. 35.
98. The discussion of "great men" in *Mysteries* may have been a fictional response to a debate between Georg Brandes and the philosopher Harald Høffding subsequent to the publication of Brandes' lectures on Nietzsche in 1889. One of Brandes' contributions to the debate was entitled "Det store Menneske, Kulturens Kilde" [The Great Man: Wellspring of Culture], *Tilskueren* 7 (1890): 1-25.
99. Birgitta Holm has developed an intriguing feminist interpretation of *Mysteries*. Pointing out Nagel's "bisexual traits"—a "sensitive, effeminate mouth," for one—she sees him as someone engaged in unmasking the pillars of society and, concomitantly, exposing the true nature of the patriarchal order. She reads the brief final chapter, showing Dagny and Martha to have developed a mutually supportive relationship, as a kind of posthumous triumph for the "halted wanderer" ("Den manliga läsningens mysterier. Knut Hamsuns roman 100 år efteråt," *Edda*, 1992, pp. 261-71, and "Hamsuns *Mysterier*," in *Hamsun og Norden. Ni foredrag fra Hamsun-dagene 1992*, ed. Nils M. Knutsen [Tromsø, 1992], pp. 105-19).
100. The most extensive treatment of *Mysteries* in relation to modernism is a section entitled "The Modernist Perspectivization of Narrative in *Mysteries*" in Martin Humpál's narratological study of Hamsun's early novels, *The Roots of Modernist Narrative*, pp. 89-104.

Chapter Two

1. "Psykologisk literatur," in *Paa Turné*, p. 51.
2. *Samtiden* 1 (1890): 8-15.
3. As far as *Editor Lynge* is concerned, Hamsun has left us an answer in his description of the novel for Albert Langen's 1894 Christmas catalogue. However bizarre it may sound, Hamsun decided to write a book "in which one finds, in prominent degree, the required qualities," having been accused of being incapable of writing such novels. However, the entry continues, he is not likely "to write more than one book in this style; but he wished to do so on this one occasion, simply to show that he could" (as quoted by Robert Ferguson, *Enigma*, p. 137).
4. Letter of November? 5, 1892, *Brev*, I: 284; *Letters*, I: 163.
5. As quoted by Tore Hamsun, *Knut Hamsun – min far*, p. 135.
6. Ibid., pp. 135-36.
7. Næss, *Knut Hamsun*, p. 16.
8. Two of Hamsun's early biographers praised the characterization of Lynge. John Landquist, calling the editor one of Hamsun's "most finished" figures, admires "the energy" of the portrayal, which blends the qualities of a "good journalist" with those of a lively, artistic nature (*Knut Hamsun: Hans levnad och verk* [Stockholm, 1929], pp. 163-64). Einar Skavlan sensibly notes that "the fur-

ther we move away from the character in time, the greater general validity the satire will acquire" (*Knut Hamsun* [Oslo, 1929], p. 183).
9. It may be noted that, after the election of 1888, in which Olav Thommessen supported the moderate wing of the Liberal Party, the comic papers began to caricature him as a "weathercock" (see *Brev*, I: 294, note 2).
10. See John 1:29.
11. Letter to Bolette and Ole Johan Larsen of January 24, 1893, *Brev*, I: 294.
12. Quoted by Johs. A. Dale, "Garborg og Hamsun," *Syn og Segn* 58 (1952): 296, from Garborg's review in *VG*, April 22, 1893.
13. Letter to the Larsens of May 4, 1893, *Brev*, I: 311.
14. Odd Hølaas, *De talte dager* (Oslo, 1946), p. 24.
15. Noted by Tore Hamsun, *Knut Hamsun – min far*, p. 148.
16. "Le Mouvement littéraire en Norvège," *Revue des Revues* 7 (1893): 721-27, 801-06.
17. Letter to Nikolai Frøsland of January 19, 1886, *Brev*, I: 63.
18. Letter to the Larsens of July 6, 1893, *Brev*, I: 323.
19. Letter to Philipsen of September 4, 1893, *Brev*, I: 330.
20. Letter to Victor Nilsson of November 1, 1893, *Brev*, I: 359.
21. Letter to Philipsen of September 4, 1893, *Brev*, I: 330.
22. Letter to the Larsens of November 25, 1893, *Brev*, I: 373.
23. Letter to Philipsen of September 4, 1893, *Brev*, I: 330.
24. Letter to the Larsens of July 6, 1893, *Brev*, I: 323.
25. Letter to Philipsen of September 25, 1893, *Brev*, I: 337.
26. See letter to Philipsen of July 24, 1893 (*Brev*, I: 326), in which he refers to books by Dostoyevsky and Turgenev, among others, with similar titles to the one he would like to use for his own novel, "Young Norway."
27. *Virgin Soil*, trans. Constance Garnett. Two volumes (New York, 1951).
28. Ibid., II: 155-56.
29. As quoted in *Brev*, I: 345, note 5, from *VG*, December 7, 1893.
30. Letter to Albert Langen of December 8, 1894, *Brev*, I: 435.
31. Letter to the Larsens of December 11, 1893, *Brev*, I: 374.
32. Letter to Philipsen of September 25, 1893, *Brev*, I: 337.
33. Letter to the Larsens of December 11, 1893, *Brev*, I: 374.
34. Letter to the Larsens of January 3, 1894, *Brev*, I: 378.
35. Letter to Philipsen of October 9, 1893, *Brev*, I: 342.
36. For further discussion, see Sverre Lyngstad, *Jonas Lie* (Boston: Twayne Publishers, 1977), pp. 125-34.

Chapter Three

1. Letter of October 31, 1893 to Bolette and Ole Johan Larsen, in *Brev*, I: 354; *Letters*, I: 179.
2. Letter of January 4, 1894 to the Larsens, *Brev*, I: 382.
3. Letter of June 5, 1994 to Albert Langen, *Brev*, I: 412; *Letters*, I: 199.
4. Letter of June 15, 1894 to the Larsens, *Brev*, I: 415; *Letters*, I: 203.
5. "Knut Hamsun," in *Skildringer og stemninger fra den yngre litteratur*, p. 49.

6. Letter of September 23, 1895 to Marie Bregendahl, *Brev*, I: 478.
7. Letter of January 11, 1995 to Elisa Philipsen, *Brev*, I: 446.
8. Letter of July 22, 1894, *Brev*, I: 418; *Letters*, I: 205. Hamsun's English is rather non-traditional in its grammar and spelling.
9. Letter of September 2, 1894 to Albert Langen, *Brev*, I: 422; *Letters*, I: 208.
10. For extensive discussion of stylization in *Pan*, see Wilhelm Friese, "Hamsun und der Jugendstil," *Edda* 67 (1967): 434–49.
11. Rolf Vige, *Knut Hamsuns "Pan": En litterær analyse* (Oslo: Universitetsforlaget, 1963); Finn Aarsæther, *Veien til verket: Om "Pan" av Knut Hamsun* (Oslo, 1997).
12. In 1985 Knut Faldbakken published a novel, *Glahn*, which is a satiric reworking of Hamsun's *Pan* on a psychoanalytic basis. Interviewed by the author in 1986, Faldbakken said that he had wanted "to show Glahn up for the self-destructive psychopath that he is." See Sverre Lyngstad, "An Interview with Knut Faldbakken, Part II," *Norway Times*, September 17, 1987, p. 12
13. "August Strindberg," *America* (Chicago), December 20, 1888, p. 31.
14. It should perhaps be noted that Glahn is aware of other, less gentle aspects of nature. In a wretched mood during which his soul is likened to a "ruined bird's nest," after Mack has discovered his affair with Eva, he describes the ocean in a storm as a fearsome "festival of ten thousand whistling devils" (II: 384). In considering Glahn's longed-for union with nature, its demonic aspects must not be neglected. Moreover, the dual image of nature presented in the novel is echoed in Glahn himself, whose split psyche is characterized by one critic, John Landquist, as "semi-barbarian," inviting disaster because of a deficiency of culture (*Knut Hamsun*, p. 123).
15. The word "erotic" in this passage did not appear in the original edition. See *Pan* (København, 1894), p. 58.
16. "Mit dem Stimmungsleben in der Natur verschmilzt unmerklich das erotische Leben" ("Skandinavische Dichter," *Cosmopolis* 4 [Berlin, 1896]: 558).
17. Letter of September 2, 1894 to Albert Langen, *Brev*, I: 423; *Letters*, I: 208. — Hamsun was familiar with artistic applications of the Pan myth in the paintings of the Swiss-German symbolist Arnold Böcklin (1827–1901) and in the poetry of Jens Peter Jacobsen, both of whom he greatly admired. Wilhelm Friese suggests that, in choosing the mythological title, Hamsun showed himself in tune with the *fin-de-siècle* as reflected in the *Jugendstil* movement, for which the myth of Pan figured as a "code sign" ("Hamsun und der Jugendstil," p. 439).
18. Patricia Merivale, *Pan the Goat-God: His Myth in Modern Times* (Cambridge, MA: Harvard UP, 1969), p. 9.
19. *The Georgics*, III: 391–393. — Robert Browning wrote a grotesque poem, "Pan and Luna," where he questions this tradition (*Dramatic Idylls*, Second Series, *The Poetical Works of Robert Browning* [London: Oxford UP, 1946], pp. 620–22).
20. Exodus 33:23.
21. For a comprehensive discussion of the function of the myth of Pan in the novel, see Henning K. Sehmsdorf, "Knut Hamsun's *Pan*: Myth and Symbol," *Edda* 74 (1974): 345–93.
22. For relevant discussion, see Ernest Jones, *The Life and Work of Sigmund Freud*, II (New York, 1955): 298. In all fairness, it should be noted that the amorous rela-

tionships in Hamsun's novel do not fulfill all criteria of what is called the injured third party syndrome.
23. A bit of symbolic action supports this view. Early on, Glahn told Edvarda about an incident in which a young lady "took a white silk kerchief" from her own neck and tied it around his. To his offer of returning it the next day, after having it washed, she responds by saying she wants to "keep it as it is." Three years later, when they meet again and he asks for the kerchief, she gives it to him "in its wrapping, as unwashed as ever" (II: 353). When on a rainy day quite a bit later, having refused and, on a dare, trampled to pieces a precious brooch with a coronet on it presented to her by the Baron, Edvarda seeks out Glahn, she offers him a "white silk kerchief" (385). Given the erotic connotations the kerchief has been endowed with, the implications of Glahn's brutal refusal of it are quite evident.
24. Øystein Rottem has convincingly argued this view in "Pan—en høysang til kjærligheten eller Tristan i jegerkostyme," in Nils M. Knutsen, ed., "Pan": Handelsstedene, novellene, illustrasjonene. Rapport fra litteraturseminaret, Hamsundagene 1986 (Tromsø: Tromsø UP, 1986), pp. 9–44.
25. Thomas Seiler reads Glahn's need for distance as a sign that he is an artist, whose creativity depends on the tension between distance and nearness. See "Knut Hamsuns Pan als patriarchaler Schöpfer-Mythos," Edda, 1995, p. 272.
26. For several of these gratuitous acts, Hamsun may have received suggestions from Dostoyevsky. In The Idiot (Part IV, ch. 7), Myshkin's breaking of the china vase produces a typical Dostoyevskian scene of scandal; in Crime and Punishment (Part I, ch. 2), Marmeladov expresses pleasure in his wife's dragging him by the hair; and in The Demons (Part I, Section 2: "Prince Harry. Matchmaking," ch. III), Stavrogin, pretending to whisper something in the governor's ear, bites it instead.
27. Let me comment on two of these approaches. In an article comparing Hamsun and Pasternak, E. C. Barksdale and Daniel Popp maintain that both these writers see nature "as a primeval pulse of strength and beauty, a reservoir of cosmic grandeur, a force which exalts and destroys." Glahn, in this view, exemplifies the Dionysian hero, a character who lives by violent emotions and impromptu actions in an Apollonian world and attains sublimity through his poetic dimensions. The critics state that Glahn's "pointless, mad death is caused by the Dionysian forces which lifted him to greatness in the forest" ("Hamsun and Pasternak: The Development of Dionysian Tragedy," Edda 76 [1976]: 343–51). Pasternak himself wrote that "he lived in a sort of feverish rapture after reading Pan" (E. Pasternak, Boris Pasternak. Materialy dlya biografii [Moscow, 1989], p. 76, as quoted by Nils Åke Nilsson, "Hamsun och Dostojevskij," in Hamsun og Norden, ed. Nils M. Knutsen [Tromsø, 1992], p. 56). James McFarlane explains the failure of Glahn and Edvarda's love by means of the Jungian anima/animus archetypes. Building on the Doctor's notion that Edvarda is waiting for a prince, McFarlane finds the crux of their estrangement in the ideal images they project upon one another, a process leading to inevitable disenchantment ("The Whisper of the Blood: A Study of Knut Hamsun's Early Novels," PMLA 71 [1956]: 589). Though both theories are worth considering, the first seems rather lofty, seeing Hamsun as the creator of a

Nietzschean type of tragedy, while the second, though superficially plausible, is rather facile. Besides, the Doctor, a shallow rationalist exposed as a pedant, is hardly to be trusted as a connoisseur of the psychology of love.

28. Asmund Lien, "Pans latter," *Edda*, 1993, pp. 134-35.
29. *The Lyrical Novel: Studies in Hermann Hesse, André Gide, and Virginia Woolf* (Princeton, N. J.: Princeton UP, 1963), p. 2.
30. In his article "Das Werther-Thema in Hamsuns 'Mysterien'," Frank Thiess sees *Pan* as well as *Mysteries* as exemplifying the Werther theme. See *Heimat und Weltgeist*, p. 151.
31. For a strongly argued presentation of this view, see Siegfried Weibel, "Knut Hamsuns *Pan*: Suggestion und De-Montage," *Skandinavistik* 16 (1986): 21-35.
32. Letter to Gerda Welhaven, *Brev*, II: 86.
33. Letter (in English) to Albert Langen of September 27, 1898, *Brev*, II: 88.
34. Letters to Georg Brandes of Christmas Eve 1898 (*Brev*, II: 109) and to Albert Langen (in English) of November 20, 1898, *Brev*, II: 92.
35. See Matthew 3:16.
36. An article by Beverly D. Eddy explores the similarities between Hamsun's use of color symbolism in *Victoria* with that of the painter Edvard Munch, whose works of the 1890s as represented by the so-called "Frieze of Life" often strike the viewer as illustrations of Hamsun's obsessive psychological themes.—"Hamsun's *Victoria* and Munch's *Livsfrisen*: Variations on a Theme," *Scandinavian Studies* 48 (1976): 158-60.
37. Atle Kittang views this as an "Orphic fantasy," namely, Johannes' descent into the underworld in search of Victoria.—"Kjærleik, dikting og sosial røyndom: Knut Hamsuns *Victoria*," in *Litteraturhistoriske problem* (Oslo, 1975), p. 216.
38. Letters to Georg Brandes of Christmas Eve and November 25, 1898, *Brev*, II: 109 & 96, note 3; *Letters*, II: 21.
39. *TLS*, May 17, 1923, p. 341; John Updike, "Love as a Standoff," *The New Yorker*, June 28, 1969, p. 93.
40. Edwin Muir, "A Great Writer," *The Freeman* 7 (Aug. 8, 1923): 522.
41. Updike, pp. 94-95.
42. Cai M. Woel, *Knut Hamsun* (København, 1929), p. 6.
43. "Knut Hamsuns Wandern durch die Welt," in *An den Grenzen der Nationalliteraturen* (Berlin, 1958), p. 265; "*Die Weiber am Brunnen*" (*Prager Presse*, January 29, 1922), in Thomas Mann, *Gesammelte Werke in zwölf Bänden* (Oldenburg, 1960), X: *Reden und Aufsätze*, p. 621.
44. *Hamsun i russisk åndsliv* (Oslo, 1969), p. 93.
45. *The Observer Review*, January 26, 1997, p. 17; *Enigma*, p. 177.

Chapter Four

1. Letter to Jacob Hegel of April 24, 1902, *Brev*, II: 197.
2. Letter to Wentzel Hagelstam of September 21, 1901, *Brev*, II: 184.
3. Letter to Albert Langen of June 8, 1902, *Brev*, II: 198.
4. Letter to Wentzel Hagelstam of December 19, 1901, *Brev*, II: 193.
5. Letter to Hans Aanrud of May 18, 1904, *Brev*, II: 266.

6. Letter to Wentzel Hagelstam of January 3, 1905, *Brev*, II: 289.
7. Letter to Peter Nansen of June 20, 1904, *Brev*, II, 269. Interestingly, the 1993 film based on the book, *Telegrafisten* (The Telegrapher), redeems this "regrettable" omission.
8. The word "sværme," related to the novel's title, *Sværmere*, means not only to dream, but also to romance, pay court, woo. For an example of this usage, see *SV*, IV: 143.
9. In his 1929 study of Hamsun, the psychoanalyst Trygve Braatøy sees *Dreamers* as a "mock" on *Victoria*. — *Livets cirkel*, p. 98.
10. P. Chr. Asbjørnsen & Jørgen Moe, *Samlede eventyr* (Oslo, 1992), I: 335–38.
11. Tore Hamsun writes that the parson's wife is not just a "product of his [Hamsun's] imagination, but an obvious portrait" of Mrs. Bergljot Hamsun. The couple were divorced two years later, in 1906. — *Knut Hamsun – min far*, pp. 199–200.
12. Curiously, in a letter of June 27, 1908, to Marie Andersen, who became Hamsun's wife in 1909, Hamsun writes, on the subject of marriage, that "perhaps the Mohammedans have solved this problem better than we have, through the institution of the harem." — *Brev*, III: 69.
13. Letter to Lars Swanström, Hamsun's publisher, of January 20, 1908, *Brev*, III: 9.
14. Ibid. and letter to Peter Nansen of February 1, 1908, *Brev*, III: 14.
15. Letter to Dagny Kristensen of March 25, 1908, *Brev*, III: 27.
16. In the letter to Marie Andersen of June 27, 1908, cited above, at a time when he was desperately wooing her, Hamsun expresses the same view of the effect of marriage on love. He writes: "Incidentally, I find it absurd that I am the one to champion the cause of marriage, I whose theory, one I have defended both in writing and speech, has for a long, long time been that marriage is the death of love. Generally speaking, I maintain that theory even today." — *Brev*, II: 69.
17. Sigmund Freud, "Über einen besonderen Typus der Objektwahl beim Manne," *Gesammelte Werke*, VIII (London: Imago Publishing Company, 1955): 67; *The Complete Psychological Works of Sigmund Freud*, trans. by James Strachey, vol. XI (London: The Hogarth Press, 1981): 166. I have made a slight change in the translation of the German text.
18. The English translation of Girard's book, *Deceit, Desire, and the Novel: Self and Other in Literary Structure*, trans. by Yvonne Freccero (Baltimore: Johns Hopkins UP, 1990), contains a reference to Freud in a footnote, but without mentioning the paper quoted in my text. After acknowledging his "anti-Freudianism," the author writes: "From a Freudian viewpoint, the original triangle of desire is, of course, the Oedipal triangle. The story of 'mediated' desire is the story of this Oedipal desire, of its essential permanence beyond its ever changing objects" (186–87).
19. René Girard, *Mensonge romantique et verité romanesque* (Paris: Bernard Grasset, 1961), p. 5.
20. *The Complete Psychological Works*, XI: 168.
21. *Knut Hamsun – min far*, p. 218.
22. Gilbert tells Benoni the date of Rosa's imminent wedding when he meets him at the general store (V: 76–77), sees Benoni at his home and is offered a drink by him the day of the wedding (96–97), and meets the bride and groom later that day (97).

23. Letter to Albert Langen of September 12, 1908, *Brev*, III: 108.
24. Letter to Lars Swanström of June 24, 1908, *Brev*, III:62.
25. Letter to Albert Langen of December 4, 1908, *Brev*, III: 122.
26. See Knut Hamsun, *Rosa*, trans. by Sverre Lyngstad (Los Angeles: Sun & Moon Press, 1997), p. 191.
27. Knut Hamsun, *SV*, II: 301; *Pan*, trans. with Introduction and Notes by Sverre Lyngstad (New York: Penguin, 1998), p. 107.
28. The reviewer of *Rosa* in the *New York Times Book Review* (Feb. 7, 1926, p. 8) describes Parelius' performance as narrator somewhat similarly. While calling him "painfully unsophisticated," he praises his keen perception, singling out his "flair for details," which the reviewer ascribes to his being something of a "poet."
29. Munken Vendt is the central character of Hamsun's long poetic drama of 1902, which takes place toward the end of the eighteenth century. Hamsun's Russian translator, P. E. Hansen, had apparently pointed out in a letter to Hamsun that, if Munken Vendt in *Rosa* was the same character as that in the drama, he would be around ninety! Hamsun writes to Hansen: "I needed him. But I have committed several such anachronisms in my books, it hasn't been criticized or mentioned.... Anyway, it doesn't matter at all if there are such 'errors.' I was fully aware of this one." (Letter of November 13, 1908, *Brev*, III: 116; *Letters*, II: 86.)
30. Interestingly, Marie Andersen, subsequently Hamsun's wife, expressed the same opinion of Rosa, to which Hamsun answered, "Women are most often boring." She doubted whether Rosa "was dear to his heart." Confessing that she had "expected to find a thing or two having to do with us in it," she continues, "One couldn't discover the least backwash from the storms I knew so well. There was smooth water in *Rosa*." At the same time she expresses wonder at "how separated his imaginative world seemed to be from the reality he was in the midst of."—Marie Hamsun, *Regnbuen* (Oslo: Aschehoug, 1953), p. 173.
31. Here is where Marie Andersen might have found what she allegedly missed in Rosa: a reflection of her and Hamsun's experience at the time he was writing the novel. A glance at dozens of letters to Marie written during the spring and summer of 1908, when he was was working on *Rosa* (*Brev*, III) will provide ample evidence of one of the main themes of the novel, the primacy of jealousy in Hamsun's conception of love at this period of his life.
32. *Mysterier*, in *SV*, I: 356.
33. As cited by Nils M. Knutsen, *Makt-avmakt: En studie av Hamsuns "Benoni" og "Rosa"* (Oslo: Aschehoug, 1975), pp. 5–6.
34. "More of Benoni," *NYTBR*, Feb. 7, 1926, p. 8.
35. *Knut Hamsun: Hans levnad och verk*, pp. 187–88.
36. "Knut Hamsun: Benoni," in *Meninger om litteratur* (København, 1929), p. 49.
37. *Modern Norwegian Literature 1860–1915* (Cambridge, Engl.: Cambridge UP, 1966), p. 182.
38. "Makt-avmakt: En studie av Hamsuns 'Benoni' og 'Rosa.'" Thesis, University of Oslo, 1973, pp. 33, 64.
39. *Knut Hamsun*, p. 264.

Chapter Five

1. These two novels were first published in English together, under the titles "Autumn" and "With Muted Strings," respectively. The volume was entitled *Wanderers* (1922).
2. According to Einar Skavlan (*Knut Hamsun*, p. 260), Hamsun did, in fact, invent a saw of this kind.
3. Hamsun's wanderers differ radically from their counterparts in German romantic literature, to whom they have been compared. Both figures are filled with longing for an intensification of life, but whereas the hero of, say, Joseph von Eichendorff's *Memoirs of a Good-for-Nothing* (1826) fulfills his dream, in a novel sparkling with good humor, joyous song and music, and youthful love, Hamsun's hero, as one critic has put it, can never be satisfied, because, as a human being, he cannot live in the dream, and as a dreamer, he cannot find rest in reality.—Axel Skagen, "Den aldrende vandrers vei mot resignasjon—bidrag til analyse av Knut Hamsuns 'vandrer-trilogi.'" Thesis, University of Oslo, 1960, p. 97.—Rebel as he may against the weakness of the flesh, the aging dreamer will inevitably reap disenchantment and end in resignation.
4. To avoid confusion between Knut Pedersen's companion and Captain Falkenberg, I am using the name Falkberget throughout for the worker.
5. See "Über die allgemeinste Erniedrigung des Liebeslebens, *Gesammelte Werke*, VIII: 78–91; "On the Universal Tendency to Debasement in the Sphere of Love," *The Complete Psychological Works of Sigmund Freud*, XI: 179–190. The translations are my own.
6. Ibid., p. 82; p. 183.
7. *The Complete Grimm's Fairy Tales* (New York: Pantheon Books, 1972), pp. 29–39.
8. The poem "Skjærgårdsø" (Island Among the Skerries) develops the same conceit, to explain the speaker's sense of communion with nature. See *SV*, XV: 190–91.
9. *TLS*, Jan. 26, 1922, p. 59.
10. *Samtiden* 18 (1907): 270–71.
11. Helge Krog, "Knut Hamsun," in *Meninger om bøker og forfattere* (Oslo, 1929), p. 36.
12. John Updike, "A Primal Modern," *The New Yorker*, May 31, 1976, p. 116.
13. Hans Keller, "The Risks of Genius," *TLS*, December 5, 1975, p. 1439.
14. Hamsun's indifference to chronology is evident from the fact that the publication dates of the two novels are separated by an interval of only three years (1906–1909).
15. *Don Juan*, Canto the First, st. CXCIV.
16. Letter to Peter Nansen of December 9, 1909, *Brev*, III: 244; *Letters*, II: 114.
17. I am not alone in interpreting Lovise's death as a suicide; see Trygve Braatøy, *Livets cirkel*, p. 186; Harald Næss, *Knut Hamsun*, p. 101; and Robert Ferguson, *Enigma*, p. 209.
18. Letter to Lars Swanström of December 2, 1909, *Brev*, III: 237; *Letters*, II: 110–11.
19. Letter to Lars Swanström of November 8, 1909, *Brev*, III: 224.
20. Letter to Lars Swanström of November 18, 1909, *Brev*, III: 229.

21. The possibility of irony is suggested by the novel's last two sentences, which betray anything but a placid contentment with things as they are. It is late in the year, and as darkness falls Knut Pedersen abandons the cave where he has sought refuge and sets out for his logger's cabin: "I wander onward, slowly and indifferently, with my hands in my pockets. I'm in no hurry, it doesn't matter where I am" (V: 423).
22. Trygve Braatøy suggests (*Livets cirkel*, p. 186) that these negative feelings of Knut Pedersen, the author's alter ego, are the key to Lovise's wretched end: she had shown him he was starting to age. The novel is certainly marked by a bias against women, of which Hamsun seems to have been fully aware. In a letter to Wentzel Hagelstam and Albert Engström of October 19, 1909 (*Brev*, III: 218), he says, "I'm writing my best book, which I'll send you both, but your wives ought not to read it—for it's not pretty." The editor of Hamsun's letters, Harald Næss, adds the following gloss: "Much of Hamsun's aggression in his letters to Marie is also to be found in the novel" (Note 2, p. 218).
23. Letter to Lars Swanström of November 8, 1909, *Brev*, III: 224.
24. Harald Næss, *Knut Hamsun*, p. 89.
25. The apparent contradiction may be due to the fact that Hamsun's view of the peasant was undergoing a change. In 1908 he engaged in a debate with the Danish poet and novelist Johannes V. Jensen, an admirer of peasant values, in which Hamsun expressed a very negative attitude toward peasant culture. He maintained, for example, that Thomas Carlyle became "creative" only after having "eliminated the peasant in himself" ("Bondekulturen," in Knut Hamsun, *Artikler* [Oslo, 1939], p. 127). Subsequently, however, Hamsun seems to have adopted a view not unlike that of his Danish colleague.
26. Letter to Lars Swanström of October 11, 1909, *Brev*, III: 214.
27. *TLS*, January 26, 1922, p. 59.
28. "A Primal Modern," pp. 116–18.
29. *Samtiden*, 17 (1906): 133–45.
30. The mention of the Reisa River (VII: 49) suffices to locate Hamsun's story in the region of Troms, Norway's next to northernmost county. The presence of Sami, or Lapps, is consistent with this setting. The description of the hut is supposedly based on an actual episode in Hamsun's life. When he visited his parents in Hamarøy during the spring of 1900, he lived in a turf hut leased from a neighbor for a couple of months while working on *Munken Vendt*. See letter to Xavier Slotte of May 24, 1900, *Brev*, II: 148, note 2.
31. Friedrich Nietzsche, *Werke in sechs Bänden* (München-Wien: Carl Hanser Verlag, 1980), III: 277. One may wonder whether the raven circling over the forest, a bird which later allegedly talks to the narrator (VII: 37), is a mock allusion to Zarathustra's eagle. Not that Hamsun's world lacks eagles. The narrator watches with rapt attention as an eagle "glides in wide circles over the valley. Large and blackish and out of reach, it describes circle after circle up there, as though around an arena. . . . Oh, it's like a melody to watch" (37).
32. Nietzsche, p. 405.
33. *SV*, II: 394.
34. "Later I learned," the text reads, "he was the illegitimate son of a telegraph operator who lived at Rosenlund almost a generation ago" (VII: 24). This

description seems to imply that Solem was sired by Ove Rolandsen, the hero of *Dreamers*.
35. In the proofs of the novel which Marie Hamsun read, Mrs. Brede succumbs to Solem. She writes: "An episode in the portrayal of a kind young mother had the effect of hitting the wrong key in the middle of a symphony. It almost felt like a personal insult. He [Hamsun] obliged me and deleted the episode" (*Regnbuen*, p. 232). Hamsun writes as follows about changes he is making in the proofs: "Among other things, Mrs. Brede doesn't do anything wrong, I was myself dissatisfied with it, and you said so too, you remember. And she had those little girls too." Letter of October 1, 1912, *Brev*, III: 421.
36. See *Pornografia*, trans. Alastair Hamilton (New York: Grove Press, 1966).
37. Several critics have noted the similar backgrounds of Ingeborg Torsen and Hamsun's second wife, Marie, who had briefly taught school before taking up acting. And the fictional transformation of Miss Torsen into a model farmer's wife parallels Hamsun's real-life program for his newly acquired wife.
38. A couple of years earlier, in 1910, Hamsun had published a blasting attack on what he saw as a tendency to change Norway into what he calls a "ridiculous and insignificant Switzerland." The tone of the article, with its sallies against those who, led by the despised "Anglo-Saxons," are turning Norwegians into a people of "waiters" for foreign tourists, is extremely strident. The assumed posture, that of a latter-day prophet, is evident from Hamsun's sense of being a "voice in the wilderness" (see Isaiah 40:3 and Matthew 3:3). — "A Word to Us," in Knut Hamsun, *Artikler*, pp. 158-60.
39. *Regnbuen*, p. 232.
40. Victor Erlich, *Russian Formalism: History – Doctrine*, 3rd ed. (The Hague & Paris: Mouton, 1969), p. 75, note.
41. See *SV*, VII: 52, 66, 68, 91, 139.
42. See ibid., p. 80.
43. It is interesting to note that, on one and the same page, the horse that Nikolai has just bought and brought home is called the "sorrel lady," while Ingeborg is compared to a "filly," her nostrils flaring, as she talks of her desire for a large family (VII: 133).
44. "Well, let us be human," the narrator remarks, seeing Solem staggering under his load of hides. And Ingeborg says, referring to how she handles her having been raped by Solem vis-à-vis Nikolai, "We don't want to be just animals, we want to be human beings" (VII: 137-38).
45. "*Den sidste Glæde*," in *Meninger om litteratur*, pp. 72-73.
46. Letter of December 10, 1912, to Peter Nansen, *Brev*, III: 429.
47. "Nye norske bøker," *Samtiden* 24 (1913): 60.
48. "Knut Hamsun—Faulkner Made Easy," *The New Yorker*, April 13, 1940, p. 80.
49. *Enigma*, p. 224; Olav Storstein, "Da den døde våknet," *Samtiden* 65 (1956): 236.

Chapter Six

1. A strong will was apparently the rock bottom of the personality, according to Hamsun. In a letter written while working on *Segelfoss Town*, he writes,

"[T]here is next to nothing left except my will to keep me upright" (Letter to Christian Kønig of April 26, 1915, *Brev*, IV: 42). Tore Hamsun says that, of all the characters in *Children of the Age*, Willatz Holmsen is the one that Hamsun "loves." And he quotes the narrator's comment on the dying Lieutenant: "An honest will to the end, a golden will" (VI: 188). See Tore Hamsun, *Knut Hamsun – min far*, pp. 240–41.

2. One wonders whether Holmengrå's name, derived from the "grå holme" (VI: 93; gray islet) where he was born, contains an allusion to the battle of Holmengrå (1139), one of many during the protracted civil wars that were to decimate the old Norwegian aristocracy.
3. The suggestion that Holmengrå is a "symbolic" figure is made in the text. At a moment when the Lieutenant sees Holmengrå approaching, the narrator asks the following question, which may as well be an instance of free indirect discourse expressing the Lieutenant's wonderment concerning the neighbor who has had such a "profound effect on his life": "Who was this man? With no family, no home, from some fairy tale, from all countries – a symbol perhaps, a force" (VI: 124).
4. Hamsun's demeaning attitude toward "acquired culture" can be traced as far back as the late 1880s. In discussing Ralph Waldo Emerson in his 1889 book about America, he decides that the New England Brahmin's criticism of Shakespeare rests on "acquired culture" rather than on "exceptional natural gifts." – *Fra det moderne Amerikas Aandsliv* (København: Philipsen, 1889), p. 107.
5. In this connection, it has been suggested, first, that Segelfoss is a "world in miniature" and, secondly, that Hamsun projects several "West-European problems" into a North-Norwegian environment "where they probably did not exist." – Terje Dyrhaug, "Kulturkritikk i Knut Hamsuns 'Børn av Tiden' og 'Segelfoss By'." Thesis, University of Oslo, 1974, pp. 9, 116.
6. "Lübeck as a Way of Life and Thought," trans. by R. & C. Winston, in *Buddenbrooks*, trans. by H.T. Lowe-Porter (New York, 1964), p. x. See also Walter Grüters, *Der Einfluss der norwegischen Literatur auf Thomas Manns "Buddenbrooks"* (Bonn, 1961) and Klaus Matthias, *Thomas Mann und Skandinavien* (Lübeck, 1969).
7. Letter to Christian Kønig of November 2, 1915, *Brev*, IV: 57. Hamsun's claim is exaggerated: Kielland did not write *all* his novels in that way.
8. Letter to Peter Nansen of November 23, 1915, *Brev*, IV: 64.
9. A German critic considers the finding of the treasure a "fairy-tale element" and, as such, an "invalid solution" to the novel's action. – Siegfried Weibel, "Der konsequente Hintersinn. Die Ironisierung des Ironikers in Knut Hamsuns 'Børn av Tiden'," in *Applikationen: Analysen skandinavischer Erzähltexte*, ed. Walter Baumgartner. Texte und Untersuchungen zur Germanistik und Skandinavistik 13 (Frankfurt a. M.: Peter Lang, 1987): 228.
10. The harshest criticism of Willatz Holmsen is contained in a study by the German critic Peter de Mendelssohn, who describes him as a "psychopath," an inwardly torn person who, with his riding whip, looks like an "unintentional caricature of a Prussian officer." Nevertheless, he considers the portrait an artistic success. – "Erleuchtung und Verblendung des Zerrissenen: Versuch über Knut Hamsun," in *Der Geist in der Despotie* (Berlin, 1953), p. 60.
11. Tore Hamsun, *Knut Hamsun – min far*, pp. 239–40.

12. It is worth noting how frequently the Lieutenant uses images of violence, especially lightning, to suggest his own pristine values (VI: 57–59).
13. This characterization of Holmengrå mirrors Hamsun's view of Americans as expressed in his notorious book of 1889, where he says that the Yankee "can pick up etiquette but be inwardly untouched by it." He will never be an "aristocrat by temperament" but remain an "upstart." — *Fra det moderne Amerikas Aandsliv*, p. 228.
14. *L'Eau et les rêves* (Paris, 1942), p. 53 (my translation). In the English translation by Edith R. Farrell, *Water and Dreams* (Dallas: The Pegasus Foundation, 1983), p. 37, "point culminant" is translated literally as "culminating point."
15. Arnold Whittick, *Symbols: Signs and their Meaning and Uses in Design*, 2nd ed. (London, 1971), p. 326.
16. "Knut Hamsun," in *Gesammelte Werke* XII: *Schriften zur Literatur* 2 (Frankfurt a. M., 1970): 386–87.
17. E. Hasselblatt, "Børn av Tiden," in *Dikt og diktare* (Helsingfors, 1918), pp. 152, 154.
18. J. S. Scott, *TLS*, November 13, 1924, p. 728.
19. Sigurd Hoel, "Knut Hamsun, I: Til 70-årsdagen," in *Essays i utvalg*, ed. Nils Lie (Oslo: Gyldendal, 1962), p. 145.
20. *Longman Dictionary of English Language and Culture* (1992).
21. Ad de Vries, *Dictionary of Symbols and Images* (Amsterdam, 1984), p. 450.
22. Hans Adolph Brorson, *Svane-Sang* (1765), with an Introduction by Arthur Arnholtz & Afterword by Karl Clausen (Strandbygaard: Skjern, 1965).
23. Daniel 2:36–40.
24. Knut Hamsun, *Hunger*, trans. with Introduction and Notes by Sverre Lyngstad (New York: Penguin, 1998), pp. 29–30.
25. Knut Hamsun, *Rosa* (1997), p. 16.
26. A variant on this thought figures prominently in Hamsun's address to the Grimstad court on December 16, 1947. See *On Overgrown Paths*, p. 191. It is also the theme of a poem, "Om hundrede år er alting glemt" (*SV*, XV: 214; In a Hundred Years It Is All Forgotten).
27. Note the casual attitude expressed in his letter to Peter Nansen of November 23, 1915, *Brev*, IV: 63.
28. Ibid., p. 64.
29. Letter to Christian Kønig of November 14, 1915, *Brev*, IV: 60.
30. Carl Nærup, "Knut Hamsun: *Segelfoss By*," in *Ord for dagen* (Oslo, 1929), pp. 131–32.
31. Sven Lange, "*Segelfoss By*," in *Meninger om litteratur*, p. 96.
32. Poul Levin, "Norge," *Tilskueren* 33.1 (1916): 79.
33. "Review of *Segelfoss Town*," *The Nation and the Athenaeum*, June 20, 1925, p. 372.

Chapter Seven

1. Franz Kafka, *Tagebücher*, ed. Hans-Gerd Koch et al. (Frankfurt, 1990), III: 846. In his diary entry of December 9, 1919, Kafka writes: "Eleseus could also have

been the hero of the book; indeed, he would most likely have been so in Hamsun's youth."
2. In his review of a novel by Nordahl Grieg (*Arbeiderbladet*, December 1, 1927), Sigurd Hoel makes gentle fun of the aging Hamsun's idea that it is dangerous to wander, that is, to be what Hamsun calls "rootless." Tempted to object that man is not a tree, Hoel asks: "Didn't Hamsun write quite good books in his days of wandering? Why not use an image from zoology occasionally?"
3. For examples of James's usage, see Henry James, *Literary Criticism: French Writers, Other European Writers, The Prefaces to the New York Edition* (New York: the Library of America, 1984), pp. 1308, 1317.
4. Letter of October 15, 1916, to Christian Kønig, *Brev*, IV: 130.
5. Letter of January 28, 1918, to the newspaper editor Thorvald Aadahl, *Brev*, IV: 205.
6. Letter of January 31, 1918, to Harry Fett, *Brev*, IV: 206.
7. As quoted by Tore Hamsun, *Knut Hamsun – min far*, p. 236.
8. Anders Österling, "The Literary Prize," in H. Schück et al., *Nobel: The Man and His Prizes*, third edition, rev. & enl. (New York, London, Amsterdam: American Elsevier Publishing Co., 1972), p. 75.
9. Apparently some aspects of Geissler's character were modeled on an actual individual, Andreas Christian Geitzler, sheriff at Hamarøy 1841-54. Mr. Geitzler, who had relatives in Sweden, like Hamsun's Geissler, was known for his sense of adventure and his bibbling habit. – Jan Fr. Marstrander, "Livskamp og virkelighetsoppfatning i Knut Hamsuns tidligste forfatterskap." Doctoral dissertation, University of Oslo, 1982, p. 259.
10. Romans 7:19.
11. This idea has been variously received. Whereas the German scholar Eberhard Rumbke finds in the novel a "quasi-apotheosis of natural man," whose "subjection to nature" results in dehumanization, to Allen Simpson agriculture as treated by Hamsun is "opposed to nature," contrary to Geissler's gospel of harmony. – "'Træskeens Tidsalder' – Regressive Gesellschaftskritik in Knut Hamsuns Roman *Segen der Erde*," in *Auf alten und neuen Pfaden* (Frankfurt am Main: Peter Lang, 1983), II: 150–51; "'Midt i Forgjængelsens Karneval': *Markens Grøde* in Knut Hamsun's Authorship," *Scandinavian Studies* 56.1 (1984): 2.
12. For a definition of these terms, see Friedrich Schiller, "Über naive und sentimentalische Dichtung," in *Sämtliche Werke*, V (München, 1972): 458–59, 489–90; "Naive and Sentimental Poetry," in *"Naive and Sentimental Poetry" and "On the Sublime,"* translated, with Introduction and Notes, by Julius A. Elias (New York: Frederick Ungar, 1966), pp. 115–16, 154–56.
13. Lars Frode Larsen claims to have found conclusive proof that Hamsun was born not in Lom but in the neighboring township of Vågå. – *Den unge Hamsun*, p. 29.
14. Leviticus 26:3–4.
15. Erich Auerbach, *Mimesis: The Representation of Reality in Western Literature*, trans. by Willard Trask (Garden City, New York: Doubleday Anchor, 1957), p. 19.
16. Aldous Huxley, "Tragedy and the Whole Truth," in *Complete Essays*, III (1930–1935), ed. with commentary by Robert S. Baker and James Sexton (Chicago,

2001), pp. 51–52. See also *Homer: The Odyssey*, translated by Robert Fagles, with Introduction and Notes by Bernard Knox (New York: Viking, 1996), p. 280.
17. Genesis 3:8.
18. For a strong argument to the effect that Isak is an "unrealistic" character, a "primordial" figure deriving from myth or fairy tale, see Kåre Glette, "Isak Sellanrå—ein truverdig figur?," *Ventil* 4.1 (1974): 10–13. In an article on the occasion of Hamsun's ninetieth birthday, Hans Heiberg calls *Growth of the Soil* a "dream book" and says, with some exaggeration, that "not a single one of the book's exploits can be accomplished in reality" ("Knut Hamsun fyller nitti," in *Peilinger* [Oslo, 1950], p. 55).
19. Genesis 4:16.
20. Carl Nærup, "Knut Hamsuns *Markens grøde*," in *Ord for dagen*, p. 137.
21. Francis Fergusson, *The Idea of a Theater* (New York, 1949), p. 31. See also Kenneth Burke, *A Grammar of Motives* (New York, 1945), pp. 39–40.
22. Allen Simpson has discussed Isak's predicament in light of Camus' notion of the absurd: the "intimation of mortality" that comes to him represents a "crisis of consciousness." But instead of "keeping the absurd alive," like Camus' absurd hero, Isak returns to his routine life, unchanged. To Hamsun, Simpson states, consciousness is "modern man's curse."—"Hamsun and Camus: Consciousness in *Markens Grøde* and 'The Myth of Sisyphus,'" *Scandinavian Studies* 48.3 (1976): 272–83.
23. See Charles Kent, "Et moderne læredigt: Knut Hamsuns *Markens Grøde*," in Knut Imerslund, *Norsk litteraturkritikk 1914–1945* (Oslo, 1970), p. 97; Sven Lange, *Politiken*, December 9, 1917, as quoted by Øystein Rottem in "Utopi på leirføtter," *Norskrift*, no. 41 (1983): 15; and Poul Levin, "Nogle Böger," *Tilskueren* 35 (1918): 89.
24. In a thorough study of the circumstances surrounding the award and the process leading up to it, Walter Baumgartner concludes that Hamsun received the prize "explicitly for his novel *Growth of the Soil*."—"*Segen der Erde* im Kampf gegen den 'Bolschewismus der Poesie': Knut Hamsun und der Nobelpreis," *Zeitschrift für Literaturwissenschaft und Linguistik* 27, Heft 107 (September 1997): 39.
25. *Weekly Review* 4 (April 6, 1921): 320; *TLS*, May 27, 1920, p. 334; Rebecca West, "Notes on Novels," *The New Statesman* 15 (May 15, 1920): 167.
26. H. G. Wells, "The Bible of Civilization, Part Two," in *The Salvaging of Civilization* (London, 1921), p. 124; Thomas Mann, "*Die Weiber am Brunnen*," in *Gesammelte Werke in zwölf Bänden*, X: 621.
27. Saul Maloff, "The Edible World," *Newsweek*, July 31, 1967, p. 75.
28. See Rumbke, pp. 139–40. The article first appeared in *Skandinavistik* 3 (1973): 39–59.
29. "Das Zeitalter des Holzlöffels—Das Zeitalter der Kartoffel. Eine ergänzende Erwiderung auf E. Rumbkes Interpretation von Hamsuns Roman *Segen der Erde*," in Uecker, II: 162, 164.
30. Klaus von See, "*Segen der Erde*—Idylle oder Utopie," *Skandinavistik* 13 (1983): 6–7.
31. "Innledning til to artikler om Hamsun," *Norskrift* 41 (1983): 9.
32. Øystein Rottem (& Ole Wøide), "Utopi på leirføtter," *Norskrift* 41 (1983): 55.

33. "Knut Hamsun, en polyfon dikter," in *Hamsun i Paris*: 8 foredrag fra Hamsundagene i Paris 1994 (Hamarøy, 1995), p. 120.
34. Harald Næss, "Knut Hamsun and *Growth of the Soil*," *Scandinavica* 25.1 (May, 1986): 16.

Chapter Eight

1. It may not be without interest in this connection that Hamsun had moved from Skogheim at Hamarøy in North Norway to Larvik in the south in 1917, shortly before he started work on *Women at the Pump*. From then one until his death in 1952 he lived in South Norway.
2. For example, a group of raftsmen trying to unscramble a logjam are compared to "ten ants on a twig." For an array of diminutive epithets and images, see *A Wanderer Plays on Muted Strings*, SV, V: 348–52.
3. See Christian Rimestad, "Knut Hamsun og hans nye roman," *Gads danske magasin* 24 (1930): 599, and Carl Nærup, "Knut Hamsun: *Segelfoss By*," in *Ord for dagen*, p. 131.
4. *TLS*, October 25, 1928, p. 778; Cyril Connolly, *The New Statesman*, December 1, 1928, p. 258.
5. This parasitic aspect of Oliver Andersen is anticipated in Hamsun's short story entitled "Small Town Life" (1903), in which an idler named Tønnes Olai assumes paternity for the illegitimate child of a pillar of society, the local consul, for a fee, after threatening to expose his affair with a sea captain's wife. For further information, see Chapter One, note 88, above.
6. John Updike criticizes Hamsun's use of the eye color motif; eventually, he says, it "grows thin as a vaudeville joke." —"Saddled with the World," *The New Yorker*, October 23, 1978, p. 179.
7. Thomas Mann, "*Die Weiber am Brunnen*," p. 622.
8. Atle Kittang has given a deep-probing analysis of what might be called the emotional underground of Hamsun's novel. Since social institutions, such as marriage and fatherhood, have become "empty facades," erotic life has been relegated to "the nightside of town life." —*Luft, vind, ingenting*, pp. 223–24.
9. See *Notes from Underground*, p. 23, and Harald Næss, *Knut Hamsun*, p. 99.
10. Genesis 18:32 & 19:29.
11. This is probably an allusion to the baptism of Jesus. See Matthew 3:16.
12. Henrik Ibsen, *The Complete Major Prose Plays*, trans. Rolf Fjelde (New York: Farrar, Straus & Giroux, 1978), p. 477.
13. Genesis 41:56.
14. Thomas Mann was the first to stress the importance of the art theme. In his review of *Women*, he says that the novel deals with "art as a life-supporting power, with life as art" ("*Die Weiber am Brunnen*," p. 618).
15. Thomas Mann, "Tonio Kröger," in *Death in Venice and Other Stories*, translated and with an Introduction by David Luke (New York: Bantam Books, 1988), p. 156.

16. According to Atle Kittang, who discerns a distinct meta-perspective in the novel, the treatment of the art theme is "ambiguous," in that Hamsun, through his identification with his "unnatural hero," represents the art of narration as "wish fulfillment." Oliver "builds his life on fiction and white lies, but thereby embodies the fundamental structure of all symbolization and creativity." However, a statement by André Green quoted with apparent approval by Kittang, namely, that creative work is predicated on a "wound or loss, a work of mourning, which the text transforms into positive fiction," expresses a viewpoint that approximates that of Thomas Mann just referred to.—*Luft, vind, ingenting*, pp. 251, 254, 261.
17. "T. S. Eliot, *The Complete Poems and Plays, 1909–1950* (New York: Harcourt, Brace & Co., 1958), p. 39.
18. John Updike faults Hamsun for what he calls "darting around and scolding" his characters, on the ground that it diminishes one's interest in them.—*The New Yorker*, October 23, 1978, p. 176.
19. Edwin Muir did not find Hamsun's handling of these intellectuals to be particularly impressive: "Prosy philosophizing is really no more interesting for being spoken by the doctor and postmaster of a small Norwegian town," he wrote in his review, summing up the novel as a "glut of commonplaces."—*The Nation & the Athenaeum*, November 24, 1928, p. 300.
20. Eivind Berggrav, *Kirke og Kultur* 28 (1921): 3, and C. J. Hambro, *Morgenbladet*, December 3, 1920, p. 6, both as quoted by Øystein O. Bentsen, "Menneskesynet i Knut Hamsuns roman *Konerne ved Vandposten*." Thesis, University of Oslo, 1975, p. 18; Poul Levin, *Tilskueren* 37.2 (1920): 485.
21. *The Nation & the Athenaeum*, November 24, 1928, p. 300; *The New Statesman*, December 1, 1928, p. 258; *The Nation*, December 5, 1928, p. 639.
22. "*Die Weiber am Brunnen*," pp. 624, 622.
23. *The New Yorker*, October 23, 1978, p. 179.
24. *The Listener* 100 (December 21 & 28, 1978): 865.
25. This is the translated title that will be used in the text. I find *Chapter the Last* to be needlessly pompous.
26. *The Last Chapter* shares this setting with Thomas Mann's novel *The Magic Mountain*, which appeared one year later, in 1924. While the chronological coincidence of the two works is an intriguing fact of literary history, apart from the setting and a deep preoccupation with mortality, they have little in common. For a comparative study, see Heiko Uecker, "Knut Hamsuns *Siste Kapitel* und Thomas Manns *Der Zauberberg*," *Edda*, 1980, pp. 205–15.
27. 2 Samuel 11:25.
28. Matthew 8:11–12.
29. Matthew 24:6.
30. 2 Peter 3:12.
31. Luke 2:11.
32. Already the second paragraph refers to a situation near the end of the novel, when Daniel, a sort of outlaw at the time, "ruled the mountain." The quoted phrase is repeated when the narrative reaches that point.
33. I have subsequently discovered similar views in the critical literature on Hamsun, from as far back in time as the 1920s. The Swede Carl David Marcus thinks that Hamsun wrote the story of the fire with "real delight," adding that

he "acts like a god" (*Knut Hamsun* [Stockholm, 1926], p. 134). Recently, Øystein Rottem has written that, in the final catastrophe, "the narrator assumes the role of a merciless Yahweh and lets the Flood strike those who by their lifestyle and behavior have broken the covenant with life's and nature's god" ("Hamsuns Dead-End?—Ansatser til en helhetsfortolkning av romanen *Siste Kapitel*," *Edda*, 2000, p. 356).
34. Øystein Rottem puts it this way: "Characteristically enough, her errant imagination will be one of the activating causes of the fire at the sanitarium" ("Hamsuns Dead-End?," pp. 358–59).
35. It is worth noting that Trygve Braatøy, in his insightful psychoanalytic study of Hamsun's works a few years after the publication of *The Last Chapter*, finds the author's technique in the novel to have "much in common with that of the young telegrapher" (*Livets cirkel*, p. 154). In a recent article, Linda H. Nesby has articulated a similar insight in terms of contemporary critical terminology. Miss Ellingsen's stories, Nesby argues, "function as a *mise-en-abysme* for the novel as a whole," endowing it with a "type of self-referentiality" ("Ironi og metafiksjonalitet i *Siste Kapitel*," *Agora*, 1999, nos. 1–2, p. 175), a "metafictional aspect" that has been further developed by Øystein Rottem in "Hamsuns Dead-End?," pp. 357–59.
36. Martin Heidegger, *Sein und Zeit* (Tübingen: Max Niemeyer, 1963), p. 284; see also *Being and Time*, trans. by John Macquarrie & Edward Robinson (New York: Harper & Row, 1962), p. 329.
37. See *Sein und Zeit*, pp. 255–60, *Being and Time*, pp. 299–305.
38. Jean-Paul Sartre, *Nausea*, trans. by Lloyd Alexander (New York: New Directions, 1964), p. 128.
39. Voltaire, *Candide ou l'optimisme*, ed. by Christopher Thacker (Geneva: Librairie Droz, 1968), p. 234.
40. Letter of September 13, 1920, to Christian Kønig, *Brev*, IV: 320.
41. In his review of the novel (*Vor Verden* I.4 [November 1, 1923]: 109), Rolf Hiorth Schøyen writes that in this instance Hamsun "overshoots the target": academic learning, he says, is not "highly respected" in Norway.
42. Aldous Huxley, *Point Counter Point*, with an introd. by Harold H. Watts (New York: Harper & Brothers, 1947), p. 351.
43. Francis Bull reports that, after *The Women at the Pump* and *The Last Chapter*, Hamsun lost his "hold on the public" for a while.—"Knut Hamsun på ny," in *Talt og skrevet* (Oslo, 1956), p. 219.
44. Heinrich Fischer, "The Case of Knut Hamsun," trans. David Maurice Graham, *New Writing and Daylight* 6 (1945): 94.
45. *The Bookman* 70 (November, 1929): 312, and the *NYTBR*, September 22, 1929, p. 9.
46. *Enigma*, p. 274.

Chapter Nine

1. Marie Hamsun, *Regnbuen*, p. 337.
2. Letter to Marie Hamsun of January 6, 1926, *Brev*, V: 32, note 4. Subsequently the Hamsuns continued the therapy together; from December 1926 to April

1927, the whole family lived in the capital. The idea was apparently Hamsun's, judging by a passage in a letter to Marie written June 1, 1926: ". . . you must come here, you need it just as much as your husband; the doctor says it's typical that both need it" (*Brev*, V: 60).
3. *Regnbuen*, p. 351.
4. Letters to Albert Langen of July 25, 1926 (*Brev*, V: 77) and November 2, 1926 (V: 82).
5. Letters to Christian Kønig of September 8, 1927 (*Brev*, V: 129) and October 18, 1927 (V: 140).
6. Letter to Harald Grieg of May 23, 1930, *Brev*, V: 319.
7. Letter to Marie Hamsun of August 7, 1932, *Brev*, V: 448.
8. Letter to Bergljot Hamsun of November 4, 1927, *Brev*, V: 143.
9. Letter to Erik Frydenlund of April 5, 1933, *Brev*, V: 487.
10. Letter to Harald Grieg of October 9, 1933, *Brev*, V: 519.
11. See Allen Simpson, *Knut Hamsuns "Landstrykere"* (Oslo: Gyldendal, 1973) and Øystein Rottem, *Knut Hamsuns "Landstrykere": En ideologikritisk analyse* (Oslo: Gyldendal, 1978).
12. See Jonathan Swift, *Gulliver's Travels*, Part III.
13. Letters to Christian Kønig of September 1, 1927, *Brev*, V: 122, and to Ola Fladmark of February 6, 1928, *Brev*, supplementsbind, p. 174. Hamsun's intent seems rather quixotic in view of his own farming experience and his knowledge of the economic conditions of Norwegian farmers in general. Five days after the letter to Kønig, he writes his brother: "Nobody makes a profit from farming in Norway now; those who have rather large farms and must hire help are bound to lose money, on the small farms, where the whole family helps with the work, it is doable, but barely." Letter to Hans Pedersen of September 6, 1927, *Brev*, V: 128.
14. Letter to Harald Grieg of May 23, 1930, *Brev*, V: 319.
15. Professor Francis Bull traces the temperamental opposites represented by August and Edevart to "two fundamental types" in Scandinavian history, defined by the Swedish romantic poet Erik Gustaf Geijer (1783–1847) as the Viking and the allodial farmer.—"Knut Hamsun på ny," in *Talt og skrevet*, p. 221.
16. I Timothy 6:6.
17. Barbara Gordon Morgridge comments that Lovise Magrete, whether seen through the eyes of Edevart or the author, lacks a "convincing reality." The "ideality" of their first meeting is pitted against the "tawdry reality" of her return, after she has allegedly been corrupted by America. Morgridge detects a clear hint of her having been sexually promiscuous during her residence there.—"Knut Hamsun's Literary Relationship to America," Ph. D. dissertation, University of Washington, 1965, pp. 281, 289–90.
18. "Psykologisk literatur," p. 66.
19. See Rudolph Erich Raspe, *The Travels and Surprising Adventures of Baron Munchausen* (New York, 1988).—Rolf Nyboe Nettum notes that Baron Münchhausen is referred to in Hamsun's teenage novel *Bjørger*; a collection of his tales sits on Bjørger's book shelf ("Ukjente Hamsuntekster," *Edda* 65 [1965]: 33).
20. Proverbs 16:18.

21. Harald Næss calls the murder of Skåro "the most intense single scene" in the entire novel. — *Knut Hamsun*, p. 139.
22. Allen Simpson defines *Vagabonds* as a Bildungsroman *tout court*; as usual, however, traditional categories fall short when one tries to characterize Hamsun's novels. — "Knut Hamsun's Anti-Semitism," *Edda* 77 (1977): 285.
23. Donald C. Riechel suggests that the "button in the snow" signifies Edevart's inability to break free of "childhood ideals." — "Dionysos in Norway. Knut Hamsun's August Trilogy," *Scandinavica* 33.1 (May, 1994): 40.
24. It is worth noting that, in his lecture "Ærer de Unge," Hamsun declared: "History consists of circles and repetitions of the few truths and the many errors" (Knut Hamsun, *Artikler*, p. 100).
25. Several comments have been made on this aspect of *Vagabonds*. Helge Krog sees no explanation why the novel should end; the story, he writes, can begin "at any time," and there is "no reason" to stop (*Meninger om bøker og forfattere*, p. 42). Eivind Berggrav makes the identical point, using the analogy of a merry-go-round to characterize the novel's narrative movement: "Everything goes around, nothing goes forward" (*Kirke og Kultur* 34 [1927]: 49). And Atle Kittang notes that there is no "real end" to the novel" ("Form og begjær i romanen: Om Marthe Robert, Peter Brooks og Knut Hamsuns *Landstrykere*," in *Møtestader* [Oslo, 1988], p. 304).
26. For references to the "broadness" of human nature, see *The Brothers Karamazov* (1991), pp. 108 & 733.
27. Noting that not all parts of *Vagabonds* are written "con amore," Helge Krog singles out the section on Karolus' madness as being one of the "delightful" episodes in the novel (*Meninger om bøker og forfattere*, p. 42).
28. Poul Levin, *Tilskueren* 44.1 (1927): 307.
29. *Meninger om bøker og forfattere*, p. 43.
30. *Life and Letters* 7 (August 1931): 150.
31. "Unrealized Realism," *The Nation* 131 (November 12, 1930): 528.
32. "Hamsun sluter ringen," *BLM* 5 (December, 1936): 797.

Chapter Ten

1. Besides the names of dead people, August's list of signatures also includes those of minors, emigrants and old-time acquaintances. August's defense of the list's inclusiveness has an intriguing similarity to the Russian landowners' eulogies of the "dead souls" they sell to Chichikov. For example, this is how August defends using the name of Joakim's dead father: "I knew your father to be an honest and godfearing man, he would have said yes at the first word" (XI: 22).
2. *A History of Russian Literature*, ed. by Francis J. Whitfield (New York: Vintage Books, 1958), p. 161.
3. See John 7:6.
4. Mark 4: 37–39.
5. Luke 5: 4.

6. Henrik Ibsen, *Peer Gynt*, trans. Rolf Fjelde, 2nd ed. (Minneapolis: University of Minnesota Press, 1980), I.ii. 22.
7. Ibid., V.ii. 161-63.
8. Ibid., V.v. 176-77.
9. *Goethes Faust*, with commentary by Erich Trunz (Hamburg: Christian Wegner Verlag, 1963), ll. 1335-36. — "A part of that power/ which always intends evil but always creates good."
10. Mark 5:1-17.
11. For Freud's view that "[t]he sexual life of civilized man is . . . severely impaired," that "civilization is built up upon a renunciation of instinct," and that "a large part of the psychical energy which it uses for its own purposes has to be withdrawn from sexuality," see *Civilization and Its Discontents*, trans. James Strachey (New York & London: W. W. Norton, 1961), pp. 52, 44, 51.
12. In an intriguing article, Knut Brynhildsvoll argues that Hamsun's portrayal of August and his world meets the requirements of a surrealist text. August's projects, the subject of what he calls the macrotext, obey the same dream logic as his fantastic tales, comprising the so-called intertext, whose improvisational quality brings to mind automatic writing. Thus August's life, empty and alienated, becomes a paradigm of creativity, in that art, in the guise of a liberated imagination, is extended into life, fulfilling the notion of a surrealist *vie poétique*." In consequence, Brynhildsvoll says, Hamsun's text acquires a metapoetic dimension.—"Not und Glanz," in *Sult, sprell og Altmulig*, pp. 130-33.
13. As quoted by Einar Skavlan, *Knut Hamsun*, pp. 217-18, from Hamsun's 1897 lecture "Mot overvurdering av diktere og diktning."
14. Edvard Beyer, "Knut Hamsun," in *Fremmede digtere i det 20. århundrede*, ed. Sven Møller Kristensen, I (København, 1967): 45; Ronald Fangen, *Dagen og veien*, p. 228; Øystein Rottem, "'Havets grøde' og 'Norges jord': Om den ambivalente fortellerholdning i *Landstryker*-trilogien," in *Om "Landstrykere,"* ed. Nils Magne Knutsen (Hamarøy, 1989), p. 14.
15. Knut Hamsun, *On Overgrown Paths* (1999), pp. 88-89.
16. See, for example, Eugenia Kielland, "Et tre-år i norsk skjönnlitteratur," *Ord och Bild* 44 (1935): 429, and Jørgen Bukdahl, "Knut Hamsun," in *Forgyldning og Svinelæder* (København, 1966), p. 41.
17. Knut Brynhildsvoll, comparing August to Charlie Chaplin, expressly states that, like Chaplin, August is a "supratemporal, mythic phenomenon" (*Sult, sprell og Altmulig*, p. 148).
18. From a different viewpoint, several commentators have criticized the bearers of Hamsun's gospel. Willy Dahl finds the "counter values" to August to be "small and weak," and its representatives, the "faithful grubbers," to be "boring and unimaginative" (*Norges litteratur II. Tid og tekst 1884-1935* [Oslo: Aschehoug, 1984], pp. 343-44). Klaus von See considers the message "contrived" and its peasant vehicles, such as Ezra and Joakim, "more colorless than their opposites" ("Knut Hamsun—Naturschwärmer, Herrenmensch, Faschist?," in *Barbar, Germane, Arier* [Heidelberg, 1994], p. 257); and Peter de Mendelssohn observes that the syntheses Hamsun attempted through Joakim and Ezra at the end of *Vagabonds* and *August* (X: 326-29; XI: 254-56) are "clumsy, cobbled together and inadequate" ("Erleuchtung und Verblendung

des Zerrissenen: Versuch über Knut Hamsun," in *Der Geist in der Despotie* [Berlin, 1953], p. 69). Finally, the poet Alf Larsen calls Ezra's gospel a "lie," while August, equated with imagination, is "our supreme divine gift" (*I kunstens tjeneste* [Oslo, 1964], pp. 107–08).
19. "Knut Hamsun's nye roman," *Tilskueren* 47.1 (1930): 251–52.
20. *Dagen og veien*, pp. 225, 227.
21. A less misleading translation of the Norwegian title, *Men livet lever*, would be *Life Springs Eternal*. The title chosen, *The Road Leads On*, is predicated on a linear concept of time, whereas in Hamsun's world time is cyclical rather than linear. The *TLS* reviewer expresses dissatisfaction with the English title for different reasons and prefers the title "Yet Life Goes On," on the ground that it better reproduces the "cynically pessimistic note" of the original (*TLS* 34 [January 31, 1935]: 60).
22. Alf Larsen raised his voice against the novel's denouement, alleging that August was "betrayed" by people and the world. Instead of "omnipotence," Hamsun demonstrated his "impotence" by plunging August into the abyss (*I kunstens tjeneste*, pp. 109–10). Øystein Rottem criticizes the ending on the ground that the flock of sheep is not August's "element"; he is an outsider (*Om "Landstrykere,"* p. 21).
23. Mark 5:2, 13, 15.
24. *Peer Gynt*, I.i. 5–6.
25. A rather special perspective on August as he appears in *The Road Leads On* is offered by the writer Jens Bjørneboe, who calls him an "old child," whose inability to grow up is allegedly a typically Norwegian characteristic ("August den udødelige," in *Politi og anarki* [Oslo, 1972], p. 205).
26. Hans Heiberg notes in his review of *The Road Leads On* that Segelfoss is "unchanged" after twenty years: the grandfathers' age is repeated in that of the grandchildren ("Knut Hamsun," in *Peilinger* [Oslo, 1950], p. 47).
27. In a commentary on this scene in the mountain, Øystein Rottem sees August's feeling of "existential emptiness" as the source of his imagination (*Om "Landstrykere,"* p. 37).
28. Luke 1:28.
29. Sigurd Hoel makes a similar statement about *August*. In his review of the book, he points to the mythic quality of time and change as portrayed by Hamsun. The causality that operates in the novel, he writes, is that of "myth and dream." We are in "dreamland" the whole time (*Arbeiderbladet*, October 1, 1930).
30. Odd Solumsmoen calls the entire *August*-trilogy frescoes of "old life in Nordland" ("Knut Hamsun," in *Norske klassikere* [Oslo: Tiden, 1985], p. 209).
31. Letter to Erik Frydenlund of April 5, 1933, *Brev*, V: 487.
32. Letter to Harald Grieg of August 17, 1933, *Brev*, V: 501.
33. "Hamsuns to siste romaner," in *Dagen og veien*, pp. 231, 233–35.
34. "Knut Hamsun," in *Veien frem*, ed. Odd Hølaas (Oslo, 1947), p. 80.
35. "Hamsuns nye roman," *Gads danske Magasin* 27 (1933): 598, 601.
36. Grace Frank, "An Elemental Novel," *The Saturday Review of Literature* 10 (June 16, 1934): 753.
37. *TLS* 34 (January 31, 1935): 60.
38. *Enigma*, p. 295.

Chapter Eleven

1. Harald Næss, "*Ringen sluttet*: In Defence of Abel Brodersen," in *Facets of European Modernism*: Essays in Honour of James McFarlane, ed. Janet Garton (Norwich: University of East Anglia, 1985), p. 316; Frederik Stjernfelt, "Hvad blir vi som ikke blir noget? Anerkendelsens strukturer i Hamsuns *Ringen sluttet*," *Norskrift* 57 (1988): 24.
2. Artur Lundkvist, seeing Abel as the "Hamsun romantic," says that he remains at a "childish level of development—in perpetual puberty dreams" (*BLM* 5 [December, 1936]: 797).
3. Erik Bjerck-Hagen, "Frihet, spatialitet og tekstualitet i Hamsun. Noen spekulasjoner om 'Dronningen av Saba,' *Børn av Tiden* og *Ringen sluttet*," *Agora*, 1999, nos. 1–2: 91.
4. Matthew 6:26.
5. Letter to G. M. Holst of January 5, 1938, *Brev* VI: 182, with a note by Harald Næss.—Hamsun expressed similar views, at some length, in an article published in the *St. Louis Post Dispatch*, December 12, 1928. Entitled "Festina lente," it contrasts American and Oriental ways and praises "contentment, the ability to do without," as he does in the novel through his portrayal of Abel Brodersen.
6. Erik Bjerck-Hagen suggests that, contrary to his previous stance, Hamsun in *The Ring Is Closed* perhaps explores the *values* of rootlessness," not its "meaninglessness" ("Frihet, spatialitet og tekstualitet i Hamsun," p. 89).
7. Letter to Harald Grieg of June 19, 1936, *Brev*, VI: 152.
8. The allusion is to Sebastian Brandt, *Das Narrenschiff* (1494).
9. See Knut Hamsun, *Hunger* (1998), pp. 187–88.
10. I agree with Jørgen Tiemroth, who finds that Abel's alleged "mediocre intelligence" is "not confirmed by Abel himself, who seems intelligent enough" (*Illusjonens vej* [København: Gyldendal, 1974], p. 286).
11. The psychiatrists who examined Hamsun after World War II cite a statement by their client that he had throughout life been "pursued by elderly ladies."— Gabriel Langfeldt & Ørnulv Ødegård, *Den rettspsykiatriske erklæring om Knut Hamsun* (Oslo: Gyldendal, 1978), p. 85.
12. See above, Chapter One, p. 14.
13. Næss, "*Ringen sluttet*: In Defence of Abel Brodersen," p. 321, note 4.
14. Ibid., 319. See also Aasmund Brynildsen, *Svermeren og hans demon*, p. 82. Walter Baumgartner says that Abel Brodersen "anticipates Kerouac" (*Knut Hamsun* [Reinbek bei Hamburg: Rowohlt, 1997], p. 118).
15. "Hamsuns ånd. Knut Hamsun: *Ringen sluttet*," in *I kunstens tjeneste*, p. 114; "Knut Hamsun," in *Norsk litteraturkritikk 1914–1945*, p. 170.
16. "End of a Saga," *The Nation* 144 (June 15, 1968): 568, 570.
17. "The Return of Peer Gynt," *The New Republic* 91 (August 4, 1937): 371.
18. As quoted from *Dagens nyheter*, August 3, 1959, by Harald Næss in "*Ringen sluttet*: In Defence of Abel Brodersen," p. 320.

Summary Evaluation

1. Hamsun himself appears to have suspected, from quite early on, that his ability as a writer deteriorated with time. See, besides the narrator/author's complaint of waning creative power in *The Last Joy* (1912) (*SV*, VII: 140–42), Hamsun's letter of November 14, 1915, to Christian Kønig, in which he says, "I probably wrote better than now in my youth," and his letter to Peter Nansen of December 10, 1912, where he claims that *A Wanderer* was "much better [than *The Last Joy*]—because I was three to four years younger when I wrote it" (*Brev*, IV: 60; *Brev*, III: 429).
2. In the case of *Dreamers*, the chosen form was obviously influenced by the circumstances of publication: the novel was commissioned as part of a popular fiction series. In a letter to Peter Nansen of June 20, 1904, Hamsun deplores having "ruined a good novel with this library book" (*Brev*, II: 269) because of the constraints imposed by the format.
3. "Der norwegische Romancier Knut Hamsun und sein Beitrag zur europäischen Literatur," in *Auf alten und neuen Pfaden*, II: 110.
4. Letter of January 15, 1929, *Brev*, V: 216; *Letters*, II: 180. The letter appeared under the title "Professor Berendsohn" in the journal *Vor Verden* 6 (1929): 10.
5. "Die Weiber am Brunnen," p. 620.
6. *Brev*, V: 215; "Professor Berendsohn," p. 9; *Letters*, II: 179.
7. As quoted by Olav Storstein, "Litt om Knut Hamsun og 'skuespilleriet,'" *Vinduet* 13.2 (1959): 158, from *Dagbladet*, January 18, 1903.
8. *Fra det moderne Amerikas Aandsliv*, pp. 69, 95.
9. "Hamsun og Hamsun-tradisjonen—'Overdådig av inkonsekvens,'" *Vinduet* 10.3 (1956): 187–88.
10. *Knut Hamsuns egen røst* (Oslo: Gyldendal, 1961), p. 113.
11. *Knut Hamsun og Amerika* (Oslo: Gyldendal, 1969), p. 225.
12. "Nature IV: Language," in *The Complete Essays and Other Writings of Ralph Waldo Emerson*, ed. Brooks Atkinson (New York: The Modern Library, 1950), p. 14.
13. *Fra det moderne Amerikas Aandsliv*, p. 91.
14. "Zu Hamsuns siebzigsten Geburtstag," in *Knut Hamsun: Festskrift til 70-årsdagen 4. august 1929* (Oslo, 1929), p. 131.
15. Lars Roar Langslet, " Rev eller pinnsvin? Hamsun, ideologi og magi," in *Rev eller pinnsvin? Tre essays om Knut Hamsun* (Oslo: Cappelen, 1995), p. 33.—Sigurd Hoel says something similar: "Part of his [Hamsun's] distinctive character consists precisely in the fact that the moods and way of thinking of the years of puberty ... lived more strongly and lasted longer in him than in most people" ("Ved Knut Hamsuns død," in *Essays i utvalg*, ed. Nils Lie [Oslo: Gyldendal, 1977], p. 154).
16. Letter to Johan Bojer of April 17, 1916, *Brev*, IV: 104, note 3.
17. *Knut Hamsun—min far*, p. 239.
18. *Werke in sechs Bänden*, III: 280.
19. "Knut Hamsun," *Vinduet* 13.2 (1959): 139. The article originally appeared in Grieg's journal *Veien frem* in October 1936.

20. Jean Lescoffier ("Lettres norvégiennes," *Mercure de France*, 1930, no. 222, p. 490) finds Hamsun's books to be deficient in ideas, while Odd Solumsmoen ("Knut Hamsun," in *Norske klassikere*, p. 209) deplores the lack of a theoretical basis to his social and cultural criticism.
21. Walter A. Berendsohn, *Knut Hamsun: Das unbändige Ich and die menschliche Gemeinschaft* (München: Albert Langen, 1929), p. 137; Peter de Mendelssohn, "Erleuchtung und Verblendung des Zerrissenen," pp. 77–78. — Mendelssohn's sweeping critique of Hamsun, whose novels he deems "unique in their formlessness . . . in modern literature," does not quite tally with his praise of *Mysteries* as a "complete masterpiece" and with his statement that, with *Hunger*, Hamsun "found his form and language."
22. Quoted by Tore Hamsun, *Knut Hamsun – min far*, p. 330.
23. "Knut Hamsun på ny," in *Talt og skrevet*, p. 213.
24. Arild Hamsun, *Om Knut Hamsun og Nørholm* (Oslo: Aschehoug, 1961), p. 63.
25. Olav Øyslebø, "Hamsuns merkverdige at-setninger, *Maal og Minne*, 1964, p. 64.
26. In my published translation, I chose to undo Hamsun's peculiar blend of discourses, finding it to be a barbarism. The translation reads: "Hartvigsen was very nervous about the Baroness and wished in a loud, clear voice, 'If only the tub were safely indoors!'" (*Rosa* [1997], p. 205).
27. Knut Hamsun, "Kristofer Janson," *Ny Jord* II (July-December, 1988): 384.
28. *Vurderinger* (København, 1962), p. 105.
29. Saul Maloff, "The Edible World," *Newsweek* 70 (July 31, 1967): 76.
30. Letter to Harald Grieg of August 17, 1933, *Brev*, V: 501.

Selected Bibliography

Works by Hamsun

In Norwegian

Artikler. Ed. Francis Bull. Oslo: Gyldendal, 1939.
Bjørger. Fortælling af Knud Pedersen Hamsund. Bodø: Alb. Fr. Knudsen, 1878.
Den Gaadefulde: En Kjærlighedshistorie fra Nordland. Af Kn. Pedersen. Tromsø: M. Urdal, 1877. Rpt. in *Det første jeg fikk trykt*. Ed. Eli Krog. Oslo: Aschehoug, 1950. Pp. 102–21.
Fra det moderne Amerikas Aandsliv. København: Philipsen, 1889. Oslo: Gyldendal, 1962.
Knut Hamsuns brev. Ed. Harald S. Næss. 7 vols. Oslo: Gyldendal, 1994–2001.
Livsfragmenter. Ed. Lars Frode Larsen. Oslo: Gyldendal, 1988.
Paa Turné: Tre foredrag om litteratur. Ed. Tore Hamsun. Oslo: Gyldendal, 1960.
Samlede verker. 8th ed. 1954. 15 vols. Oslo: Gyldendal, 1992.

Translations

Novels

August (*August*, 1930). Trans. Eugene Gay-Tifft. New York: Coward McCann, 1931.
Benoni (*Benoni*, 1908). Trans. Arthur G. Chater. New York: Knopf, 1925.
Chapter the Last (*Siste kapitel*, 1923). Trans. Chater. New York: Knopf, 1929.
Children of the Age (*Børn av tiden*, 1913). Trans. J. S. Scott. New York: Knopf, 1924.
Dreamers (*Sværmere*, 1904). Trans. Tom Geddes. New York: New Directions, 1996. Earlier trans. by W. W. Worster, 1921.
Growth of the Soil (*Markens grøde*, 1917). Trans. Worster. New York: Knopf, 1920.
Hunger (*Sult*, 1890). Trans. with an Essay and Appendix by Sverre Lyngstad and Foreword by Duncan McLean. Edinburgh: Canongate Books, 1996. Earlier trans. by George Egerton, alias Mary Chavelita Dunne (1899) and Robert Bly (1967).
Hunger. Trans. with an Introd. and Notes by Sverre Lyngstad. New York: Penguin, 1998.

The Last Joy (*Den siste glæde*, 1912). Trans. Sverre Lyngstad. København & Los Angeles: Green Integer, 2003. Trans. as *Look Back on Happiness* (1940) by Paula Wiking.
Mysteries (*Mysterier*, 1892). Trans. with an Introd. and Notes by Sverre Lyngstad. New York: Penguin, 2001. Earlier trans. by Chater (1927) and Gerry Bothmer (1971).
Pan (*Pan*, 1894). Trans. with an Introd. and Notes by Sverre Lyngstad. New York: Penguin, 1998. Earlier trans. by Worster (1920) and James W. McFarlane (1955).
The Ring Is Closed (*Ringen sluttet*, 1936). Trans. Gay-Tifft. New York: Coward McCann, 1934.
The Road Leads On (*Men livet lever*, 1933). Trans. Gay-Tifft. New York: Coward McCann, 1934.
Rosa (*Rosa*, 1908). Trans. Sverre Lyngstad. Los Angeles: Sun & Moon Press, 1997. Earlier trans. by Chater (1925).
Segelfoss Town (*Segelfoss by*, 1915). Trans. Scott. New York: Knopf, 1925.
Shallow Soil (*Ny jord*, 1893). Trans. Carl Christian Hyllested. New York: Scribner, 1914.
Under the Autumn Star (*Under høststjernen*, 1906). Trans. Oliver Stallybrass. Los Angeles: Sun & Moon Press, 1998. Earlier published, together with *A Wanderer Plays on Muted Strings*, as *The Wanderer* (New York: Farrar, Straus & Giroux, 1975). First English version of the two novels, by Worster, appeared under the title *Wanderers* (1922).
Victoria (*Victoria*, 1898). Trans. Oliver Stallybrass. Los Angeles: Sun & Moon, 1994. Earlier trans. by Chater (1923).
A Wanderer Plays on Muted Strings (*En vandrer spiller med sordin*, 1909). Trans. Oliver & Gunnvor Stallybrass. København & Los Angeles: Green Integer, 2001. For earlier trans., see *Under the Autumn Star*, above.
Wayfarers (*Landstrykere*, 1927). Trans. James W. McFarlane. Los Angeles: Sun & Moon Press, 1995. Initially published by Farrar, Straus & Giroux, 1980. Earlier trans. as *Vagabonds* (1930) by Gay-Tifft.
The Women at the Pump (*Konerne ved vandposten*, 1920). Trans. Oliver and Gunnvor Stallybrass. Los Angeles: Sun & Moon Press, 1996. Initially published by Farrar, Straus & Giroux, 1978. Earlier trans. by Chater (1928).

Other Works

"August Strindberg." *America* (Chicago), December 20, 1888, pp. 29–31.
The Cultural Life of Modern America. Trans. Barbara Gordon Morgridge. Cambridge: Harvard UP, 1969.
"Festina lente." *St. Louis Post Dispatch*, December 12, 1928.
In Wonderland (*I æventyrland*, 1903). Trans. with an Introd. and Notes by Sverre Lyngstad. New York: Ig Publishing, 2004.
Night Roamers and Other Stories (*Livsfragmenter*, 1988). Trans. Tiina Nunnally. Seattle: Fjord Press, 1992.
On Overgrown Paths (*På gjengrodde stier*, 1949). Trans. and with Notes by Sverre Lyngstad. København & Los Angeles: Green Integer, 1999.

Selected Letters. Ed. Harald S. Næss & James McFarlane. 2 vols. Norwich: Norvik Press, 1990, 1998.
Tales of Love and Loss. Trans. with an Introd. by Robert Ferguson. London: Souvenir Press, 1997.

Hamsun Biography and Criticism

Alm, Kristian. "Knut Hamsuns *Sult*: Å fremkalle ord av tomhet." *Kirke og Kultur* 94 (1989): 403–27.
Alverdes, Paul. "Knut Hamsun: Zu seinem 75. Geburtstag." *Das innere Reich* I (August, 1934): 616–29.
Arntzen, Even. "Hamsun og Strindberg." In *Hamsun og Norden*. Ni foredrag fra Hamsun-dagene på Hamarøy, 1992. Ed. Nils M. Knutsen. Hamarøy: Hamsun-Selskapet, 1992. Pp. 13–32.
Bale, Kjersti. "Hamsuns hvite hest. Om *Victoria*." *Edda*, 1997, pp. 292–302.
Barksdale, E. C., & Daniel Popp. "Hamsun and Pasternak: The Development of Dionysian Tragedy." *Edda* 76 (1976): 343–51.
Baumgartner, Walter. "Intertextuelle Mysterien: Hamsun, Brandes und Dostojewski." In *Ästhetik der skandinavischen Moderne*. Ed. Annegret Heitmann & Karin Hoff. Bernhard Glienke zum Gedenken. Frankfurt am Main: Peter Lang, 1998. Pp. 301–25.
———. *Knut Hamsun*. Reinbek bei Hamburg: Rowohlt, 1997.
———. "Nagel und Minute im kommunikativen Clinch." In *Der nahe Norden*, ed. Wolfgang Butt & Bernhard Glienke. Festschrift for Otto Oberholzer's 65. Birthday. Frankfurt am Main, 1985. Pp. 251–72.
Berendsohn, Walter. *Knut Hamsun: Das unbändige Ich und die menschliche Gemeinschaft*. München: Albert Langen, 1929.
Berg, Leo. "Knut Hamsun." In *Zwischen zwei Jahrhunderten*. Frankfurt am Main, 1896. Pp. 100–29.
Beyer, Edvard. *Hamsun og vi*. Oslo: Aschehoug, 1959.
———. "Hamsun und das Hamsun-Problem." *Nordeuropa* 11 (1978): 49–65.
———. "Knut Hamsun." In *Fremmede digtere i det 20. århundrede*. Ed. Sven Møller Kristensen. Vol. I (København, 1967): 29–49.
———. "Knut Hamsuns *Mysterier*." In *Profiler og problemer* (Oslo: Aschehoug, 1966), pp. 38–58. Rpt. in *Søkelys på Knut Hamsuns 90-års diktning*. Ed. Øystein Rottem. Oslo: Universitetsforlaget, 1979. Pp. 122–37.
Beyer, Harald. "Knut Hamsun." In *Nietzsche og Norden*, vol. II (Bergen: Universitetet i Bergen, Årbok, 1959): 94–106.
Bien, Horst. "Knut Hamsuns vei fra krisen til katastrofen. *Edda* 76 (1976): 129–38.
Bolckmans, Alex. "Henry Miller's *Tropic of Cancer* and Knut Hamsun's *Sult*." *Scandinavica* 14 (1975): 115–26.
———. *Individu en maatschappij in het werk van Knut Hamsun*. Antwerpen, 1967.
———. "Knut Hamsuns August-trilogie: Een picareske roman?" *Studies in Skandinavistiek* (Groningen: Brouwer International, 1977), pp. 103–19. Festschrift for Amy van Marken.

———. "Le Romancier norvégien Knut Hamsun et sa contribution à la littérature européenne." Etudes germaniques 28 (1973): 433-43. German version in Heiko Uecker, ed. Auf alten und neuen Pfaden II (Frankfurt a. M.: Peter Lang, 1983): 97-111.
Borgen, Johan. "Nagel." Vinduet 13 (1959): 118-28. Rpt. in Ord gjennom år (Oslo: Gyldendal, 1966), pp. 174-88.
Boyer, Régis, & Jean-Marie Paul, eds. Présence de Knut Hamsun. Nancy: Presses Universitaires, 1994.
Brandes, Edvard. "Knut Hamsun: Mysterier, 1892." In Litterære Tendenser: Artikler og Anmeldelser, ed. Carl Bergstrøm-Nielsen (København, 1968). Pp. 125-29.
Brandes, Georg. "Knut Hamsun. Et kritisk essay." Edda, 1990, pp. 118-27. Afterword to a 1911 Russian edition of Hamsun's Collected Works (vol. 13), trans. from the Russian by Martin Nag.
Breiteig, Byrge. "Det erotiske i Sult." Edda 72 (1972): 329-35.
Briseid, Audun. "Opprør og tilpasning: En strukturell studie av Knut Hamsuns Mysterier." Thesis, University of Oslo, 1977.
Brynhildsvoll, Knut. "Hamsun auf den Kopf gestellt: Plädoyer für eine neue Lesart des Romans Sult." In Arbeiten zur Skandinavistik, ed. Heinrich Beck. Frankfurt am Main: Peter Lang, 1985. Pp. 21-43. Rpt. in Sult, sprell og Altmulig, 91-107.
———. "Not und Glanz: Metapoetische Aspekte in Knut Hamsuns August-Trilogie— im Lichte surrealistischer Kunstanschauungen." Skandinavistik 19. 2 (1989): 81-99. Rpt. in Sult, sprell og Altmulig, pp. 127-48.
———. Sult, sprell og Altmulig. Alte und neue Studien zu Knut Hamsuns antipsychologischer Romankunst. Frankfurt am Main: Peter Lang, 1998.
Brynildsen, Aasmund. Svermeren og hans demon. Oslo: Dreyer, 1973.
Braatøy, Trygve. Livets cirkel: Bidrag til analyse av Knut Hamsuns diktning. 1929. Oslo: Cappelen, 1954.
Bull, Francis, et al., eds. Knut Hamsun: Festskrift til 70-aarsdagen 4. august 1929. Oslo: Gyldendal, 1929.
Burkhardt, Hans. "Hamsun und die skandinavische Welt." Die Waldhütte 31 (October-December 1971): 5-15.
———. "Das ironische Verhältnis zum Fortschritt und zum Tod bei Hamsun (Das letzte Kapitel) und bei Thomas Mann (Der Zauberberg)." Die Waldhütte 41 (April-June 1974): 4-19.
Buttry, Dolores. "The Friendly Stone: Hamsun's Pathetic Fallacy." Edda, 1979, pp. 151-56.
———. "Music and the Musician in the Works of Knut Hamsun." Scandinavian Studies 53 (1981): 171-82.
———. "The Passive Personality: Hamsun's Hamlets." Symposium 36. 2 (1982): 99-114.
———. "Perception of the Physical World: Jean-Jacques Rousseau, Knut Hamsun, and Nature." Edda, 1981, pp. 347-58.
———. "A Thirst for Intimacy: Knut Hamsun's Pyromania." Scandinavica 26 (1987): 129-39.
Cease, Julia K. "Semiotics, City, Sult: Hamsun's Text of 'hunger.'" Edda, 1992, pp. 136-46.
Christensen, Hjalmar. "Knut Hamsun." In Unge Nordmænd: Et kritisk Grundrids. Christiania: Aschehoug, 1893. Pp. 117-42.

Dahl, Willy. "Knut Hamsun og datteren på Sirilund." In *Perspektiver: Essays om norske klassikere.* Bergen: Eide, 1968. Pp. 55–81.
———. *Stil og struktur.* Oslo: Universitetsforlaget, 1965.
Dingstad, Ståle. *Hamsuns strategier: Realisme, humor og kynisme.* Oslo: Gyldendal, 2003.
Doma, Akos. *Die andere Moderne: Knut Hamsun, D. H. Lawrence und die lebensphilosophische Strömung des literarischen Modernismus.* Bonn: Bouvier Verlag, 1995.
Downs, Brian. *Modern Norwegian Literature 1860–1918.* Cambridge, Engl.: Cambridge UP, 1966. Pp. 174–88.
Dragvoll, Johan. "Hamsun, *Pan* og Schopenhauer." *Edda*, 2000, pp. 15–25.
Eddy, Beverley D. "Hamsun's *Victoria* and Munch's *Livsfrisen*: Variations on a Theme." *Scandinavian Studies* 48 (1976): 156–68.
Edschmied, Kasimir. "Hamsun und die europäische Literatur" (1920). In *Frühe Manifeste* (Hamburg, 1957), pp. 44–62. Rpt. in *Auf alten und neuen Pfaden* II: 1–19.
Eggen, Einar. "Mennesket og tingene: Hamsuns *Sult* og 'den nye roman,'" In *Norsk litterær årbok*, 1966, pp. 82–106. Rpt. in *Søkelys på Knut Hamsuns 90-årsdiktning.* Oslo: Universitetsforlaget, 1979. Pp. 55–76. German version, "Der Mensch und die Dinge," in *Auf alten und neuen Pfaden* II: 43–70.
Endres, Fritz. *Knut Hamsun: Welt und Erde.* Tübingen, 1931.
Enright, D. J. "Blossoms and Blood: On Knut Hamsun." In *Man Is an Onion.* London: Chatto & Windus, 1972. Pp. 52–58.
Epifani, Silvia de Cesaris. "Una rilettura di *Pan*." *Istituto orientale di Napoli. Annali, Sezione Germanica* 8 (1965): 175–200.
Eriksen, Anita Sævik. "Epilogen i Knut Hamsuns *Pan* med hovudvekt på vandrarfiguren." *Eigenproduksjon* 19 (1983): 75–86.
Evensen, Per Arne. "'L'orgue saigne' où le démon de l'écriture." Trans. Régis Boyer. In *Présence de Hamsun*, pp. 73–94.
Fechner-Smarsly, Thomas. *Die Wiederkehr der Zeichen. Eine psychoanalytische Studie zu Knut Hamsun's "Hunger."* Frankfurt am Main: Peter Lang, 1991.
Fechter, Paul. *Knut Hamsun.* Gütersloh, 1952.
Ferguson, Robert. *Enigma: The Life of Knut Hamsun.* New York: Farrar, Straus & Giroux, 1987.
Fischer, Heinrich. "Die Welt Knut Hamsuns." *Neue Schweizer Rundschau*, New Series 18.2 (June 1950): 83–94.
Friederich, Reinhard H. "Kafka and Hamsun's *Mysteries*." *Comparative Literature* 28 (1976): 34–50.
Friese, Wilhelm. "Hamsun und der Jugendstil." *Edda* 67 (1967): 427–49. Rpt. in *Auf alten und neuen Pfaden* II: 71–96.
Fürstenberg, Hilde. "Die Frauengestalten in Knut Hamsuns Werk und Leben." *Die Waldhütte* 27 (October-December, 1970): 1–26. Appeared separately as *Die Frauengestalten in Werk und Leben Knut Hamsuns.* Mölln in Lauenburg, 1971.
Gabrieli, Mario. "Knut Hamsun." *Rivista di letterature moderne e comparate* 3 (1952): 41–48.
Giersing, Morten, John Thobo-Carlsen, & Mikael Westergaard-Nielsen. *Det reaktionære oprør: Om fascismen i Hamsuns forfatterskab.* København: GMT, 1975.
Gimnes, Steinar. "Knut Hamsun: *Benoni* og *Rosa*." *Edda* 76 (1976): 139–47.
Glette, Kåre. "Isak Sellanrå – ein truverdig figur?" *Ventil* 4.1 (1974): 10–13.

Gorki, Maxim. "Knut Hamsun." *The Adelphi* 2.11 (April 1925): 887-91.
Gouchet, Olivier. "*Børn av Tiden* av Knut Hamsun og *Buddenbrooks* av Thomas Mann." *Hamsun i Paris*: 8 foredrag fra Hamsun-dagene i Paris 1994. Ed. Régis Boyer & Nils M. Knutsen. Hamarøy: Hamsun-Selskapet, 1995. Pp. 55-68.
Granaas, Rakel Kristina. "Ironi of ideologi: Ein analyse av Knut Hamsuns *Børn av Tiden*." *Norsk litterær årbok*, 1979, pp. 56-76. German rpt., "Ironie und Ideologie: Eine Analyse von Knut Hamsuns *Kinder der Zeit*," in *Auf alten und neuen Pfaden*, II: 295-318.
Gustafson, Alrik. "Man and the Soil: Knut Hamsun." In *Six Scandinavian Novelists*. Princeton: Princeton UP, 1940. Pp. 226-85.
Hagen, Erik Bjerck. "Frihet, spatialitet og tekstualitet i Hamsun: Noen spekulasjoner om 'Dronningen av Saba,' *Børn av Tiden* og *Ringen sluttet*." *Agora*, 1999, 1-2: 67-95.
Hamsun, Arild. "Ein Dichter und sein Verfolger." *Die Waldhütte* 46 (July-September 1975): 1-15.
———. *Om Knut Hamsun og Nørholm*. Oslo: Aschehoug, 1953.
———, ed. *Ni artikler om Knut Hamsun*. Arendal, 1976.
Hamsun, Tore. *Knut Hamsun – min far*. 1952. Oslo: Gyldendal, 1992. German translation: München, 1953.
Haugan, Jörgen. "Knut Hamsun – det ubevisstes poesi." *Nordisk tidskrift för vetenskap, konst och industri*, New Series 49 (1973): 36-51.
Haugstvedt, Børge. "Forholdet mellom vandrer og fastboende i Knut Hamsuns *Ringen sluttet*." Thesis, University of Oslo, 1976.
Herzfeld, Marie. "Knut Hamsun." In *Menschen und Bücher*. Wien, 1893. Pp. 54-71.
Hitschmann, Eduard. "Ein Gespenst aus der Kindheit Knut Hamsuns." *Imago* (Vienna) 12 (1924): 336-60. Rpt. in *Auf alten und neuen Pfaden* I: 1-29.
———. "Knut Hamsun und die Psychoanalyse." *Die psychoanalytische Bewegung* I (1929): 318-24.
———. "Von, um und über Hamsun." *Imago* 14 (1928): 358-63.
Hoel, Sigurd. *Knut Hamsun*. Kristiania: Olaf Norli, 1920.
———. "Knut Hamsun: Til 70-årsdagen." *Samtiden* 40 (1929): 339-52. Rpt. in "Les 70 ans de Knut Hamsun." *Europe* 21, no. 81 (September 15, 1929): 5-20, and in *Essays i utvalg*, ed. Nils Lie. Oslo: Gyldendal, 1972. Pp. 132-48.
Holm, Birgitta. "Hamsuns *Mysterier*." In *Hamsun og Norden*, pp. 105-19.
———. "Den manliga läsningens mysterier: Knut Hamsuns roman 100 år efteråt." *Edda*, 1992, pp. 261-71.
Humpál, Martin. *The Roots of Modernist Narrative: Knut Hamsun's Novels "Hunger," "Mysteries" and "Pan."* Oslo: Solum Forlag, 1998.
Haaland, Arild. *Hamsun: Spenninger og slør*. Illus. Oslo: Universitetsforlaget, 1987.
———. "Knut Hamsun: Kontakt, konflikt og tragedie." In *Hamsun og Hoel: To studier i kontakt*. Bergen: John Griegs Forlag, 1957. Pp. 45-98.
Ingwersen, Faith, & Mary Kay Norseng, eds. *Fin(s) de Siècle in Scandinavian Perspective: Studies in Honor of Harald Næss*. Columbia, SC, 1993.
Jacob, Hans. "Knut Hamsun und Thomas Mann: Eine kunstwissenschaftliche Untersuchung an Hand der Romane *Das letzte Kapitel* und *Der Zauberberg*." *Philosophischer Anzeiger* 3 (1928-29): 200-42.
Jensen, Johannes V. "Knut Hamsun." In *Den ny verden*. Kjøbenhavn & Kristiania, 1907. Pp. 175-86.

Johnsen, Egil Eiken. *Stilpsykiske studier i 1890-årenes norske litteratur*. Oslo: Gyldendal, 1949.

Kanthack-Neufelder, Katharina. "Idee und Form im Werke Knut Hamsuns." *Zeitschrift für Ästhetik und allgemeine Kunstwissenschaft* 33.3 (1939): 202–25. Rpt. in *Auf alten und neuen Pfaden* I: 73–101.

Kaunas, Tarmo. "Knut Hamsun og Nietzsche." In *Hamsun i Paris*, pp. 27–37.

Ketelsen, Uwe-K. " Das Zeitalter des Holzlöffels—Das Zeitalter der Kartoffel. Eine ergänzende Erwiderung auf E. Rumbkes Interpretation von Hamsuns Roman *Segen der Erde*." In *Auf alten und neuen Pfaden* II: 159–65.

Kirkegaard, Peter. *Knut Hamsun som modernist*. København, 1975.

Kittang, Atle. "Form og begjær i romanen: Om Marthe Robert, Peter Brooks og Knut Hamsuns *Landstrykere*." *Møtestader*. Oslo 1988. Pp. 301–35.

———. "Knut Hamsun's *Sult*: Psychological Deep Structures and Metapoetic Plot." In *Facets of European Modernism*. Ed. Janet Garton. Norwich: University of East Anglia, 1985. Pp. 295–308. Festschrift for Walter McFarlane.

———. *Luft, vind, ingenting: Hamsuns desillusjonsromanar frå "Sult" til "Ringen sluttet."* Oslo: Gyldendal, 1984.

Knudsen, Jørgen. "Knut Hamsuns dilemma." *Dansk Udsyn* 43 (1963): 248–60.

Knutsen, Nils M. "Eine nordnorwegische Feudalgesellschaft: Eine Analyse der sozialen Machtstruktur in Knut Hamsuns *Benoni* und *Rosa*." *Skandinavistik* 4 (1974): 25–36.

———. *Makt-avmakt: En studie av Hamsuns "Benoni" og "Rosa."* Oslo: Aschehoug, 1975.

Kolloen, Ingar Sletten. *Hamsun: Svermeren*. Oslo: Gyldendal, 2003.

Landquist, John. "Hamsuns Held und Dostojevskijs Gestalten." *Die Waldhütte* 40 (January-March 1974): 2–5.

———. *Knut Hamsun: Hans Levnad och verk*. 1917. Enl. & rev. ed. Stockholm, 1929. German ed. Tübingen: Fischer, 1927.

Lange, Wolfgang. "Hamsuns Elementargeister." *Euphorion* 50 (1956): 328–40. Rpt. in *Auf alten und neuen Pfaden* I: 157–73.

Langslet, Lars Roar. *Rev eller pinnsvin? Tre essays om Knut Hamsun*. Oslo: Cappelen, 1995.

Larsen, Hanna Astrup. *Knut Hamsun*. New York: Knopf, 1922.

Larsen, Lars Frode. "Dikteren og døden: En studie i Knut Hamsuns forfatterskap og livssyn." Thesis, University of Oslo, 1980.

———. *Den unge Hamsun, 1859–1888*. Oslo: Schibsted, 1998.

Lavrin, Janko. "The Return of Pan." In *Aspects of Modernism*. London: S. Nott, 1935. Freeport, N. Y.: Books for Libraries Press, 1968. Pp. 93–111.

Lien, Asmund. "Pans latter." *Edda*, 1993, pp. 131–37.

Lowenthal, Leo. "Knut Hamsun." In *Literature and the Image of Man*. Boston: Beacon Press, 1957. Pp. 190–220.

Löwenthal, Leo. "Knut Hamsun: Zur Vorgeschichte der autoritären Ideologie." *Zeitschrift für Sozialforschung* 6 (1937): 295–345.

Magris, Claudio. "Gefangener der Vitalität." In *Werkbuch über Tankred Dorst*. Ed. Horst Laube. Frankfurt: Suhrkampf, 1975. Pp. 181–205. Italian version, "Il prigioniero della vitalità." In *Dietro le parole*. Milano, 1978. Pp. 78–86.

———. "Zwischen den Spalten des Ichs. Hamsuns *Mysterien*." *Edda* 78 (1978): 345–54. Rpt. in *Auf alten und neuen Pfaden* I: 319–32.

Marcus, David. *Knut Hamsun*. Stockholm: Fahlcrantz, 1926.
Marken, Amy van. *Knut Hamsun*. Illus. Groningen, 1977.
Marstrander, Jan. *Det ensomme menneske i Knut Hamsuns diktning: Betraktninger omkring "Mysterier" og et motiv*. Oslo: Det Norske Studentersamfunds kulturutvalg, 1959.
———. "Von den *Weibern am Brunnen* zu *Der Ring schliesst sich*. Ein Essay über die sozialen Romane Knut Hamsuns." In *Auf alten und neuen Pfaden* I: 217–45.
Mazor, Yair. "The Epilogue in Knut Hamsun's *Pan*." *Edda*, 1984, pp. 313–28.
McFarlane, James W. "Knut Hamsun." In *Ibsen and the Temper of Norwegian Literature*. London: Oxford UP, 1960. Pp. 114–57.
———. "The Whisper of the Blood: A Study of Knut Hamsun's Early Novels." *PMLA* 71 (1956): 563–94.
Mendelssohn, Peter de. "Erleuchtung und Verblendung des Zerrissenen: Versuch über Knut Hamsun." In *Der Geist in der Despotie*. Berlin: F. A. Herbig, 1953. Pp. 17–121. Partial rpt. in *Auf alten und neuen Pfaden* I: 123–56.
Miller, Henry. "*Mysteries*." Review of Gerry Bothmer's translation in *NYTBR*, August 22, 1971, pp. 1, 30.
Mishler, William. "Ignorance, Knowledge and Resistance to Knowledge in Hamsun's *Sult*." *Edda* 74 (1974): 161–77.
Morburger, Carl (pseud. for Josef Schossberger). *Knut Hamsun*. Leipzig, 1910. Norwegian edition (Kristiania & Kjøbenhavn: Gyldendal, 1910), trans. by Einar Skavlan.
Morgridge, Barbara Gordon. "Knut Hamsun's Literary Relationship to America." Ph. D. dissertation, University of Washington, 1965.
Musarra-Schrøder, Ulla. "Monologisk og dialogisk fremstilling i *Sult*." In *Studies in Skandinavistiek*, pp. 137–50.
———. "Tankegengivelsen i *Sult*: Et bidrag til jeg-fortællingens teori." *Edda* 74 (1974): 145–59.
Myhr, Petter. "Raskolnikovs fornuft og Nagels mysterier." *Ergo* 13.4 (1982): 203–15.
Nag, Martin. "*Forbrytelse og straff* i norsk litteratur." In *Dostojevskijs roman om Raskolnikov*. Ed. Geir Kjetsaa. Oslo, 1973. Pp. 154–75.
———. *Hamsun i russisk åndsliv*. Oslo: Gyldendal, 1969.
Nesby, Linda H. "Ironi og metafiksjonalitet i *Siste kapitel*." *Agora*, 1999, 1–2: 151–78.
Nettum, Rolf Nyboe. "Fantasiens grøde: Et aspekt ved Knut Hamsuns diktning." *Nordisk tidskrift för vetenskap, konst och industri*, New series 56 (1980): 89–96.
———. *Konflikt og visjon: Hovedtemaer i Knut Hamsuns forfatterskap 1890–1912*. Oslo: Gyldendal, 1970.
Nilson, Sten Sparre. *En ørn i uvær*. Oslo: Gyldendal, 1960. German trans.: *Knut Hamsun und die Politik*. Villingen: Ring-Verlag, 1964.
Nilsson, Nils Åke. "Hamsun och Dostojevskij." In *Hamsun og Norden*, pp. 55–68.
Norseng, Mary Kay. "The Startling Vagueness of Knut Pedersen (From an American Point of View)." *Edda*, 1979, pp. 157–73.
Nybø, Gregory. *Knut Hamsuns "Mysterier"*. Oslo: Gyldendal, 1969.
Nærup, Carl. "Knut Hamsun." In *Illustreret norsk litteraturhistorie*. Siste tidsrum: 1890–1904. Kristiania, 1905. Pp. 91–121.
———. "Knut Hamsun." In *Skildringer og stemninger fra den yngre litteratur*. Kristiania, 1897. Pp. 1–56.

Næss, Harald. "American Attitudes to Knut Hamsun." In *Americana Norvegica* III: Studies in Scandinavian-American Interrelations. Dedicated to Einar Haugen. Ed. Harald S. Næss & Sigmund Skard. Oslo: Universitetsforlaget, 1971. Pp. 338–60.

———. "Der Fall Hamsun," in *Faschismus und Avantgarde*, ed. Reinhold Grimm & Jost Hermand. Königstein, 1980. Pp. 66–82.

———. *Knut Hamsun*. Boston: Twayne, 1984.

———. "Knut Hamsun and America." *Scandinavian Studies* 39 (1967): 305–28.

———. "Knut Hamsun and *Growth of the Soil*." *Scandinavica* 25 (1986): 5–17.

———. *Knut Hamsun og Amerika*. Oslo: Gyldendal, 1969.

———. "*Ringen sluttet*: In Defence of Abel Brodersen." In *Facets of European Modernism*, pp. 309–22.

———. "A Strange Meeting and Hamsun's *Mysteries*." *Scandinavian Studies* 36 (1964): 48–58.

———. "Strindberg and Hamsun." In *Structures of Influence: A Comparative Approach to August Strindberg*. Ed. Marilyn Johns Blackwell. Chapel Hill: University of NC, 1981. Pp. 121–36.

———. "The Three Hamsuns: The Changing Attitude in Present Criticism." *Scandinavian Studies* 32 (1960): 129–39.

———. "Who Was Hamsun's Hero?" In *The Hero in Scandinavian Literature*. Ed. John M. Weinstock & Robert T. Rovinsky. Austin: University of Texas Press, 1975. Pp. 63–86.

Nørgaard, Felix. *Knut Hamsun*. København, 1940.

Oudry-Henrioud, Béatrice. "Le Personnage féminin de Knut Hamsun: Son évolution." Dissertation, University of Paris-Sorbonne, Paris IV, 1988.

Popperwell, Ronald G. "Critical Attitudes to Knut Hamsun, 1890–1969." *Scandinavica* 9 (1970): 1–23.

———. "Interrelatedness in Hamsun's *Mysterier*." *Scandinavian Studies* 38 (1966): 295–301.

———. "Knut Hamsun and *Pan*." *Scandinavica* 25 (1986): 19–31.

Przybyszewski, Stanislaw. "*Mysterien*." *Die Zukunft* (Berlin) 8 (1894): 603–09.

Reinartz, Hubert. *Der junge Hamsun*. Berlin, 1936.

Rekdal, Bjarte. "I Grenseland: Hamsuns Abel i eit psykoanalytisk perspektiv." *Edda*, 1989, pp. 233–41.

Riechel, Donald C. "Dionysos in Norway: Knut Hamsun's August Trilogy." *Scandinavica* 33 (1994): 23–44.

———. "Knut Hamsun's 'Imp of the Perverse': Calculation and Contradiction in *Sult* and *Mysterier*." *Scandinavica* 28 (1989): 29–53.

Rottem, Øystein. *Hamsun og fantasiens triumf*. Oslo: Gyldendal, 2002.

———. "Hamsuns *Dead-End*? Ansatser til en helhetsfortolkning av romanen *Siste kapitel*." *Edda*, 2000, pp. 346–60. Rpt. in *Hamsun og fantasiens triumf*, pp. 168–94.

———. "'Havets grøde' og 'Norges jord.' Om den ambivalente fortellerholdning i *Landstryker*-trilogien." In *Om "Landstrykere"*. Ed. Nils M. Knutsen. Hamarøy: Hamsun-Selskapet, 1989. Pp. 7–38. Rpt. in *Hamsun og fantasiens triumf*, pp. 195–226.

———. "'*Humbug*, cela aussi, rien que *humbug, humbug* de décadence moderne...': Nietzsche, Hamsun et la grande illusion." In *Présence de Knut Hamsun*, pp. 15–35. Rpt., in Norwegian, in *Hamsun og fantasiens triumf*, pp. 68–89.

———. *Knut Hamsuns "Landstrykere."* En ideologikritisk analyse. Oslo: Gyldendal, 1978.

———. "*Pan*: en høysang til kjærligheten eller Tristan i jegerkostyme." In "*Pan*," *handelsstedene, novellene, illustrasjonene*. Ed. Nils M. Knutsen. Tromsø: University of Tromsø, 1986. Pp. 9–44. Rpt. in *Hamsun og fantasiens triumf*, pp. 90–124.

———, ed. *Søkelys på Knut Hamsuns 90-årsdiktning*. Oslo: Universitetsforlaget, 1979.

Rottem, Øystein (& Ole Wøide). "Utopi på leirføtter." *Norskrift* 41 (1983): 13–64. New version in *Hamsun og fantasiens triumf*, pp. 125–67.

Rumbke, Eberhard. "'Træskeens Tidsalder': Regressive Gesellschaftskritik in Knut Hamsuns Roman *Markens grøde*." *Skandinavistik* 3 (1973): 39–59. Rpt. in *Auf alten und neuen Pfaden* II: 135–57.

Sandberg, Hans-Joachim. "König Midas und der Zauberer oder die Weisheit des Silenos. Von der 'Sympathie' mit dem Tode zum 'Lob der Vergänglichkeit': Knut Hamsun und Thomas Mann." In *Thomas-Mann Studien* 7 (Bern, 1987): 174–212.

Sehmsdorf, Henning K. "Knut Hamsun's *Pan*: Myth and Symbol." *Edda* 74 (1974): 345–93.

Seiler, Thomas. "Knut Hamsuns *Pan* als patriarchaler Schöpfer-Mythos." *Edda*, 1995, pp. 267–77.

Simpson, Allen. "Hamsun and Camus: Consciousness in *Markens grøde* and *The Myth of Sisyphus*." *Scandinavian Studies* 48 (1976): 272–83.

———. *Knut Hamsuns "Landstrykere."* Trans. Jan Fr. Marstrander. Oslo: Gyldendal, 1973.

———. "Midt i Forgjængelsens Karneval: *Markens grøde* in Knut Hamsun's Authorship." *Scandinavian Studies* 56 (1984): 1–35.

———. "Theme and Narrative Perspective in Knut Hamsun's *Landstrykere*." Dissertation, University of California, Berkeley, 1968.

Skagen, Axel. "Den aldrende vandrers vei mot resignasjon: Bidrag til analyse av Knut Hamsuns 'vandrer-trilogi'." Thesis, University of Oslo, 1966.

Skavlan, Einar. *Knut Hamsun*. Oslo: Gyldendal, 1929.

Soleim, Kjell R. "Kristianias merke: En studie i Hamsuns *Sult*." *Edda*, 1987, pp. 141–56.

Stenström, Thure. "Gammal och ny Hamsun-forskning." *Samlaren* 94 (1973): 41–69.

Stjernfelt, Frederik. "Hvad blir vi som ikke blir noget? Anerkendelsens strukturer i Hamsuns *Ringen sluttet*." *Norskrift* 57 (1988): 20–60.

Stragnell, Gregory. "A Psychopathological Study of Knut Hamsun's *Hunger*." *The Psychoanalytic Review* 9 (1922): 198–217.

Thiess, Frank. *Das Menschenbild bei Knut Hamsun*. Schriften der Knut Hamsun-Gesellschaft. München, 1956. Trans. by Ragnhild Fearnley as "Mennesket i Hamsuns diktning." *Vinduet* 10 (1956): 169–77.

———. "Das Werther-Thema in Hamsuns *Mysterien*." In *Heimat und Weltgeist*. Jahrbuch der Knut Hamsun-Gesellschaft, ed. Hilde Fürstenberg. Mölln in Lauenburg, 1960. Pp. 133–52.

Tiemroth, Jørgen E. *Illusjonens vej: Om Knut Hamsuns forfatterskab*. København: Gyldendal, 1974.

Torp, Sigfred Hennum. "Friedrich Nietzsche og den norske litteratur i 1890-årene." Thesis: University of Oslo, 1946.

Trana, Nils Filip. "Knut Hamsun: *Victoria*. En analyse." Thesis, University of Oslo, 1961.
Turco, Alfred. "Hamsun's *Pan* and the Riddle of 'Glahn's Death'." *Scandinavica* 19 (1980): 13-29.
Uecker, Heiko. "Knut Hamsuns *Siste kapitel* und Thomas Manns *Der Zauberberg*." *Edda*, 1980, pp. 205-15.
———, ed. *Auf alten und neuen Pfaden: Eine Dokumentation zur Hamsun-Forschung*. Two volumes. Frankfurt am Main: Peter Lang, 1983.
Unruh, Kathryn I. "The Long Dark Summer in *Segelfoss Town*." *Edda* 77 (1977): 263-72.
Vige, Rolf. *Knut Hamsuns "Pan"*. Oslo: Universitetsforlaget, 1963.
Weibel, Siegfried. "Knut Hamsuns *Pan*: Suggestion und De-Montage." *Skandinavistik* 16 (1986): 21-35.
———."Der konsequente Hintersinn: Die Ironisierung des Ironikers in Knut Hamsuns *Børn av Tiden*." *Applikationen. Analysen skandinavischer Erzähltexte*. Ed. Walter Baumgartner. Frankfurt am Main: Peter Lang, 1987. Pp. 195-236.
Wellershof, Dieter. "Das Mysterium der Nerven: Über Knut Hamsuns Roman *Hunger*." In *Literatur und Lustprinzip*. Köln, 1973. Pp. 27-37.
Wells, Marie. "A Narratological Analysis of Knut Hamsun's Novel *En Vandrer spiller med Sordin*," *Scandinavica* 42 (November 2003): 239-54.
Wessely, Kari. "Knut Hamsuns *Pan*, erotiken och det Onda." *Edda*, 1999, pp. 232-44.
Wiehr, Joseph. "Knut Hamsun: His Personality and His Outlook upon Life." *Smith College Studies in Modern Languages* 3 (1921-22): 1-129.
Winsnes, A. H. "Knut Hamsun I & II." In Francis Bull et al. *Norsk litteraturhistorie V: Norges litteratur fra 1880-årene til første verdenskrig*. Oslo: Aschehoug, 1937. Pp. 266-300, 468-86.
Woel, Cai M. *Knut Hamsun*. København, 1929.
Wolfert, Raimund, ed. *Alles nur Kunst? Knut Hamsun zwischen Ästhetik und Politik*. Berlin: Arno Spitz, 1999.
Wøide, Ole. "Tilværelsens udlænding." *Norskrift* 41 (1983): 65-99.
Øyslebø, Olaf. "Gjentakelse som lyrisk middel i Hamsuns prosa." *Edda* 65 (1965): 1-26.
———. *Hamsun gjennom stilen. En studie i kunstnerisk utvikling*. Oslo: Gyldendal, 1964.

Index

(The works of Hamsun are listed under his name.)

Aadahl, Thorvald, 360n5
Aanrud, Hans, 352n5
Aarsæther, Finn, 350n11
Absurd, the, concept of, 16, 342n39, 361n22; sense of, 35, 73, 104, 118, 333
Absurd hero, the, 16, 325–26
Absurdist comedy, 246
Alexander (the Great), 228
Ambiguity, 59, 71, 120, 161, 168, 213–14, 236, 253, 282, 292, 299, 312, 363n16
Andreas-Salomé, Lou, 61, 350n16
Angst, existential, 35
Asbjørnsen, P. Chr., 353n10
Atmosphere (mood), 104, 106, 217, 230, 321
Auerbach, Erich, 206–7; *Mimesis*, 360n15
Auster, Paul, 342n41

Bachelard, Gaston, 173, 359n14
Balzac, Honoré de, 4, 39; *Lost Illusions*, 15; *Père Goriot*, 15, 258
Barksdale, E.C., 347n86, 351n27
Baumgartner, Walter, 347n89, 358n9, 361n24, 369n14
Beckett, Samuel, 246
Behrens, Carl, 1
Bentsen, Øystein, 363n20
Berendsohn, Walter, 329, 334, 370n4, 371n21
Berggrav, Eivind, 363n20, 366n25
Beyer, Edvard, 367n14

Bible: general, 9, 206, 286, 294; FIGURES FROM: Abel, 325; Abraham, 238; Adam, 10, 325; Cain, 14, 325; Esau, 205; Ezra, 278; Isaac, 205; Jacob, 205, 238; Jesus, 68, 238, 278, 309–10, 362n11; Job, 14, 225–26; Joseph (in Egypt), 229; Lazarus, 26; Martha, 26; Mary, 26; Moses, 62; Pharaoh, 229; Rebekah, 205; Uriah the Hittite, 237; Yahweh, 9, 62, 205, 364n33;
CITATIONS FROM: Daniel, 185; Exodus, 10, 62; Genesis, 207–8, 225, 229; John, 42, 191, 278; Leviticus, 206; Luke, 239, 278, 301; Mark, 278, 294; Matthew, 26, 32, 67–68, 228, 238, 312; 2 Peter, 238; Proverbs, 269; Psalms, 10; Romans, 203; 2 Samuel, 237
Bjerck-Hagen, Erik, 369n3
Bjørneboe, Jens, 368n25
Bjørnson, Bjørnstjerne, xii, 3–4, 21, 25, 37, 45
Boccaccio, Giovanni: *Decameron*, 144
Böcklin, Arnold, 350n17
Bohème movement, the, 14, 45–46, 191
Bojer, Johan, 370n16
Bolckmans, Alex, 329
Braatøy, Trygve, 343n45, 353n9, 355n17, 356n22, 364n35
Brahms, Johannes, 24
Brandes, Edvard, 1, 5, 14, 29, 340n12, 342n35, 347n87

Brandes, Georg, 1, 7-8, 341n21, 346n83, 348n98, 352n38
Brandt, Sebastian (*Das Narrenschiff*), 369n8
Bregendahl, Marie, 350n6
Brontë, Emily, 259; *Wuthering Heights*, 63
Brorson, Hans Adolph: *Swansong*, 183, 359n22
Browning, Robert, 350n19
Brynhildsvoll, Knut, 343n48, 367nn12,17
Brynildsen, Aasmund, xii, 339n5, 369n14
Bukdahl, Jørgen, 25, 367n16
Bulgakov, Mikhail, 80
Bull, Francis, 336, 343n55, 364n43, 365n15
Burke, Kenneth, 361n21
Buttry, Dolores, 340n17
Byron, George Gordon, Lord, 135; *Don Juan*, 355n15

Calverton, V.F., 273
Camus, Albert: *The Myth of Sisyphus*, 16, 361n22; *The Stranger*, 326
Carlyle, Thomas, 356n25; Carlylean yea, the, 140
Cervantes, Miguel de, 96; *Don Quixote*, 254, 283
Chaplin, Charlie, 367n17
Characterization, 22, 79, 86, 89, 156, 210-12, 232, 272-73, 284-87, 322, 334-36; ambiguous, 168, 228-30; of authorial mouthpiece, 41, 230, 324-25; based on inconsistency as a fundamental trait, 22, 37, 69, 267, 324; bifocal, 182; black and white, 48; changing perspectives in, 140-41, 310, 313; conceived as the creation of "characterless" characters, 8, 334, 341n24; by gesture and other demeanor, 71, 75, 87, 170, 212; humorous, 163; as reduction to one dominant trait, 284, 334-35
Characters, types of: anti-hero, 15, 20, 26, 307; Christ figure, 278, 342n34; Christ figure, parody of, 14, 26-27, 191; ingenu, 105; natural man, portrait of, 98; parody of, 112; the outsider, 9, 64, 123, 253, 298, 318, 325; positive hero, 49, 197; raisonneur, 118, 179, 203; romantic hero, 14, 175; vagabond, 123, 261-62, 264, 266, 281; wanderer, 7, 98, 104-5, 122-23, 128, 145, 202, 244, 256, 355n3; wandering persona, 129, 155
Charles XV, 165
Christ, 13, 17, 19 (*see also* Characters)
Christianity, 17, 84
Cinderella, 85
Clairvoyance, 28, 292, 346n80
Connolly, Cyril, 218, 233, 362n4
Conrad, Joseph, 88; *Heart of Darkness*, 8, 26, 231, 341n28, 345n74
Consciousness (mind, psyche), divided, 9, 19, 22, 214, 262, 342n36
Contingency, 19, 27-28, 245, 262
Crime, 224, 231, 239, 321

Dahl, Willy, 367n18
Dale, Johs., 349n12
Darwin, Charles, 8, 140; Darwinism, social, 43
Death, 78, 80, 136, 151, 181, 244, 276; awareness of, 331; as confrontation with mortality, 6-7, 10, 16, 271; as critical event, 235; Dance of Death, 237; and eros, 331; and life's uncertainty, 269-70; love-death, 63, 71; revolt against, 235; transcendence of, 73; wish for, 31, 151, 235, 313
Death-in-life, 77, 98
Defamiliarization (*ostranenie*), 141, 160, 247
Dickens, Charles, xi, 339n2; *Great Expectations*, 15, 258
Disillusionment, pattern of, 68, 80, 190, 255, 260, 308, 325
Doma, Akos, 339n2
Don Juan, 41, 44
Dostoyevsky, Fyodor, 5-6, 8, 19, 30, 34, 68, 315, 329-30; *The Brothers Karamazov*, 9, 26-27, 30, 272; *Crime and Punishment*, 16, 29, 116, 341n27,

Index

347n89, 351n26; *Demons*, 27, 344n59, 345n65, 351n26; *The Idiot*, 26–27, 326, 329, 344n63, 345n77, 347n92, 351n26; *The Insulted and the Injured*, 29, 344n59; *Notes from Underground*, 224, 341n24, 344n61; *Poor Folk*, 2
Double, the, 19, 30, 76, 124 (*see also* Dostoyevsky)
Douzette, Charles, 345n65
Downs, Brian, 119,
Dreams, 25, 30–32, 35, 61, 72, 76–77, 126, 367n12
Dyrhaug, Terje, 358n5

Eddy, Beverly, 352n36
Eggen, Einar, 342n39
Eichendorff, Joseph von, 355n3
Eidsvåg, Inge, 339n6
Eliot, T.S.: *The Wasteland*, 230, 363n17
Emerson, Ralph Waldo, 330, 358n4, 370n12
England and the English, satire of, 151, 156, 357n38
Engström, Albert, 356n22
Erlich, Victor, 357n40
Eros/desire: celebration of, 221, 331–32; centrality of, 95; and death, polarity of, 98–100, 112, 331–32; divided, 122, 125–26, 170, 285; expressed through musical images (*see also* Imagery), 79, 173; fable of, 32; as mediated, 96–97, 101; repression of, 83, 125; spontaneous enactment of, 259; sublimation of, 32, 77, 129, 171; and *thanatos*, 171; as a universal force, 71, 77; vagaries of, 69, 84
Existentialism, 229, 244–45, 326

Fadiman, Clifton, 157, 233, 249
Falck, Arne, 345n69
Faldbakken, Knut, 26, 345n69, 350n12
Fangen, Ronald, 290, 306, 339n2, 367n14
Farrell, Edith R., 359n14
Fatality, 27–28, 32
Faulkner, William, 176, 357n48
Fechner-Smarsly, Thomas, 342n42

Ferguson, Robert, xiii, 26, 80, 157, 249, 306, 339n2, 348n3, 355n17
Fergusson, Francis, 211, 361n21
Fett, Harry, 360n6
Fischer, Heinrich, 339n2, 344n60, 364n44
Fitzgerald, F. Scott, 253
Fladmark, Ola, 365n13
Flaubert, Gustave, 4, 96; *Madame Bovary*, 174, 320
FORM, STRUCTURE and STYLE. FORM: circular, 57, 319; musical, 9, 35, 79; problematic, 23; significant, 16; spiral, 102; by way of recapitulation, 102–3; weakness of, 143, 167, 288–89; STRUCTURE: episodic, 254; through leitmotifs, 57, 64, 79, 102, 173, 177, 190, 232; recurrent figures, 102, 320; recurrent motifs, 228, 270, 279, 336n23; ricorso, 186, 320; sexual triangle, repetitions of, 318–19; STYLE: general, 65, 289, 336; burlesque, 13, 43–44, 91, 120, 141, 164, 169, 179, 182, 227, 267, 294; fairy-tale, 32, 78, 85, 126–27; folksy, 85, 103, 157, 287; grammar, attitude toward, 336; grotesque, 9, 20, 99–100, 164, 233, 305; influenced by Whitman, 330; maximal expressiveness, search for, 287, 289–90, 336; oral, 103, 209, 336; parody, 10, 15–16, 26–27, 31, 93, 141, 228, 238, 289, 294, 319; self-parody, 15, 17, 105, 328; and tropes, 10, 44, 47, 74, 89, 145, 151, 221, 283, 297, 318, 324
Frank, Grace, 368n36
Freedman, Ralph, 64, 352n29
Freud, Sigmund, 18, 32, 96–97, 126, 350n22, 353nn17–18, 355n5; *Civilization and Its Discontents*, 281, 367n11
Friederich, Reinhard H., 345n72
Friese, Wilhelm, 350n10
Frøsland, Nikolai, 340n8, 349n17
Frydenlund, Erik, 340nn10,15, 365n9, 368n31
Fürstenberg, Hilde, 346n82

Garborg, Arne, 1, 44, 349n12
Geijer, Erik Gustaf, 365n15
Geijerstam, Gustaf af, 340n20, 341nn22–23
Geitzler, Andreas Christian, 360n9
GENRE, MODE and FICTIONAL TYPES, INDETERMINATE BLENDS of: apprenticeship novel, 66, 71–72; autobiographical fiction, 129; Bildungsroman, 270, 307, 366n22; character novel, 159; comedy of love, 83; counter-development novel, 121, 151, 196, 307; detective fiction, 234; family chronicle, 166, 218, 231–32, 270; generational novel, 159, 166; Künstlerroman, 78; lyrical novel, 64; novel of disillusionment, 18, 40; novel of everyday life (*bytovoi roman*), 176, 270; novel of manners, 159; novel tragedy, 23, 29, 46, 83, 121, 143, 159, 239, 332, 352n27; period novel, 159, 165, 176, 270; picaresque, 254; regional novel, 270; *roman à clef*, 37, 44; *roman-fleuve*, 252, 254, 271; romance, 27, 29, 43, 129, 234, 265; *skaz'*, 154; small-town novel, 217; urban picaresque, 122; utopian fantasy, 208, 214, 328
Gide, André, 341n30, 352n29; *The Immoralist*, 8–9, 331
Gierløff, Christian, 330
Girard, René, 96–97, 353n19
Gjesdahl, Paul, 119
Gladstone, William, 344n61
Glette, Kåre, 361n18
Goethe, Johann Wolfgang von: *Faust*, 280, 367n9; *The Sufferings of Young Werther*, 28, 63–64, 79–80, 346n82, 352n30
Gogol, Nikolay: *Dead Souls*, 276, 366n1; *The Inspector General*, 276
Gombrowicz, Witold, 149; *Pornografia*, 357n36
Goncourt brothers, the: *Germinie Lacerteux*, 8
Gratuitous acts, 9, 28, 64, 351n26

Grieg, Edvard, 21
Grieg, Harald, 365nn6,14, 368n32, 369n7, 371n30
Grieg, Nina, 21
Grieg, Nordahl, 306, 326, 333, 360n2, 368n34, 370n19
Grimm brothers, the, 126, 355n7
Grüters, Walter, 9, 358n6

Hagelstam, Wentzel, 352nn2,4, 353n6, 356n22
Hambro, C.J., 363n20
Hamsun, Arild, 336, 371n24
Hamsun (also Goepfert), Bergljot, 79, 353n11, 365n8
Hamsun, Knut: acquired culture, criticism of, 165, 180, 296, 358n4; in America, 3–4; American culture, opinion of, 282, 289, 359n13, 365n17; and anarchism, xi; anglophobia of, xii; antifeminism, 324; anti-Ibsenism, 45, 140; birth, 2, 204, 340n3; and the Bohème movement, 45–46; childhood and early youth, 2–3, 53, 340n4; and circumstantial realism, 206, 289; and determinism, 241; didacticism of, 37–38, 43, 50, 121, 137, 143, 159, 191, 200, 327; and emigration, 254, 261–65, 285; and expressionism, 19–20, 75, 322, 343n48; fairy-tale elements in work of, 32–33, 35, 72, 87, 128, 174, 185, 358n9, 361n18 (*see also* Style); and fascism, xii; and fecundity, theme of, 147, 153, 193, 221, 275, 301, 332; fictional aesthetic of, 20–22, 34–35; hard times, 3–6; illness, 4; and impressionism, 20, 334; and infanticide, 196, 199–201; and jazz, 298, 304; *Jugendstil*, relation to, 350n17; literary apprenticeship of, 2–5; and magic realism, 35; and modernism, 35, 64, 80, 246, 326, 329, 348n100; modernity, critique of, 254, 283, 294–95, 299, 333; name, change in spelling of, 340n9; and naturalism,

15, 17, 45, 113, 182, 225; Nazism, involvement with, xi–xiii, 327; and the Norwegian Resistance, xii; and panpsychism, 145; pantheism of, 331, 333; paradise lost, dream of, 331; in Paris, 38, 53; and philosophical naturalism, 119, 140, 333; and politics, xii–xiii; progress, skepticism of, 244; in psychoanalytic treatment, 257; and quietism, 119, 139, 188; and race, 296, 298–99; religion, satire of, 225–26, 231; revivalism, comedy of, 304–5; and sentimental education, theme of, 82, 103, 196, 267; and stylization, 54, 66, 78, 350n10; and subjectivity, 19–20, 327–28; surrealism, relationship to, 20, 35, 91–92, 104, 367n12; teleology, the question of, 225, 238, 245; theodicy, negative, 26–27, 129; and unanimism, erotic, 221; urban culture, satire of, 241, 254, 332; utopian ideas of, 143, 207–8, 214–15; and vagabondage, 214, 264, 266, 284; and "writing one's life," 14

— WORKS: NOVELS

August, 252, 254, 268, 275–90, 313, 318, 366n1, 367nn11–12, 367nn17–18

August Trilogy, The, 123, 252–54, 271, 287, 290, 303, 328

Benoni, 81–104, 106, 109, 119–20, 171, 175, 182, 328, 353nn12,16

Bjørger, 3, 365n19

Chapter the Last (The Last Chapter), 217, 234–49, 251, 269, 321, 323, 333, 335, 363n26, 363–64nn33–35

Children of the Age, 119, 159–75, 177, 179, 182, 184–85, 190, 193, 222, 248, 299, 332, 335, 357–58nn1–5,9–10, 359nn12–13

Dreamers, 82–89, 92, 103, 105, 179, 328, 353n8, 370n2

Editor Lynge, 37–47, 159, 327, 348nn3,8–9,11

Enigmatic One, The, 3

"Frida," 3

Growth of the Soil, 119, 152, 193–215, 217, 233, 253–54, 264, 328, 331, 359–60nn1,11, 361nn18,20,22

Hunger, 1–2, 5–21, 51, 54, 71, 81, 106, 122, 124, 187, 213, 323, 325–27, 329, 337, 341nn22,24, 342nn34,39, 343n48

Last Joy, The, 82, 121, 143–57, 193, 196, 202–3, 234, 248, 279, 300, 328, 333, 335, 356–57nn30–31,34–35,37–38,43–44, 370n1

Mysteries, 20–35, 38–39, 54, 71, 73, 81, 122–24, 129, 192, 209, 218, 235, 249, 262, 326–27, 329, 332, 343n50, 346nn79–82, 347nn88–89,92, 348nn98–99

Pan, 53–65, 71–72, 83, 90, 104, 116, 122, 130, 144, 146, 175, 179, 209, 235, 329, 332, 350nn12,14,17, 351nn25,27

Ring Is Closed, The, 273, 307–26, 335, 369nn2,5–6,14

Road Leads On, The, 252–53, 275, 280, 290–306, 332, 337, 368nn21–22,25–27,29–30

Rosa, 72, 82, 89–91, 104–20, 175, 179, 182, 196, 235, 242, 308, 316, 328, 336, 354nn28–31, 371n26

Segelfoss Town, 119, 159, 166, 175–92, 197, 202, 206, 217, 230, 235, 248, 252, 254, 275, 277, 295, 303, 333

Shallow Soil, 37–38, 45–51, 159, 191, 327

Under the Autumn Star, 121–30, 139, 143–45, 179, 355n3

Vagabonds, 251–73, 275, 280, 284–85, 295–96, 303, 317, 320, 365nn13,15,17, 366nn21–25,27

Victoria, 53, 65–80, 83, 85, 105, 297, 308, 328–29, 332, 352n36

Wanderer Plays on Muted Strings, A, 82, 121, 130–44, 153, 157, 159–61, 217, 235, 299, 328, 335, 356nn22,25, 370n1

Wanderer Trilogy, The, 121, 144, 235, 328, 334, 355n3

Women at the Pump, The, 217–34, 236, 243, 247, 249, 253, 286, 301, 307, 317, 333, 335, 362nn5,8,14, 363nn16,18–19
— WORKS: MISCELLANEOUS
Brushwood, 81
Cultural Life of Modern America, The, 1, 358n4, 359n13, 370n8
"From the Unconscious Life of the Mind," 8, 20
"Honor the Young," 366n24
"In a Hundred Years It Is All Forgotten," 359n26
"Island Among the Skerries" (Skjærgårdsø), 355n8
"Literary Movement in Norway, The," 45
Munken Vendt, 81
On Overgrown Paths, 282
Queen Tamara, 81
"Small Town Life," 362n5
Wild Choir, The, 81
In Wonderland, 81, 340n4
"Word to Us, A," 357n38
Hamsun (née Andersen), Marie, 154, 251, 353nn12,16, 354nn30–31, 356n22, 357nn35,37,39, 364–65nn1–3,7
Hamsun, Tore, 38, 98, 169, 332, 340n12, 348n5, 349n15, 353nn11,21, 358n11, 360n7, 371n22
Hannibal, 228
Hansen, P.E., 354n29
Hardy, Thomas, 79, 242
Hartmann, Eduard von, 23, 29, 344n57, 346n83
Hasselblatt, E., 359n17
Hegel, Frederik, 3
Hegel, Jacob, 352n1
Heiberg, Hans, 361n18, 368n26
Heidegger, Martin, 244–45, 364nn36–37
Hemingway, Ernest, 11; *The Sun Also Rises*, 230
Herzfeld, Marie, 345n65
Hesse, Hermann, 175, 352n29, 359n16
History: circular concept of, 366n24; downward spiral of, 186; lack of stringency in treatment of, 303; Ovidian conception of, 185; viewed as a matter of natural cycles, 165–66, 270
Hitler, Adolf, xiii, 344n60
Hitschmann, Eduard, 342n45
Høffding, Harald, 348n98
Hoel, Sigurd, 175, 359n19, 360n2, 368n29, 370n15
Hølaas, Odd, 349n14
Holitscher, Arthur, 345n64
Holm, Birgitta, 348n99
Holm, Helge Vidar, 214
Holst, G.M., 369n5
Homer: *The Odyssey*, 194, 206–7, 361n16
Humpál, Martin, 339n8, 342n40, 348n100
Hutchison, Percy, 249
Huxley, Aldous, 206, 360n16; *After Many a Summer Dies the Swan*, 182; *Point Counter Point*, 249, 364n42

Ibsen, Henrik, 4, 21, 243, 260, 362n12; *A Doll House*, 48, 140; *Peer Gynt*, 279, 367n6; "Terje Vigen," 72; *The Wild Duck*, 228, 321
IMAGERY and SYMBOLISM.
CHARACTERS, SYMBOLIC DIMENSION OF: general, 332–33; Andersen, Oliver, 229–30, 362n14, 363n16; August, 275, 280–81, 283, 293–95; Bårdsen, 191; Gregersen, 323; Holmengrå, 162, 358n3; Holmsen, 162; the organ grinder, 320; FAUNA: general, 43, 110–11, 155, 287, 301; anthill, 217–18, 224–25, 243–44; ants, 278; aurochs, 156; bear, 193; beast of prey, 242; bullock, 242; cat choking on a fish hook, 31–32; cygnet, 173; filly, 287, 301, 357n43; flea circus, 218; hens, 169, 325; horse, 152, 155; insects, 16, 112, 249; insects dancing, 112; magpie, 176–77, 189; mare, 155; rooster, 186; snake, 191; swan, 173–75, 182–84; vermin, 9, 115; worms, 9, 44, 99; FLORA: general, 198, 269; flowers, 22, 60–61, 70–71, 128, 178;

garden, 79; mimosa, 22, 343–44n55; rootedness, 214, 271, 313; rootlessness, 21, 284, 311, 343n50, 369n6; roots, torn, 184, 198, 215, 262; FOLKLORE AND RELIGION: Ashlad, 85, 87; the biblical serpent, 150; evil apocalypse, 238, 293; the Fall of Man, 322; fire, apocalyptic, 6, 238; like fire and sword, 44; giant, 76; Norns, 183; Valkyries, 183; water troll, 194; wood nymph, 302; MISCELLANEOUS: abyss, 151, 236, 291, 293–94; bleeding, 71, 76; blood, 71, 77; button in the snow, 270, 366n23; cave, 79, 191; color, 71, 73–74, 352n36; dance, 70, 76–77, 112; diving, 76; falling, 11, 33; fire, 6, 173, 317; fishing, 32; fog, 203, 205, 253; horsemanship, 167–68; the hunt, 31, 43; the hunter/hunted, 32; labyrinth, 16; lightness, 283; microcosm, 240, 283, 321, 358n5; music, 31–33, 70–71, 76–77, 110, 119, 173, 209; sea, 72, 76, 79; seafaring, 44; ship, 321; song, 68, 70, 111, 173, 182, 209, 298; theater, 188; warbling, 70, 173, 182–83
Injured third party, the, 28, 62, 96–97, 350–51n22; "unworthy" third party, 114
Irrational, the, 9, 50
Irrationality, 28, 35, 63, 69, 102

Jacobsen, Jens Peter, 330, 350n17; *Niels Lyhne*, 342n38
James, Henry, 198, 360n3
Janson, Kristofer, 4, 8, 341n26, 371n27
Jæger, Hans, 14, 45
Jensen, Johannes V., 356n25
Johannesson, Eric O., 341n24
Johansen, Krøger, 330
Jones, Ernest, 350n22
Joyce, James, xi; *A Portrait of the Artist as a Young Man*, 16

Kafka, Franz, xi, 197, 345n72, 359n1; Gregor Samsa, 16; the hunger artist, 17–18

Kayser, Wolfgang, 34
Keller, Hans, 355n13
Kent, Charles, 361n23
Kerouac, Jack, 369n14
Ketelsen, Uwe-K., 213–14
Kielland, Alexander, 21, 119, 166, 358n7
Kielland, Eugenia, 367n16
Kirkegaard, Peter, 25
Kittang, Atle, 18, 342n44, 352n37, 362n8, 363n16, 366n25
Kjær, Nils, 45, 354n33
Knutsen, Nils M., 120, 354n33
Kønig, Christian, 358nn1,7, 359n29, 360n4, 364n40, 365n5, 370n1
Kristensen, Dagny, 353n15
Kristensen, Sven Møller, 336, 339, 367n14
Kristensen, Tom, 290, 339n2
Krog, Helge, 130, 273, 355n11, 366nn27,29
Krohg, Christian, 45
Kuprin, Aleksandr, 342nn32–33

Landquist, John, 119, 348n8, 350n14
Lange, Sven, 119, 157, 192, 359n31, 361n23
Langen, Albert, 54, 61, 348n3, 349n30, 350n9, 352nn33,3(ch.4), 354nn23,25, 365n4
Langfeldt, Gabriel, 334, 369n11
Langslet, Lars Roar, 370n15
Larsen, Alf, 326, 368nn18,22
Larsen, Bolette & Ole Johan, 340n11, 343n50, 347n94, 349nn11,13,18,22,24,31,33–34,1,4(ch.3)
Larsen, Hanna Astrup, 339n8
Larsen, Lars Frode, 340nn3,5, 360n13
Lavrin, Janko, 345n75
Lawrence, D.H., xi, 339n2; *Lady Chatterley's Lover*, 332
Leporello, 41
Lescoffier, Jean, 371n20
Levin, Poul, 192, 359n32, 361n23, 363n20, 366n28
Lie, Jonas, 21, 119, 140, 328, 349n36; *Evil*

Powers, 166–67; *Niobe*, 50; *The Visionary*, 346n80
Lien, Asmund, 63, 352n28
Lowenthal, Leo, xii, 339n4
Lundegård, Axel, 5
Lundkvist, Artur, 273, 366n32, 369n2
Lyngstad, Sverre, 349n36, 350n12

Maloff, Saul, 340n19, 361n27, 371n29
Mann, Thomas, xi, 17, 80, 213, 220, 233, 329, 331, 352n43, 358n6, 361n26, 362nn7,14, 363n22, 370n5; *Buddenbrooks*, 166–67; *The Magic Mountain*, 249, 363n26; *Tonio Kröger*, 9, 230, 362n15
Marcus, Carl David, 363n33
Marstrander, Jan Fr., 360n9
McFarlane, James W., 339n2, 346n80, 351n27
Mæling, Per, 343n46
Melodrama, 23, 49, 57, 67, 201, 247
Mendelssohn, Peter de, 334, 358n10, 367n18, 371n21
Mephistopheles, 280
Merivale, Patricia, 350n18
Metafiction, 78, 155, 213–14, 230, 325, 363n16, 364n35, 367n12
Metamorphosis, 10
Metempsychosis, 127
Michaelsen, Aslaug Groven, 343n51
Michelangelo, 10
Miller, Henry, 26, 33, 326, 345n71
Mirsky, D.S., 276
Moe, Jørgen, 353n10
Molière: *Le Bourgeois gentilhomme*, 107
Morgridge, Barbara Gordon, 343n47, 365n17
Mörner, Karl Birger, 345n65
Muir, Edwin, 79, 192, 233, 352n40, 363n19
Munch, Edvard, 343n48, 352n36
Münchhausen, Baron von, 267–268, 365n19
Myth (mythic), 14, 54, 61–62, 64, 85, 174, 185, 193, 205, 207, 214, 283, 303, 343n48, 361n18, 367n17, 368n29; of Pan, 57, 61–62, 350nn17–19,21
Mythomania, 15, 92, 229, 253

Nag, Martin, 80, 330, 341n27, 342n34, 343n49
Nansen, Peter, 47, 353nn7,14, 355n16, 357n46, 358n8, 359n27, 370n1
Napoleon, 228, 255, 270, 279; the Napoleonic motif, 15
Narrative technique: apostrophe to characters, 323–24; authorial intrusion, 248; center of consciousness, experience as refracted by, 19; cutback with looping, 88, 189; delayed exposition, 66; deviation from realism, 305–6, 324; episodes recollected and transformed, 68; foreboding, 101, 238; foreshadowing, 32, 101, 239, 301; free indirect discourse (*erlebte Rede*), 34, 75, 88, 224, 232, 248, 284, 288, 324, 347–48n96, 358n3; incremental exposition, 310, 313; interior dialogue, 19; interior monologue, 9, 20, 34, 91, 284, 288; involuntary memory, 57; limited omniscence, 34, 88, 232; memory sequence, 88, 102–3; monologue, 71–72, 110, 218; narrative voice, protean character of, 168, 174, 187, 248, 285, 305; omniscience, 160; prefiguration, 28, 30; retrospective point of view, problem with, 138, 239; shifting point of view, 103, 106, 285, 287–88; stream of consciousness, 34; suspense, 28, 55, 101, 109, 131, 239; tense shift and narrative distance, 20; unreliable narrator, 58–59, 65, 105
Nature: cycles of, 270–71, 304; eroticized, 61; mystical sense of union with, 31, 61–62; paradoxical relationship to, 60
Naughton, Charles, 233
Nebuchadnezzar, dream of, 185
Neeraas, Caroline, 344n62
Nero, 6
Nærup, Carl, 2, 25, 53, 130, 136, 143, 192, 218, 345n67, 359n30, 361n20, 362n3

Index

Nesby, Linda H., 364n35
Næss, Harald, 215, 224, 330, 339n8, 340nn6-7, 345n65, 346n83, 348n7, 355n17, 356n24, 362n34, 366n21, 369nn1,13-14
Nettum, Rolf Nyboe, 341n25, 365n19
Nietzsche, Friedrich, 8, 29, 329, 346n83, 347n86, 348n98, 356nn31-32; *Also sprach Zarathustra*, 144-45, 333, 370n18; and tragedy, 352n27
Nilsson, Nils Åke, 351n27
Nilsson, Victor, 349n20
Nobel, Alfred: Nobel Prize in Literature, xi, 53, 201, 213, 215, 217, 290, 360n8, 361n24
Norheim, Pål, 343n55
Nybø, Gregory, 345n66, 346n81

Ødegård, Ørnulv, 369n11
Olsen, Hans, 2
Österling, Anders, 360n8
Øyslebø, Olav, 371n25

Passion love, 28-29, 63, 65, 73, 110, 125, 259, 313, 332
Pasternak, Boris: *Doctor Zhivago*, 204; and Dionysian tragedy, 347n86
Pasternak, E., 351n27
Pedersen, Hans, 365n13
Philipsen, Elisa, 350n7
Philipsen, Gustav, 29, 347n90, 349nn19,21,25-26,32-35,
Picasso, Pablo, 17
Pontoppidan, Henrik, 217
Popp, Daniel, 347n86, 351n27
Primal scene, 18, 106
Proust, Marcel, xi, 96
Psychopomp, 77, 183

Quisling, Vidkun, xii-xiii

Randers, Kristofer, 345n68
Raspe, Rudolph Erich, 365n19
Reincarnation, 128, 225
Ribot, Théodule, 341n25
Riechel, Donald C., 366n23

Rimestad, Christian, 306, 362n3, 368n35
Rost, Nico, 345n73
Rottem, Øystein, 214, 347n86, 351n24, 361nn23,32, 364nn33-35, 365n11, 367n14, 368nn22,27
Rougemont, Denis de, 63, 346n82
Rousseau, Jean-Jacques, 54; *Emile*, 224; concept of happiness of, 268; and pantheism, 331
Rumbke, Eberhard, 213, 360n11, 361nn28-29

Sarraute, Nathalie, 343-44n55
Sartre, Jean-Paul: *Nausea*, 35, 245, 326, 342n39, 364n38; *regard d'autrui*, 88
Sayers, Michael, 326
Scene, handling of: genre scenes, 95, 98, 100, 260-61; humorous-pathetic scenes, 210-12; scenes of scandal, 19, 24, 34, 68, 86, 99, 190, 297-99; three-way scene, 285-87
Schiller, Friedrich, 203, 360n12
Schopenhauer, Arthur, 29, 346n84
Schøyen, Rolf Hiorth, 364n41
Schück, H., 360n8
Scott, J.S., 359n18
Sehmsdorf, Henning K., 350n21
Seiler, Thomas, 351n25
Shakespeare, William, 358n4; *Hamlet*, 263
Simpson, Allen, 360n11, 361n22, 365n11, 366n22
Skagen, Axel, 355n3
Skavlan, Einar, 120, 157, 348n8, 355n2, 367n13
Skram, Erik, 2, 5-6, 30, 38, 331, 340n18, 343n50
Slotte, Xavier, 356n30
Solumsmoen, Odd, 368n30, 371n20
Sørensen, Johan, 340nn13-14
Stallybrass, Oliver, 79, 130, 233
Steiner, George, 7, 80, 340n19
Stendhal, 96
Sterne, Laurence: *Tristram Shandy*, 323-24
Stjernfelt, Frederik, 369n1

Storstein, Olav, 357n49, 370n7
Stragnell, Gregory, 343n45
Strindberg, August, 4, 62, 142, 170, 246, 260, 329-30, 341n24, 343n48, 350n13; *Miss Julie*, preface to, 8; *By the Open Sea*, 345n65, 346n83; *The People of Hemsö*, 119; *The Red Room*, 341n24; self-description of, 59
Strømme, Johannes Irgens, 251
Sub(un-)conscious, 8, 11, 18, 22-23, 25, 31, 34-35, 37, 50, 61, 63, 76, 125, 344n57
Suicide, 16, 23-28, 30-33, 39, 43, 46, 49, 63, 116, 136, 146, 161, 183, 187, 235-36, 299-300, 355n17; mental reservation of, 27, 262; vicarious act of, 56
Sunne, Richard, 273
Swanström, Lars, 353n13, 354n24, 355nn18-20, 356n26
Swift, Jonathan: *Gulliver's Travels*, 182, 253, 365n12; Swiftian satire, 121, 141
Swiss, the, satire of, 136, 153, 156, 357n38

Tennyson, Alfred Lord: "Tithonus," 182
Thiess, Frank, 346n82, 352n30
Thommessen, Olav, 21, 38, 40, 47, 349n9
Tiemroth, Jørgen E., 369n10
Time: chronology, casual handling of, 66, 78, 165, 189, 271; contradictory data of, 303; the created moment, refuge from, 74; cyclical, 271, 368n21; end-time, 238; eschatology, Christian, 238; evolutionary, 128; as experienced, paradox of, 57, 271; human, 238, 244-45; linear, 57, 271, 368n21; mythic quality of, 368n29; narrative time, circling back of, 57, 319, 325; simultaneity, 189; transience, 31, 243-44, 271
Tolstoy, Leo, 38, 170, 192, 259; *Anna Karenina*, 18, 174, 213
Tourism, satire of, 147, 357n38
Tristan and Isolde, story of, 63, 351n24

Turgenev, Ivan: *Rudin*, 27; the superfluous man, 26, 59; *Virgin Soil*, 47, 349n26
Tveraas, Svend, 340n6
Twain, Mark, 4, 34, 340n9

Uecker, Heiko, 363n26
Unanimism, erotic, 221, 331
Uncanny, the, 10, 33, 35, 269, 346n80
Updike, John, 26, 79, 130, 143, 233, 345n71, 352n41, 355n12, 362n6, 363nn18,23

Vige, Rolf, 350n11
Virgil, 62
Vogt, Nils, 79
Voltaire: *Candide*, 105, 245, 256, 364n39
Voyeurism, 49, 125, 286; as an element of narrative technique, 106, 121, 131, 149, 153
Vries, Ad de, 359n21

Wais, Kurt, 80, 352n43
Walsøe, Laura, 3
Walsøe, Nikolai, 3
Weibel, Siegfried, 352n31, 358n9
Welhaven, Gerda, 352n32
Wells, H.G., 213, 361n26
Weltschmerz, 31
West, Rebecca, 213, 361n25
Whitman, Walt, 330
Whittick, Arnold, 359n15
Woel, Cai M., 352n42
Wøide, Ole, 361n32
Wood, James, 339n1
Woolf, Virginia, 18, 342n43, 352n29; *Mrs. Dalloway*, 188

Young, Stanley, 326, 369n16

Zahl, E.B.K., 3
Zane, J. Peder, 341n22
Zola, Emile, 4